Dedication

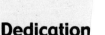

In honour

Thank you for providing for my survival and growth
against the most impossible and horrific of odds.

I respect your guts, your sacrifices
and most of all your suppressed pain
in the name of safety, love and freedom.

Time to settle, peacefully.

Your son – *Mickey*

It's been said that we are all 'mirrors' for each other. I echo a lot of
what Mickey says here, to my parents and family. I have always
wanted to dig deeper. Have spent hours trying to figure out the things
lurking in the family cupboards, and talked endlessly with my Mum,
and now exploring with my Dad, the stuff that seemed to be round my
ankle like a ball and chain.

Don't know what more to say. Except that what I express here must be
a reflection of myself. I only realised recently that I have spent my life
running from my own darkside. So, where I see snobs, there is a clue
to my own snobbery. Racists, my own racism. Anger, fear. You get the
picture?

So, here's to the Dark and the Light. *Ed*

WARNING! NOT FOR THE FAINT-HEARTED...

Disclaimer Statement.

The language we sometimes used (on tape) was raw, brash and quite rude/harsh. We've transcribed it just as it came out, there and then.

It contains references to/descriptions of sex, drugs, (rock & roll!), violence, our personal experiences, our personal opinions and absolute honesty. Everything that we have said is true, to the best of our knowledge. We have taken advice from our lawyers (at great expense!) and have changed place names and identities in order to protect those involved.

Nothing in the book is intended to be malicious, everything in the book feeds our exploration of life. We have openly explored our philosophies and the ways we live(d) them, therefore this book is not intended as a gratuitous display of sex/'naughtiness', however these and other themes are fundamental to the things explored in the book.

This is not a 'how to' book of advice – though hopefully you will not have to learn your lessons the hard way, if you can learn from our experiences in any shape or form!

To those who may be offended by any of the content – we apologise.

To those who believe themselves to be characters within the book, we have done our utmost to endeavour that the only person that might recognise the characters - are the individuals themselves. Where possible, we have sought consent from the characters.

DO NOT BUY / READ THIS BOOK UNLESS...

(We are very serious – and sincere – about this.)

You are over 18.

You are not easily offended.

You commit to reading it to the end.
If you stop reading it prematurely, you will really miss the point. You could seriously damage your relationship with yourself, as well as your relationships with other people.

You are up for a change in perspective.
Facts don't usually change, but our relationship to, or understanding of them does. We've dug up, pieced together and grown (up!).

You do not expose anyone.
All names have been changed – apart from the famous – to protect 'the innocent'. It's fine for the authors to expose themselves and reveal their own secrets, but they do not have the right to expose anyone else. So, please play fair and don't try to find out who/where any of the characters in the book are. If you do know who they, or anyone else in the book is, please keep it to strictly to yourself – or Email personal@menspeak.co.uk if you really need to tell someone – and save your own karmic little arse in the process.

You are ready for a good laugh/cry!

Enjoy

Acknowledgements

With thanks to my brother Caetano - for dropping everything and being there, when I 'lost it'.

Billy, Eva, Freya, Gina, Lisa & Yannis, Simon & Anna - for love, safety, belonging and support in my life and work.

Gina's Dell Latitude LS laptop, John's 256MB magical memory stick, Rob's Apple Mac iBook - for hardware, software and no major disasters along the way.

All at the Hoxton Biblio-tech - for my website, generous business, training and IT support. (With added gusto from the Flaming Archer)

Sarah, whose legal expertise went way beyond Chapter 56 - for her belief in this project, generosity with time and patient hand-holding.

Dan and Darren - for their belief in me, in my work and putting their resources at my disposal. Your inspiration has helped me get fit, in every way.

Dr Andrew Parker, Dr William Bloom, Michelle, Mike and Mike - for being friends, mentors and role models. Not to mention my courageous clients!

Mr Poonchie (Rob) with whom I began my pathway; Flatie-pate (Lui) with whom I added the shadow; Trevor (and the plums) - for being my best friends (ex-worst enemies) in the world!

All those (mis) named in the book/my life, for playing their roles on my stage, helping me learn my lessons (one way or another) and pick up my tools (as I un-learn the un-helpful); and for not drawing attention to us in or out of court, so that life remains private, peaceful and free!

And finally, my co-author Ed Seeker. A man amongst men, with a strong will and the courage to find and live his truth to its' max - bugger the consequences!

Mickey Elias

MEN Speak the Unspeakable

This signed and numbered limited edition

by **Mickey Elias & Ed Seeker** *is*

published by

Michael Elias Networks
www.menspeak.co.uk

"MEN Speak the Unspeakable"
is published in the UK, in 2004, by
Michael Elias Networks
239 Old Street, London EC1V 9EY
Email: business@menspeak.co.uk
www.menspeak.co.uk

A CIP catalogue record for this book is
available from the British Library.

ISBN 0-9549095-0-X

*Printed and (perfect) bound in Great Britain
by Bookmarque Ltd, Croydon, Surrey
on non-bleached recycled paper.*

About the authors

Mickey Elias (38) was a nice Goan Catholic boy, whose idyllic childhood in post-colonial Uganda came to an abrupt end at the age of eight. Fleeing death threats, he arrived in the UK, Fatherless, finding himself in 'barbaric' rural Wales via refugee camps and familial emotional abuse. This is where he stops and claims his manhood after years of workaholism, travel, study and perpetual 'fleeing for his life'.

Mickey is my best friend. In fact, I am perfectly happy in the sound knowledge that he is the best friend anyone could ever have; even though I still wish I'd never met him, on a fairly regular basis!

We've had pretty much daily contact for the last five years, and although it has been fraught with conflict and chaos, I have grown; in ways I myself, and the people that knew the 'old' me, would have thought impossible. I attribute this to my relationship with Mickey, not just because of the contact, but because I want to be like him, and try to be – all the time.

Like a child, Mickey wants more. Of everything. All the time! Especially when it comes to love, relationships, wisdom and life in general.

Sometimes it's exciting; fun; inspiring; motivating; and lots of other good stuff – sometimes it's just over the top and I begin thinking of unpleasant ways of making him shut up – but that's usually when he's telling the truth (again) and I don't like it!

There is one thing Mickey always is – different. This is what I really love about him. He has a gift of awareness, and he loves to share it.

As the global representative for the phrase 'the truth shall set you free', Mickey has unshakingly demonstrated it to be… well… the truth!

One possible flipside is the truth becoming an obsession, which I don't recommend, and sometimes need to remind my best friend.

The vulnerability, honesty and openness on these pages changes lives – and if we would all do it even just a bit, it would change life on earth as we know it. But don't take my word for it - or Mickey's, or Ed's - try it! I dare you!

Lui Judge (Mickey's best friend) London, January 2003

Ed Seeker (37) was a middle-class golden boy; no financial pressure, no real direction, spiritually, emotionally, creatively frustrated. After the explosive break-up of his marriage he went into a tail-spin, crash-landing head-first into everything he had ever run away from. A former sex addict, solicitor and local government officer - he is a part-time Father, artist and masseur.

Ed is my son. Ed and I are now, I believe, good friends, probably understanding one another better now than at any previous time. We've certainly had quite difficult times, particularly, perhaps when living in the same house as adults. Not an uncommon situation. We can both be somewhat short tempered and this has led to a number of flare ups.

I've viewed Ed with a mixture of frustration, admiration and love for many years. Frustration because he seemed to have no real game-plan for life, moving from one sphere to another without what seemed to me to be clear goals, in spite of time apparently spent on detailed analysis of needs. I was always aware that he had many talents, including considerable artistic ability and also tenacity as evidenced, for example, in slogging through Law School and qualifying as a solicitor. So this accounted for part of the admiration.

Love, not simply because he is our son but he is a charmer and has good people skills. He has a wide circle of very supportive friends. He has been excellent company on, for example, car trips abroad. I hope his navigational skills and good sense of direction translate into life generally!

There have been many apparent conflicts, for example that between his wish to 'be his own man' and being firstly heavily influenced by others and secondly between that wish and the seemingly fatalistic attitude engendered by the Buddhist teachings. He does now seem to be moving towards taking firm steps to influence events and away from unrealistic expectations and sometimes what seem to be unfortunate acquaintances!

The recent initiative of his in setting up our joint visit to Paris was very successful, I think, in improving our relationship; frank talking demolished a number of misreadings, of, I believe different behaviours and we shared some very relaxed moments and the spirituality and indeed, sheer theatre of Mass at the Sacré Coeur. Openness and frankness, however, like too much self analysis, needs to carry a health warning!

So it's been a bit of a rollercoaster ride these last few years but in the right direction for all that. I hope that the somewhat zigzag course Ed has followed leads him to a way of life which can reconcile his spiritual needs with the need to earn a living!

Daniel Seeker (Ed's Dad) Silchester, February 2003

Mickey and Ed met at the 'Sex & Spirit Conference' at the Findhorn Foundation, Scotland and became 'unlikely friends'. They allowed this book to express itself, over a period of fourteen months, as they de-briefed their eccentric adventures and everyday woes and bared their souls into a Dictaphone. Whinging and blaming over - the new life begins...

Edward Seeker

1524
———
3000

Preface

"This book is the form of my unanswered questions and disjointed thoughts, taken in a snap-shot of time. A time of confusion, exhaustion, poverty, fear, depression and shock, as I emerge from the self-medicated dragon-smoke that kept me safe, numb and vague enough to 'hold it together'.

Serious soul searching, intense therapy and laser eye surgery stimulated focus, clarity and the barriers (glasses) and suffocation (lenses) to shift.

The foul language, raw emotion and extreme perspectives were my truth, there and then, as it all came out for the first time. As you will soon see, I use anger and babble to protect my vulnerability. Hey, at least I finally got there!

This record of my transformation - from 'am I?' to 'I am' – causes me sheer terror. What will my parents think? My brother, best mate, friends, family, communities; the public at large will all hate and reject me and spit salt into my opened wounds!!!

The colossal boulder that had been blocking my path is being given a tangible shape and form. The depressed 'pause buttons' that strung my boulder in place have suddenly come into my consciousness and this book is my reaction to the unknown. The uncovered. Blasting my boulder and its shadow; erasing my unconscious script.

To my parents, family and friends. Please help me to remember - and tell me the truth. I need to cut the chords. I need to go places and express who I am, by finding out who I am not. Please help me."

'I think I've just dumped some major baggage, while scribbling this preface on the London Underground. I just walked off the Jubilee line at Baker Street without my day-bag (my security blanket). £100 towards my unpaid rent. My diary, all my contacts, 'special' dowsing rods, pendulum and compass. Brochures on who I am and what I do. Ian Duncan's 'Lucifer' (unread) Lui's favourite book and my birthday present from the man incarnate. All gone!

I've lovingly stored my tatty old rucksack that was 'home' for many years of travel through Europe, Thailand, Australia, New Zealand, Fiji, Singapore, Bali, Goa, India, Mexico, America, heaven, hell and back. I ran - clutching my faithful rucksack - from a (minor) kidnapping in Delhi, drunken brawlers after my blood (for various reasons) in Fiji and the countless times I have moved, in search of home.

The baggage at my parents' home — crammed in, on, or under internationally decorated and lovingly adorned refugee furniture and hoarded cases — weighs heavy on my chest. We were only allowed hand luggage as refugees without a Father, who was left in Africa, to probably die. The pushing and shoving on the gangway up to the plane split me from my family. I was petrified of losing the bag entrusted to me. I had recently lost my home, my dog, my school, friends, church; we were suddenly 'in hiding' from the killer Secret Service. No wonder I work as a feng shui consultant, creating homes and communities!

My large, lost Mambo day-bag eased the pain of my shoulders with its weight. Who will I be without my baggage? Let's see...'

Check this out! My bag was returned to London Transport!!! Everything intact minus £40 out of the £100 that was there. That makes me £60 up, as if I had it returned I would have given them the cash anyway - but with no name or address... Nice to lose yourself (and get over it) once in a while, eh!

Chapters

This section was previously entitled *'Curse Of The Mummy's Boy'*

With special thanks to Padmal de Silva & Stanley Rachman, for use of excerpts from 'Obsessive Compulsive Disorder - the facts' (Oxford University Press); and Robert M Young, for use of excerpts from 'Ideas In Psychoanalysis - Oedipus Complex' (Icon Books).

Prologue

(Mickey's parents' house, Welshpool, February 2004)

You and my Father had a really good chat while I was on the phone to… was it Matthew?

Yeah, yeah. It was really great! In the past I probably would have thought, 'well I'd better not speak my mind. I'm in his house and I don't want to cause a disagreement or an argument!' but I just thought, it was important to explain to him how much impact the book has had on me and my family.

That's what the conversation was about?

Pretty much, yeah. Yeah, what it boils down to was he was saying, okay, he was saying, basically, that *"You have to turn the page on the past and move on."* And I was saying "Yes, to an extent, *but first of all you have to see what's written on the page."*

Yeah, yeah!

I just felt very adamant about it.

That's very very well put.

Yeah. Otherwise, it's just, it's buried.

Suppressed… and ruling the life.

And my next counter-argument – why am I sounding like a lawyer today? Must be a legal sort of day, m'lud.

Hm hm hm

That's right, he was then saying "OK, fine to dig and delve, but do you have to share it with the whole world?" and I think, just as you were coming off the phone, I was saying to him "Before I would have agreed with you. I had doubts about the book. I wasn't just doubting - I questioned the whole process. But now I definitely agree with Mickey. Because, it kind of shows people... what's possible."

Yeah

I mean it is 'speaking the unspeakable'.

Wanking

(Mickey's bedroom, Muswell Hill, weekend daytime November 2002)

Aah, you've been sticking your photos up!

Yeah, that's for women over there; and this area is men. Caetano my brother, Rob, pointing to a sign in Halcyon[1] saying 'No matter where you go, there you are!'; Lui and Mark and the people we used to live with in Tooting - we all went to stay in a yurt[2] in Hammlet.

Hammlet?

Yeah! This is Suzi, I went to stay with her in Wimbledon before I flew back to Australia and Mark just turned up from Bristol. He heard where I was and that I was flying the next day and he turned up to stay – he didn't know where he was staying or anything – just to hang out. Us dancing with Vinny, who committed suicide; and this is his half brother.

God, he committed suicide?

Yeah, all sorts of addiction, his Mother died and there were messy secrets, lies and misunderstandings. Kevin, Suzi, Sebastien, this guy I used to hang out with in Calcutta. I worked with Mother Theresa over Christmas and New Year one year and we used to hang out loads! He's French and we communicated brilliantly over there, it was so cool! In this country we just couldn't. Everyone else is speaking English here, so I suppose in comparison we were speaking the same language over there. When he moved here, I helped find him work and stuff, but he was 'too much work'. He had his girlfriend with him anyway.

What language did you speak over there then?

English!

Aah

But out there no one spoke English that much. Everyone else was speaking their language, broken English or an Indian English; Timmy and I, Jane, and a guy we met in, um, where was it, the top of Australia somewhere. Coomba? *'Living In The Light'*[a], years ago, that's when I first went away, abroad, since moving into England, on my own, with some friends. I was reading 'Living In The Light' sitting near the pool and Tim snuck up behind me while Mark took the shot.

Where's that bottom one?

Delhi!

What's that huge...

Taj Mahal...

Is that the Taj Mahal?

Yeah, so it's not Delhi then is it? It's Agra. Vi-agra...

Huh huh.

I was sitting in my favourite little rooftop café, just watching the kids playing on the roofs, stuff like that, and it all looked fucking gorgeous, so I just took a photo. See that little kid in there? *(laughs)* I'll tell you why I have this picture of the Taj and the kid in my 'man' area... I was watching the kids play and someone from the table behind me said *"That little boy's having a wank!"* And the guy was just facing the wall, had a quick little wank and then just carried on playing with the rest of the children. How cool and honest is that! So I thought 'fucking-ace, that can go in my 'man area'. Ha ha ha ha ha... Natural, normal wanking!

As it should be.

I don't know. I don't know that I'd wanna know that one of my friends had just 'popped one out' and now he's come back to me to hang out…

Remember I was telling you about that mate who, um, I cut off - Jude? When I was about fourteen or fifteen? We used to talk about wanking – I mean, never quite "I've just been to the loo and had a wank!" But – it… isn't that normal?

Yeah, I think that's cool…

Yeah, that's what I mean, that's exactly normal.

Not that I've really had that. Or properly talked about stuff like that… Kind of, not really, not at all. Well, I didn't used to do it properly, even deny doing it! Too bloody Catholic.

That's something I really admire about Margaret. She's got a kid who's nearly fourteen, and an eleven or twelve year old son; and the older one, she's very very aware of boundaries. She always knocks when she needs to go into his room.

That is sooo good.

She's superb with them. I was just suddenly thinking about wanking when I was – how old would I have been? Twelve to about fourteen or fifteen. It's that weird thing again, like parents don't know what's going on. I used to wank against all sorts of things, like bed clothes and the curtains in my room – I used to, like, clean myself up on my curtains…

I never did that! Any of that!

…thinking that my parents wouldn't know, and they must have known. I remember once when my Mum washed my curtains. She very deliberately took them down and - like they weren't like actually stiff, but…

OH MY GOD!

…but how did I think they wouldn't know? And what did they think? Again, it was like there was no – maybe they didn't need to say

"Ed, I think you're going to have to stop creaming against the curtains." I mean that would be potentially even more embarrassing. But that's it, again, no one knows how to handle it, there's no parents to say "Look, ok, you're going to want to wank, here's a box of Kleenex[4] – don't do it against the furniture, son." Do you know what I mean? Fundamental, really…

The confrontation side of things with parental communication…

I remember you saying that you didn't really used to wank!

No, not at all…

Is that because you didn't know about other people doing it, or…

No, quite the opposite! Well, no, I didn't know other people were doing it. When I was really, really young, I kind of discovered it myself. I wasn't ejaculating or anything, it was just such a nice feeling! I was so paranoid; even then, I so wanted to not do it, to stop myself, because *I was so convinced that I was going to get pregnant.*

From wanking?

I didn't know how babies were made. I had no idea, I was so young, that somehow I just put my dick and pregnancy together, even though there wasn't a woman involved, and I thought, 'fuck me I'm gonna get pregnant! And then the doctors are probably going to cut me up and see what's up with me and they'll ask me how it happened and I don't know what I'm going to say; I'll have to come up with a really good story because I can't explain, or whip it out and go there! So I'd have to come up with some logical explanation…'

Ha ha ha… How bizarre! How old were you at this point? Twelve, or …?

No, no, no, no. Pre-teens.

So when did you start wanking? Or playing around? Ten? Eleven?

No, I'd say it was, around… I don't really know. Nine?

Nine? That seems young!

Mind you I wouldn't be surprised if its'… I remember one day, when I was in school, thinking, remembering suddenly that I had a dick and that I hadn't seen it for ages! Not having any idea what it looks like or anything, and you know I probably, obviously peed every day, washed and whatever but never looked, never thought, it just never crossed my mind.

1. Halcyon, California. HQ of The Temple Of The People, intentional community. www.templeofthepeople.org (and in England http://homepage.ntlworld.com/creedsdisappear/index.html)

2. Yurt. A temporary dwelling made generally from cloth or canvas and large poles. Originally from Mongolia, made from skin.

3. 'Living In The Light'. Shakti Gawain (New World Library) 1995. www.shaktigawain.com

4. Kleenex. A brand of tissues.

Worth

I find that's something I get a lot when I've been smoking dope[5], that I actually process things so quickly that I get beyond actually needing to express it. I'm thinking, 'I should have expressed that...'

Ha ha ha – it all happens so quickly in your head!

Yeah!

But I find that's what dope does. You go so round-and-round in circles in your head that on one hand it's really creative, and really quick and really clear and stuff; but on the other hand you can go all over the place and forget the point. Or you could have these great insights and everything; and once you're not stoned any more, it just floats off in this bubble, this huge creative bubble that you have no connection to, 'cos you're down again. Further down than before because you 'owe the energy back'. So, vague, with no energy to think straight – leave alone bloody do anything.

Hmmm

But more than anything, I'd say, for me, it cuts me off emotionally.

It cuts you off?

I would say that for most people it's an emotional buffer, so you can observe and think and get into your head and stuff and not really feel. But for me I find it brings me 'down here', rather than keeping me so in my head in concepts. More down into the physical through, basically, breathing into my body.

Hmmm, yeah, breathing, breathing.

(drift away silence...)

And again it's that thing, that elusiveness of achievement, of success, what does it actually mean and how do you measure it, how do you know? Robert Bly[6] talks about this in *'Iron John'*[7], that Fathers have nothing to show their sons.

In what way?

Well, he was saying, in traditional societies, even up until the early 19th or 20th centuries, generally people were either agricultural or they lived above a shop or above a smithy[8] or whatever, where the children could actually see what the Father did...

Yeah

...now, as you said, you know, some people occasionally take their child to their office for a weird day out. Well, how do you explain, "Well, I'm a corporate decision maker," or...

And it's not about quality, service, relationships, community - it's all about money! Competing. How to rip off people! How should I best rip-off people? *What kind of a cunt[9] are you? Oh, that gives me perfect license to be this kind of a cunt then, because that level of cunt-ism is accepted, in fact expected in our business community.*

Or, it's reacted totally against – I mean, that's what I feel I've done. In fact, my brother and sister, to an extent

In what way?

Well, its like you were saying, about money, and not knowing how to handle it. Its almost like 'money is evil'. Whereas it's probably a lot to do with models that we were shown; the way that people use money or power or – oh, I don't know – in not knowing what they are achieving. I've never really known how it works with my Dad. It's always been, he's always had money, they're wealthy, though they have a fairly poverty-conscious mentality.

Do they?

In some ways, yeah! They don't know quite how to live lavishly. They don't know how to enjoy their money. They fall into my Dad's parents' pattern, buying cheap, mediocre stuff, from catalogues - its really odd – penny-pinching mentality. My Mum hardly buys anything for herself, she buys for me and my brother and sister, when we let her. And then it's lavish. As if she's saying "I know how to lavish!" She can spend on other people, but not on herself.

My Father used to do that. But then, in a way, is that them doing something good and clever, by saving some money? Are they being tight or are they being shrewd? But then don't people over-perform something, rather than being in a relationship with it? Not knowing when to stop being clever because it's not clever any more? Like him telling jokes, its funny the first time, but when I witness him telling it to everyone, all the time, it's so fucking boring…

Yeah

…especially when I'm expected to act like it's the first time he's telling it. But it just becomes a sad lie – from me!

Absolutely

People becoming performing monkeys for each other. 'I will do whatever I need to do, or be whoever you want me to be in this company, but you don't find out who I really am – and you won't reject me.' Surely sex comes into it in a way, there. Its like, 'ok well if that's what you want, as long as you look after me and feed me and whatever, then I'll do this, and this, 'to' you to make you feel safe'. There's no meeting and enjoying being intimate and playing and stuff together. It's more like, well sex is expected now, I suppose. Typical 'Married With Children'[10] – the Bundies! Know it?

Yeah…

What about that guy we met at Findhorn[11]? If there's one thing I did at Findhorn, it was speaking with that guy who was so cut up about his wife and how she never had orgasms. She always hassled him, "You don't know how to treat me", "You don't know how to bring me to orgasm", "Sex is crap!", blah blah blah and his posture was all, he was a broken man with a twisted spine. He was obviously very very nice. He had dignity. But there was something missing. It was so sad. Like a shadow cast over him. I didn't think. It was quite a risk for me to take to say the truth, and I said, "Well, has she given herself an orgasm?" Hmmmm, no! "Does she know what goes on down there? Has she had a look or a play herself?" Hmmmm, no! *"Aah… so she's totally avoiding her own sexuality and beating you up for being scared of her own fucking fanny!* Tell her to take responsibility and something might happen, yeah?!"

That's so incredibly truthful…

Yeah, he's an old man and he's probably had this all his life. I wonder where this came from? I wonder what his family was like, or what his first sexual experience was. Or even experiences that weren't even necessarily that sexual, because it's obviously not about those two. They probably don't feel right about something that comes from further back in their pasts.

So how was it for you then?

I remember in the early days – I've never been a really good kisser, I don't think – because it's not something that I do, it's something by which I like to express how I feel. It's a really intimate thing – far more intimate than shagging! But, um, I wouldn't kiss so much, but I'd feel – in the early days – that I'd need to perform sex. What positions, in what way, how, I wasn't feeling or enjoying or anything; in fact it was easier to hold her hard and close because then I wouldn't need to make eye contact. It's like we weren't there. 'Let's get this act out of the way'. Sure, I enjoyed some of it some of the time, but it's not what I want now. Now I am a lot more comfortable and mature and it is about fun and sharing, rather than all the lies that blokes tell and all the crap you see on TV.

Well yes, there is the liberation of just being with somebody and not having a point in mind. When you were a teenager, the obsessions, well, the cultural obsessions with sex as a sort of starting and finishing point. You learn how to do foreplay and kissing, then get your clothes off, penetration, orgasm – preferably both, preferably her first, followed by you... So there's a far bigger menu, isn't there? Than the set dinner.

Well, different for me, because we weren't allowed genitals in the house and there was no such thing as sex, because we were teased. Anything that my parents were embarrassed about, emotions, sex, whatever secrets and lies; we were manipulated so they would never come up. Basically, my parents would tease my brother and I if there was kissing on the TV because they were very embarrassed and hadn't matured as adults, or even young teens, sexually, so we missed out on ours and it was all very taboo and stuff.

Presumably your parents had sex in the dark...

I don't know. I'd be astounded if they had a good sex life. I remember a couple of little rows that they had, where things were said, partly in code but I could always understand a bit; hence I thought, or believed that sex was something that men did to women that women don't want done to them. Something painful, or a sacrifice. Heavy.

That they were prepared to give, because, as you said, it was part of the contract...

Yup

'...you feed me, you clothe me, you give me children, you protect me'

Exactly! 'She makes my meals and I have to do this, or do that'. And also for me, it wasn't a 'normal' sex life. Over and above my parents, I was obsessive-compulsive[12], so the whole idea of kissing, or anything intimate, was contamination and was just plain dirty. Plus being coloured, just being checked out and different and whatever; plus my own issues, I was fat, I was hairier than most of the other guys, I had never really seen bodies or anything – it was all taboo – and because I was fat or whatever, the most embarrassing thing I have had all my life was inverted nipples! I thought 'no one is going to see this!' I would rather not! And to an extent, it's like I'm not going to shag until after leaving home – and I was so many years behind, sexually totally unaware anyway, it just got into, well, its been so long, or I've hidden from this for so long, that now I've got to be right. You know, I need to do something about my body. Learn some new tricks or whatever. But then it just started happening. But I've never been... I don't know, maybe I've just never used sex as a fix. It's been something over-serious. Maybe, respected. Yeah, sex was never something to share or enjoy. And the way that men talk about it, or maybe lie about it, makes it sound like something you aggressively 'do' to someone else; it doesn't even sound pleasurable. So many of my friends have been saying that they go out, on the pull or whatever, they get drunk, they pick some 'thing' up - it's not even a person by then, and it's certainly not attractive, and the only way of justifying it to yourself and other people is "I was drunk – and it's nothing to do with me" and then they take 'it' home and they just know pretty-much exactly what they are going to do, how they're going to do it - lift her up here, fling her around there, whatever – cum, and then just totally disconnect.

Disengage…

Yeah!

How do they get the person out of their bed, or how did they get out of that person's bed?

They - the blokes - just don't want to be touched, under any circumstances, after cum-ing. So it's like open the door, get a fix, total 'vamp'[13], then close the door and run away! Where's the pleasure? What's the point? And am I missing out on something?

Ha ha ha

He he he

We're not a very pleasure-orientated society, are we? As you have said already about the work and the money. Those are the important issues.

Say that again?

I don't think pleasure is really something we are taught to look for. Again, this is...

It's a class thing again. Working class people can't afford pleasure!

I know, but, ironically, I think historically, they were more free sexually.

Exactly!

So that was their free leisure. Sex.

Through poverty, you don't buy sex, you share it, enjoy it. Being really intimate, rather than some sort of a paranoid power trip.

But *do you think poverty is noble?* I don't think it necessarily is...

No, not at all. But well, it can separate people. Look at the working class these days. They've got more courage. They can get credit – or whatever – and it separates them. They're not sharing any more, they're competing with trainers and gadgets and everything the so-called wealthy have used to fuck themselves up with. But how fucked up? I don't want to play any of this any more – I don't believe in it. Where do you go? What do you do?

That's the kind of nub of it. What do you do? What are the alternatives? You know, you can talk about community, I mean... I lived in Wilmington for a year and a half, the 'intentional community' in Wessex; and that's one thing. But with you, you build yours around you and you have done wherever you've been – in Sydney, Fiji, here,

wherever – and you've kept being able to do it. It's about belonging, isn't it? And not belonging – that's where that desperation comes from. It's that desperation again, I've got to 'be' somebody. I've got to make my mark.

Who do you want to prove it to? What do you want to prove? Let's deal with that!

I think there is a Dad element in there, but I think it's – it is the kind of comparative thing - you know - that we can rationally talk about all the things we've talked about; being separate and in competition and how it seeps into you without you realising. I guess my point is that in talking about it, saying it's a bad thing, I have never been more aware of other people's success; and everywhere I look there seem to be celebrities, everyone is trying to be famous, you know, like the cult of being famous, like *'Big Brother'*[14] and *'Pop Rivals'*[15] – whatever they are called – *'Pop Stars'*[15]. There is an obsession of being 'better than'.

Being someone...

Yeah, but it must be quite a strong drive, or it's always been really encouraged.

Well, do you know, a couple of days ago it crossed my mind, why do I want – over and above sharing my awareness and my purpose and all that wank – why do I want to do this book, TV, whatever? OK, I want to live in Australia. Then I thought, 'well, as a child, what did we do? Watch TV'. That's how we avoided life and that's how we lived our lives through other people. That's how we were connected. So what would be the ideal thing for me to do? Well, one of them was working with Mother Theresa, because with my parents' poverty consciousness and the Catholic shit and the rest of it – that's the way, Mother Theresa. Hmmm... I now realise that wasn't the intention – I didn't realise until years later – so I scored marks with that one! Where do I get my next brownie points from? Well, what were they addicted to, other then poverty and Catholicism?

Well, TV. Ha ha ha ha ha. That's where you think the drive comes from?

Well, maybe – that's part of it or something?! Maybe… And other people that are on TV. What have they got in common? Probably from a TV family, probably didn't really get that much attention or be able to join in at a normal day-to-day level at school and other places, so this is their way of performing – or dominating? Or being in a position where they can't (or want to) have stones thrown at them? Do you know what I mean? How to 'be someone' for themselves, or to feed, or react to the past.

Yeah! Untouchable, higher than…

Yeah, all the big issues – and a lot of it is child abuse as well; and I was thinking about this. And I was thinking, was I abused as a child? *Psychic people have pretty much all been abused, from what I've heard!* I remember a woman who I met that a friend took me to - who knew about my background and the psychic stuff and whatever - and she said "Yes, he is psychic and this and that and whatever, but it doesn't make sense because he is not gay and all psychics are; one way or another – bisexual or they've had some sort of an abusive 'thing' happen where they have had to leave their bodies and 'go somewhere' while it went on. There is that common denominator…"

5. *Dope. Cannabis, marijuana, grass, spliff, ganja, blow, draw, pot.*

6. *Robert Bly. US author and poet. www.robertbly.com*

7. *'Iron John' Robert Bly (Vintage Press) 1990.*

8. *Smithy. A blacksmith's workshop.*

9. *Cunt. A nasty person of no honour (in this context).*

10. *'Married With Children' (1986-1997) US cult sit-com.*

11. *Findhorn. (Forres, Scotland) Intentional community/educational facility. www.findhorn.org*

12. *Obsessive-compulsive (disorder) / OCD. Neurosis, where the sufferer is driven to repeatedly perform particular acts, such as washing, counting, checking, tapping, etc.*

13. *Vamp. (A 'Mick-ism'. Taken from the word vampire) One who steals emotional / mental / psychic energy from an unsuspecting host.*

14. *'Big Brother' Reality television show.*

15. *'Pop Rivals' & 'Pop Stars' Reality television show.*

Fathers

(still sticking pictures up...)

This is a really cool picture of me...

That's your Salman Rushdie[16] expression.

Which one?

The orange T shirt...

That one! Ha ha ha ha ha

But I think you've changed! I mean, in that picture – it's kind of recognisable, but it's not! That's more a... kind of 'girlie?'

Hmmm...!

Silvikrin[17] advert.

Yeah, being 'nice'. Hmmm – being a 'good' Mummy's-boy!

When you got off the bus today, I was thinking - I just kind of had this feeling, I mean I looked at you and thought you seem more manly!

Yeah!

Well the same with Bob actually... To a large extent, last night. It was just like, fear. A lot of the fear seems to have gone...

We're growing into our own. But then again, that's the whole thing about – this always happens to men when their Fathers die. I don't want to wait!

Absolutely!

I don't want to play small for approval or 'be silly' in that way.

But I think the other thing - you know you were saying about your family and TV and fixes - I guess when we grew up, TV was just becoming a really big thing. Not taking part – I mean the office that I work in; it's really strange to hear them talking about *'Eastenders'*[18], or they all went to the pub, or they did this. I guess it's that kind of thing about being on the edge...

What do you mean?

I guess I want – I want to live amongst people who have community, or be in a community where it's not all kind-of 'love and light' like the community where I lived, or like Findhorn. But it's also not the sort of bond together by getting pissed-up at the pub or workaholic straight-heads. Creating something new... But not even new, maybe recreating something that we had in old communities.

Yeah, or the principles of, because there is natural progression.

Hmmm.

Fuck that's lovely! That is just, such a happy door... Smiles and people, gorgeous! It's unbelievable, just one panel! I have had such a fucking good life.

So what are you fucking whinging about then?

Ha ha ha – I WANT MORE! But a lot of these photos are... not in England. It is not within this structure. In fact all of it, including my close friends who are in England and things that happened in England. It was when we were 'breaking the rules and being close', being friends and being trusting and not being competitive. Most of these – looking at them – are overseas, or people who have moved abroad. Just that special spark of acceptance, trust... bloody hell!

I guess its interesting that we are taught that if you are not competitive you are 'soft' and you don't have any edges, but it must be possible. That cooperating can actually – fuck, I can't even express it – its like you were saying earlier, not everyone needs to know how to do everything. In a functional society - a cooperative society - everyone has roles to play - and not just one role.

It's too hot in here…

Too hot? In here? Well, you can turn it down – or turn it off…

Man I never remember that I can turn the radiator on or off in my room.

Bet your Dad never showed you how to do that, either!

Ha ha ha – cunt! Fucker… The heating and lights were hysterically monitored.

That's the thing with my Dad, I mean, I can remember that he would start off trying to be a patient teacher or mentor, but he'd get so impatient and frustrated really quickly – was it the same with you?

(Nods)

Yeah, he would take over like 'let's mend the puncture on your bike. Let's go out and do it'. I didn't know what the fuck I was doing, it wasn't explained clearly, I would get really frustrated and he'd say "Oh, for God's sake!!!"

Exactly!

I'd almost prefer it if he just pushed me physically out of the way, throw me aside – some real, tangible violence, rather than this kind of real fucked-off hovering… Uurgh!

Exactly… It is so much worse when they are pretending not to be angry and they are suppressing it; and you are living in absolute fucking fear! I wish they just did it…

Well, it's all there, isn't it? *The clenched fists and calm talk through gritted teeth and hateful eyes.*
"No, you are doing a really good job. That's fine. I'm really enjoying

showing you how do this."

I suppose it's the same as wife beating. It is better to be beaten sooner rather than later. You know it's going to happen; and the longer you have to wait the worse it's going to be and the more painful it is now while waiting.

Exactly, it just kind of brews and brews and gets more and more - ugly.

Twisted! - I am doing exactly what I want clients to do.

Feng Shui[19] their rooms?

Wouldn't dream of getting them to stick so many up in such a student-stylee, obviously! Yeah, with the right photos, the right images. - Yeah, my Father was a fuck-wit like that. Always ridiculously angry, brewing – wouldn't say – you'd never know if he was happy, or sad, or if he was going to smile, or growl or what! What kind of a tension is that for anyone to live in, leave alone bring up your own children in. But you know, they denied it "Everything is fine!" Deny that there is an issue, meanwhile, we're learning that this is 'real life'. We're suffering like shit from their suppressed darksides – this becomes our lives. I have always said that we haven't had our own lives. All we are doing is living through my Father's childhood. Then, on the other hand, I always say 'poor fucker!' Must have been bad – must have been tough – but that's no excuse! To not 'deal with it' and to take it out on us!

Don't you want to hear your Father's story told – not in exact terms, but without self-pity, without the kind-of, oh...

Without the justification

...look, 'this is how it was, this is how I felt, this is what I experienced, this happened; and there it is'. I always got my Dad's story from my Mum – and it was always completely smothered by "well, you've got to understand...; and he had a bad...; and his parents didn't...;" and I just want to say... "Oh for fuck's sake!"

She had to understand him, to justify staying with him. It doesn't mean you've got to justify it to us, because we know YOU'VE FUCKED UP!

Ha ha ha ha ha... 'And I get to leave home, legitimately and you have to stay here with him...'

'And worse than that, you get to manipulate us for abandoning you, because you're stuck with this fucker that we have to give our whole lives to'; and pretend it was all okay. And what have we learned from it? Be a fucker, or don't go anywhere near girls because you – all men are like this; I was brought up to hate men for most of my life – *I*

hated men!

Yeah, absolutely... and *I was fearful!*

Exactly! And I would never be accepted by one. Whose 'stuff' is that? I'm not sure how much is my Mother and how much is my Father – that's quite new. You know, I believed my Mother – how could I not, she was the victim...

And probably quite a martyr as well...

Definitely! Both parents played martyr. But, yeah, now I'm thinking, well how much did my Mother control any communication and make sure I didn't have a relationship with my Father, because otherwise who has she got? She's scared of him, probably scared of even bonking him; I feel I was in the middle of my parent's relationship to keep them apart. So they don't need to deal with their own intimacy issues – well where the fuck does that leave the rest of my life?

Mm. Yup!

Didn't even know how to be 'nice' to each other. Basically nice; how do I know where dead centre is with this picture?

Thing I read this morning with that Robert Bly book – and I mean, now, I've heard all this stuff about *'Star Wars'*[20], the Tao[21], Yin Yang[22] and whatever – I've never thought about the fact that Darth

Vader[23] was a pun on Dark Father.

Aaah, dark fucker!

Vader, that's a German or Dutch word. V-a-d-e-r.

The dark invader...

Hmmm. Do I want, to be truly happy? *(whispers)* **I don't know what to do...! But that's the other thing. Yeah, and Mothers will carry not only their own pain and fear of abandonment, as they have been taught to do; but they take it for their men as well. So no wonder it has spilled over on to us.**

Yup...

Or we were made surrogates.

Hmmm! Well, we are the most powerful generation yet – I'm not sure every generation is – because we have choices, where they didn't so much, they kept schtum, they carried on; and let in the pervy way – because they weren't allowed to express it any other way but pervy and twisted. But we don't have to come from the darkside. And, um, we communicate. We say "No." We can. We're not dependent, like they were. We don't have to be together to survive. We can take loans and use our credit cards - and then not talk to each other about how much we owe; does that look centred? From the centre of the mirror?

Yeah, I would say that's okay. I love it when it gets dark up here...

I just love this room, you can just see – you can be part of nature. What's cooking in the garden and what's happening with the sun and the moon.

Is there a new moon on Wednesday?

Yes!

16. *Salman Rushdie. Author of 'The Satanic Verses' (Random House) 1988, amongst others.*

17. *Silvikrin. Brand of shampoo.*

23

18. 'Eastenders' Soap opera set in London's East End.

19. Feng Shui. Ancient Chinese system of harmonious surroundings, which bring health, happiness and prosperity. (Aligning us with heaven and earth).

20. 'Star Wars' (1977) George Lucas, US.

21. The Tao. Religio-philosophical system from the 'I-Ching' ('The Book of Changes')

22. Yin & Yang. The two complementary and opposing principles of Chinese philosophy.

23. Darth Vader. Principal character in 'Star Wars'.

Living space

Evil little fucker!

Me?

You look like a little black boy from the ghetto!

That is, um, the prison. Alcatraz[24]... so I assumed the –

Probably the expression of most of its inhabitants...

Yes!

'Angry black person.'

Huh huh huh huh...

Yeah, you know you have been talking about yoga. I have been doing it now, for what, four years. I could teach you the rudiments of it...

What type do you do?

Well I started off doing Iyengar, which is one of the more... well, I don't know if it's traditional!

I thought that was quite new! A lot of stretching and...

Yeah, you spend quite a lot of time getting into the postures and aligning your body with... but actually I think a proper teacher is necessary.

Yeah, to start with... That looks okay, doesn't it?

Yup, I'd say that's pretty perfect.

Outrageous!

You've got an eye for it… Something interesting here, having your own pictures, when I was staying, and looking after my friend Elizabeth's house, I noticed that she didn't have any pictures that didn't have herself in them. Part of me was like, that's really egotistical; but actually, it makes complete sense.

Hmmm.

I mean, whose life are you living?

Yeah! Huh huh huh huh huh…

Actually, something I was really aware of last night, when Lisa was explaining something. When she was talking about that workshop she went to. And I got totally distracted, because she was just saying "you" "you" "you". Instead of 'I' or 'me'.

Yeah. In panic, people don't always remember to 'own' what they say, do they?

Hmmm…

When it's something personal, that's when it's most important to de-personalise.

What do you think…? I mean, I must admit, one of my reservations about living in Bob's place is that feeling of confinement. People living above, either side, across, feels grotty – it feels… Not his house – the actual space I quite like. And the woman upstairs *"You fucking little cunt, shut up!"*

I haven't heard all that. To her kid…?

Well I actually, funnily enough, I stayed – how long? Ten days? And after about the third day, I thought 'I can't… I can't just listen to this. This is children, being talked to like this.'

Yeah…

And so I talked to some of the people I was doing fund-raising with. As it turned out, we were doing fund-raising for the National Children's Home[25]. Again, it's that sharing with people – I explained to my co-workers. 'I don't want to go to her door as, this kind of, well-spoken, middle class pseudo-social worker…'

Ha ha ha ha ha ha ha

"The NCH[26] run centres for single parents who might not be coping, blah blah blah." So it's like this perfect way. I went to her front door one morning, having heard this stuff the night before, just rang the door bell, the woman's grown up daughter came down and said, "Oh no, you want my Mum…" So her Mum came down and I thought, 'what the fuck do I say?' "I've been living downstairs for a while and it sounds like things can get really stressed in your house." And then she kind of looked at me like, 'what are you talking about?'

Hmmm

And I said, "You know, I don't want to interfere in your life; I work for the NCH and they have places for people, if they are feeling a bit stressed, they can go to see other families, whatever…" I gave her this leaflet and it was like, she didn't know what to do with it!

Ha ha ha ha ha…

She said "Aaow, fanx…!"

"You're not 'ere for a fight ven…"

I know. That's what amazed me.

Yeah. The 'shock' of caring…

Yeah! Yeah, not coming from the, sort of, humbler than, or better than, or…

"This is how I deal with emotions and boundaries and therefore WE HAVE TO HAVE A FIGHT!" Right – poo tiiiiime! *(Mickey goes for a shit…)*

(Ed, alone) 'Trouble is, I don't really feel safe. There is something hanging over me, so much of the time, a giant hand, some almighty – almighty something about to whack me! Knock me back. Down into place. Some background darkness. Darkness. The border… Water's trickling next door'

How wonderful that you're taking time to wipe your arse. All the things that I don't know – I didn't even know if you were doing that!

Hmmm…

I was suddenly thinking, God! About the way that we are taught to rush everything, wipe your bum quickly, and get out of there, and flush it and wipe it away – it's just this train of thought, what we were saying about creating something. About creating a community.

In what way…?

So many people that… I was thinking about Indian life, I was thinking that maybe their life is more meditative and better paced – and then I thought, oh well, that's romantic-ness, or whatever… But then I was also thinking about how so many idealists rush off and then feel that they have to make this kind-of 'renunciation'. Give up everything and live in poverty. So they go and live in a community that's got to be sort-of centred in the woods in a run-down old shit-hole of a house. I thought, God! I want to do that, but with abundance. Create a community… With wealth – not necessarily billions and billions, but just to do it well. I don't want to live in a shack in the middle of nowhere…

Yeah. Poverty. What's the term? Poverty is next to Godliness. No – that's cleanliness.

Oh, poverty is probably in the same region.

That was Mother Teresa's thing… that totally defeated the object of the exercise. It's not only working with the poorest of the poor, but it's about being and living; and the only way is to 'be' the poorest of the poor. And basically, all she created was a recycling machine. When I was working with dying people, it was the same old bloody people that were on death's doorstep, come in, she'd save their lives, sort them out, put them back in the same situation as they were in which they would survive for a while, then they would get another infection, back in here as gangrene sets in to join the other nasty diseases they had. It would eventually get the better of them and it would go on and on until they finally die – I suppose. Where she wouldn't give money to them, to send them back to their homes which would be in another part of India, where they could have started a new life and been OK and out of the cycle. But that would have been extra money and against the rules.

So she was propping that up!

Uh-humm. And the only reason is usually that people from different parts of India, who end up pulling a rickshaw, then having a cycle rickshaw, living and sleeping on the rickshaw as they pay someone else for the use of the rickshaw – whoever their boss or master is – and then sending the money back to their families. But because they are always earning money to pay their rent for the rickshaw and to send money back, they never have any. If they get a sore or a cut, they will carry on and it will go septic, gangrene will set in, maggots would move in and they still wouldn't look after it because they would have to work to have enough money and they'd end up with us. We'd just keep recycling them. Meanwhile, she used to give money to women, for dowries, so that they could get married!

Really?

How 'Catholic Church' is that?! But that used to go on…

But, I mean, she had loads, didn't she? A huge amount of abundance – homes, money…

Didn't it just go to the Church?

I don't know a lot about her, apart from her reputation as a living saint.

Living saint, but bloody hell, she was the most focussed person I have ever met. Totally stayed focussed, and so clear about it all – but, she also knows how to disconnect and switch off! She will stay with you and talk about something until your are done, no matter how many people are waiting; but like, for instance, I was talking about – don't remember what I went and said to her then – and in the end she got into a loop and said that "A family that prays together, stays together." I said, "OK, but I live in Australia, my brother is in Germany, my parents live in Wales! It wasn't quite practical here and now, so what about real life?" It was like, 'yes – but…' and then she decided to stop listening. And I found that she did that every now and again, when it suited her, and ordinarily, you know she is too holy to question. And with people like that, they just, you know, smile and say something silly; and if it was your child or your friend or your husband or wife you wouldn't really think anything of it, but because it's this holy person, or this famous person, or this smart-arse, you think "Oh, wooow man…!" Even though everyone has been telling you that stuff for the last twenty years. But she is a real battle-axe!

Ha ha ha ha ha

But funny you should mention that, because the last time I went to Wales was in June; and it was after months of getting on well with my parents. A few months after being more honest and truthful about who I am, how I am, and that there actually isn't enough money, and it's difficult, it's a nasty world, people aren't nice, ha ha ha. You know, just the truth, rather than 'fine, fine, everything's fine!' Which is what they really want, because then they don't worry and that way I don't… which isn't the truth. So, great! So I went and hung out, and um, to cut a long story short, that incident with my Father, when he left us on the roadside so he could go and make beef burgers for the Welshpoolians; my god Mother with her crutches, my Mother with sciatica[27], no shelter and no where to sit, and it seemed normal, because that kind of behaviour was normal. And, I realised, there and then, that it just wasn't. Rather than 'playing the Father' and telling him off and sulking around, I just withdrew, basically, until I left. And our relationship hasn't been the same since. But then I just thought, 'no, this is not acceptable.

You are crossing my boundaries; if everyone else wants to accept being treated like that, that's up to them. But they need to communicate or do something, but I'm not playing any more'.

Hmmm. Breaking a pattern...

24. *Alcatraz. San Francisco ex-maximum security prison, now tourist attraction.*

25. *National Children's Home. UK charity for child welfare. www.nch.org.uk*

26. *NCH. National Children's Home (see 25.)*

27. *Sciatica. Painful medical condition, affecting sciatic nerve in lower back and legs.*

Shitting

And from that time, I realised that I was constipated all my childhood. But I didn't know. It was hell going to the loo! Really painful. Horrible! Bleeding and shit.

Hmmm.

And pushing and straining…

Yeah…

But I thought that was normal. I thought everyone shat like that! Because we didn't talk about shitting.

Who does…?

Hmmm.

Christ!

Hmmm. And I came back and it was exactly the same. When I shat here, it was really painful. I even had piles once or twice when I was a kid there – and since – and I just thought, 'fuck it!' When I travelled in India for a bit, *I knew that at some stage I'd have to shit the Indian way,* squatting, without toilet paper but with water, and I remember about a week or so before I knew I'd have to do that, I just practised without even having a shit. Squatting there, would I fall over? And it wouldn't be a big scary deal – because if I fell over I wouldn't be covered in shit. It was only practise…

Hmmm.

And I kind of got into it, and I thought, 'fuck it, I'll do it that way so I don't have bleeding grapes'.

Ha ha ha ha ha

So I have been doing it the Indian way ever since and loving it, because ordinarily, I hate cleaning my arse. I screw my face up and want it done as quickly as possible!

Well, you screw your face and your arse up, don't you?

Yes, it's just tense and horrible… But this way, I really like – getting to know myself in a way! Washing the Indian way is great! I don't squat though. Oh, I think it's fantastic! I don't know why I'm telling you about all my shit! Oh I know, its because you said you heard the water trickling…

Yeah…! …and I don't know. Even though I have that same kind of retentiveness, I think it's really interesting to talk about! It's not even interesting, it's just – is!

Oh, he he he he he…

Oh, fucking hell, it's like… shit!

It's a secret! No one knows that I wash my arse. Huh huh huh huh huh… And I've got a little bottle and towel that I hide in the bathroom.

But it's so fundamental, isn't it? Never mind which part of the body you hold up to this or that, or represents whatever, a-la Louise Hay's book[28]; it's unhealthy not to just sit on the loo, you know just la la la la la, breathe a bit and out it comes!

Yup!

Actually, one of my breakthroughs was reading that Barefoot Doctor book[29], and he just talks about breathing into your stomach. Well, that's something else - I've always been straining and leaning forward. Ungghhhhhhhhhah!

Oh, when you're shitting?

Yeah! But no one teaches you how to shit, I mean I've noticed, now that Malaika is three and she is using the loo, she "unggggggggggggggghah" strains, but, I don't know. I wouldn't know how to explain to her…

Maybe you need to know whether she's constipated or not? Because with my parents, it probably didn't click! Because I was in there for ages and they probably thought it was because I was obsessive-compulsive more than anything.

Well, she's not! Because it's always fairly quick and fairly healthy, and she eats loads of fruit and dried fruit and whatever. I was just thinking, there are also practicalities, apart from all the emotional stuff, like drinking litres of water per day helps as well. Water is bloody good!

When I was a kid, I used to be constipated, I had obsessive-compulsive disorder BIG TIME! Touching things, checking, everything from my pockets to the doors, the windows, whether everyone is in the room, counting them, make sure that everyone is breathing, that doors are closed, fuck knows… that the heating is on and the taps are off and the fire has a guard in front of it, touching things, winking, making funny noises, twitching – and with all that, try finding the time to conk out! I'd get into panics, sweats – and think great, I'm sweating, this means I must be losing weight, because when you do any exercise, you sweat away your weight! Somehow, I must have put the two together, I told myself that I was using all that reserve energy and I must be losing weight.

It was probably a cold sweat, wasn't it?

Yeah! Probably, I'm not really sure what it is, but it was a sweat. I had mood swings – and that was low blood sugar.

I have a bit of that as well!

Yeah?

28. Louise Hay's book. 'You Can Heal Your Life' (Hay House Inc) 1984. www.hayhouse.com

29. Barefoot Doctor's book. 'Handbook For The Urban Warrior' (Piatkus) 1998. www.barefootdoctorglobal.com

Changing rooms

And funny you say about the fatness as well, because I think that's a very Mummy's-boy obsession.

Really? Mummy's-boys are usually quite chubby!

Yeah, well, girlie-looking!

Yeah, well fleshed out…

I was terrified because I was quite fat. I'd got these tits… And I remember once – I was sitting having lunch, and my Dad reached over and pinched my waist and said "Hmmm, getting a few rolls of flab there, Ed." The shock of that – I only realised how big a shock that was recently. The shame! I don't even remember anyone specifically pointing it out… Except that time. But it was just, looking around and seeing that other kids didn't seem to have them…

Well I didn't even dare look at other boys in the changing rooms; and I didn't want anyone to look at me! I wouldn't dare, in case anyone saw me looking at them. I was too scared to look. It's like, not even a sex thing or I'll be caught, but it's just like – no way!

Did you not even look surreptitiously?

Not really!

Kind of stealing from the corner of your eye?

Not really, not until probably – probably, the only ones I'd look at were the ones that were really hiding under some; I remember there were one or two boys who had these huge towel things, with a loop that they put over their heads, so they can change in their own tent.

Oh?!! Did they not get the piss ripped out of them?

Not really… That's when we were really really young and unaware – of anything.

Especially not knowing why you are doing it. Yeah!

I remember the first time I looked, and I was just changing and stuff; and my friend kept looking at me and making eyes to look at someone else. And there was this older boy there and he had this big dick and it was all hairy and stuff and we thought, 'fucking hell, what is going on there!?'

Ha ha ha ha ha

It was scary. It was like, 'What's going on? Surely that's not going to happen to us!' But it didn't register that all that had happened was that things got bigger and hairy. 'Are there extra bits there? Is it a monster? Is he in pain? Is it…'

Like a mythical creature has walked into the changing room.

Yeah. I had just never seen anyone naked like that. And my parents were just so anal and hiding, pretending to be comfortable but it was all weird. But how sad. I mean the shock that a man's body could freak me out like it's a monster from another planet, at that age! 'Was there something wrong with that guy and it's only him that's like that, or is it normal?' I didn't even know that… Ha ha ha ha ha! 'Has he got some secret disease that no one else knows about?'

They're powerful places, actually! You could write a whole book about changing rooms, couldn't you?

Hmmm.

They are about the only place in our culture where men are naked, but then it's mostly either peeking 'oops, and then not getting caught' or blanking, 'I'm not looking at all…' or sometimes, the kind of – well the gay thing! You are allowed to look, you are allowed to make eye contact.

Really?

Well, that's the beginning of it. It's like, you can make sexual contact. I mean you can in any situation...

Oh, but in that case it is looking more, because you want some, rather than looking because it is just healthy and normal to look.

Yeah, the preparation for 'doing' something. It's like, *'I want you, do you want me, so let's meet up and fuck or whatever.'*

So, is all this judging-looking then?

Well, I guess so!

Evaluating whether I fancy you or not...

Or kind of catching somebody in the radiance. 'You take my fancy, do I take your fancy...? Yeah, okay.'

Right.

But at school, I don't remember that. Although I do remember – I can't remember if I have told you, but I drew my own 'gay porn' from an early age. Or rather sex, or men's bodies.

What age?

Probably about puberty... Again, it was like the kind of... partly because there was so much there, in your face, but you weren't allowed to look. A bit like my Dad thing, when I used to watch him walk naked to the bathroom and thought he didn't know. Yeah! Peeking through the crack in the door... and one day, he stopped – he wasn't angry or anything – he just said "I can see you." ...maybe this ...I don't know. It sticks in my mind...

Oh?

Well, I drew pictures – and I was always being fucked by teachers.

Older men…

Really?

In changing rooms! That is total fantasy, by the way… At one point, even going into a changing room, the smell would totally excite me. Wow!

So what was your connection with the others? Did you feel like a 'lesser' boy? I felt like a lesser boy. I wasn't tough, I wasn't a bully, I wanted to be invisible, especially being the only coloured boy, I just didn't want to be stared at, or noticed, or taken the piss off, I just wanted to keep my dignity.

Yeah,

So I'd make myself invisible rather than compete. I just never joined in. And it was all a blag! I remember coming home from school after the hugest traumas of my life in changing rooms; first time I went to the swimming pool – I'd never been swimming. So I just put my trunks over my underwear and thought 'fuck it, I'm not going to get naked or change, I don't know how to do that'. It was so traumatic. And when I came out of the swimming pool, I'll just take my trunks off and I will be in my underwear. Ha ha ha. I would be totally preoccupied about how to hide myself in the changing rooms; leave alone check anyone else out. I just didn't want to be checked out. So I think the school teacher had to help me out – I haven't got a clue what happened, but she must have had to help change me somehow, or done something. Well we were refugees anyway… And that was the first time I had ever been in a changing room.

Fuck!

My parents didn't used to talk about anything that was scary. We never talked about changing rooms, but I remember them asking me if I had noticed anything 'different' about the other boys? They were almost like, 'he he he!' I don't remember whether I said 'yes', or 'no', but it was just so traumatic to even talk about – and especially with them, or my perception of them coming from 'he he he' – which is probably what

I'd expect anyway, with my own paranoia. Then they talked amongst themselves – or so it seemed – rather than saying – because I didn't know what they were referring to – maybe it was just the colour, maybe they've got two dicks... what was wrong with me?

Size, maturity, hairy...

Years later, I realised that what they were referring to was circumcision. Obviously, I had never heard of all these things. Why didn't they just tell me before?

Why was it such an issue for them?

Exactly... And especially not to explain what they are on about. It left me paranoid because for most of my young life I thought I was deformed. Like I told you when we first met at Findhorn. Not realising that other people have that fraenulum thing[30], that looks like a deformed, not properly broken away piece of stray dick-skin!

Do you know, this is really funny, I just suddenly thought – Findhorn, 'find horn' Ha ha ha

No exactly, how can you possibly find something like that out, unless you check out other boys and stuff; but then I didn't want to go anywhere near other boys, or girls. Boys in changing rooms, because I was obsessive-compulsive anyway – I was fucked up! I had fucking inverted nipples, and coloured, and Catholic...

Yeah, I know, but at least you've got all those excuses. I don't have any, apart from being poncey, clever, Mummy's-boy. Yeah, well it's no wonder, I mean Jesus Christ!

And then, thinking about it, my first day in the changing rooms in secondary school – everyone scared the shit out of me about secondary school – a guy attacked me verbally and physically! He started abusing me, about racist stuff, do I fuck white girls – I didn't even know what fucking was! I thought you just lie there with your dick inside her – and what happens if you want to pee?

Ha ha ha ha ha

And what's the great fun in that? Just lying there, and...

We had this discussion in our class once, it was so naïve, looking back at it. 'So, um, how do you get the sperm into the woman?' It basically transpired that nobody knew that you had to fuck them. It's like, we all thought, because we all wanked, we thought that what you did was that you wanked, then somehow you transfer it, very carefully, like from in your hand to her cunt...

Ha ha ha ha ha

Ha ha ha ha ha

I didn't even know that anyone else wanked. I remember being given a little book, from my parents, or my school or the Church or something. It basically said that if you get a stiffie, you should turn over and think pure thoughts like about the Virgin Mary and stuff. Say your Hail Mary's until it goes away! Huh huh huh...

More like thinking about fucking the Virgin Mary!

Ha ha ha ha ha

Which, of course, is probably what you start doing anyway. It's like when you're told 'not' to do something, what do you fixate on? Doing it!

Yeah, exactly...

Except it's all so twisted and forbidden. And of course Mary is the ultimate in all Mothers. So they are already making it about fucking your own Mother.

30. Fraenulum thing. 'Fraenum'. Piece of skin under the glans of the penis, connecting it to the shaft.

Class

My Father and Mother both pushed their families away.

In what way?

Well, my Dad absolutely reviled his father for being working class.
And my Mother, I think, well, the whole shit with her family.

Your Father had a thing with his family for being working class?

Mmmmmmmmmm.

Did he feel like he needed to...

Desperate to be middle class!

But did he help them out? Give them? Share with them?

No! No need. They were quite capable. They owned their own home
in the 1930's and 1940's, in London, and I suppose that was quite
unusual. But I think he hated his Father because his Father was, you
know, a solid...

Working class bloke!

...yeah! Absolutely. But he, my grand Father wanted to be an artist
and a journalist. And now he's got a grandson who's a journalist and
one who's an artist.

And that's what your Father wasn't into?

Yeah, yeah...

And that's what his sons turned into.

Yup! It skipped a generation. He ran off to sea to do the kind of...

So you are your Father's replacement for his Father?

Oops! Fucking hell, I never thought of that!

Maybe?

Maybe, I've always thought of being my Mother's replacement for her Father – maybe I am both! Jesus, what a burden! And wasn't that interesting, what Bob said about that fight between his parents? Do you remember? Where his Mother threw the cup...

Yeah!

...and then she said "Help us, help us!" to him.

Yeah, yeah!

I thought, 'how incredibly revealing!' I mean, it's almost like, what a slip!

Yeah, totally!

You rarely get that degree of 'this is what this is all about'.

Yeah. Honesty.

Yeah, amazing.

And what a trip...!

Exactly!

That means, right! You're on duty for good now. And *bang goes your childhood.*

Yeah. You're the keeper.

Exactly...

You're the parent.

Yeah...

But it is, it's the rejection of the Father. You know, coming back to what I have been reading in the Robert Bly book; you know, when we were talking yesterday about the Father having something to show his son – that sounds like something Bob's friend Dave's got with his Father.

Just really... love of the land, and of nature, and relationship to every thing and every one.

Absolutely!

Meanwhile, ours was demonstrated as quite the opposite. Fear of everything and every one!

Yeah.

Don't belong... Competitions... Who are we...? Not good enough... Tossers...!

Hummm. Ha ha ha ha ha. No identity!

Hmmm.

My Dad hasn't really got an identity. Well he's not working class, but he's not really middle class.

So, why is he not middle class?

Umm, because he's got the trappings. I suppose he has succeeded in becoming middle class. He's sort of erased the past bits – but where did that leave us? I mean, we all did the – going off and becoming Socialists[31] and Communists[32] and rebelling against successful Dad – well, financially successful Dad.

So was his becoming middle class partly a lie – and you guys didn't buy the lie?

I think so, yeah...

Or a blag?

Hmmm... I think it was done so unpleasantly as well. I mean, it wasn't as if he tried to; this could be my sister's memory playing up or whatever, but she says it must have been the 70's. My Dad was really into exploring 'foreign' food and that's all about being middle class. Or was then...

Hmmm...

He took us on foreign holidays to Brittany – how fucking middle class can you get? But she says that we were having lunch once, when my grandparents were over and we had baguettes – which I suppose was quite unusual in those days, in Surrey. And, um, apparently my grand Father got the bread knife and started to cut it and my Dad just said to him, with complete disgust, "You don't 'cut' it – you 'tear' it!" Aaah - and she said it was like acid, so venomous. Visits to my grandparents were horrendous. He was so abusive. So angry...

Really?

Oh, and they were just like frightened deer. They wanted to give – give – give. But he just would not accept. Could not accept.

So they were good, honest, working class people?

Yeah...!

And he was a competitive, middle class...

Bastard!

Ha ha ha ha ha

Ha ha ha ha ha

And what was his work? Was it something corporate in British Gas or something?

My sister's always said he was just a good arse-licker.

Really?

Which I think is true! I mean, then again, when he talks about his childhood, he is really nostalgic. But, it's like, the reality of it, when we were growing up, was awful. We couldn't wait to get away from my grandparent's house. All of us. My Mum, desperately trying to smooth things over. So yeah... I wonder really...

Yeah.

It's really fucked up!

My Father was an arse-licker, but I think that's quite a working class way. He was always paying back the community for accepting us. He paid with 'our' lives. The only way to get on... and you expect to be bullied; and you're trapped; so what are you going to do – get another job? And, my Father needed to be accepted, and be someone, whatever – so it was a 'love me – love me' thing. Fear of abandonment - so he licked arse...

I hung out with a mixed bunch of boys and girls at the beginning of sixth form, then I mainly hung out with this really cool bunch of girls – they were all Mod-ettes[35], they really liked music and they went to clubs and they drank – so my initiation there was by girls, of my own age; after not knowing quite what to do when faced with a hot girl who wanted some form of sex.

Didn't the blokes talk about sex and stuff?

Yeah! But I completely abandoned my set of friends when I went from college to university. *Oh God, it's so horrifying to see that I have repeated all my Dad's patterns; and my Mum's patterns!*

Really?

Yeah, just the whole thing. It's just never really occurred to me in such clear detail. At every stage of my life, I have moved on – and quite brutally.

46

What, "I want better people now!"

Yeah, 'they're clod-hoppers, they're sort of country idiots, I go to university, I'm really clever, they're really stupid, they're going to fuck their lives up…'

And all of which, surely at some level, was "I need to be good enough for my Father, so I'll dump the working class…"

Yeah…!

So is that what you're saying?

Well, Haversham is an interesting town as well, because I guess it's a bit of a satellite of London. A lot of people there were of very similar backgrounds to my Dad. You know, lower middle class or upper working class made quite good, living in modern 60's, 70's estates and feeling pretty good about the fact that their children are going to be well educated. They've arrived. But, yeah, the undercurrent – snobbery, ugliness really. But yeah, I mean I haven't got any friends from university left, because they've all either gone or… Yeah, and no one male friend since that bloke Jude.

Really?

No. Apart from my brother. I think it's hard to be best mates with your brother.

Yeah.

But it's good to have a good relationship with your brother; but no real strong bonds since Jude.

Tell me about Jude again?

Oh God! Shit! Well he was my best friend before sixth form. I basically kicked him away when I needed to join the 'cool crowd' who were into music and trendy clothes and all that sort of thing. He was my hanging-out friend. Running about in the woods, camping and making tree houses and stuff, talking about wanking and how we

47

never had girlfriends, wondering what the blokes meant by fingering[34]; and I was quite brutal really. I just dropped him, because he was embarrassing and it was basically him, or my new 'desirable' friends. I think he was really bitter – and hurt. I never spoke to him again. He became a really nerdy sciency sort of geek at college. Funny how this conjures up a picture of my Father and grand Father here, with my tongue getting browner by the second.

So who's next? What about male friends and strong bonds?

31. *Socialists. Those who work for the good of all, rather than purely for personal gain.*

32. *Communists. A more extremely political version of the above.*

33. *Mod-ettes. A female 'mod'. 1980's revival of 1960's youth cult.*

34. *Fingering. Slang for stimulating the clitoris / vagina with fingers*

First sex

From the Mod-ettes, I went to university and then into my relationship with Ayesha. All the energy going into the relationship.

So, from this guy was the social climbing into the cool group...

Yeah,

...and it didn't really work there; and then it was the group of girls – Mod-ettes.

Ah, well, I also had a group of mixed blokes and women, some of whom were in the band, where another complicated little sexual scenario with my best friend Charlie, who, yeah, I was good friends with actually. We hung out a lot, played music together and; he had a relationship with a girl called Diana. She was a draaama student. Quite lovely! They finished and I ended up sleeping with her – I think we were talking about this – not having a clue how to – you know, eat her pussy, or anything like that. And she was shouting *"Eat me, eat me...!"* I was in complete sheer terror, in my parents' house...

So, again, 'sex and what the fuck do I do...'

Yeah, completely! I mean, it was all functioning, you know, things were going well, but I didn't know what to do next. It's not like I can say that I wasn't told what to do, because most people figure it out, don't they?

Dunno! I'm really not sure – I think shit loads of men are scared of eating pussy; because it's like – what is it that goes on down there and different girls are different; their equipment is different, they're into different things, they like different things, they are challenged by different things – I've come across loads of men who are scared... I've got a book called *'Sex For One'*[35] about women and their fannies – it's for women, written by a woman. I have loaned it to a load of female clients, but I have also loaned it to a good few men to check out fannies. 'This is what it looks like. This is what you can guess and work out.' It's not a sex manual, but you can check out what's what, where and how...

Hmmm...

Which is important to know about.

You must have done that as well, just by...

Aww, I was scared for years. I didn't know what the fuck is going on down there or what to do with it.

I mean with Ayesha it was a complete revelation because she'd never had sex with anyone and we lost our virginity together. I basically – well wouldn't say conquered her, but we explored each other and it was quite gentle.

The best way, surely!

I can still remember the first time I put my hand up her skirt. She was so shocked and then she started laughing. She said, "Oh, no one has ever done that before!" I said, "I've never done that before" – well, I had done it, but no I would always be naked before, but that was more like the fumbling that I should have had before...

Yeah, yeah... It's like, the other way around...

...yeah, and like honestly, 'I don't know what I am doing, but this feels nice.'

Surely that's the best way. Playing and exploring, rather than 'doing' each other.

35. 'Sex For One' ('Sex For One – The Joy Of Self-loving') Betty Dodson (Crown Publishing Group) 1986. www.bettydodson.com

Trapped Fathers

I still feel such a grief that I fucked that up so badly! With Ayesha. But, again, it's like, too young. If you only have one major sexual experience with a woman, from eighteen onwards, it's going to bubble up, isn't it?

Yeah... So, did you fuck it up? Or have you claimed your own life back to go where you need to go to...

Well, yeah!

...and do what you need to do?

But it's a process again, it's like maybe that was the final kicking away. The final; this is the last time I want to do this. I don't want to be driven by this patterning any more – kicking people away.

And if you were there, entrapped, you would take it out on both Ayesha and on Malaika.

Yeah, yeah!

Be like most Fathers, surely. Trapped in a situation that they hate; cheating, out drinking, hanging out with their mates, whatever, shagging around, abandoning the kids, abandoning the wife, feeling really guilty...

Yeah, you're right actually – it's *liberated fucking up!*

I wish my parents had split. I'm sure it would have done them both the world of good! It would have done me and my brother...

Did you think that when you were young?

No, when I was young I wanted my Father dead.

Hmmm.

Not just because it was the simplest, easiest way to deal with things; I just couldn't figure out why he was being such a bastard.

Hmmm.

There was always a tension like he was going to explode. And he did explode. He couldn't communicate, he couldn't loads of things.

What was your Father's Father like?

Umm, don't really know! From what I understand, he wasn't around the home a lot, because he used to build railways...

Well really? That is so freaky! I knew that he was involved in the railways. I wrote it down – and I don't think you ever told me. That is so weird, because I was writing this thing about - it was almost like a letter to Fathers or grand Fathers - and I started off saying, to my grand Father, "You were an East End boy who had an alcoholic Mother, a 'fucked up' gentle Father, had to go out and be the bread-winner when you really wanted to be a journalist and artist," and I started to say to him – it was kind of an addressing to all grand Fathers – and it was like, yours "You were working on the railways in Africa..." and then I stopped because I thought, well, I don't know any more...

Ha ha ha ha ha. That's exactly it! They were in Kenya and he was building railways. I think he had something to do with bombs as well. It just never occurred to me until now, that my Father's first job and what my Father really always wanted to do was be a railway driver – a steam train driver.

Really...? And that's what all boys are supposed to want to do, isn't it?

Then, in Britain or Wales, he got into working in explosives, which is what his Father did. He blew up a bridge or something, when the Indians were attacking Goa and taking it over from the Portuguese!

Really, when was that?

My grand Father happened to be there and happened to know about bridges and explosives and he just blew things up apparently!

Wow...

So he did the hero thing! Same as my Father did the hero thing in lots of ways. Fuck! I think my grand Father was probably a 'wuss' because he was 'never there'. He didn't stand up to my great grand Mother; and I don't know whether it is his Mother or my grand Mother's Mother, but she just fucked everyone's lives up in that family, her second marriage! And in those days, apparently she was a real known character in Africa because she would teach the young African kids, she would look after people, not as a Mother, but she was a hunter, she would go out hunting — she was one of the men. She was like the chief of the tribe. You wouldn't mess with her.

Matriarchy...

From teaching, to hunting, to fuck knows what else.

Yeah,

Apparently, fucking up every one in the family — totally fucking them up. I don't know the details, but these are the things I want to find out. Like, get this Email relationship with my Father going, so at least we have a way of communicating, with him being able to think and talk in his own time, without worrying about his stammering and without feeling constantly challenged or confronted. So let's see!

Are you going to see him by yourself?

No, no, no — Email.

Aaah. But that feels like what has to be done. It's like Bob had his Dad down for the weekend; it feels like we all have to claim that.

Make peace rather than waiting for them to die.

Yeah, absolutely. It feels like the desperation has passed; like this is

going to happen and we're going to make this happen.

Yeah. My Father used to say, a few times, that his Father never said "Well done!" or anything like that. But then, neither has he. He is full of threats. They are meant as "Well done! Be careful!" but they just come out as threats and criticisms – that's all he knows. Maybe it's all he's ever been around. And he'd always say to Caetano that he and his brother used to be close – maybe he didn't even say that bit – "but then we hated each other", blah, blah, blah, "don't become like us". So that's how we became!

Ooh...

But most of it was because of the way my parents behaved, not stuff between Caetano and I. Our misunderstandings and our reactions to their behaviour, their inability to communicate, or be parents, or adults, or raise us, or to be emotional, or anything. So, the misunderstandings were handed down to us. And now we get on fine, but they are still 'living' the problem.

Huh!

It was my Father's projection. When his brother was the Mummy's-boy - like me - and loved by everyone, he didn't even realise he totally sold out to be the wuss, to stay out of the matriarchal firing line.

Oh really, aah...

Meanwhile, my Father is the one in the firing line, because they already had a Mummy's-boy.

That's exactly like my Dad and his brother! When he died, apparently he was the golden boy, the favourite, the younger, died in a car crash, mythologized; and here is poor old fucking Daniel to take the shit!

Yes.

How interesting... There are so many links, because my grand Father - I don't think he blew anything up in the war but - he shunted trains in the Docklands Gas Works in East London. Amazing! I love all this

stuff, the connections. And my grand Mother's Mother was a very strong woman; and her husband was a bit of a kind of 'rake', a gambler who went off to America and came back again...

It would make life so much easier and everything would make so much sense if our parents could be honest about who they are, where they have come from; so we don't dedicate our lives to undoing their fears. Finding out 'why' and surviving it... and then starting our lives!

But the sad part is that they probably don't know, because I mean, I think one of the classic – I mean I've done it, I know I've done it, I remember I told you I got some memories back, it's like – you don't even know you've lost them. Don't know that you don't know. So you can't look for them.

Yeah...

So it's about their 'back seat' past?

Yeah, their generation – and it may be a cultural thing, a Catholic thing, a Goan thing, a British thing – is to put it behind you and move on. Don't upset other people. In fact, sell out to lick their arses so that they don't reject you.

Yeah.

They don't reject the people that are fucking you up the most – seek their approval and carry on being hurt; without protecting your own kids, leave alone yourselves.

Well, they don't know how, do they?

But maybe this is where our generation comes in. We don't stand for shit. We have got a lot of power.

Yeah. Yeah. But it was interesting, John's girlfriend was saying last night about almost having to do a test to be a parent. Do you know what I mean? I know she was joking, but you do think; it's just complete carte blanche, parents can do whatever they like, almost. I know there are all those theories about how we choose our parents,

we choose our destiny, for the lessons we have to learn, but you'd think a little safeguard would be nice.

But it would be socially unacceptable – so many people say "You're never 'ready' to be a parent; when you're a parent, then you're ready." Because I've asked a lot of people if they were ready and most people say "No". Very few say, "I waited until I felt ready" and I think a lot of people that say "No, ha ha ha you're never ready," what they are really saying is *'I didn't really give a fuck about kids or anything, but right then I needed to be loved, I needed sex, I needed a fix, I needed to trap someone, I needed to be trapped, I needed safety and all that shit; and a child was just a by-product that we had to deal with.'*

Yeah. Well I can relate to that, absolutely!

Sexuality

Are you saying that's you?

Yeah, I would say that it was. I mean, I was really resistant to the idea of even having children. Mainly because I thought there are sexuality issues, like, this is going to be too much. I can't take that responsibility. It's all about responsibility.

Like if you're gay?

Yeah, or bisexual or not having fully explored it, always kind of flirting with it, having casual sex and half-hearted relationships; like with a bloke who was a manager at Big Royale Burgers...

Really?

Yeah, I met him on Clapham Common. We had a really passionate relationship. He was a lovely man. He wanted me to leave Ayesha and go and live with him.

Really? It was a proper, big relationship!

Oh yeah, absolutely! The first big 'heart' one with another man. And again, I so was indecisive, push pull, push pull, maybe I will, maybe I won't, eventually he was saying *"Fuck off, I don't want to see you again..."*

What was all that about? Because you were so pushing and pulling?

Yeah! I couldn't commit myself to, er...

Was he gay, or bi, or hiding, or not sure, or...

I think he had had some sexual experiences with women, but, I think another Mummy's-boy! Brought up a Catholic and his sister had become a lesbian, and actually, born in the same week as me – same year.

Really?

Amazing! Oh no, five days before, the 18th of October.

Wow! What are you the week of in *'The Secret Language Of Relationships'*?[36]

Eh...? Um...

(both) Drama and Criticism!

It's like a script! I suppose the bottom line, is I want a relationship with – another 'week of Drama & Criticism' Lui, one way or another. Or just to go to – rather than holding back like a good Catholic; and then exploding with non-sense, whatever a relationship means, take the barriers away - like Lui and I set - and see where or how or whatever it goes. And probably, like we both want, ultimately, we will both meet women, not lose our relationship; like our dream has always been, like for years, to walk along Manly beach in Sydney, with our women and kids, on the way to, or from somewhere and just be hanging out.

Wow!

Being relaxed and being a family, a community.

That is so superb.

Yeah, that is 'the picture'. Everything, in life, in a way for both of us, is dedicated to that picture. Which is a big thing, with another individual. How – fucking – scary is that? And another bloke?!! From another country? Who happens to be my 'relationship akin to marriage'. Ha ha ha ha ha...

Do you know, I feel almost like my Mother is 'hunting' me. It's almost like, kind of avoiding her; and the more I avoid her, the more she,

kind of...

I feel we are finally escaping our Mother's clutches.

Hmmm.

And our Fathers are probably waiting helplessly - without knowing what the fuck to do - and it has been up to us, because we are the untouchable, special little golden boys, Mummy's-boys, whatever... And like I was saying, with my Mother, is my Father going to be punished here? Is he going to suffer? For me being a man, finally? Where, I was brought up anti-men; they are bad people, who do this and that and the other. And also, the way that my Mother used to punish my Father – I'd generally know why and think, 'well of course that's wrong and of course he deserves punishing'. I was on her side. I was one of the women, basically, and I think from really early childhood – I don't know whether this is you as well – from very very early, it was *you*

either join the women, or you get fucked up by the women, the way that you see them fuck every one else

up. And as a child, probably as an adult it would have been very easy; how did I know not to join the women?

Well, who knows what they are, really? I mean, if that's where your strongest programming is coming from...

Were you 'saving' your Mother as well as 'joining' her? I was!

Oh, God yeah!

So, totally played the victim, stayed in control, punished people with their own pain, blah blah blah...

Well, like I say with my Mum, it's been coming in the last year – more than the last year, actually, just the connection between her Father dying, me being born just before he died – it's just become so clear to me that she has been using me as her Father's replacement.

Yeah, I bet it's like the throne. Probably bypass Charles and straight to

Harry... Ha ha ha ha ha ha

Actually I think it's Prince William next in line! But I see what you mean about bypassing my Father.

36. *'The Secret Language Of Relationships' Gary Goldschneider & Joost Elffers (Element Books) 1997*

Jack-off buddies

But then, I thought, with you, with me, with a lot of my friends, we all have that in common. We want male company, we all love girls, but we want to be accepted by the men - which we never were, or earlier on by the boys - and how could we be? Mummy's-boys aren't!

Well, we don't know how, do we?

Check this out... I have been chatting to men on the internet about all sorts of things, from sex and sexuality, to parents, childhood, death, money, girls, pussy, dick, the whole caboodle. It's been absolutely amazing!

I suppose it's a way of connecting with men at all different levels, ages, situations, paradigms; so it's not all about wanking then...!

Anyway, I had this really nice, long conversation with this guy. It was amazing, clear – it wasn't wise, or deep, or schmaltzy or anything like that. He was just an ordinary bloke, in America, mid to late 20's; and we were just chatting, where have you been, what are you doing, da da da, where we live, how we live, then we got into wanking. To cut a long story short, he has wanked with all of his roommates.

Really?

Each and every one of them. And in America, roommates probably means more share a flat than share a room; according to him, that's what guys do. Plus, um, they fool around in the changing rooms – he was in the baseball team or something or other – and apparently, it is very very normal. We were just talking about it and I said, "Well, I didn't really do that." He said, "Well, it's kinda normal." It just blew me away – and he is a 'blokes bloke'. A proper bloke, rather than something feminine or obviously dysfunctional.

What, he still does that? Or was he talking about when he was younger?

Apparently, he does it with his present roommate. I mean, I don't imagine they both rush home and wank, but every now and again, if they're drunk, or there is a porn movie on, or whatever – they naturally fall into that. It expresses closeness if you do it with a girlfriend or have sex or whatever; but they don't have sex or anything. They wank! But what he said, is that this is 'male bonding'. Is that what they have been talking about all these years? *Is that what male bonding is?* That you wank with each other?

Hmmm…

So I said, "So that's what male bonding is?" And he said, "Well, once you've jacked off with someone, you know that you can rely on that person one hundred per cent with your secrets and stuff…" But it seems that, that is the… It kind of made sense, because when I was at school, I couldn't figure out why these blokes were absolute tossers and didn't quite like each other or anything, or get on. But they would stick together, there was some sort of a bond.

Hmmm. So do you think that they may be…

I mean, what do I know! I didn't 'do' changing rooms when I was in school.

Well also, they kept a very strong barrier. They attacked! I mean, I was never really a target, but there were definitely – you know, kind of – the weaker, smaller or more kind of feminine blokes at school who were the target from those people; as you say, the ones who were 'doing it' – they are the ones who would throw around all the accusations. I mean, it's almost like they are untouchable. No one can accuse them of touching each other up, or farting around, fiddling around. They are the ones who – it's almost like when someone does a really smelly fart! You point the finger and insist "YOU must have done it!" Do you know what I mean?

It's quite vicious! Yeah, and it struck me when I think about my school and college – how some of them would stay over, especially when I was a bit older – and it never crossed my mind. I didn't fancy them, I didn't want to see them naked, it never entered my mind, and it wasn't like that. They were like, company. But they were also Mummy's-boys – each and every one of them – smothered by their Mother, not one of the lads, didn't do the sports thing, it was the other side. And they were the ones who had the fingers pointed at them, as 'poofs' or whatever.

Hmmm.

They are the ones that didn't 'do' anything! Then I thought about them and I've heard about quite a few of them; most of them look like they've turned gay!

Really?

Yeah! So maybe, I don't know. What's going through my mind is that maybe this is some sort of a male initiation. Something like we used to have in the old days, within communities, acceptance by the men. And then, you go to the women. But we never had that 'acceptance by the men' bit.

Hmmm. So by default, we crave the older man and end up not having a woman, because you are too busy having the men! But not in the way that you want to have a man.

Yup. So we had, probably, about an hour's wank together.

You and this American guy?!!

Yes.

Over the internet?

Yes.

Because you can see, of course, with that web cam thing…

We can see each other. We were chatting and stuff, typing.

Blimey!

And it wasn't – and it was cool! We were just chatting, saying stuff.

What…? I don't know.

I have never, really enjoyed wanking. Well I have… but it was all Catholic guilt and my Father might burst in, my Mother might burst in, someone's watching me, yadda yadda yadda, everything 'down there' is just not to be touched; and I never really explored it. Other blokes probably did, together – you know – but because I had… Maybe it was the refugee/coloured thing, blah blah blah, could have been.

Hmmm.

Maybe it's quite simply Mummy's-boy's stuff, I don't know. Maybe I'm just not much of a wanker! Ha ha ha ha ha ha ha ha

Well… Hmmm! Yeah…

But, you know, these are the things that probably… It is always the public school boys that the fingers are pointed at. Maybe because they did it.

Yeah, it's almost like a national institution. The whole sort of 'fag' system. Fucking, buggering each other. Well I don't know if they even do that? More like, a sort of pecking order.

It's just wanking together as far as I know. Which isn't necessarily anything to do with sex. I mean, there's been a huge distinction. Because with this guy, we talked about pussy for ages. Eating it, what we like about it, what we've done… it was really good to talk! And question. With someone like that, about that, in a fun way – in lots of different ways. So 'up for it', but this was a different… part, of – I don't know – male bonding, or closeness, or something. And it wasn't like I wanted to fuck him or anything. He has a dick. Huh huh huh huh huh… But it was…

Amazing!

Check this out! John rigged-up his computer to my computer, when he first gave me his mate's web cam. He was tinkering for ages and went to work chuffed with himself, because he could get to his home computer automatically from work, and he was telling all his work mates, "Guess what I've done! You'll never believe this – come and watch this…

Oh, ha ha ha ha ha

"…I've got the computer at home networked and I can call up my computer…

Ohhhhhhhhhh nooooo

"…from here!" *My screen flashed up, me, big 'cock shot' with me naked,* I don't know who else was on the screen, whether there were other guys, or women, or what was going on! Only I 'always get caught with my pants down'! They know that I've got big naturist tendencies; but now they know just how big…

Ha ha ha ha ha

So they all saw me, us, got a shock and switched it off! And that's it – but, you know, when that happened, I thought, in the old days it would have been 'well, that's the end of my life!', but I just thought, 'what the fuck! What a relief…' in a strange way.

Masculinity

This reminds me about what you said about one of your friends. A guy who said something about his not being able to properly explore bisexuality because of what he'd experienced...

He hasn't got that clear, clean relationship to explore his sexuality. But I imagine that if anything 'not quite right' happens, no matter who it happens with, in your early days – whether its with male or with female – if there's something 'wrong', then that will become a block - and a depressed pause button - or the other extreme, an addiction, and that would be your reaction to it, do you know what I mean? If this 'thing' hadn't got out of hand, he could have properly explored his sexuality. But it did, and his 'natural' growth has been blocked. Stopped. So the way he lives his sex life expresses his reaction to this.

Hmmm.

I just think, whatever. I'm not scared of judgements, you know, gay, straight, whatever, whatever, I'm easy with it. When Lui and I talked about touching and closeness and whatever, um, one day last week – and that was interesting, because he can't bear anyone touching him, male or female or anything like that; and for me, like with you, or my male friends, my female friends, whoever, I am not a great toucher. But I touch people, people touch me, we lean on each other and stuff like that and we don't even really notice it, but with Lui – it's more like a big decision. And, um, hitting is the touching that we had, mainly. Um, as time went on, we were playfighting and me being bullied by him. It was the only touching that we could have, I suppose. And I suppose playfighting can be intimate, you hold each other - you know - hit each... whatever. But it's contact. It's physical contact. And it's nice with force. I'm not sure about – it's nice, it's nice playfighting and pushing and being pushed and stuff. I'm not sure about being overly gentle with men...

No... Well no, that's the difference, I think. I mean you can use your strength, because it's usually kind of equal. I mean, my memory of playfighting with Sandy was that he would always, kind of, attack me, and I would kind of, be like a big sort of sheep dog and let him jump all over me and kick around and whatever. Um, but not sort of seeking it. Again, it's the Mummy's-boy thing. Nice boys don't fight! And they certainly don't jump on their younger brothers and start fighting and whatever.

Don't hurt yourself, don't hurt anyone else, don't break anything, don't make noise, don't this, don't that... Be perfect, listen to all the judgements about every one and don't 'be' any of them, because you'll be judged like them, which leaves absolutely no space... to be anyone. *How do I 'be' me right?*

To explore... While you were talking, I was thinking about – a huge element of my relationship with Steven was 'playing'. It was fun! You know, we just had a lot of fun together and it was like; I remember you saying actually, "What would have happened if it hadn't gone sexual?" I mean, obviously, it's another life, another story...

Yeah...

I mean I do think, it wasn't really about fucking - as you observed at the time - it was more about surrendering. And sort of, you know...

'This is what I'm, this is the only connection I am allowed. That I deserve to have.'

Yeah, and yet it had much more to it than that. Not even under the surface, but – yeah, it was still a lot of fun and a lot of physical contact. His Mother was abandoned by his Father while he was actually in the womb – I mean, that was, talk about...

Wow

...possessive. I mean, she really was possessive!

So he is a Mummy's-boy?

Yeah! Completely. You know, his ex, Cynthia, always said that he was very good at all the touching and the physicality with her, sort of looking after, but sex was a bit like 'Well, what the fuck's that all about?'

For me it's been fear of hurting them.

Fear of letting go, I mean, I just love – I love making noise, thrashing, and really – fucking! Not just kind of "Let's make lurve darling...?" I mean, I actually, I can't bear that phrase!

It's nice to get really animalistic, sometimes. But I am generally very gentle, quiet, sensual, generally more multiple orgasms, rather than acrobatic banging! But then I suppose the acrobatic banging comes with playfighting.

Well, also, a man can take it. It's like, however small or weak, a bloke can pretty much take strength for strength; whereas with a girl, it's like – you know – my experience when I was little was like, push them and they fall over and they start crying; whereas boys...

You recover!

...well at least he might fall on his arse and say "Ow!" but get up again and come back at you.

Yup!

You learn very quickly with girls... "Ow...? Boo hoo!"

And that's it. Men are brash! They tell you whatever they can tell you, where with the girls, it's emotional manipulation.

Hmmm.

So, maybe this 'gay' thing – you know, I've been 'on one' with this thinking – right, so maybe that's the difference between Mummy's-boys and non Mummy's-boys; the boys who have wanked together and not wanked together. Over and above playing sports, because that must be another bonding thing.

Hmmm.

So, maybe a lot of the gay boys want acceptance by men; I mean it is obvious to me that a lot of gay men were abandoned by their Fathers, therefore they're gay.

Hmmm.

But maybe its where this Mother's all-absorbing thing, maybe by being Mummy's-boys they couldn't get acceptance from the other men, so it's like starting another male 'thing', where the only men they can get acceptance from are similar to them, therefore that's where they go! Do you know what I mean?

Yeah! Yes, it does make sense... I'd be really interested to look at cultures where having sex with men as well as women was the norm. Like Greece, or Turkey, or the Middle East.

But it's just the norm, isn't it? And is it even labelled as having sex a lot of the time?

It probably isn't. It's interesting you picked up on that, because... Yeah, I mean, from what you're saying, is, is that it's bonding. It's just, kind of...

Being together!

...yeah. But I mean, the fact is that blokes have their hands in their pockets most of the time, anyway. Fooling around, you know, through their trousers.

I don't do that sort of thing in my pockets –
do you really?

Do you not? I remember when I was in art school – this is interesting actually, it brings up...; this guy Ben made the comment that I am

thinking of, but I did a series of close-up 'arty' - with mirrors and stuff - photos of my cock, erect, but I thought they were really good in the end. I put them up in the corridor...

Ha ha ha ha ha!!!

...as you do...

Ha ha ha ha ha!!!!!

...and the head of department, this bloke took them down overnight and there was a big hoo-hah about it; and being the kind of rebellious art students that we were, we had this seminar to discuss it...

And *you had a seminar to discuss your cock!?*

Yeah!

Displaying it to everyone?

The censorship of this thing, was it right, was it wrong, whatever. And I remember this guy saying that what he liked about it was the fact that – he wasn't even talking about hard-on's or whatever, but he said that "Blokes have always got their hands in their pockets and they are fiddling." And I think that's true! Like, in our culture, I've always been conscious that if a woman looks at me and I'm doing it – I'll stop! But if I'm talking to a bloke, I'd just carry on doing it. I think girls do it as well, I mean, some of my female friends who are confident with their bodies will just sit with their hands 'down there'. I do it when I am by myself - all the time - where I'm constantly just fiddling with my dick and stroking pubic hair; but not with any intent! Just touching, really. Just like when you kind of stroke your face, or whatever. So much of it is hushed up.

Yeah, exactly. But what is it? What is it that turns into perversions, because it is hushed up and it has to be totally totally denied? I mean, in this country, it's not that long ago that it was like you were describing Greece and Turkey. The working class had no running water at home, and so they would go to 'slipper baths' as I think they were called, the men with the men and the women with the women, or the family would go in a room together and they would wash together. Even when I was in Calcutta, when I would go to work with Ma T, on the way, it was quite early in the morning, every tap, everywhere there was water, there would be a crowd of men washing together. And the women would go and do theirs somewhere else. And they would wash each other; but then, I imagine, 'I wouldn't be able to reach my back very easily', or 'I would like my back scrubbed' – 'normal' towards each other. Maybe it's like in this country, it's the same as passing a spliff[37] to each other. It's like, we're all together, we're doing something, the same as women making a quilt or something. Sports, saunas, holidays.

I am very easy, in bathrooms. If I want to have a shower and there's say three or four people in the house, I'll leave the bathroom door open and just go in the shower; it doesn't bother me if someone comes in and has a shit, or piss or whatever. But, there is that – it's not knowing. There's no, sort of general, 'that's fine!' Or not. It's that thing, we all come from different families. What may be completely normal to me, might be completely outrageous to somebody else. You know, that to me is normal; maybe not so much men and women. It's almost like a compensation. Public baths… I can remember my brother and my Dad and I – I think my sister must have come, but my Mother would never come swimming – we used to drive about forty minutes to an hour to the nearest pool, when I was growing up. I was fascinated by that, it was actually the only place where you could see fully grown men, completely naked…

"Hey son, have you ever seen a fully grown man… naked?!!" Ha ha ha…

Ha ha ha – 'Airplane!'[38] Yeah, why the fuck is that funny? Close us down even more, why don't you! But some of those blokes were really comfortable and others just did the kind of prissy British thing with the towel, you know, they kind of put their pants on under the towel. Others would just strut about, happy as Larry, standing in the showers… I found it; I think that's one of the other things. The excitement of it was completely out of proportion! Because it should be normal, but because it's like a steam valve, where when you turn the handle and let this huge explosion out, builds big associations – forbidden fruit, men, fixate, fixate, you know, and especially looking at 'cocks', because they are visible, they are very, you know, they have dark hair, there is this cock hanging down, before I'd reached puberty, or any of us had. You know, it's electric! It's just completely electric.

I have never had that. My Father would hide – both my parents would hide. They'd act. There would be an atmosphere. A very strange atmosphere. And it was all secrets, and wrong, and bad, and dirty, and God knows what else. But it was all hidden. Same with when I was in school in Africa. Then suddenly, it was completely the totally opposite here! I hadn't seen a dick or anything like that. And, um, I hadn't even looked, really. I was so used to 'looking away' with my family. I was so paranoid of being caught looking. Also, it never occurred to me, for such a long time, that anyone had a dick; including me. It wasn't an issue. It wasn't there. The bottom line with it is, *at what age did you become 'straight', or at what age did you become 'gay'?* Because before that, we are all bisexual or asexual. It is not a sexual thing.

Hmmm.

So at some stage, surely, the individual will either choose, or be told, or taught, or – you know – something changes. Restrictions are put up in the name of, identity? Or fitting in? Or safety? Or what the family will demand that you are, to gain approval from 'their' friends and family.

It must be, it must be, um. I don't know, there must be huge amounts of reasons for it. Obviously procreation feeds society. Children make workers, whether it's capitalism, industrialism, communism, feudalism, the family is the basic unit – fuck me, I just got side-tracked into politics! Ha ha ha...

Going back to what we were saying before, I wonder if there are cases of men that have been gay, so called, for a while; then, in a way, 'got over it' because they have had the acceptance that they wanted from 'mainstream' men rather than just 'gay' men - or maybe just gay men - and then decided, now that they have picked up that key, or that part of their initiation; naturally gone back to being straight – or wherever along that scale is their truth.

Who did '2-4-6-8-Motorway'[39], Tom Robins?

Tom Robinson[40]…

Classic! I mean I think he labels himself 'bisexual' now, but he is married with a child, or he was a few years ago, I don't know what's happened; and there was a huge out-cry, the gay community wanted him to be 'in their camp', which is ridiculous, because they've fallen into a trap of providing this – I don't know – polarity, you know, kind of… It has to be so defined, it's like you said at Findhorn, if you want to be feminine, or expressive, or creative, you have to go off into the gay camp; if you want to be a stockbroker, or, you know, have a mortgage, 2.4 kids and blah blah blah you have to go off and be straight. It's almost like it's a kind of logic of the exclusiveness of the straightness that created gayness.

Hmmm

As you said, there's no middle ground. And yet, there is – it's going on everywhere, like between the cracks. Like you are discovering on the internet.

Yeah, it's interesting, the gay and the straight thing with this guy on the net. We were chatting a bit, talked about fannies for ages, and, um, you know, we did – it's after we had a wank as well. And I said, "OK, so what's going on with you? Are you gay? Are you straight? Are you bi? What sort of sex are you?" And he said, "Hmmm – tell me about you first." And I said, "Well, maybe, the most accurate would be, straight, and curious about bi…" but it was almost unidentifiable. I mean neither of us saw each other as gay, neither of us saw each other as bisexual, we both saw each other as straight, because we were talking about fannies; no, because – forget about the 'women' side –

because we were talking about dicks and we were showing ourselves and being open and stuff, then surely part of the 'gay' label must belong to us, but which parts of what we do would be under the 'gay' label, which would be under the 'men hanging out' label, which act, or words, or whatever, would be under which 'jurisdiction' – ha ha ha – 'dick' being the operative syllable – ha ha ha ha ha.

I think a lot of it comes back again to the kind of, maybe the kind of sex, the differences maybe between the kind of sex that women are supposed to 'like' having, and the kind of sex that men are supposed to 'like' having. And then I'm thinking again of, I've suddenly got this image of Clapham Common. Sometimes you would see two blokes fucking. You know, they'd be quite out in the open about it – sometimes they would go off into the bushes. And it's just so, it's like watching animals. You know, there's no finesse, no 'darling I love you', or sort of pretending.

It's just the raw physical.

Yeah! Which is great, in a way, because it is just so necessary.

And I feel that without male initiation – because Mummy's-boys don't get dirty, or play rough games, or aren't very practical, etcetera, etcetera, except for generally one or two exceptions to the rule – and I feel like now I am trying to get 'into' the physical; but not blag it, build my own relationship with it. Not be scared and think about doing things and how I am going to do it, but get involved, or 'muck in' basically, and that's new!

I suppose...

Deep, deep, deep in my subconscious, if I broke my arm, or hurt myself in any way, whatever, *'my Mother is going to worry, my Father will be angry; and I will cause pain.'*

Hmmm...

Rather than my own, 'I don't give a fuck, and other people are responsible for their reactions to this, but I fancy jumping off' – well, maybe that's how come I fell into all the danger sports. Bungee jumping off a cliff, parachuting out of a plane, walking on fire, feeding sharks, fuck knows, whatever! Which was totally not like me and only 'bad people' or 'stupid people' did that kind of thing. Or so the parents said, so they don't have to worry! Or, maybe, so, if I get hurt, they won't feel guilty. It's like... who owns what here? And... let's all pretend we haven't got genitals! Ha ha ha ha ha

Like Action Man[41] toys! Hah hah

Crazy!

Hmmm. But it's interesting, again I was thinking about the different ways in which it manifests. Thinking of, Bob, for example... He's quite clearly got a lot of Mummy's- boy traits and yet he's had male friends that he's had for years, very solid strong relationships; um, I suppose my thing with Ayesha, you know, I was generally able to have very physical, really good sex. And it always puzzled me, 'so why do I still crave men? What the fuck is going on here?' But with me, my kind of Achilles' heel[42], if you like, the panic of 'how do I support this woman, I don't want to go off and do the 9 to 5 shit!' That just didn't feel right – and she ended up supporting me. And I end up fucking her and gradually that all falls apart, because, I want to be fucked. But maybe even more so... to be looked after.

Yeah

Because she becomes more masculine and goes out and does the breadwinning...

Well, you don't want to be the man with the breadwinning, do you, but she probably respects you being a man by living your truth, rather being a '9 to 5 anyguy'. *Women absolutely love men living their truth!*

Well, yes and no, as long as they are being – not looked after, but there is an element of at least equality I think, otherwise it slips into a kind of dependency.

But then, I think, most relationships I have come across are co-dependent. 'No matter what is going on sexually inside, I am a man and this is who I'm supposed to be; I am a woman and this is how I'm supposed to be. I am supposed to get married by this age, and I'm lonely and I need to feel safe, protected, and I also need a 'fix' of this, this, this, this and this. It's better economically, my family will be off my back, I'll have sex regularly, or at least if I don't want sex ever again or I am scared of sex, then it's only between the two of us and it's not something…'

Hmmm…

All these fears and things to cross off the list, *from finances to fat*, all for the wrong reasons.

From finances to fat – that's a great quote!

…to fanny! The number of conversations I have had with men who have been so scared of fanny…

Hmmm

…until they have built a relationship with it. They have gone there! But, so many – like, some of the guys I have chatted to, they are not bisexual, they are gay! And they are scared shitless of fanny, or interaction with women physically, but treating them like queens, or goddesses, or Mothers, or 'head girls' or whatever – fine, as long as it is not intimate…

Fanny-ocracy! Ha ha ha

…but, how terrible, that any man, through sheer fear, doesn't go there.

So do you think, this is what I've been thinking about lots since Findhorn. Well, what the fuck is gay? I mean, there is that kind of, very prissy, effeminate, lisping gay-boy; and I wonder if that's different

from a lot of men who think they're gay, but in fact are probably just Mummy's-boys who are scared.

Yeah.

I mean, maybe there is this huge overlap as well; maybe this is it, you know, I am - we're all - so fucking conditioned to put sex into boxes. You're this, you're this, you're this... and once you're in the box, that's IT.

Was it what you have done, what you have thought, your first sexual experience with a man or a woman, needing certain fixes, to be held, it could be to get rough, it could be to... you know, anything.

37. *Spliff. Rolled up 'joint' of cannabis, marijuana, grass, dope, ganja, blow, draw, pot.*

38. *'Airplane' (1980) Jim Abrahams, USA.*

39. *'2-4-6-8-Motorway' (1977) Tom Robinson.*

40. *Tom Robinson. Pop star, songwriter, radio presenter.*
www.tomrobinson.com (bisexuality links)

41. *Action Man. 1970's cult toy – doll for boys!*

42. *Achilles' Heel. A person's weak, or most vulnerable point.*

'Women' bits'

All the 'defining moments'. It's fucking mind-blowing. I can't believe it
was only January when I was in New York, staying with my friend
Misha and I never, for a moment fancied her, and God knows how it
happened, but I ended up in bed with her, and, kissing. And starting
to – she is just not someone that I find physically attractive – but there
was something happening. And she was wearing this, kind of,
antiquated nightie, and I was kissing her tits, basically, and suddenly it
all stopped – again, it's the 'Mother thing' – and I remembered being
with my brother, in bed, with my parents – I don't know eight, nine,
ten years old – and we were wriggling around in bed, the two of us,
Sandy and I, and our parents were half asleep on a Sunday morning
or something – and we both came down the bed to my Mum's bum. I
have never seen my Mother naked. I have never seen anything more
than her forearms or when she wore a swimsuit. And we were both by
her backside, giggling and calling it the 'giggling stone'.

Ha ha ha ha ha

More than that! There was a kind of slightly cloying perfumey smell,
but she was wearing this nightie. Exactly like – well not exactly, but in
my mind, like the one that...

Oooh My God!!!

...Misha was wearing! It was just so fucking weird.

So did you go down to her arse and giggle? Ha ha ha ha ha

Ha ha ha ha ha... No, but I remember she said – I don't know what
she was expecting, she wasn't looking for a relationship, just probably
wanted a shag because she hadn't had one for a while, but she said –

"I am so sick of men who haven't got over their Mothers. I just can't bear it!" Ha ha ha ha ha

Fuck-ing-hell! You know, these things that we are probably discovering, most people that we know, or people whose paths we cross, it would come to them in a second; but they just assume that we probably know all this!

Mmmm. Or they probably think they are fucked, or they're weird, or – you know – old. I mean that's the thing, you've often said things and I haven't really thought of the fact that a lot of things that I have assumed were 'normal'; I mean, for example, I – I don't know where this comes from – I don't sit on the loo and wipe my arse - I think it came up in conversation - I stand up and wipe it.

Mmmm?

I don't know where I was – I think I was with my sister – and I made some comment about how inconvenient it was, and she said "Just hang on…"

Ha ha ha ha ha

Suddenly, like, the spotlights turned on me!

Ha ha ha ha ha

"Doesn't everyone do this?"

Ha ha ha - well who wiped your arse when you were a kid in a standing-up style?

I don't know… Now that would be interesting to, er…

Ring-ring, "Mum…" Ha ha ha

You're going to get the truth out of Mum? I don't – fucking – think so…

And who knows, maybe your Mum cleaned you different to your Father, to your Aunt.

Yeah… When I am wiping Malaika's bum, I realised it was much easier with her sitting down.

That's true… Did you stand her up and clean her arse?

Yes, and when I was doing that I though 'this is really hard'. It's much easier when she is sitting on the loo, with her bum spread out, just to wipe it. And she is happy with that – you know, it's what Ayesha does. I imagine…

Fanny

One thing that surprised – and kind of excited – me when I went to bed with Maria the first time, um, she immediately started wanking... herself. Even though I was inside her...

Mmmm. I love it when they do that...

...she was like – but I have not experienced that before. Such an assertive woman. And I actually said to her – I had to check in with her – I can't remember what I said, I said something like, "Is this alright?" "Are you enjoying this?" She said "y-e-a-a-h..."

Ha ha ha ha ha

But for me it was like 'inadequate', 'inadequate', you know.

'You're not big enough. You're not hard enough.'

Yeah...

I love it so much man. I love eating it. I was telling this guy specifically about one time when I was with Becky, and we were on the beach, it was the naturist beach...

Oh yeah, Studland!

...on the beach, in the sand dunes, she was on her back and I had my finger just like 'tickling quickly' like it's a goldfish, playing around nice and slowly with her G-spot, while with one hand I was just holding her fanny wide open and I was just going crazy with my tongue torturing her clitoris and she was just cumming and cumming I mean fuck what she was doing, I WAS LOVING IT! And I was so lost in that minge – it was great! I have never – she has changed my relationship to fannies!

She had the best best fanny! Everything was just – it wasn't overly neat, or gentle, or polite, or in place or anything – it was just there!

Hmmm

It was raw, it knew what it was, it wasn't messing around, it was just there and it worked and I just loved it in every way! The only one I have actually, totally – I was totally besotted by her fanny! And I have never felt like that about a fanny. There had always been something a bit hidden, or a bit smelly, or a bit this, or a bit that, but that one – un·bel·ieve·able!

Heh heh heh heh heh

Fucking amazing! And I used to think that from the time I take my clothes off, to the time 'she' leaves in the morning, I am supposed to have a stiffie.

Oh my God, yeah, that's another great fucking myth! And if it starts to go down, panic – and that makes it go down even more. And then usually silence…

It's like, *who needs a stiffie when you're eating snatch?* You're not thinking about what's going on – you're there!

It's glorious…

The 'family curse'

All those things I was thinking about when I was younger, it's like faaaking hell! Meanwhile, we didn't talk about it; probably the guys that wanked with each other – of course they talked about this, and everything else. Probably lied to each other, I don't know how it worked for them, maybe it was great, maybe it wasn't. Maybe some told the truth and they had a great time. Lucky bastards.

Were you very popular with other people's Mothers?

Totally! Parents loved me, I was an adult.

Perfect! Well mannered, well behaved, an example, better than their boys. There was that whole thing going on, at a subtle level, 'Why can't my boys be more like you?'

Well, as Mummy's-boys, we know that we are 'superior'. We are the most superior beings that ever walked the planet...

Ha ha ha

...basically. Now what kind of a fucked up attitude is that for a Mother to give a child and then send into the world?

Mmmm... Yeah, "You will succeed."

Somehow, you are better, you don't need to, you are special – you know – you are exempt from this, this and this, because you can do that, that and that – you know – you are 'golden'; and everyone else is fucked! And we believed that for how many years? We live it, without even realising we are living it, and then we wonder why we are not included, or – in certain places – how can you have someone like that included? Because once we get older, we're the ones that they dump!

Then they don't want anyone like that around - complete tossers, because buttons are pressed. Ha ha ha

Hmmm... Well it's as if the one magic gift is enough to sustain you in any situation. I can remember – I can't remember, did I hear it? Or overhear it? – I think I kind of overheard it, but I was meant to overhear it. My Mum saying to my Dad "Ed will always be alright, because he can get through any situation with his charm..." And it's only in the last few years that that's, kind of *(kisses teeth!)* blown apart, because of situations where I have, actually, stepped into a situation and not been charming. Actually allowed people to, hate me and dislike me.

...to tell the truth! Yes, because it's a 'life sentence'. It's her saying, "Ed's going to be in situations in which he is going to have to be charming to prove me right."

Hmmm

...so that's exactly what you will do.

Yeah, you're right, it is. Absolutely. It is the weirdest 'sentence', isn't it?

Like my Father. Basically, putting the willies up all of us about money. 'There won't be enough, the day will come, don't come running to me when..., I won't bail you out..., blah blah blah blah blah...' I have been spending most of my life either running away from that day, or living that day, or fearing that day. Thanks for the script!

Can you remember – I mean, was there a key moment, or phrase or literally just...

There is one, but I don't quite remember it. But they were always a bit – because that was his relationship with money. Plus, 'Let's teach them good things, by demonstrating the bad, by putting the fear of God in them, by criticising – you know – like giving negative feedback so they 'act' positive; rather than positive feedback to 'feed' the positive.'

Oooh, God...

But then, you know, the poor bastards. They had none of the positive feedback or positive parenting stuff.

Well exactly, what else could they do?

But thank God that it's our generation that is going to turn this all around. Because I have not wanted kids yet. Because, something has not been right; and I haven't known what it is. And the more I understand all this, the more I feel comfortable about bringing a child into the world. I feel that I am getting more and more ready, and comfortable, and looking forward to having kids, as I think in this way and realise that it's about my own life – and that I know I can attempt to deal with myself now, and not pass my version of the 'family curse' to my own kids.

Hmmm

And maybe subconsciously, I have known that there is a lot of shit that isn't right, that I wouldn't want to pass on to my kids. It's only in the last, week? That I am doubting my Mother as a manipulator and what she's done and how she has edited things, and been in control. A week – that's nothing!

When you say that you've been doubting…

It just never crossed my mind that she used to watch everything that my Father said, or did, or wrote; or that the way that I was brought up as a 'special boy' was desperately destructive to me and actually took my life away. But it gave her safety, and love, and everything else.

Hmmm

All in the name of love, done with love and sheer ignorance of the consequences on us…

And it's interesting, because I've always had that knowledge. My sister has always been there to mirror and point out that, that I would always 'protect' my Mother. And always stand up for her.

My Mother always told me, in a nice asking way, "…you will never abandon me", "…you won't send me in a home", "…you'll look after me," yadda yadda yadda; and, as a little child, well of course I will. I couldn't imagine life without my parents! Especially my Mother who loves me so much. So, you know, who wouldn't? I didn't know there was such a thing as 'fanny'…

Hmmm?

Or 'freedom', or having a 'fucking good time' in any way. I just wanted to be tucked up in bed, told how lovely I am, talk nicely…

Exactly!

Yeah, and that's when it started. 'Programming' maybe.

I actually remember, a few years ago, before Malaika was born, I suddenly realised, it's like this kind of lead weight dropped on my head and I said to Ayesha "One of the reasons I don't want to have children is that I don't want my parents to be the grand parents. I don't want them to be around."

Yeah, hmmm.

Yeah but deeper than that, I think you said at Findhorn, it's about not passing the family karma on, yet again.

At the back of my mind, I haven't wanted my Father and Mother laughing at my kids, the way that they laughed at me. Because they're nervous little — you know how vicious kids are, they just giggle at everything in the playground? That's my parents. They didn't even know what they were laughing at half the time.

Hmmm.

Or teasing. Teasing non-stop. I didn't want my kids teased, or manipulated. You know, the whole thing — I didn't even know what it was, but same as you, I knew something was wrong; and I didn't want to bring kids into this… whatever.

87

I know. Because, again, it's the irony – we've talked about having a tribe or a bunch of people who are a very strong influence on a child. I want people like that. You know, if my parents are ruled out, then it will have to be friendships – community?

In Australia, I've got a friend, Bruce, who was a young boy when I first met him. I remember, he wanted to spend his ninth birthday with me, so he must be fourteen, fifteen now? His Father was absent, Bruce is actually a fucking excellent guy, one of my best ever friends, and I remember saying to him that when I have kids of my own, I want him to be a really good influence on my kids. Because he will be a sort of halfway house between my age and my kids. And my boy may not be able to talk about all things with me, or play sports; Bruce is great at basketball, skateboarding, he comes from the right place and he is great! Lui and I have talked about this so much. It's just normal, that I want Lui, and Bruce, and my friends Nick and Martin around to influence my child, my son, or my kids. There is so much that probably they could do that I couldn't. I'm crap at football, but I'm not going to say that football is 'bad'. I'm not going to be scared that my child is going to say *"My Father is crap at football."* The child needs educating, not for me to be in the playground subconsciously thinking, 'well how am I going to get back at the child now'; or how can I avoid this from happening.

Yeah, and also by appreciating other people's skills that they can put forward, the child will presumably be able to appreciate your skills. Because you are honest and open about what you are allowing them to do with other people. They will be able to say that Dad is really good at this, or this, or this.

And even then, I mean, this is the way my mind is changing. I don't even want to think about that anymore, because all the child needs is love; *the child doesn't need to love me more than it loves Lui, or my wife, or his brother.* The child does not need to respect me more than anyone. I'd rather the child had – if I could provide the community, and the safety, and the love for other people as well, then the child has got loads of men and loads of women to choose who he wants to be like, or who is going to stimulate the parts of himself, inside of him, that can then come alive. And maybe I don't have any of those. Maybe I'll have lots of them. But I can't 'need' to, or 'have' to be 'number one' for my kids, like a lot of people do. That's theft...

Yeah, yeah.

...and I know so many people, like we were saying before, like men become Men when their Fathers die. So many people remember the time when they realised that they've outgrown their parents; they've realised that there are better ways than their parents' ways. And they get angry, they get upset, they get insecure, they get into a huge state when they realise that. I want my kids to know that all the time. That they've got a lot of people to ask, and they need to find their own way, over and above mine. I'd like to be able to give them mine, as 'this is my way', rather than use mine to manipulate them, prove myself right and make them play small behind me.

I don't know, it feels...

Even so, I might get addicted to my child as soon as it is born! Huh ha! Fall in love with the girl and do the Oedipal thing as soon as it is born; or want my son to be my best friend and do everything I didn't do, etcetera etcetera.

But doesn't the intention go a long way towards creating it?

And I can't imagine – I can see a half a dozen of my friends, off the top of my head right now, who'd say, "What are you doing to your child, get a grip!"

Hmmm

Man do I value those friends. Not the ones that are going to play the same games, and we're all going to have the same lies, and we're going to compete. What's the point? What do we gain out of that? I need to be criticised, because then I've got some feedback that could be better for myself and my kids. Kids! Huh ha ha ha ha ha

Wow! Got any plans?

Best friends

Last Christmas was one of the best I have had. It was me and Steven and an empty house; and the sex was starting to disappear. For me, it was kind of like 'why are we doing this?' It was nice, but, the thing I enjoyed the most was getting on our bikes and cycling along the seafront on Christmas Day. Really sunny – you know, that kind of crisp winter's day, it felt like two boys on their Choppers.[43]

Ha ha ha ha ha…

It's quite weird, and then going back and fucking on a fur rug in front of the fire. And actually, that evening I plunged into a real darkness. Yeah, 'why are we having a sexual relationship?' And that was the evening I most consciously said to him – now what was it I said? – "I surrender." Hmmm… I think I said to him, "Blindfold me. Tie me up! Fuck me!" And that was like, kat-o-o-ng!! That broke it! Somehow that was just sooo clear. And talking to you about it after, you said "You're not prepared, any more, to do just anything to get your Dad's attention."

Did I? Was it like, 'there you go now, you can have everything you want. I am not going to play this attention game!?' So no more chasing… of your Dad.

Yeah! But saying that, the thing with Steven was so about, well, about climbing trees, going for walks, cycling…

Best friends stuff.

…yeah!

No need to wank with our mates!

Hmmm. Unless we want to.

(Both) Ha ha ha ha ha

But who would have thought? I've never looked at my – since coming back to England this time, and speaking with Emma, what a couple of years ago? She said, "Fuck! Your friends, there were always HOT; HOT men around you!" I didn't know, they were just my mates. I didn't know that the girls really fancied my mates!

Hmmm

Same as, through my life, I never looked at my friends, or other blokes; I've looked at other blokes and thought, 'fucking hell, I wish I had that bloke's belly' most of the time, because he only had one! Mine felt like it was hanging all over the place. He he. And that's how I would look at men and their bodies. 'I wish I had that and I wish I had that.' Plus, I wanted to be 'normal'. My shape and size and everything is slightly different, because I'm not English. Do you know what I mean? A foreign body.

You're more kind of squat, aren't you?

South American looking, or you know, that kind of thing I suppose. Which you don't see in the media or around generally.

No…

So of course I've looked at others, especially when I was older, or in pictures and stuff. In the changing rooms, I just wasn't really interested really. I didn't want to, well actually thinking about it, I probably couldn't see anyone because I wore glasses.

Hmmm

Even if I put them on they would be steamed up anyway… Ha ha ha ha ha

We didn't wank together – we might as well have. But it was with Jude – my friend, do you remember who I was saying, that I cast out like an

old shoe – and that was great! I mean, that's the closest I can imagine getting to that, otherwise…

Is that where Steven carried on, maybe, where Jude left off!

Yeees! Hmmm. Totally. And now, friendships. I was thinking, well if I said to you, "Let's have a wank" that would be totally 'do-ing' it. Wouldn't feel right…

And also, I don't think we'd be able to 'get it up!' And it would be 'do-ing'. Some types of physical stuff just needs to happen naturally. And it turns out – and I can't believe this, I have only realised this recently – that my Father's social life revolved around the Church, the local council and his community meetings. There was an agenda, structure, etcetera, etcetera, etcetera. I've turned out the same. It's not just 'hanging out and being normal'.

Oh no, you've fallen into the same trap!

Agenda, structure, doing this, doing that, doing the right thing, not making our Mummies worry about us, etcetera. *Anyway, I don't want to fucking wank with you…*

Well fuck you then!

Ha ha ha ha ha

That whole thing about sex in the woods; I just wanted to take all my clothes off just then - in Highgate Woods - and have a wank. No one around me, it's not like I wanted to be seen, or shag someone or anything; I'm not even sure that sex comes into it.

I remember, when we were really really young, my brother and I would go to the woods and stuff like that, and I did that a couple of times. Just got naked, not wanking! It felt 'normal'. I think I asked my brother if he wanted to, and he didn't, but I didn't need for him to. It wasn't sex or anything, it was 'charging up'. Nothing to do with him. Do you know what I mean?

Absolutely!

No wonder I'm turning 'naturist'! So, was a lot of your sex in the woods?

Hmmm.

So, do people go to woods; rather than, I thought it was more toilets.

My sense is there's like, different... There are some people who seem to enjoy that sort of thrill of standing at a big porcelain urinal, having somebody, like – not knowing who's coming in, who's coming and going, there is even more of a thrill of danger there, I guess.

But it's not committing!

No...

Because you can pretend not to be there really; where if you go to the woods, you're, because you're in a 'gay place', you're committing to being part of that tribe.

Yeah, and there's more, um. There's more control I suppose, in the woods, because you get a chance to check people out, see them from a distance, walk around them.

Oh, so you know for sure that everyone is 'wise' as to what's going on?

Yeah, you know who's there, by-and-large; and there's parts of the commons, or downs, or woods, or graveyards where everyone knows it, like, the gay area. There's that place in Clapham...

And other people don't go there?

...well, the other thing is, in gay magazines, there's actually listings of cruising places. And there's whole books, like guidebooks for cruising. A complete, sort of, counter-culture.

So how does it work with the police, then?

I've never really understood. I've never – well, not that I go there anymore – but I have never had any trouble, or even any single encounter with them. But they know…

Exactly!

I think, well in Silchester, I've been told by people that every now and then they'll be seen to be policing the area, they'll come around with big searchlights, sometimes helicopters!

Ha ha ha

Just to fly over the woods; but it's mostly to scare people. I mean, I don't know if they arrest anyone.

Scare people, so, because… so they are saying that they will catch people if they carry on?

It's like, my sense of it is that it is tolerated. Everyone knows it happens!

But they can't be arsed…

Yes, yes, exactly. To be seen to be doing something. But it's so half-arsed – they can't be bothered, but I don't think they're really interested – but it doesn't stop it. It just kind of flushes people out for a while, you get a sense that there has been a sort of 'raid'. It would be like a sort of illicit club, where people would stay away for a couple of weeks and then gradually start creeping back. But Highgate Wood feels different. It doesn't feel like there is any, cruising energy, or a cruising area… It's weird.

So, disappointed?

I was on Surbiton station platform the other night and there was this guy standing on the platform. We kind of checked each other out. And there was a part of me that was like, I could feel a sort of arousal, heat. But in my mind, I thought, 'I don't want to do anything with this guy. What would I want to do? Just go off to his flat and, fuck?' So it all happened really fast in my head, like a sort of, memory of what I used to do. And then I thought, 'what I would really like to do is have a real wrestle with somebody', do you know what I mean?

Hmmm. You mean playfight?

Yeah, I never did that. Not really... I was holding back with my brother.

I didn't do it with my brother. But I did with a bloke who used to work with me, Jake – we were mates before and then he worked for me afterwards. Blah blah blah. And we used to smoke dope and just playfight a bit. And Lui and I do.

Really?

But, it is a power thing. Lui is not into being overpowered. It used to be the only form of touch between us, which is the other thing. The other day, we spent some time. I was just very mellow, I had loads and loads of things going on in my head, um, just so much, not really being able to work, or to move, or to think, or anything. I hadn't even slept in my bed for like two weeks. I've been sleeping there, in the living room. It's like my den – 'on' the heater, in my corner, but so snug, it's like a little tree house, it's cool.

Hmmm...

43. *Chopper. Recently re-launched 1970's kids bike.*

Men expressing emotions

So I've been sleeping here, not sleeping, it's been weird. So, yeah Lui was here and I was just lying on the settee, just hanging out – and it's different because I've got my own space now. Before I'd always be doing something. Endlessly be doing something. Work, panic, money, holding it together, people, you know – being responsible for everyone's emotions. And, nothing in particular, but he came over – you know, we were just chatting, chatting – *and then he touched me on the shoulder.*

What was it?

It was quite quiet. Very mellow. He really must have 'touched me', and then he just walked away, *and then I started crying.* Something happened... But it was different, it was not like I did; it's like my face or my body or something was, crying. Gently. Where in the past, it has always been manic boo-hooing.

It's different, isn't it? I'm discovering manly crying! I cry now, really quietly, deeply, it's like a sort of meditation.

Yeah?

Not the sort of public 'come and rescue me!' And this is what this sounds like, with you...

Mmmmm. Mmmmm.

A sort of... aahhh, release...

Hmmm.

Release, rather than attention seeking!

Which is very, very different.

How did he touch you? Was it very - kind of - casual...

Lovingly.

Yeah?

We didn't 'do it'. It was, we were both so, so clean; so clear. There was no funny shit between us or anything at all. We were just together.

Hmmm.

And he didn't, purposely, he was just, totally there for me. No he wasn't – it wasn't about him being 'there for me' or anything like that. We were us.

Hmmm.

And it's cool. And, um, we chatted a bit, he sat with me, I wasn't 'broken' or 'needy', it was just 'different' it was real. It was really excellent.

Just men being with men.

Man being with man. And I realised that, for most of my life, I have been scared of men. Or men touching me. Totally. And...

But wanting it as well?

No, not at all. Absolutely not!

Wow...

No way. I didn't want them to come near me. But what, what would I want them to touch me for? Plus, they generally smell a bit funny, of stale smoke, sweat, dirty, musty, hairy rough things. It's like what the fuck do I want there? Don't forget my obsessive-compulsive stuff too, eh.

Ah, yes...

And I suppose kids and boys and stuff as well before. I was totally cool touching and being touched by girls, until I got a bit older. Maybe until puberty! And then it was no one. Because if I was touching girls, then it would be abuse. So touching no one was clean, or safe, or I would be aware of who I had been touching and I would go and wash and whatever.

So the OCD caught you really young?

I also realised that all my emotions, at home, were in the toilet. Go in the loo, lock the door, and I was there alone. And that's where it was. It wasn't allowed anywhere else.

What, no one could sort of 'break down'?

And also, from the last time I went to Wales, I came back, very very painfully constipated. And it hurt! And I had to shit it out, like it was the greatest force. It ripped me apart.

Jesus!

And I remember that throughout my whole childhood, shitting. That's what it was like. I would bleed like fuck, every time; and I could not shit, throughout my childhood, in that house. But I didn't know that was weird... I thought everyone's was like that. Just part of being human. So I realised the difference this time, and um, yeah, shitting. And emotions and the loo, quiet, my Mother – no one could get to me, or touch me, or to pretend that it's not happening, or it's okay.

Shit.

And like you were saying, even with crying. Crying would happen inside. Sobbing, inside. I could feel it, it would almost feel – I don't know – water or tears, moving inside. But no one would know, by looking at me...

That you're barely holding it all together?

Yes, so even now, I wonder - when I'm angry, or upset, or I need space, or whatever - all my life, *I've locked myself in the*

*loo with a spliff; and that way, I can shit
properly, 'let go'* and it's all out of me. And especially in the
winter, I'm just pissing and pissing! As soon I leave the house – I can
piss just before I leave the house, but then I need to piss in no time
once I'm out of the door, and I'd know that the nearest toilet on the way
to the Tube – there's one there; and then I wouldn't be able to piss until
I get to wherever I'm going, so my bladder would be full when I am
nearing Camden Town, so I'd think right, I know there's a toilet there,
so I'd have to get out and go to the loo – and I'm not cool going to
pubs and Big Royale Burgers, I just feel too conspicuous, and I'm all full
of pressure carrying piss around anyway, panicking...

"Can I use your loo?"

I can't stop pissing in the winter. And, um, it's tears. Needs to come out
somehow. I always go funny in the winter – a right moody bastard – it's
when most of my shit hits the fan!

It has to come out from somewhere!

But *what a strange way to cry! I mean, it's
like it's my dick crying!*

Ha ha ha ha ha

One difference between my relationship with Rob, as my 'best friend'
and Lui, as my 'best friend' is that with Lui we have feelings. Fucked up
expressions and reactions, but when I was crying with Lui; I realised
that with Rob's and my relationship no feelings were allowed. It just
didn't happen. We loved debate and exploring our heads, but never
felt the vulnerability of 'taking part' in society. Neither of us knew how
to cry. Once, when I cried through sheer pressure, after huge fuck-ups
and injustices with our business landlords-financiers, at the end of a
huge meeting, I went out and I started crying. Rob, was confused. He
just didn't understand – to explain to him that I am upset, this is why
and at this point I feel that I don't have any words or I can't express
myself – I've got a build-up of something that needs to be released, you

know, it's intellectual. He just didn't get it! When my grand Mother died, I got a phone call when I was at work and Rob was there. I had to phone a couple of people and tell them, um, and when I put the phone down, Rob said, "…look, I know you're upset and everything, but I need to go soon and this is really important. Do you mind just checking my CV[44] one last time so I can make sure that it's OK?" And it's not like he's bad, or he meant it, and it was totally safe for us . because I couldn't, I didn't have to get into any feelings then. The only times there were feelings – actually this is the same as Lui! – the only times we have had real tears, or feelings, is betrayal. Either I've betrayed him, or he's betrayed me. Because that's 'the ultimate', same with Rob I suppose… Very rarely otherwise. My feeling with Lui, there'd be feelings – with both of us I suppose, it's a bit mixed up, because it seems to be the trap of 'what's going on here?', but it taps into something from the past. But yeah …funny that! Same as home. No emotions, no genitals *(sly laugh)*, no nothing. Safe. Hmmm.

I just, I think it's, it's, happening anyway, but I got to noticing, since we've been talking, more focussed – like this, this is so present in society. The whole thing with children. The whole repression. So early.

Hmmm

You know, squeezing them down and making them silent. And the touch thing as well, I mean I, I gave Maria a massage last night and this morning she said she felt really stiff – and we were just like shaking and moving. When do people touch in this society, I mean it's almost like – you know, people can't fathom, say domestic violence, but that must be – it's like you pissing tears – it's the only way that people can express things…

Exactly!

…is through violence.

Yeah – because it needs to come out somehow – and if that's the only way it's allowed – or, you know, hold it 'til it bursts – but in the same way, it would be unnatural for people to suddenly start touching each other.

Hmmm…

They'd need to… undo their shit I suppose. Because when I used to touch 'a lot!' after just not touching all my life, it was the other extreme, of huge hugs; but a huge hug is no connection. There is no… nothing.

Hmmm

It's, the opposite extreme of avoidance. It's either too low or too high.

Yeah, you've got to have a balance, of actually 'feeling it' – and less… 'prattling on'… Hmmm, yeah! It's like the phrase "'lovemaking' – ooh, it's so wonderful to be able to touch…" *(in choir-boy voice)*

Yesterday, for the first time, seeing my parents – it was tough! I wasn't sure whether I was going to go through with it, ummm; if Rob and Carrie weren't there I don't know whether I would have gone!

Are they over from the States? They're over?

Yeah!

Oh, I didn't realise!

Yeah, yeah… That's how come I hung out with them. Rob was like a son to my folks as well, but they hadn't met for a long long time. So perfect, kind-of, um, deflection. Handy work, and we all got on, when there was someone else there – when there was a guest. When there were no guests, it was weird. No one knew what to do.

Really…? This wasn't the session with your brother that you were talking about, where you were going to talk to your folks? That's – is that going to happen?

Oh no, that's when they come back from Goa. So we've decided to just hold it together – basically, for me, I'm just saying to myself for a couple of weeks, 'hold it together' until, yesterday, after seeing (my parents) Angela and Tony. So what we agreed, was to keep a lid on it – and really, seeing them yesterday was for them, so they don't feel fucked up because I didn't see them before Christmas and going away. When they come back, we can take them into family therapy; and rather than getting into anything, it will be 'let's discuss the ground rules'. Errr, so everyone has a forum, or some sort of a structure within which to communicate, rather than, just avoiding everything.

Let's do it!

…*Whoever 'abused' my Mother, or whoever 'fucked up' my Father,* but rather than 'anger' and 'poor me', it's more like 'ah, right – so…' It's like clients, I can so easily sort clients out, because they know their past, or they can feel, or I get a sense and I question to confirm whatever – the picture's there and it's sorted out! Quite easily and quickly. I can't for me, because I don't know, and this is what I am trying to find out! I'm not 'coming to me' from an outside perspective.

Yeah…

…and there are just so many different huge 'lost pockets' and secrets and things. Sub-plots.

Hmmm. It reminds me of a conversation I had with this woman Elvira, who runs the Five Rhythms[45]**; and she was saying, it's almost like, she had a sense it was happening more across the board, but there are people in families who are almost like an 'agent', to break the karmic pattern…**

Yup!

…or whatever you want to call it…

Yup!

It's not about saying 'you fucked me up!'. 'You're to blame!'

Yeah, but breaking the 'family curse'.

Yeah… enough! Big thing you said about, after Findhorn, to me.

"You don't want to pass all your shit on to Malaika...!" That's interesting, I was thinking, you know you said, about, we talked about abuse, I think in the summer. How we had a sense, that it was like, an atmosphere from the past. Me, and my brother and sister, have often puzzled over... Well, we had a 'happy' childhood and yet... there's a gloom, melancholy hanging around. No wonder, with my Mum, abandoned by her Mother; and my Dad's family 'sitting on the corpse' of his brother. Jesus! Nowadays, it's like, 'was it abuse - wasn't it abuse?' But, again, it's like, *what's the classic thing that abusers are supposed to say to children?* "This is our little secret, don't tell anyone..."

Exactly!!!

So even if they are not, then, actually touching your cock or sticking their finger up your arse or whatever – it's still 'it's our secret'...

Hmmm

...and somebody's the 'power broker' in the family, and I think that our common thread, again, is the Mother.

I wish my Father would communicate... He has a minor speech impediment – which is a huge thing for him, but unnoticeable and not an issue for others – and all through my life, he never entered into conversation, arguments, discussions, anything, because, of it. He wouldn't be able to communicate, and he would be found out 'wrong' or 'bad' anyway, so why bother?! Poor guy...

Hmmm...

So, his behaviour told me, all my life, up until now, that 'yes, he's admitting to it – whatever the 'it' of the moment is - and he knew he'd be found out anyway', because, what else is communicated to me by that? He'd look guilty, he'd act guilty, that's what he'd bring upon himself so how could I know anything else? He'd dig his own grave – and jump in it feet first! It's all he knew.

That's quite revealing; interesting isn't it!?

Yeah… Totally! But my Mother, none of us touched, or could touch. And for years, I've been like, covering my crotch with my arms, or crossing my legs when she's around. Feeling funny. I didn't want to be touched by, or touch my Mother too much, but she was so… if I didn't I was abandoning her, and she was like this helpless little thing that was in panic, in the city or in the street or amongst people, wherever she could be harmed or felt threatened. So, I don't know, 'how comfortable am I shagging hard?' Do you know what I mean? It follows on…

Hmmm!

And, um – not that I haven't – and, also attracting girls who have been abused. To keep me in that pattern…

Hmmm

How else could I fall in love with my Mother – unless I find another abused girl, I suppose… So, yeah, funny that – about being scared about being touched by men; and not sleeping in my own bed, pretty much.

What, recently you mean?

Yeah, I have not been sleeping in my own bed recently…

I wonder what that's all about?

Quite often… dunno. But, I was thinking, that's why I want regression therapy.[46]

Hmmm…?

I'm sick to death of trying to find out from other people, different stories of whatever, whatever. At the end of the day I want 'my' experience – that was my reality; and if it's wrong, then fine, I can deal with it and move on.

Hmmm.

44. *CV. Curriculum Vitae, resume, profile of career. To seek employment / funding.*

45. *Five Rhythms. Gabrielle Roth's authentic, inspired, catalytic dance therapy / meditation. www.5rhythms.com*

46. *Regression therapy. Technique to take client to time and place of emotional block.*

What sex am I allowed?

I was speaking to Lui, as well, about – um – everything! About his experiences – um – and me, cottaging, stuff like that – I don't think I've told you this either, but… I've got a criminal record.

You have?!!!

Yup.

Seriously???!

Yeah.

I mean, you told me about going and having a nose around the loos at Angel, Islington.

Yeah, none of that's…

That, that…

But all this, you know - cottaging, going to saunas, whatever - I didn't even look at other people, properly. I was pretty-much invisible, being around, not really wanting to be touched, or take part, but I suppose just… It's almost more comfortable being in a sauna, a gay sauna – than a straight sauna or changing rooms, because everyone's so uptight!

Yeah.

Looking, not looking, talking crap, not talking, not being relaxed, not being… it's all such a show! It's just – I dunno, it's not safe, it's not comfortable.

Again, that's where the gay thing comes from… It is extreme, but it's

kind of relaxed, I suppose. It's the only place you have permission to – as you say – overtly look.

Exactly! But then, if you don't want to get involved – you don't! If you do, you do; it's okay to touch, you don't have to look or pretend that you are not looking; and because of that, there is really nothing to look at.

You know, it just gives you permission, doesn't it?

Yeah, well it's not pervy; where, in an ordinary place it's a bit pervy because you are pretending and you are so uptight, but with this you can just get on with it and… whatever! But no, I've never actually taken part or been interested in taking part, or it's not really… I've never been really that interested in men, sexually. But fuck, I remember when, when I was in Catholic Primary school, someone - a girl's Father - coming to me and saying *"Stop fiddling with my daughter in the mini-bus, otherwise I'll tell your parents!"* And I totally forgot that in the early days, I would always be chasing the girls, and fiddling, and I was just so fascinated and I just wanted to touch them and tickle them and – it was playful! It wasn't sexual or abusive or – as far as I know… And this one girl was really not attractive, and I didn't… And, you know, she kind of joined in – or I let her join in a little bit, just through sheer charity.

Hhhhuh huh ha…

Maybe she did it because she felt left out, or wanted some attention. But it stopped me. Because, again, touching girls is equal to abuse and I don't know where to draw the line. But, you know, I was quite fascinated but I never wanted boys near, because… That was obsessive-compulsive – they were filthy! I didn't want to touch them.

Which is, kind of, presumably – a sort of reflection of feeling that you were filthy. If boys are filthy; if you're a boy…

Yes, and the way that I cleaned, and cleaned and cleaned. I suppose my Mother told me that I was filthy, because all men are. She'd laugh at their bodies, laugh at their smell and laugh at their ugly toes and their big noses and their hairy backs, and, you know – what is left?

Ummm...

I am, you know, once she notices that I am male, then she is going to abandon me.

So you have to... 'girlify'.

Yup!

So, did that man saying that – the Father – was that kind of a defining moment when you stopped...

Which Father?

You know, the one who said "Stop fiddling with my daughter or I'll..."

Yeah. I forgot about that. But that was such a shock! That was huge...

(whispers and mumbles then says clearly) A huge panic!

...don't touch girls.

Well, funnily enough, I've...

And the big thing is, 'parents shouldn't know!' ...that I've even got a dick. Forget about anything else – I HAVEN'T GOT A DICK.

But that's so natural! I mean, that's what children do at school!

I wished that mine was tiny – and wouldn't show. Because then it wouldn't be... making the place filthy. Or it wouldn't be abusing my Mother. Huh huh huh huh huh... Can you imagine that? I sooo hated it! It was...

Jesus! If that's what you got from her, imagine what your Dad must have felt like!

Fuck! Poor guy...

Hairy, smelly, masculine,

Yeah, he's just male!

Yeah. He's just there.

Hmmm.

Now I had a similar – only came to me, recently, as a defining moment. I was talking to George, the American coach guy who I did some stuff with earlier in the year. And I remembered, at school, this girl called – I think it was Judith Saatchi I think she was called... and another girl called Sally-Anne Honeywell, and me, and we all played 'doctors & nurses' and got Judith naked - I don't know what we were doing or when - it was like in the cloakroom. She was naked in this plastic bath and we were examining her.

How great!

Yeah, exactly. You know, she was – I can't remember the details. I remember, she was either naked or part naked – and we were discovered by our teacher! It was like, this is going... Almost that thing of 'the whole school will find out'...

Yes.

"You're sick!"

Exactly.

"Perverts!" Not in; not so much as in yours, like 'you're a filthy boy'; but 'you're just disgusting children!' 'How can do you this?' 'You're vermin...'

Yeah. Yeah.

Terrible. But it's the same... I mean, last night, at the museum – at the Tate Modern. This big trumpety sculpture thing. Maria and I were making lots of noise – it's great! We played! It's what you want to do. And the only other person who did it – spontaneously – was a child;

and his Father went "SsschhhHH!!!"

Nnnnnooooo…

And I started clapping the boy, cheering him on – 'cos I thought, *'Fuck you, you bastard - don't… repress that child!'* and the Father looked 'really' sheepish. He kinda went 'Oh, did he do something good?!'

HA HA HA HA HA… Yeah!

How dare you… tell this child to stop!

Yeah. First 'kill' the child!

…I know! I came back from Highgate Wood, coming through the gates and this little boy was playing with the gate. I said, "Oh, are you the gatekeeper?" And he laughed; and his Mother said "Oh stop fooling around!" Aaah… Jesus Chrjst!

And we were such well-behaved kids, Caetano and I. We never – before we saw Angela and Tony, we met the night before. We were just chatting about various things… Uuum, and he said something about – I said "I think it would be really good to get together beforehand, so that anything that we're angry about, or you know, we can just; I want to chill. I want to go to my acupuncturist before I see them so that I'm just 'clean' and I don't 'dump' whatever I am feeling on them, because it's not going to help anyone." And he said something about, "Yeah you and I were a bit childish the last time we were all together, because we just sent texts to each other you know, we had to do something." And I said, "Well, in a way, it's about time, because we never were, when we were kids. Ummm, and what's so bad about that?" It was OK. But we so forget that we are… supposed to be the children.

Hmmm.

And we're the ones that were supposed to play and have tantrums – but there was no space for our childhoods. The same with so many clients that I've met. 'Rescue your child, your children, and let them have the childhood – stop stealing it from them because you haven't had yours. That's not fair!' You know, men going around and shagging women all over the place, um, women 'love-addicting' their sons and 'avoidance-addicting' their daughters, who have an Oedipal thing with their Father, who is out shagging and 'being the boy', so the boy is too much of a little dweeb because there is no space for another boy, the boy role is being taken by the Father, blah blah blah, it's just so natural, *no wonder the kitten shits on the best rug –* do you know what I mean?

Ha ha ha

It's got to be expressed by someone in the family!

HA HA HA HA HA

Ha ha ha ha ha

Community

I mean, I guess I keep thinking 'what's it all about?' Is it a cultural thing, something to do with the way that society 'has to' operate. You know, you can't have 'emotional' people operating machinery or doing jobs on production lines, or working on computers – you've got to hold it all together, so you have to be... dulled down, kept in, suppressed.

This is how it is now, but I hope... What I believe, is, you know, before – I don't know – the Land Lords (butchers!) or Christianity or whatever it was, surely the Pagans[47] or whoever would 'be' in communities as best as they could, where everyone was just 'living together' and everyone was inspiring each other and didn't need 'your son to totally love you and keep your secrets...' because he was free to love everyone and everyone to love him; and I don't imagine there were so many perversions and therapists because *everyone was 'naked'* – physically, emotionally, mentally – and just sharing 'the life' together and feeding each other. You know, being 'normal'. *Now, we are just so separate and competitive and paranoid...*

Hmmm

...suppressed and therefore it just comes out in weird ways; but that is the only way. For me, that's the answer. It kinda makes sense, I think...

What, the Pagan thing?

Yeah! Whether it's Pagan, or any community. There are communities these days that work, surely. In the old days, I imagine – you know, when they first appeared – places like Findhorn, The Temple Of The People, up in Halcyon, what's that one up near Pondicherry, in India…?

Oh, um – Auroville![48]

Hmmm, yeah. *'Diggers And Dreamers'*[49] – there are so many communities, but, it can be a pain in the arse, because, it's a real commitment to find out – and going to join one – rather than 'this is how I choose to live my life' – and I'll attract people, like this house, because look at who it attracts. People just meet people, and share whatever they want to, and… it's wonderful!

I think the whole community thing has a lot to offer, but it's, it's… It's a kind of 'doing' community, something deliberate…

Exactly!

…you never know who you're going to end up with; not that that's exactly a bad thing. But I think, from Findhorn, from the *'Sex & Spirit Conference'*[50] and also from my experience at Wilmington, there's no body; nobody really knows how to contain the darkside[51]…

Yeah, it's denied!

Yeah…

You're not allowed it. 'If you bring it in here, you're out!' Same as the family. Maybe, it's different at the Zegg Community[52] – and I would love to check it out.

Well there's, yeah, the openness and the sex.

Hmmm. And more and more – you know – now that I've applied for Incapacity Benefit and Housing Benefit – did I tell you?

No…

It's just the most embarrassing thing! I could die, because I have to do this, because I still don't have enough money to survive.

Hmmm

Uum, but, I don't come from a rich family. There is no one to look after me and no means to support me, so *I've got no choice... But to choose, not holding it together.*

Yeah, it's almost like having a breakdown...

Exactly!

Allowing...

Yup. Let's see what's going to happen.

And then again, you know, I, my sense, recently, I'm actually – in a bizarre way, I feel like doing this shit job is actually, completely appropriate, because I am seeing that – most people, most people are in the same situation; they don't want to be doing half the crap that they are doing.

Hmmm

But, I suppose underneath it all is the big question of, 'what's the meaning of life?' What – the fuck – are people doing?

We are doing things differently, because you haven't done this type of work before, which is what most people do...

Hmmm

...and I have always been over-working, workaholic, smoking dope, panic, umm, being responsible for everyone's emotions – and now I am doing 'nothing' which is my opposite. So we are going to find the space that we've been avoiding, so see what it's... who we are!

Hmmm

The bits that need feeling, fuelling, filling...

Hmmm, hmmm... But most people are just barely holding it together. You know it's like, I find it quite laughable...

Yeah

...but it's, it's actually inspiring, you know. I can, I can see why people go off into the spiral of total self-annihilation – the drink, the drugs, cigarettes, whatever – oblivion. Or, you can look at it and say 'Wow! There's a chance to use it creatively...'

Hmmm

...which is not always easy – huhhh – because you have to 'live it'! And I just feel, I feel just such a huge compassion for people, especially, having a child or being around children. Looking at them in their, sort of, pure state...

Yeah

...and thinking, 'they' were all like this! Everyone was like this in the beginning...

Yeah

...and somewhere along the line, once, twice, however many times – you know, you get 'hit over the head' so many times by a hammer until you surrender.

I was looking at kids, um, recently, because there are more kids on the Underground – you know, school's out! People taking them shopping. And what a difference between the kids who aren't being 'vamped', who are still bright-eyed and looking around the world and learning; and the kids who are so being 'vamped' that they don't have their own personality. They are a product of the Mother's or the Father's worries. Or fears. Or whatever it is, so 'don't this, do that, whatever, whatever...' it's terrible. It's shocking!

Ummm

And they're not doing it because they're bad – they're totally unaware! They haven't got a clue! Just like me, I was a pawn – ha ha ha ha ha – I was 'up for service' basically.

You're right! It's a complete lack of awareness — that's at the root of it.

47. *Pagans. Those who actively live with(in) the cycles and laws of nature.*

48. *Auroville. (Pondicherry, India) Intentional community / educational facility. www.auroville.org*

49. *'Diggers And Dreamers' Annual directory and website listing intentional communities worldwide. www.diggersanddreamers.org.uk*

50. *'Sex & Spirit Conference' Findhorn Foundation annual conference.*

51. *Darkside. The part(s) of ourselves that we disown, through fear, shame, lack of awareness.*

52. *Zegg Community. (Belzig, Germany) Intentional community / education facility. www.zegg.de*

Upsetting sex

I remembered, also, that when Rob and I slept with a girl. I wasn't 'that' up for it.

What, the two of you and a girl?

Yeah…

Sounds like fun!

Loads of girls wanted to do that with us because we were so 'in-tune' – I was so sexually unaware anyway; and that must have been so attractive, because I wasn't playing games or manipulating or needy. And it just 'happened' with this girl, and she was – we'd talked about it, uum, she was drop-dead gorgeous, a model from Sweden, perfect in every way, uum, it didn't really work. I mean, I was alone with her, Rob was alone with her; and, I wasn't - I didn't even get a stiffie through the whole thing!

Which isn't necessarily a bad thing!

No, well, except it took me a long time to get over it. It took me a long time to get over the whole experience – but I didn't find it exciting. I did find it very scary, but then, I found sex scary.

So, what happened, he basically… fucked her, and you watched?

No no no, the three of us were there, kissing, playing whatever. I'm not sure I knew how to do it. How to join in or anything. Uum, and Rob was not emotionally there at all. He was physically there, and rampant, uum, I think I was emotionally there, but emotionally didn't make any sense. It seemed abusive. And, I think she was, gagging for it, or wanting an experience, or, I think she wanted love. Big time! But she

didn't know how to accept love. *She could only accept...*
being fucked. And if I was with her, alone, I would have
wanted something really soft and gentle and nice. I don't think she
could have gone there. So there was me wanting hugs and kisses and
soft and sensual, and, you know, that kind of stuff; Rob wanting to fuck
her; and her only knowing being fucked, I imagine...

Hmmm

...and me being scared of sex anyway. And the same as those two,
therefore they just fuck and don't meet emotionally anyway, where I
couldn't do that because I was, you know, I've got the 'abuser' issue –
so messy, too messy!

Hmmm

And one thing that really upset me – the other day – was that Lui
reminded me of something; and I don't remember him ever saying to
me, uum, but we went out somewhere, party, club, whatever – came
home with a couple of Australian girls – *and we were all on*
Ecstasy and just stayed up and chatted and whatever, and I don't
remember knowing that, they both wanted to shag Lui. I hadn't even
met them all night, they were just girls that Lui met. I didn't know. And
we were even outside his bedroom saying "What shall we do?" or Lui
saying "What shall we do?" and I said, "Well, I don't know... I don't
know how these things work. I suppose, hang out with them, or tell me,
or whatever. I haven't got a clue!" I was on Ecstasy and I'm not used to
Ecstasy, or situations like this or anything like that, plus, sex is something
that 'harms women' – and my parents shouldn't find out about. So, I
didn't know. Apparently, they were looking at, or one of them was
looking at Lui, saying, with her eyes, "What's up? What's up?" and Lui
just looked down and avoided the situation. And then he told me later
and I had this horrible horrible feeling; and I have had that feeling
before and I recognised it. I think that it was a similar feeling to, when,
Rob and I and the girl were sleeping together and it was like – I don't
know – this is wrong, there is something 'sinister', um, and recently I

have realised, recently like today, that my parents must have shagged on a Saturday morning when we were downstairs watching kids' TV.

Ummmmm

Whatever…

What, did you feel like…

Never heard a thing, if I remember.

Oh my God, no… 'silent sex'

There was a really sinister, weird atmosphere. And the only way I can describe it, was the feeling of my Father being really really angry – but me not knowing why. My Mother being really really frozen, and some secrets. And some pain – something like that. But, obviously it wasn't happening, because every now and again I'd shout upstairs "…can I have another packet of crisps?" Or "Caetano's doing 'this'!" Or "Caetano's doing 'that'!" What I would do on a Saturday morning, is, it would be my special treat for everyone, or, my job, or whatever, that I'd clean the fireplace, lay the new fire, do all the dusting, do all the hoovering, just clean. Clean the whole downstairs of the house; and Caetano was supposed to do it with me. And I was – you know – I was a do-er. He was a proper, ordinary child. He wanted to watch TV; I wanted to watch *'Swap Shop'*[53], because… blah blah blah, because, I was being a good boy; Caetano wanted to watch *'Tiswas'*[54], where I'd never actually watch anything on TV or even read a book, because 'I was never there!' I was thinking about everything that was fucked up and how I am supposed to be making it better.

53. *'Swap Shop'* 1970's kids television show hosted by Noel Edmonds.

54. *'Tiswas'* 1970's kids television show hosted by Chris Tarrant.

Self-acceptance

And that's what they must have been doing. And it was such a horrible feeling. They never touched, they never smiled at each other, they never anything.

It was like a sort of mechanical act...

Hmm. So yeah, funny stuff around sex. ...and all the girls that I've 'shagged' chased me like fuck! And they've been – I realise that there were so many situations when girls have, you know, girls in bed with me, after pretty-much fighting to stay, in a way; umm, that I didn't realise what was going on. I remember one time, I had a big party and this girl was just all over me and I didn't realise; I just thought that she was being nice. Because I was still a little boy - and why would any girl, you know - I didn't realise I was a man, or fuckable, or anything – I was just a little boy. And she stayed, and, umm, I just made sure that she didn't touch me and she wanted to fuck the living daylights out of me. It was so obvious, looking back. I didn't know, I didn't believe it, I didn't know how to deal with it; it just happened in Australia again, with loads of girls on my case and 'nice' me, totally oblivious – it was crazy – recently it's been quite full on! But the *criminal record*, uuum, years and years and years ago, I was busting for a piss, as I always was in the winter...

Ummm

I remembered that there's a; I was outside London if I remember. I remembered that there was a toilet in Harrow-On-The-Hill station, dashed to the loo and I was standing there. There was an Asian man, and, I thought - I never saw my Father's dick - and I always thought I was deformed. I couldn't figure out, after my Father saying, or my parents talking about "Were the other boys different?" or "Did you notice anything?" and all that kind of stuff. And my parents always hid themselves. It was all very... terrible to see, you know, God knows what, so it did cross my mind, I thought 'I wonder what his dick looks like?' Not that, I could check if it's okay or something like that, but I thought nothing of it really. Um, I was standing there, and pissing and pissing and pissing, and then I stopped and I was just freezing cold. Um, and then I looked at him and he was just standing there and whatever, I didn't think anything of it. And I stood there to see if there was any more to come out, and just shaking myself, whatever – and it must have been a while, because, when – when it's bad like that, in the winter, when I go and go, as soon as I leave, I want to go again. Where if I wait for a minute, then there'll be a load more, and then it's clear. And before I knew it, he touched me. And I didn't even look at him or anything. Um, not that it didn't cross my mind, because like I said, it's like, there's a brown-skin, I wonder what; 'am I okay?'

Hmmm

Next thing I know, *the police burst in.*

Jesus...

And they'd been watching from a sky-light. They needed, apparently, to get a certain quota... of people... from there. They thought I was younger, and it seemed that they were looking for younger Asian men, or boys, or whatever; or to say that there are men hassling boys – this is a long long long time ago. And for most of my life, it's been as if it never happened. Even after I left then, it's like it never happened. And I looked – like I look young now – I looked really young then. Um, so they thought they were getting their quota of paedophiles or something. Or for – nastiness, but they wanted young Asian boys and older Asian men, so I didn't quite fit the bill, but I got a criminal record out of it anyway. Plus, one was saying to the other "Do you recognise him, you know, do you know who he is?" and it just made sense from everything that they were saying that – maybe one of them actually said – one of 'the squealers' had been cottaging to get to know everyone around.

Well they do...

Who to take? Why, why, would they want to do that?

Well, apparently, they've always sent out the prettiest young coppers – I don't think they do anymore...

But why? And why would they want to go out and cottage...

Because why are they doing it? Because it's illegal! Why is it illegal? Dunno! Just because... Hmmm. Judaeo-Christian bollocks. The Bible?

But weird! So, after I finally left, it felt like it didn't happen after a little while. I wasn't sure that it actually did. Until, I don't know how many weeks later they turned up at the door and started harassing. And I was in bed, and Rob, and another friend of mine Chloie were sleeping in my room with me. All of us in bed. Not mine though, I don't remember, we were just all over the place, we'd been hanging out. And I answered the door with a quilt around me and they started with my name and was I... oh what's it called? I wasn't even arrested...

Oh, what, you got a warning?

No, I had to go to Magistrates' Court. 'Gross indecency with another man' that's what it was. Aaam, which is a bit over done – ha ha ha – but then on the other hand, there were other times...

But that's standard!

... when I looked at people, people looked at me, you know whatever it was, you know, even someone touching me or whatever.

Hmmm

I should have been caught for that! 'That' was 'gross indecency'! But the interesting thing was that the one time that my 'Father' was there, is the one time that God said 'Right - ha ha ha - this is why you're here' or 'deal with this' or whatever it is, and that's the one I was caught for – not doing anything, while I was busting for a piss. And, because of my colour – which I have never really had direct 'colour stuff' that way, unlike other people who come from 'coloured communities' or from cities...

Hmmm

And for looking young. Fucking weird.

Hmmm. Interesting bit of karma... I need a piss, actually.

The great outdoors

It's funny, when you were talking about that thing with Rob and that woman. I was just thinking, it's interesting, that whole thing about sex; the comment you made earlier about the self worth. I think it's, again, that thing when we're children, we are, we're just unconsciously letting our light shine, aren't we? We are just being radiant in the world. And then somehow we learn that that's bad, and whatever; and then I think that a lot of my sex addiction and the whole thing with seeking men, that – it was a bit like you said with Lui, that you know that he knows that he's got those good looks. I knew that I could go to just any of these places and immediately people would be…

You wouldn't be rejected.

Yeah! Like flies to shit.

Right…

And whether, you know, taking anything, whatever.

Hmmm

Just, as long as, I don't leave there rejected and unsatisfied.

And were you satisfied, always?

Well, sometimes – I remember one day – it was interesting – at Wilmington; and I was just feeling so pent up. I was really, getting a kind of desperation to be fucked by a man. So I went all the way from Wessex to Silchester for one day…

Really?

Yeah, to this sort of, the cruising part of Silchester. Uum, and a guy that I didn't even fancy was sitting in a car, I saw him – it's so classic…

People sit in cars?

Yeah… In this place in Silchester – well I think they do everywhere – they drive up and just sit there. And there's like signals, I mean, *there's a whole sub-culture of signs and language.* Yeah, you kind of make yourself available by looking in a certain way, or standing…

Hmmm

So he follows me into the woods, and, hummm…

So you get out, you were walking?

Yeah, no. I was on foot. I had come from the station.

And he was in a car?

Yeah…

So you looked at each other in certain ways, then you walked into the woods and he followed?

Yeah…

And it was like having quite a detailed conversation?

Yeah, without any words. It was completely psychic. If you look at somebody…

Facial expressions.

…they look at you, you walk past, you kind of both look back, it's like that's the first stage. Then one of you follows the other and you go off somewhere. But, there's a kind of; it's interesting watching, it's like a kind of dance. Some people, you can see, are really being pursued and are not that interested. The other person hasn't read the signals – 'I'm not looking at you, fuck off! I'm interested in him, and he's interested in him, and...'

Huuuh

...it's quite bizarre!

So, after all that, *if you're not getting who you want, can you go back to your first reserve?*

(Both) Ha ha ha ha ha...

Sometimes, I mean yeah I've ended up with people who I'd sort of rejected at first - maybe old or ugly or whatever - sometimes I'd almost... sounds like I was Mother Teresa, but I'd almost sometimes give someone a handjob, because it looks like they wouldn't get anybody else. If I hadn't found anybody, or even some – this one day in particular, this guy basically fucked me up the arse – it was really painful because he had a huge dick...

Hmmm

...and I shut my eyes at one point. Next thing I know, these two other guys, one of them was watching and the other guy was trying to stick his dick in my mouth... and it was really 'odd'. I had actually left, and this guy pursued me.

...the one who was shagging you...

No. He disappeared. The other guy who had been trying to stick his dick in

...you mean you had walked off mid shag?...

Hmm!

...you didn't say anything...

No. It's all very silent, and, er, so, he

...I don't believe it! Mid actual shag!

Well pretty much!

…You stand up and walk away…

Yeah!

Faaack! That is, um, surely that's quite liberating…

Hmmm…?

…that you had started - but you didn't have to carry on?

Hmm!

…Is that where people can get violent, because it's like, you know, 'I'm wide open and I'm doing this… you can't reject me now!'

Not really, I think it's sort of passivity. I've never come across it…

Had you ever seen violence there, or – so no one exchanges words, so obviously no shouting.

No.

What about sex noises? Groaning, and…

Well, I feel like I went there as a kind of 'un-holy innocent' in a way. Just, um. I'd do whatever I fancy doing. Like some men make it quite clear they don't want to kiss, others go straight for the, you know, hand on the crotch.

Hmmm

Others will follow the leader, almost. You know, I'd – again, it comes back to that thing. I would want to take all my clothes off.

Hmmm

And for a lot of men, it was, like, 'WoW! This is great. This is really unusual'.

So they would as well?

Yeah!

Because you did it, you gave them permission.

Yeah.

Were you more of an 'act' for other people, because you were naked? And that was unusual, or did other people sometimes get naked?

Not so much down in Silchester. But like I said when we went to that party in Clapham, I remember, years before, on the Common – there was this sort of, yeah it was like an orgy I suppose. And near the centre of this, sort of heaving mass of forty or fifty men, there were naked blokes. Weird… But, um, yeah I think it's – those people don't go there for intimacy. And I think that's what I craved. I wanted intimacy with men. Sex was a big part of it…

Are you sure about that? Or maybe they gained intimacy through being rough. What they got was a 'fix' of intimacy through being - as long as they were - like Lui and I. Fight! That's touching. It's all we could allow.

Hmmm

Maybe that's all they'd allow themselves to feel, or something.

Yeah, well it's like, I mean, again, coming back to children. They want to be rough and playful and whatever, as well as, sort of tender and…

Hmmm

…I remember this one guy – who, apparently, I heard from another bloke, was quite notorious for, wanting, to 'abuse' people. He said to me, "I'd like to see you naked, lying on the floor with a group of men wanking over you." It was quite bizarre.

But then, that's what, um, I know a guy who does, they call it 'dogging' or 'car park fun', and they agree, or arrange to, well, I think with a lot of people it's just luck. They know each other or something. But, otherwise, you arrange to meet up, people have web sites – this guy I know through the internet. And I've met him. He took me to that naturist place for the first time, Rio's – in Kentish Town. Um, so you arrange to meet up, a load of men know where, what time, and a girl turns up, with her boyfriend – or whoever – um, he's got a camera or a video or something, and, um, they just – apparently I think it's all silent, no one talks or very little talking. And then, the object of the exercise is for men to wank over her, or she can suck someone off if she wants, or let someone fuck her if she wants, but generally it's all of them wank over her. Maybe there's one lucky one that's going to be sucked off. And the boyfriend makes videos of it. People pay to see it on the internet. And that's it. They do it in car parks and call it dogging. Never checked it out myself, but this guy's well into it.

No wonder all those places are so fascinating. I mean I don't know if you've ever…

There's a vibe!

…yeah. It's the after dark thing, somewhere a bit illicit…

Yeah

…where you're not supposed to be, yeah, you kind of notice people who are loitering.

So there's a vibe in car parks, in the woods, toilets, graveyards and in very sacred places, generally, there is a very similar vibe I find. There's a really high energy. And maybe it's the thing, where, near every sacred place, in the world, pretty much, right next door to it there's the opposite.

Profane.

Prostitutes and Churches. Findhorn and the American airbase. Uuum, very very often it's where there's drugs and prostitution there's either something really nasty happen there or there's the equal and opposite 'high'.

Well again, it's like you said, it's all the 'darkside stuff' that doesn't get

let out. I feel like we are kind of scraping on the surface of this, you know what I mean? It feels like there's something really...

Brewing!

Cock-suckers

So, um, another thing that happened. I have been chatting a lot on the internet. Very very very interesting people. Uuum, intense, quite deep, emotional, honest conversations about childhoods and abuse and sex and whatever. There is this one guy who just seemed, so cool. Not that much chatting, really nice picture on his profile – so you can check people out on their profiles, and see, aaam, if they look really dodgy. You know, you can look at someone's face and say, 'you're safe!'

That's one thing I've never done – anything on the internet! I know what you mean though, about 'knowing' when someone is safe and 'knowing' a bit of rough; or maybe even a looney or a nutter.

So with this one, the bottom line is, he loves giving people blowjobs. Uum, and that's it.

What - men, women, whatever…

Men!

Oh, men?

Yeah, yeah! And he pretty much always has – didn't get into any detail with him, but with other people, it's really interesting. That's what's been up. Men who like giving blowjobs. I've met some.

Hmmm…?!

On the internet, chatting. And that's what they did in school, that was their status, a lot of them have had the whole rugby team, football team, the boys that are into this all know, but the ones that don't, no one knows; their girlfriends – you know, small towns, where so many of the men know, so many don't, none of the women know, the girlfriends don't know, they get married, blah blah blah and they still love to give other men blowjobs, which is… fair enough. But, with this guy, he was in an area where I was going to be, we just got on. I thought, yeah, this will probably never happen, but whatever. Interesting, nice guy. I ended up going to his place, aaand, just had the best, ever, blowjob. And he was just a really cool guy! Uum, and he says that he's got, a few — and it's not, he didn't necessarily, he was totally serving. Uum…

And he knew what he was doing, presumably.

Exactly. He was aware. He knows what it feels like! Lovely.

He knows what it feels like to have a blowjob, because a woman never can. I don't know whether it's…

Yeah, yeah, there's that. *That's why he gave a very good blowjob.* It was very very very different for me. Because, sex has always been 'How do I perform?' 'How do I make it right? Do it good? Whatever whatever whatever…' So totally receiving, in a really nice, clean, no manipulation, doesn't want to Mother me, smother me or anything! And I have, and it was honest, what was going on.

Hmmm

You know, I was saying with cottaging or going to saunas or whatever, I didn't take part, didn't even look that much, or pretended not to and I was invisible. In a way, similar with sex, earlier on, or in the beginning, or whatever — and certain things are just… can't receive. Lui and I can't receive love, so we have dramas to prove that we're not being loved and push those who want to love us, away. Then make up and vamp the appropriate fix, without vulnerability or moving forward. And with this, not only was it receiving, he didn't even get his pants off! And, it was connecting, and acknowledging that this was what was going on. And, it was totally different. I was actually 'there'! Ha ha ha ha ha. Rather than 'What am I supposed to; what do I have to do next?'

Yeah

But there was something totally different about this. It was, unconditional. It was totally fun! 'This is what you want, this is what I want, it matches.' Really excellent, clean, intelligent cool guy...

Wow!

...and, we made eye contact while he was sucking my dick. I don't, not actually clear that I've done that before.

Hmmm

And it wasn't rough, it was masculine.

Hmmm

I could not, would not treat a girl like that. Or maybe I would now, I dunno... Fuck-in-ell that's weird, innit!

Yeah, but I told you about that. You know Matt, the guy that I met through Luke in Findhorn. He gave me that Joseph Kramer[55] video, and he talked about this massage that the men were doing, and, I don't know, it's like the men weren't particularly... well, one of them looked like he was made of luncheon meat. He was a very odd, pinkish colour. But what they were doing was, was the whole Taoist thing. And he was basically saying, "A woman, and a man, can't do this. Because it's masculine energy." And it wasn't about, actually, how quickly can I jerk off... which is another thing. Something Maria said yesterday about sex – is a way of... because we're so repressed, because we're not allowed to scream and shout and cry and touch each other. Sex becomes the only outlet. The kind of, only way you can get friction and get moving. And then it all becomes about having the orgasm. Sort of, 'towards' something. Whereas something like that, is just about energy exchange.

Yup.

No agenda, it's just pure energy.

Yeah. And I wouldn't have gone there or liked it if he was a wuss!

Yeah...

He was a healthy – he turned out to be a gardener, quite 'aware', just a lovely guy.

Hmmm

Healthy, eats well, you know, exercises in the garden whatever, just a fucking ace guy.

...and he does a bloody good blowjob.

Ha-ha-ha-yeah yeah! Maybe, it's not so much that he does such a good blowjob, but maybe I allowed myself to have one.

Well, yeah. There is that, I guess! Yes, well, as you say, just being present. But that's what it says on this video, it's really amazing. 'Can you receive and give sexual energy, without fantasising and without going off into a 'I've got to cum – he's got to cum"

'Quick quick get it over with!'

Yeah. In fact, I think in that whole Taoist school of thought, look, there's no failure but if there was failure, it's when somebody cums.

And if there's failure, it's as soon as you get your kit off, because it's an insult - if you haven't got an instant stiffie - then, you don't fancy her!

Hmmm

And it stays stiff for the rest of your two hour, a week, day, month, year-long relationship. Whenever it's not stiff, it's you know, 'you don't love me anymore.'

I know... Well I found that even last night. Even with all this awareness, after I had given Maria a massage, it was kind of, 'and now what?' We were staring into each other's eyes, started kissing, and I did feel really turned on, but I was really conscious. There was a split. The 'present' part of me was enjoying it and the other part of me

was, like 'but I'm not getting a hard-on...' And then it was, like, 'she's moving over, putting her thigh on me, uh-ooh it's not stiff. Fuck!' But I just gave into it. But there was that moment where – I don't know who's experienced this – where it's kind of, you just allow it to just not be stiff... and accept it. And wait for her to say "Oh, what's the matter?" Or, or my usual pattern is to go, "I'm really enjoying this, but... for some reason... I'm not getting a stiffie!!!" Like the panic mode. Explain. Get everything clear...

But it's always, 'What's the matter?' 'What's wrong?' 'Something's wrong!'

Hmmm

Rather than 'This is how I am, if you want something, do something; if I want something, I'll do something, you know...'

Hmmm

Ha ha ha ha ha. So, that was one thing...

Wow... sounds amazing!

Yeah. But he said that all the guys that go to him are just like totally cool guys, not a problem, mostly married. They wouldn't get blowjobs like this from their wives and they like hanging out with, you know, male company. What do they do? Lie about who they are and have a crap time at work. Go home and have to shag the wife and pretend that she's everything and they don't want for anything else or anyone else, there's no space for them, or maybe they don't do sports – because they haven't got the time, with the panic of the money they have to earn to prove that they love everyone.

55. Joseph Kramer. Runs the New School of Erotic Touch, California. www.eroticmassage.com

Sitting 'round the fire

Yup. Yup. Well, that's one of the things about a lot of these cruising areas. I would say, people have told me, and I guess I can feel it, that at least half the men there are married. So it's the same thing, it's men desperately searching for a way that they can connect with men, that's not going to the pub, getting pissed…

Telling lies!

…telling dirty jokes – yeah, exactly, lies!

Or going anywhere else, to pretend. I suppose, it's like I said, in changing rooms, for instance. It feels better in a gay one, 'cos no one's gonna look at… I feel that no one's going to look at me, unless I'm looking back. Because if I'm not finding them attractive, nothing's going to happen. What do they want to look for? Look for the next one. Surely, that's what happens. Or that's what 'feels' that happens. So I can either be invisible, or very visible, as I want. Where, otherwise, invisible, no connection, no talking – unless there's something 'macho' – is the way it is in a 'male' changing room. A 'straight' changing room.

I guess that's the thing, often, just hanging out with men, it is – I find it fascinating! Really, to compare, to contrast, to just be curious.

Be normal, surely.

Yeah, I mean, like when I was in the park. There was a guy, who was obviously jogging, he was covered in mud, stopped – and again, it's interesting because of the old patterns, for me, going to the woods for me was all about sex. And I found myself watching him. It was very different; there wasn't any – I had no sense of 'I want to do something with this bloke'. I was just looking at his legs thinking… 'Yes, he looks really well toned'; but that was it, you know. If he had then turned around and, sort of, eyed me with a 'let's go into the bushes' sort of thing, it would have been a bit of a shock. It really was literally just being there, and... and noticing. Because we are not even allowed to 'notice'. A funny thing happened at work last week. Where I work at the moment they are taking out asbestos, and we've got these big windows. They'd kind of fenced it off and there's all these 'working class beefy blokes' coming in and out, getting changed out of their protective suits, or whatever. A week before, this woman, Joan, who is in her 40's, a very 'proper' married woman, said "Oooh my goodness, it's a naked man!" And like, all the women stood up and looked; and I noticed the guy opposite me, very surreptitiously going 'like that' *(Ed cranes neck)*, because he sits right opposite me and I thought, 'well, yeah, I don't want to make it obvious. I don't want to turn around'. Next day a similar thing happened and I just looked around, you know, really like – 'wow, let's have a look'. And, there was like banter going on, and this other bloke said something, and he – and I was looking, then he said, "Chantelle wants to know, why are you looking Ed?" And I just said, "'cos I'm curious." I thought, 'I don't want to get a reputation, because it's a very stuffy little office. Being like a poof, or a queer, or whatever'. But, and I thought, 'well, I've been caught...'

And if it was a woman, would they not look?

...'course they would!

The women?

Yes. Well, I don't know, would they? It gets into that thing 'You're a lezzie – you're a poof'.

They'd check out cellulite; what would we do? I'd look at how big's his belly! Huh, has he got a hairy back? Hmmm, am I thinner than him? You know, I'd compare! What's different?

I know, but that was it. It was all this conditioning...

And was his dick bigger? And they would compare, I imagine, you know, tits and how much muff[56] is there?

Ha ha ha

Do I shave mine okay? Ha ha ha

It's the thing – you're not allowed to look. You are doing something wrong. You are making people uncomfortable. But probably because they are desperate to look as well. I mean, I'm sure this guy – who said it – was desperate to look as well; but wouldn't. Almost like the lack of awareness thing, where he probably didn't even know that he wanted to look. Yeah, so repressed!

Shut down – autopilot? Yeah… same, in school, I remember – I've been getting so many memories – fitting things together, now I've had some space. I never went for a piss in school. Not once. Or even in college. I started going to the toilets in college but I'd go in a cubicle – keep it private! And in the changing rooms, I wouldn't look. I couldn't see anyway because I had bad eyes – or glasses that would steam up. I didn't look, because I didn't want to be looked at, because I wanted to be invisible. Meanwhile, the 'boy' boys would look, but they were the ones in the teams, that would be sucked off from this guy that used to meet them in their neighbouring town, apparently met them under some bridge from what I could gather.

Surreptitiously… I just remembered… Steven used to – he actually couldn't piss with another man standing next to him.

The stories I have heard since, from some of the other boys at school, about what they'd get up to in the changing rooms – they'd wank together or get sucked off together or whatever it was; while pointing the finger at some of my friends - who'd never even touched a dick - calling them 'poofs'. I was treated differently – I think, because of my colour – and checked out more. My friends weren't aggressive bastards. They were more Mummy's-boys, looking after everyone's emotions; and they didn't get up to wanking together or changing together or checking each other out or anything. But they turned gay.

There was definitely something funny about the 'bully' sports master too. Was he shagging the female sports teacher fuelled by his favourite boys in the changing rooms? He used to love bursting in and surprising us, after listening to 'the blokes' talk from outside.

Hmmm

Or so I've heard.

Uuh!

And it's only, like, three, four of them. Uum, but they were the blokes that I would hang out with. And... they weren't! Well, maybe they were in the closet or something, but...

But then again, like you said, what does that all mean? I used to... when I was at secondary school, I think they must have built the sports hall quite recently, but there was something – I mean I always associate that smell, to feeling – it wasn't even 'turned on', but it was just like the vibe of all these bodies, together. Yeah, I guess there is a bit of a tension; and actually Maria said to me that the school she went to, the male sports teacher showered with the boys!

Apparently that happens in America.

Really?

Hmmm...

But, I mean, how liberating. Again! Well, if you're allowed to look. If it was all open...

Then, on the other hand, it would take a certain type of man that would want to shower with a load of boys.

I suppose, in our culture, yes. I mean... because it's suppressed.

Because of someone that didn't do it when he was in school, or was loved, because he had the biggest dick and everyone could look at it and play with it, like I said about that other guy. Same as speaking to people on the internet. There's this one guy who I spoke to, who's a scout leader or something...

Hmmm...?

And he just sucks everyone off! He did when he was in school...

All the boys?

Yup, all the teams. And, he's a scout leader. No one in scouts knows, just the older men (now) and boys (when he was a kid).

I imagine, some of whom send their boys...

Or, maybe avoid sending their boys to...

Well, yeah!

But he's getting married soon. No one knows. Everyone in the town knows – well, those that are 'into' all of that.

That's it! I mean, where else do people have to go but the closet? I mean, I was just so curious about – well about the grown ups. I never really looked at blokes of my own age. It wasn't any kind of 'oh, let's experiment and wank each other' apart from this one guy, Jude, who I just talked about it with. Yeah, I mean all my fantasies were about the teachers...

Hmmm

Because it was all so forbidden and closed off.

A bit like your Father I suppose.

Yeah...? Yeah!

It's all linked, so they, eh...

Yeah! What about games like rugby? That was... really exciting! Because as we said, there's the tension. You know, and - did you play rugby at school?

I wasn't into it, because I was – I was painfully cold. It just hurt.

Hmmm

Changing, washing, water on my skin; and it was too aggressive. Being touched, I was obsessive-compulsive! I did not want to be touched, or touch anyone. Male or female. No, I did want to touch girls. I didn't want to touch men. They were just – filthy! Ha ha ha – I couldn't deal with it.

But, I mean, there is – I forget exactly what it is – because I really; it was the only sport I liked. I think partly because, it was so sort-of...

I think it was too rough for me. And also because of wearing glasses.

Yeah, it would have been a disaster for you! But there is one thing, I can't remember what it is and who does it to who, *when you get to the scrums, you actually put your hand on the crotch.*

Really?

Yeah! And it's part of 'the move'. To me, it's like the only, sort of safe ritual. Like men are allowed to do that, because it's all nice and contained 'and we're not really doing this'.

And maybe it's all some men need.

Hmmm

Maybe to some men, they can 'vamp' that way, what they need, and getting a 'fix' of; and with other men, you know, they were so okay at home, or in their town – no male issues.

Yeah, yeah. Then they all go and sit in the bath together; God knows what happens then!

Ha ha ha ha – maybe not always, by any means!

Yeah

The other day, I had – I was going through so much in my head. I needed something. I just wanted to be held, touched, male company. But it wasn't – it was like being around a camp fire in the woods, actually. That's what...

That's what you wanted, yeah.

And, I really wanted to go to a sauna. Plus I was cold and I do that to warm my bones up. Even here, I go to the sauna at my local gym, but it's not sexual. But I need to warm my bones up – and think, like meditate. But all of it, I wanted to go to a sauna; and I was told by a few people on the internet that Chariots[57] is cool – check it out!

Oh, in Shoreditch...?

Yeah. Near Liverpool Street. So I went there, and it was different, because... I could see. Post laser-eye exploits. And I realised that it's going to be different now, because I'm not going to be invisible. And I'm going to look at people and people are going to look at me and, you know, I'll 'be' there!

People are visible to you as well...

Yeah, exactly! I can now see, and I know that it's safe to go to the sauna again because I've had my eyes tested, so even if I'd wanted to before that, I couldn't have and I wouldn't have. Not straight after the eye op. So I went, and... it was interesting. I... didn't... fancy anyone. Or want to be sexual or anything like that. Uum, and I didn't want the lights on, it was too bright. I was, it was, it was about me. What do I want? And... being relaxed.

Hmmm

56. *Muff. Slang for (unshaved / unwaxed) 'women's bits'*

57. *Chariots. www.gaysauna.co.uk*

Poking at the embers

So there's this quite dark steam room, I went and sat in there, a couple of men doing stuff to each other, whatever, and – but it was cool. It was dark, it was relaxed. I could sit and sweat like a pig, whatever was going on; and it was excellent. And a few men came on to me and I just gently pushed them away. I'm just not...

Not here for that!

And they were just generally unattractive and I was generally not interested! I just didn't find, you know, the sexual thing happening at all. And, a lot of them were older. And I was aware that, there was some... different vibe with the older men. Uum... not a sexual thing – almost, remembering when I was a kid, white older men, they were either 'being nice' or giving us some sort of 'charity' and we needed to show them that we're good people; and do the 'ha ha...' or 'yes... no...', or say something interesting. Like when we were in Africa, we were an Asian family happily beautiful and living in Africa, and, whatever exchange there was, the white people would be ex-pats or something similar. And then here, suddenly, we were just 'Paki' refugees from Uganda and blah blah blah big story, so they would be the 'established gentlemen of the country', so we would be respectful and act in a certain way – which is just bollocks! Being nice – and always being scared of them. Needing to - because they are old as well - not relate to them as people at all or hang out in any way. Being in a certain way was like, we were programmed to allow them, and lots of other people, to 'vamp' us. Especially, old men. Which is strange. So, I – that just came up and I just had no time for it, or them – and that would be charity. Being an old man and acting that way allowed them to express themselves within their forum and totally sell out and give them your power. Basically...

Hmmm, hmmm… interesting…

So, they were all after cock and I was just thinking about that – HA HA HA HA HA

HA HA HA they wouldn't have dreamed in a million years what was going on in your mind.

I was just in there for ages, people coming and going and I wasn't even paying much attention to what was going on. I had my eyes closed for quite a while, thinking 'right, I'll keep these eye balls moist because of the op'' you know, not so much being visible, but just relaxing in the heat – it was great!

Hmmm

And there was this young guy sitting in the corner. Um, he looked quite cool and quite, invisible. Like me, in the past. Not really taking part or anything, being quite invisible, just sitting there – and it was cool. So, I just reached over and I touched his leg and, it was just like, brothers. Or Father and son. It wasn't sexual. And as soon as we touched each other once or twice – and men started coming around and checking us out – it was weird. Really weird… And we weren't sexual. And so, you know, it was just cool and natural. Rather than him sitting all crouched up, he stretched a leg behind me, where I wasn't sitting and his other one was resting on my leg, and it was… comfortable. And it wasn't sexual – it was nice. And it was a huge relief, for him, I could feel it. That I wasn't expecting or wanting sex from him, at all. And I obviously didn't want it from him. I just wanted to – hang out. And it was great! And then, after a while – and he couldn't really look me in the eye, but he kind of looked at me, but couldn't connect. Probably this guy was scared of himself, or shy, or – you know, how I was.

Hmmm

And for me, it was just to realise that I was there, being 'me'. *I wasn't there to get my rocks off,* or get a fix, or vamp, I was there to be me and to get to know who I am. So, not a threat to him at all. It was just fucking excellent.

Wow

And, um he was massaging my shoulders a bit and stuff, just like hanging out on the beach! Then, after a little while – and the room was empty a couple of times, and I said "Look, are you comfortable with this – because it's a bit weird with blokes trying to check us out?" He said he was cool, but he obviously wasn't because he just left soon after. I guess it was safe in the dark corner and that's where we stayed.

So what did you do next...

You chat about something... I've been chatting for fucking ages!

Well no, it's interesting 'cos for me I haven't experienced that sort of place. It's the sort of place I've never been to.

Really?

Nooo, I guess I felt like I got a lot of that out of my system in, you know, woods and the odd foray into a toilet or, ummm... I don't know what it was about those places - like saunas - maybe it was too real, whereas the rest of it... it's nice to, sort of, off in the dark and...

Oh, so the woods were in the dark?

Often, yeah!

Oh, I just imagined the woods would be 'really real', because, you're wearing your clothes, you're in normal daylight, seeing each other, talking, walking...

In Silchester, it tended to be in the daytime. In Clapham Common, only really as far as, well yeah, there's usually a few people hanging around, but it's mostly a night time thing.

Same as when you pick up girls in a nightclub. *It doesn't matter if they are ugly, because they're okay*

in the dark.

Yeah, it's almost like – a vibe? I mean, it depends, sometimes I remember there were nights when it was so dark, it was literally just like 'what was that shape like?' No - huh huh - it must be more than that, I guess it was like a sense of somebody.

Hmmm

I don't think I ever really went for anybody who then didn't feel right. Although I know there was one time where, um – I don't know why it was, it was that night when there was this big, sort of melée, this sort of orgy of people and this guy was standing on the edge, looking at me, and I went back with him to my flat. And as soon as he was in there, I felt that I had made a mistake and that all he wanted to do was say "I'm going to fuck your arse!" It was all like talk and it felt really really uncomfortable, and I don't know what it was, but it was like; that was one of the more obvious Father types. Sort of, not really like my Dad, but sort of bearded, and quite hairy all over, and I just – told him to leave. (heavy breath) He did, but... um. Yeah, I don't know what it is, really about that; I don't know why I didn't check out the saunas and the... because it sounds really int. - it sounds like it's as close as you can really get in the mainstream to, just male intimacy. If that's what you've gone there with a clear intention to do.

Hmmm

I think maybe people sort of 'graduate' as well, you know. From what I gather, there are different times for different things. Like people discover, like I did, that people loiter in public toilets, but it's a pretty horrible vibe, really.

Yeah

It's smelly, cold. Then from that, people hear about the woods – 'ah, next step'.

People don't talk, do they?

Well, they do! Not kind of long conversations, but…

Yeah, like 'How's your wife…?' Ha ha ha ha ha

Yeah, 'Watch the sport this weekend?'

Ha ha ha ha ha 'Watch any football?'

No but, I mean, I can't even think. I guess it could be something like a throwaway comment, like "Do you want to go to the woods… because it's more private…" or whatever?

So, do people do that? Do you say to someone in the toilet "Do you want to go to the woods?" and then walk to the woods together…

I did!

…and then you go to the woods together, and you chat, while you're walking…

Yeah!

…so it's not uncomfortable walking?

Nooo

Because I thought that the whole thing was quiet. Not saying anything or doing any; so that doesn't mean that you have to have some form of relationship when you are going from place A to place B.

Yeah… yeah…

Or am I just getting in my head about it?

A lot of the 'not talking' is, yeah, it is keeping that distance. It then becomes a body or an object, or a cock, or whatever. But yeah, there's a few, I guess only a handful, about three or four blokes who I took back to the flat I had at the time in Stockwell. There was talking, because we'd drive back in their car; I'd usually walk to Clapham Common or catch the Tube.

Ummm?

Yeah, you do, as you say, immediately start to have some form of a relationship with somebody if you were talking to them. Because it makes them into a real person.

Do you talk or make any noise while you are having sex? Or is 'that' the quiet zone?

Oh, in the woods? Aaam, no I suppose it was fairly quiet. Keep it quiet, sort of…

Same as my parents. Totally suppressed.

Yeah. Yes, because, I suppose there is nowhere you can really go and be as noisy as you want, is there? But I was thinking, it is interesting about the way that things are expressed – you know I've mentioned my friend Elizabeth. She's got this bloke staying with her, and, um, I had an interesting experience with this guy. He's a masseur, from America, he's English and I went to Five Rhythms, and he was there – I've never seen him there before – and, we had this amazing dance and it was, again it was…

With him?

Yeah! I'd only ever spoken with him before and we were both – I think he had taken his top off and I was just in my… pants - ha ha ha… I'm afraid - 'cos I sweat like mad – and I just like, well, why not be naked? Yes, it's as close as you can get to letting it all go. Being completely naked, jumping around…

Hmmm

And people do engage, you know it's like encouraged by the…

I find that more intimate, than… anything.

Dancing with someone.

It's amazing!

Even with clothes on, I can't deal with that level of intimacy.

But then again, it, because it's, I suppose in a way it's possibly like the sauna - I'm not sure, but because there are, there are kind of in-built boundaries I mean, I don't know if there are Five Rhythms or dancing where people end up... fucking, or whatever. I don't think there are.

Do you end up shagging?

Huh?

Shagging there and then?

Naaaw. No I don't think that happens, because it's got this sort of boundary thing. I think maybe people sometimes go off afterwards and can pursue it, but; yeah! It was really intimate, but it felt like there was nothing we had to do with it. You know, I guess that if I met him in a sauna or a club or whatever, the next thing would be touching and then who knows what, probably sex. Because it felt like there was just a really, massive vibe – and I couldn't say what it was. It wasn't like he was the woman and I was the man, or he's the man; 'I wanna fuck you - you wanna fuck me', it was just – a dance. And it was very elegant, flowing, sort of very masculine.

Hmmm

Just amazing. And because there was nothing to do with it, it was complete in itself. Well, I think a lot of other times, like you say, you know, talking to this guy in the sauna, means... that 'something' now has to happen. I can't explain that. I just find it really powerful, the whole dance thing, and again, its like, we have to create these spaces where you can go to be intimate with people.

And know how to, not have to carry on.

Yeah.

How to stop. How to have boundaries.

Exactly. Yeah, because we're not taught that.

And I imagine – and *that's probably why I'm crap at dancing. Because you need to negotiate boundaries and I don't know how to have boundaries – I'm only just learning.*

Hmmm

And not to feel rejected. Not to feel like I've abandoned someone. Can't move for all that fucking baggage and 'am I?' self-consciousness.

It's very good for that. I mean I think a good, um - teacher's the wrong word - facilitator can be amazing in Five Rhythms. Because, yeah, that's exactly what it's about. It's about, almost playing with the whole thing, but taking it seriously at the same time. There is a sort of tension, a paradox in the whole Five Rhythms. Because you are, as you say, it's not 'I'm going to dance with you – and I've got to dance with you all evening' like if you go to a club with your girlfriend or whatever.

Hmmm Hmmm

Yeah, there'll be people dancing and you might want to join in, rather than just being tied to the one person.

Fucking

But I felt, again - and this is going off on a slight tangent - last night, I was really clear that I didn't want to sleep in the same bed as Maria. I said "That was great — now, where am I sleeping? Is there a spare bed?" She made no fuss about it; but I was saying to her, you know, *women should live in women's houses and men should live in men's houses.* Get together, fuck, whatever. Then - "Cheers! See you." I mean, the whole thing...

When you want to.

Yeah!

When you both want to.

But no wonder all our parents — well, not just our parents, but — become bored with each other. It's like it's so mundane.

Hmm.

And I don't think that's, kind of, thrill seeking. It's just 'over exposure'.

And that's one of the main things that I hate about being in a relationship. When I am wide awake and my woman is so mellow, she wants to cuddle up — and I just want to do stuff! And I have to 'play dead' there, while she snuggles up?

Um-hmmm.

It kills me!

Mmmm.

Or... I mean I'm over this because I've got other people now, but in the old days, I'd be up, dying to go somewhere, do something, have fun that I'd want to share with this person – and I was younger, so I thought it had to be this person, and no one else – and if she doesn't share it all and enjoy it with me, then there is something wrong. Ha ha ha... But, you know, now I can deal with someone who's lazy in the mornings and hang out with other friends. But if I want to do things or share things – "You lazy bitch!" Ha ha ha ha ha ha ha ha. "Get up, I want to play!"

Yeah.

Be my mate!

Meanwhile, back at the...

Either that, or you stay in bed and, as you say, go off and...

Yeah! Now I've got mates. Now I realise I'm allowed to do that. Because then, being young, she'd think "He's abandoning me!" "He's supposed to be here!" "He's supposed to want to fuck me!" Or "He's supposed to want to not fuck me, because he loves me too much he doesn't want to hurt me, just hold me and make me breakfast and show me he'll be my Father!"

Ha ha ha

Or, "Fuck me hard because I was abused!"

Absolutely. Do you know, I think that's one of the best things I got out of reading David Deida[58]... he talks about how *women will test you for your purpose.* Because I knew I said that I was going to be here about eleven o'clock-ish, Maria and I were fooling around and I just had the sense it was time to go. I was sufficiently aroused again, thinking, 'yeah it would be nice to have a quick fuck', she said "Just let's have a quick one!"

Huh huh huh *(like Beavis)*[59]

And she was sitting on me, rubbing herself against me, just rubbing my cock. I just sat there and said "Well I'm not going to be distracted from my purpose – you've got two minutes to do whatever you want..."

Ha ha ha ha ha

"And then I'm going!" Ha ha ha

Struth!

And it was like she said "Oh no, the pressure's on, and I don't know what to do!" Ha ha ha... And so I then, literally, I thought it must be two minutes, so I threw her – not violently – but I picked her up and said "That's it, I'm off." And I said "Isn't it great to leave it when you want more, rather than – oh, let's just satisfy ourselves."

I remember that with Emma once. I was so gagging for it one morning and she had to get up. We were having the best sex that morning and I still wanted more and she just looked at me and said "Right..." because I was just nagging, and she was like, "Ok, you've got five minutes!!!" so I just... did everything that I wanted to do and it was fucking excellent! For five minutes, it was the BEST! Then she just looked me in the eye and just said "Stop! I'm getting up. Game over!" It was fucking excellent...

Hmmm

Because we were there, we were playing, it wasn't 'I have to perform – she has to perform – yadda yadda yadda'

Totally liberating.

But, sex changes when the relationship changes.

Yeah.

You bribe and punish and communicate through – our relationship got, in the end, that the bed was the only place we were meeting or communicating. Because all our stuff was coming up! I was 'being' her Father, her Mother, she was 'being' my Father, my Mother, swapping, our shit, what does this mean, what does that mean, we were young...

Hmmm

So, we fucked!

Hmmm

We fucked all our anger away, because that's what 'fucking' is all about. In the beginning we couldn't get enough. Honeymoon period. She turned from scary sex-kitten to someone I could touch and connect with and get a stiffie from smelling her pillow. Sex and the relationship were great, so obviously paranoia set in and I had to give her that one extra orgasm, so I knew that I was better than all the others and she won't go around telling her friends that I'm crap and 'you're not gonna leave me, ever, and abandon me because you can't, because it's the best sex you've ever had'.

Hmmm

Sometimes, if you fancy a fuck, then that's cool. But if that's the only way, then you're not; like a lot of my friends have said, they get pissed, they know what they're going to do, which is either collapse into cozy oblivion, or you'll follow the usual sex-script of 'this, then this, then this, then you flip her over, for this, and this, with that bit in the air... and then cum.' And then "...don't fucking touch me" and sleep. And then, you know, get the fix and feel like shit in the morning and rush off from the 'ugly cow'. 'What have I done? *It wasn't me it was the alcohol*, but I needed a fix so I vamped you – and you vamped me so it's cool.' Cold...?

Icy.

58. David Deida. US author of 'The Way Of The Superior Man' (Plexus) 1997, amongst others. www.bluetruth.org

59. Beavis. Beavis And Butt-head, cult US cartoon.

Touch

So, yeah, these two guys back in the sauna… I was listening to them
walk down the stairs in front of me and they were nice, 'normal', young
guys - one was from South Africa, the other one I couldn't really tell –
and they weren't coming from their shadow[60] or hiding or, you know,
sinister, or sneaky, or vamping or anything. So I got my dry towel from
downstairs, so I was going back up the stairs and I didn't even – I
hardly noticed the other guy until he was right in front of me and
coming down. Not the South African, the other bloke. So I thought
'cool' and smiled at him when we walked past each other, and then
after he was half way down the stairs, it clocked that he just touched
my hand. And I thought, 'Oh fuck me, that means something, doesn't
it?'

Aaahaa…!

I forgot that, you know, well we dashed each other; I would have been
totally unaware. So I looked around as if to say 'Wooow! You just
touched my hand' not thinking what it might mean or anything. And
then he looked around and smiled and I thought… 'Fuck! This is one of
'those things' isn't it?'

Aaahaa – 'gotta do something…'

'Am I supposed to follow him?'

Umm humm…!

So I thought, 'hmmm? This could be interesting!' So I went downstairs,
followed him, and they had these cubicle things all over, the door was
open, I went in, he didn't have his towel on, huge stiffie, really nice
body, exactly the type of body that I used to always look at. That's

what a young body looks like and I've never had one of those. Flat stomach, hairless, little abs, that kind of thing, but it was like a 'boy body'. And I thought; it didn't feel sexual to be honest. Not anything like that at all.

But he was presenting himself like an offering...

Yeah, and this is, or that was, that's the body in all the magazines and television, films, you know – that kind of a body. And, um, he was standing on the bench with his cock out obviously wanting me to suck it. Inside, I was just in stitches!

Ha ha ha ha ha

I was just on the fucking floor!

Ha ha ha ha ha

I wasn't scared, still not sexual or anything. And also I spoke, very recently, with a very very close friend who I would not have imagined anything like this. He said that, yeah, the opportunity arose once and he stuck a dick in his mouth to see what it was like. And I just thought 'WHAT?' It just never crossed my mind and the opportunities had never arisen, but then they wouldn't because that kinda stuff was not on my mind so why would they? But then, it is that simple and that normal, where the boys that used to do that in school, you'd never think that they'd ever done that and thought that. But they're the ones that teased, so therefore fooling around with each other was never an option, in case they'd find out – but they were the ones that were up to it.

I, actually, you see, that's something I never enjoyed. Giving a man a blowjob.

...Well I stuck it in my mouth...

It's big!

...yeah exactly! It was...

Gag!

...because it doesn't taste of chocolate, you know, nuts and raisins would be nice...

And it hasn't got the smell of cunt – you know, that sort of moistness and – mmmmm!

...I had it in my mouth for a bit and did whatever and; not for very long because I was like – I took it out and looked him in the eye and said *"First time I've ever done that!"* And he said "What?! Really?" And we just got chatting for ages, we just lay down and hung out and had a really excellent time...

It's almost like you broke the spell, because you just...

Totally!

And going into kind of *(slurpy noises...)* Like, 'I've got to do this until you cum.'

Yeah!

That's obviously what the script says.

And then we were chatting about it; and he said "Well ok, check this out, maybe try this, or try that, sometime, no big deal." I didn't get a stiffie through the whole thing. Not one, anything. So he said, "What's up with you? You haven't got a stiffie or anything? How come you haven't?"

"How can I help you siiir?" *(In a camp, lispy American accent)*

Ha ha ha... and um, I said "I imagine I must be scared or petrified or uncomfortable..."

Or maybe it's not that exciting...?

...obviously I would be, because I haven't done this before. And he said "Yeah, probably are then." But like you say, maybe I just wasn't sexually excited. Maybe I wasn't, but that would have killed it somehow. Or that would have been...

You couldn't say that to him, yeah.

He he he he he he he he. Well, it wouldn't make sense, because that was the body I used to always look at, but not that I wanted to shag. That's what I wanted on me.

Yeah. I think that's the interesting and really complex thing about attraction. But, yeah. Those kind of places – it's not just the cock, it's what's attached to the cock that's important.

And the guy, that first time I listened to him talking to that other guy, I could feel he was open and honest and pure and lovely. When I suddenly saw him in front of me and our eyes met, it was like a shining light. He was clean. There was no nonsense.

You were sharing your energy with him.

Didn't even think about that; it was just…

Oh no, that's just post Findhorn

'…two lights looking, two lights passing' that are on the same frequency, and then it's out of frequency as you pass. So, it was cool. Happens to me on the Underground all the time, with all sorts of people. Like Wim Wenders'[61] angels in *'Wings Of Desire'*[62].

But it's funny. I was thinking about my 'one night stand' with Luke Gallagher, at Findhorn. I was quite bored. Sex was not really very interesting. Like going into his room, again it was the quiet thing; it's funny, I remember him saying something about, "People might… you know, this is where all the other teachers - or whatever you call them - are. We had better be discreet." Well why? This is the Sex & Spirit Conference. It's meant to be a bit 'wild', isn't it?

Ha ha ha ha ha ha ha ha

What he said to me, when I contacted him, after the conference, was that what he really appreciated was the fact that the next morning I got out of bed and into bed with him. I snuggled up with him.

Warm?

Yeah!

You know, saints do it, mice do it, probably even cockroaches do it.

We were lying there at one point, he was demonstrating this thing where – I can't remember how he did it, but it was like – I was on my front; and it wasn't fucking but it was like, he must have gobbed on his hands and he moistened my thighs and he was doing this kind of in and out thing and I... Again, you know, you can't say these things. I wanted to say *this is really boring!*

Ha ha ha ha ha ha ha ha

You know, it was like the whole energy, like the kind of excitement of, 'Yeah, it's gonna happen, go to his room, blah blah blah,' and almost from that point on, it was like 'this isn't very interesting!' But I really liked him as a person, I enjoyed hanging out with him and, just sitting there with him and, you know, fiddle with his chest hair or, you know, tweak his nipples or rubbing his arse or whatever and it was like, that was enough! The same with Steven, the relationship with Steven. There would be times when we would just play with each other. Idly, casually, like little kids do.

Hmmm.

And it wasn't like, you've got to cum, or...

Not aggressive sex – just hanging out!

...as you say, a good person, despite the cock!

Yeah, and actually, that guy in the sauna. Ummm, it was so nice, because he was like a little child, touching my face a couple of times. His hands...

So nice!

I didn't mind, in fact it was quite nice. No one had touched my face

161

for a while and it wasn't vamping or sexual, it was – clean. Honest. Normal. You know, basic touching. In; for all my life, if anyone had bare feet, I wouldn't want to be in the room. I couldn't sit on furniture because I saw someone's bare feet on that part of the furniture, but 'contamination' spread to the whole thing, so until I knew the servants had cleaned, or someone had cleaned, or I'd seen someone 'decontaminate' it, I couldn't go there. This guy, it was comfortable for both of us, for his feet to be on my legs. And it was cool. You know, basic 'brothers hanging out on the settee,' basic normal honest stuff.

When I was around here that time with Lisa and – that Yugoslav guy –

Yannis

When we were all sitting around...

I kept thinking about you saying that

...yeah! It was just, like you say, like a 'golden moment'.

Name it.

All I remember is, having had enough spliff to feel like I was quite mellow, not wanting more; and he, he just leaned against me at one point. Not like even his head on my shoulder, but just his back against my shoulder. And I just felt a complete... bliss is the wrong word, but it was like – 'aaah...'

Hmmm

Relaxed

Relief

Yeah! Thank God, you can just do this. He didn't kind of go, "Oh, sorry" which is what most people do, don't they?

Yes

And I noticed, the same evening, Bob was lying there and it was like we were both being really careful to avoid... legs touching? And at

one point, I think I, I touched his leg and I think we both, kind of, just like, I think our legs just moved really quickly away. That's weird! I'm sure that both of us were really comfortable with it... yet... 'zap!' We jumped apart. Fear?

60. *Shadow. Carl Jung's term for the darkside.*

61. *Wim Wenders. German film director. www.wim-wenders.com*

62. *'Wings Of Desire' (1987) Wim Wenders, Germany.*

Intimacy

I find now, with Lui and I, we touch a lot more. Um, and, we don't have to.

Hmmm

It's okay, like if he doesn't want to, or I don't want to, or he wants to, but it's not even that it's okay; there's just nothing to think about. It's cool now. It's changed. From before, when I was crying, from then. We just don't vamp, or, it's just, even he said; because I said it was totally cool for him to come over for Christmas. And I know that he wants to; needs to spend it with his ex-girlfriend. Because she's alone, and whatever, and within their relationship let them do what's right. I always had a problem with her. Nothing against her, but it – it's totally my Mother.

Hmmm

She is *(Frank Spencer*[63] *voice)* weak, needy, oh little girl, 'oh, I'm very pretty, I'm alright, yes, I'm a woman, I'm strong…'

Hmmm

Get real. Um, and, in the old days, I would have loved – absolutely adored her! Now, I don't want my Mother around, I don't want a victim around me, looking – you know – mouth down-turned, looking pretty and sweet, but just a victim. And even the tone, every tone is like 'hmmm?' – like that. So Lui said, "Well, can I bring my ex?" And I said, "I'm not sure…" and rather than getting into talking about it, he said "Well, if you're not sure, then let's not even go there…"

Hmmm

Then it's clean. And in the past, I would have, "Let's talk about it, just so you understand, yadda yadda yadda" – no need. We are just so clear, it's not a problem. And, I was aware. I thought that maybe at some stage I'd say, "Well it's because my... Maybe it's all my projection and I should deal with it..." there's just no need. It's good for me to know.

It's justification!

And it's good for me not to dislike her for being like my Mother, or get into any drama about how it has to be, and I need to accept her, or don't, or whatever – the bottom line is, I never really wanted to be around her...

Hmmm

...because of that; and I didn't do the 'should', because of Lui. Other times, they were very big, important things. It would have been more than, it would have been normal to have 'met', when Lui and I were re-doing the 'marriage stuff', or big changes, or after a huge bloody fight, with the police and bites and scars; then it would be normal for the girlfriend to have got involved, I would say. Any of those things. Marrying her boyfriend so he can stay in the country? Hearing from him that she feels that I have total power over her life and her happiness; meanwhile, there is nothing for us all to get together about? Let's pretend it's not happening? That pissed me off! Again, that was my Mother's avoidance, secrets and lies I suppose. Um, with all of this, it's just fine to think, 'well, I'm dealing with my Mother, I don't have an issue here, it's cool'. It's fucking excellent!

Yeah, you just don't need to be around her.

Still, going back to the sauna, going back to that little room with that guy, sexual stuff just didn't really kick off. But, we hung out, and talked about stuff, and he said, no, I think I said to him, "How old are you?" and he said to me, "How old are you?" and I said...

"Guess!"

Ha ha ha ha ha – no, I was totally honest with him. I know that I look young for my age, and it's silly just to pretend that I don't, and play that charade. And I said "Yeah, I look good for my age but I'm 38." And he looked at me and said, "What, you're kidding!" And before I could get into, "Yeah, yeah, yeah... I look young" he said, "So am I!" And I went "What!" And he said "...most people think I'm like 23!" He does look, like 23!

From what you've described, Jesus Christ! Does he shave his body?

No! Just hairless! And like, you know, abs and stuff, uum really flat belly and a thin line of hair going down to his pubes...

Not shaved, but pruned, I imagine!

No, not at all.

Good God! Peter Pan...

You're doing the 'Oh yes, well, I'm the Aunty!'

Well Christ! I'm just surprised! I've seen shaved men, it shows. I suppose if it didn't show...

And it was 'the body' that I wanted to have. *That's the body I should have, in order to be acceptable.* And I always felt that once I've 'got that body', then I'll probably partake in sex because 'I'll be good enough'.

A-ha...

Until then, I had inverted fucking nipples, that I felt my parents would laugh at and my cousin would laugh at and I didn't know what was gonna happen; and in my twenties, I went to the doctors and said "Look! What the fuck do I do?" And, he kind of said, well, "I don't know. Um, I don't think they will do you any harm."

Did you realise that you had a normal body?

No. Not my dick. Now, yeah! Now, fuck me! Try and stand in my way! But then, it was interesting, when I went to Fiji, the first time 'living' in another country, the first time staying at a backpackers, in dorms, stuff like that; and I was very comfortable. I never took my shirt off but I was quite normal, you know – I didn't know 'how it was', but I wasn't totally hiding, but I certainly wasn't going around naked. Just normalising with all of this. And, it was really weird but something happened. My chest changed. My nipples came out! And it was really sensitive; I remember once in the morning I went to the shower and there was this strange, 'film', like a thin piece of plastic, that I peeled off my nipple and it was in the perfect shape of a nipple, and it must have been, it's like a wound had healed, or something. It must have seeped something or other. And it was just so sensitive, because it was, a part of my body had just come out. I would have loved to have heard from someone that this is normal and this happens and it's what goes on.

What?! Just one of your nipples, or both of them? I don't...

One, more than the other. The other one was almost fine, pretty much. And then from there I had it pretty much – you know, it was very sore and very sensitive - but after a while it got to what I imagine was normal. But a whole lifetime of being checked out and something being weird – it's a deformity!

Hmmm... Bizarre!

Basically. And not only did I have one visible deformity, and then I had the invisible deformity which was my dick, that I didn't know was normal. Plus I felt fat and hairy! And a different shape to the people of this country.

And your Dad wasn't going to be able to guide you...

And he was obese! He was totally in denial of his body, or exercise, it was just like – that was not how I want to be. Was that what I was turning out like? Apart from two minor deformities. Minor? Fuck!

How amazing though, that that kind of, level of healing could take place.

Yeah! And it was the first time I was 'normal', with other people of my age, or younger, or older, changing, or not changing, mixed shared showers, dormitories, sleeping in the same room, you know 'Who switches off the lights?' Or maybe there isn't a 'rule', and – you know. How does it work? Or do they stay on all night because everyone is too shy, or is there someone non-English to say something? Ha ha ha ha ha – who wears or doesn't wear what? Boundaries, whatever. So yeah, he was 38. And he said "Fuck! I just, I saw your body and I thought, man I wish I had that body. *Listen, you look like a man! You've got hair on your chest, you've got a big chest, you've got hair on your belly, you've got strong legs, big shoulders...*"

Validation!

Yeah! – "...you look like a man!" Then I said "Fuck! Your body - that's the body that I've never had and always wanted on me, when I was younger. Yeah, sure, I'd have my body, but not until I've had your body, because I haven't had all the things, the part of life that that body would give me." So we were just chatting about that and he was saying, "Well, I used to have, you know, not so much of a lot of weight, but I had some and I just did bodypump and I was the only girl in the - the only boy in a class of girls, and they thought 'He's a perv! He's just a boy wanting to look at our bodies. Then they realised I was gay, or thought 'maybe he is', we became mates and we all hung out; and it's a really good workout, and I've got abs and my body is just really good, but *I can't age! I look too young. I want my body to change...*" Man, he talked!

Wow!

"...and I want to grow hair; and I want the body that's like yours."

I wonder what's happened to him now. I guess it was like a big change for him.

Hmmm. But he was obviously stuck – and then we got into, yeah, he was abused by his step-Father who beat him, and his parents split when he was three, blah blah blah, and he's had girlfriends; and he asked me "Does anyone know that you go to saunas?" and I said, "Well, no, no, people who I was chatting to on the internet – because we can be honest there and talk about deep stuff, but with my friends, they're not totally honest, but I tell some, and, you know, they're being more honest about themselves; not so much that they've done stuff, but who they are. Rather than cutting them off and scaring them, or whatever it is" – and he was saying, when he used to go out with girls, he'd love it, but men suck dick better, and he loves sucking dick, and he loves men as well, but he knows he prefers girls now, but some people just don't. They just like to go to the sauna and hang out with men sometimes; but they love their wives and families. This is just a part of themselves that they have to keep secret, because other people just wouldn't understand.

Hmmm

Or, would feel in competition. So we just talked and talked and hung out and talked about spiritual stuff, and emotional stuff, and just normal things. We were just mates, hanging out, like in a tree house. Absolutely nothing else. It was, fucking excellent. And, um, I said "Ah, fuck! I'm going to have to go before 8pm, I'm meeting my brother before seeing my parents..." Got to talking about parents and how he dealt with his parents. You don't do that normally. And his sister, and his brother, and how he told people that he was gay, and how cool it was, how not, and how he didn't look at other people – other men – and how he was paranoid about, um, he used to be really paranoid about sucking people off, and disease, and how he feels about all that. And just, like 'Okay, here's all the information I know about looking after myself and having fun and what means what, how to play the games that they play in the playground, out of this playhouse, out of the tree-house' – do you know what I mean?

Hmmm

It was just excellent! The whole Mother thing, and the Father thing, and the brother thing, communicating, and lies, and beating, and being responsible for emotions – totally fits the picture to everything that we are saying pattern-wise – and his friends as well...

Oh God

...and just talking about, me saying what a great house I live in, I just love being naked at home, what great mates and girls I have around me, and all that stuff. And him saying that he is looking for somewhere to live and if I know of anywhere. He was just so clean, and honest, and respectful. So it was mates.

Yeah

So, um – we kind of fooled around a bit, but... not really. It was, just in the beginning. And it was, to check out, or it, it would have been weird not to. It would have been shut out. So all through – we were on a, kind of like a bench thing, and it was clean, someone had just cleaned it, and we were just lying there. Um, against each other, type thing. Umm, and not really thinking about how we're lying, or what we're talking about, not really aware of what we're doing.

Ummm

We were 'be'ing. It was fucking excellent!

You hadn't gone there with any particular intention, had you?

No, no. I didn't really go there for sex or for anything in particular. I just needed to, sit around a camp fire and chill out, and be warm, and – ha ha ha ha ha

I think that's the interesting thing. Often, when you stop looking for something, it's like when you – not even when you give up. Yeah. Stop the desperate searching. As soon as the desperation goes, things start falling into place.

He was talking about things like, I asked him about – because there's something on the internet, um, about the male clitoris being up the bum.

Oh yeah, the prostate!

Discussion groups and things. And some naturist thing or something I belong to would chat about this and that, and if there's anything interesting in the heading that I'm interested about, then I'd check it out. And I'd been thinking about a couple of friends, older men who've had prostate cancer. What is the prostate about? What part of us does it represent, as the liver holds anger and rage; and the kidneys and bladder our fear. And is it a part of a man's body that he needs to get to know. Whatever, physically, emotionally, sexually, whatever. Because if he denies it, then he'll get prostate cancer. Do you know what I mean – or a part of himself emotionally. And *if it's pleasurable, then surely that's a clue that you're supposed to go there?*

Uummm-huh!

I don't like stuff up my arse, anything, I'm just not into that, it just…

Have you ever had anything up there?

Not really, I mean, once I remember sticking a candle up it a bit, just for the sake of it, just to see what it was like. But I wasn't that interested. Ha ha ha. My fucking luck! My brother walked in. It always happens to me! Don't know if he realised what I was up to…

No, but I think that there must be a technique to it. I mean…

Probably.

I used to stick carrots up my bum.

Really! You were probably free to explore and experiment and have some fun! I was just, God was watching me, my parents were watching me, my brother was going to walk in, whoever knows will tell everyone and I may as well commit suicide just there and then. Because no one else is sexual. It's wrong, and it's bad, and it's dirty.

So that's the thing. Because it's so secret, no one is able to explain, I mean. I think the key with anything to do with your arse is preparation. A good Boy Scout motto. I'm sorry! I'm sorry! Ha ha ha

Ha ha ha

I mean, there's also a different type of – I notice, people who have obviously, fucked people up the arse, stuck things up their arses, had it up there, they know what they're doing. I mean, I had, I once had – the only time, actually – I once had, um, an orgasm, just from some – no wanking – from this guy, just being up my backside. And he did this thing...

What, with his dick?

...his dick.

Really?!

...It was like – it's hard to describe it – as a person, yeah I was attracted to his energy, whatever, blah blah blah, but he really knew what he was doing. Not like cumming into a woman. But being penetrated... To the heart? To... oblivion? Fuck – it's hard to describe. It was like there was complete preparation, I just really wanted it, and he didn't just – it's like with a lot of men and women, you know, you're not going to get an orgasm if you just stick it in and thrust it endlessly. It's kind of like, feeling into it. There is a point...

It's meeting somewhere...

Yeah!

And then going to the pleasure zone...

Absolutely! And a lot of people are so panicky about...

Because most people don't ever meet, if you ask me...

No...

They just wank hard against each other, and get all their frustrations, and anger, and fear, and embarrassment out through being hard – and then, cut off.

Yeah. It's amazing. I mean, it's painful as well. Because, it's not 'meant' to have things in it, it doesn't go moist - like a cunt - but it obviously… As you say, it's a clue, that if it's pleasurable…

But what…? Maybe, maybe, I don't know…

Maybe not being fucked. Maybe, the whole hand thing, you know, just… lovingly… gently…

For all I know - I mean, I haven't really gone there, ummm, just working it out, because I haven't had the head for it - but maybe it's the prostate that's stimulated, but not directly from up your arse, but it gets indirectly stimulated, as you 'act' in a certain way, as you 'are' in a certain way; it's like, recently, I've been, as I've opened up more with Lui, crying, uum, or other times, just thinking, and feeling, whatever. I really felt my heart open. And it's been so different.

Hmmm

It's been wonderful!

Hmmm

Other times, having orgasms while 'making lurve to ma laady'. It just… bursts! Out of the top of my head. And it just fills the whole of my body with such energy. It's fucking amazing!

Hmmm

When I'm doing healing work on friends and clients, I just feel the palms of my hands, my hands feel like they are on fire, or – you know – so many different things with healing. And it's pretty much indescribable. So maybe it's the same with the prostate. That's it's not – maybe it is shove something up your arse, no matter what, maybe it's another way, because *I don't do anything to the top of my head when I cum, but that's where it*

happens.

No, that's probably true. Well, it's about, yeah, opening to people. I mean, last night, I felt like I could put my whole hand inside Maria's cunt.

Hmmm

Started off with two fingers and it was just... it was exquisite! And like you said, a total body thing. I felt like...

Hmmm

I was her.

Yeah, yeah, yeah, you connect at that level and you both, check in at...

Like I'm having her orgasm with her.

...like you 'go to' that orgasm together. Bliss!

> 63. Frank Spencer. Effeminate character from 1970's sit com 'Some Mothers Do 'Ave 'Em' played by Michael Crawford.

Infidelity

What a day. Draaaama!!! Fuck, just when I thought it was all over…

So come on then… tell the story…

Well I felt I had to, you know tell her - Ayesha - about Maria.

So what is she - what part of your life, who does Ayesha represent?

Well half my 'life'. But now… she's the past. It's just trying to get the balance between… So I told her I'm seeing someone and she said, "Well I wish you luck" in her 'bright and breezy' tone. So I said, "It's a woman", and suddenly as I knew it would, the atmosphere, the room… went cold, tense. *She'd assumed, because of the stuff with Steven that now I was 'gay for life'.* You know, how we talked about putting people in 'boxes'.

So where was this all taking place? Had you rung her on the phone, was it face-to-face?

Oh, face-to-face. Dropped Mallie off, back at her, Ayesha's parents' place

From the old life is there anything, anyone that you're taking with you - apart from your daughter?

Oh God, I wouldn't, I… just, abandon her

No, that's just not an option.

God you know how to nail me… Well I was going to say my brother, but… he's got away…

What he ran away from the family drama?

Yeah probably had the right idea. And yeah, last time I saw him, when he was home from the Far East, I said to him, that I'd realized I was almost resentful, because me and my sister were in the 'front line' at home, I took all the shit with my Dad, I was always battling for everyone, shrilly defending everyone against the 'tyrant'…

So, bottom line is… Malaika is now the only 'constant' from your life before the bust-up?

Yup. I mean telling Ayesha what I told her on Friday was really the final kick, because when I told her about Maria the Sunday before, it was like she did her usual thing of not really getting angry, but letting out poisonous little sparks, remarks

Isn't that passive-aggression[64] anger, rather than…?

Yeah, just like my sister, just like my Mother, just like so many women I've known

And men! I've got an 'O' level in that. Didn't bother with the 'A' level - I thought that would really fuck 'em up. Heh heh heh.

You stayed at home and sulked instead…

Heh heh heh

Ha ha ha… What I wanted was a full-on - I don't know - screaming, plate-throwing… something I could get involved in and fight back against, or 'see', instead of that… urrghh. You know, tell me to 'get the fuck out of the house!' And I started to explain about why I thought it hadn't really worked out, and she said *"I don't want to hear about how much better this woman is…"* That really stung me, like what, I am so insensitive? I stewed with that all week, and the Friday, told her how pissed off I was, and she was like, "I said don't tell me what's different or explain or…" it all got tense again. And I just said really, um bluntly "I would rather, I would prefer that I didn't have to see you at all…"

Whoaaaaa!!!!!

…I know! And it was like I'd punched her in the stomach. I felt awful and… but, then…

So you don't see each other now, or talk or hang out?

No, there's nowhere left for us to meet, or anywhere to go, and to be fair, our basic, bottom-line agreement is to keep things - we want to keep things - as good as possible for Malaika's sake. The thing that's been this week is the conflict between that - 'doing it for Malaika' - and my own emotions, wanting to withdraw and…

So you don't talk or discuss, or…?

Well, I might say to Ayesha, "What you do when Mallie really strops?" or "How did you deal with her that time when..?"

So why did you tell her about Maria! And after how long? Was it…

Three, or four, or …five months

Whoaaaa!!!

I think I didn't tell her before because I was trying to protect her.

Protect her? Get real! From what…

I don't… really… um… God… I can feel myself squirming here. It was like when I saw Angus and Elizabeth a couple of weeks ago, and we got talking about, I told them I was still seeing Maria and it came up that I hadn't told Ayesha, and they both were… Well I started to come up with, with all sorts of… excuses. And Angus said, "I don't buy that mate" and so it was like my next reason, and he was "Well that smells a bit fishy too…"

Heh heh heh

"What's the real reason?" and I was just "Oh, fuck off !!!"

Aaaarrrggghh !!!" Ha ha ha. And yet at the same time, with people like you, and him, men who will not accept my bullshit, is really, just so...

Is it men, or is it just anyone who won't accept your bullshit?

It's more men now, because I think women accept more of it, because they don't want to be abandoned...

And they get, they get fed by it, some of them.

Yeah, and I mean I guess Elizabeth, Maria - yeah Maria - pretty much and Margaret are three women who won't, or don't.

So what was it like? Why did they 'make' you tell? Was it sleazy, or, manipulative?

No, no, God no. They are both into David Deida in a big way and into truth and all that. No, of course not. And I knew them separately, so all that was going on. The 'couple', me... and well, they are so meant to be together. But I just felt like connecting. And my shoulder still hurts so I just said, "Look will one of you take my feet, and the other take my hands and just... stretch, pull me..."

Oh, so totally for the highest reasons. Clean. So what are they? Are they 'New Age hippy' types? Or are they into the land, proper earthy, 'Cornish fishermen' types?

Ha ha ha!

Do you know what I mean? Farm types?

Oh, not at all. Well I mean they're into, she does lots of things and he is basically a builder, but also both really into bodywork. So she says, "Why don't you get on the massage couch and we'll both massage you." And it was, amazing. Just ...whoaaa. Yeah, great. And we took it in turns and swapped over. We had a real laugh too!

So, tell. Set the scene for me.

Okay, well I was feeling like, I haven't seen them for a while, we're all sitting round talking, and, um when I last saw them they weren't together. They broke up about the same time as Ayesha and my counselling failed.

Failed?

Well, not failed but you know, it…

So if you were still having counselling now, you'd be successful? Or if you were living with her now, it wouldn't be a failure?

Hmmm. Yeah. No… I thought you were just going to gloss over it, you know, ha ha ha.

Yeah. Tell me about it!

Yeah, I guess I still feel somehow, I've still got this idea that's obviously deeply ingrained, *we should be together for Mallie's sake.*

What have you just, just, within the last five minutes finished reading?

Erm… oh, what you mean the Pia Mellody[65] thing?

Emotional. What's our 'duty' to pass on to the poor fuckers… after us?

Ohhhhh. Oh… Hmmmm… Funny you should say that, because… I read the bit that says it's not just Mothers and sons, it's Fathers and daughters, like they become 'Daddy's 'little girl'.'

Which is what you've done. Mmm hmm

Have I?

Well, now, of course, she's 'Daddy's little girl' because you're not having a relationship with the Mother. Who still wants to have a relationship with you, one way or another. And so do you with her, theory, fantasy, would you say that's fair to say or am I just shooting off?

Yeahhhhh. No, you've... rumbled me. Ha ha ha

Heh heh heh heh. So you tell me what you, what you think the reality may be? And...

What, now?

Yup! And where does Maria fit in and...

That's a good question! So Doctor, how much did you say your fees were?

All the royalties, you're bolloxed! Heh heh heh.

You wish! We're not gonna get paid per word you know! So what is the reality? The reality isssss... She's got a new bloke who I had guessed about, I even knew who he was, just put the pieces together, so I'd assumed she knew about me and Maria, or had worked it out, but no, seems she hadn't a clue, which is what amazed me, because I thought she had picked it up!

Oh come on, cut the crap! You're just, blah blah blah! First and foremost, why did you not tell her, that you're seeing a girl? Or that you're even seeing anyone?

Protecting her, protecting myself? Um....

Whoa, whoa, one by one! How were you protecting her?

By, erm, because it felt really cruel to... umm. How does that work?

It's a... woman. She's a woman. A man is safer because a man isn't competition.

Yeah

...because she hasn't got a dick, so she can't compete with a man.

Well, when I told her, she said straightaway, "Oh, well I'm seeing someone too..."

No!! You were both holding back!

Yeah!

Why?

Well, I knew she was seeing somebody, because she seemed different, happier, more feminine, like she was probably having some good sex, or really being appreciated.

So what about… She hadn't guessed? Hadn't Malaika mentioned anything? You know "I saw Daddy and Maria".

Oh, yes, well, Maria has been mentioned, but Ayesha seems to have assumed it was just a woman friend, or…

So you both had an ulterior motive or three. Sooo… is it possible you would get together? Is it a fantasy? Could it be a reality?

I think it has… it does still lurk there. I think because I didn't have the guts to say, 'this isn't going to work because I can barely hold things together', or move back in together, or look after you like I feel I'm supposed to, or live in suburbia, or…

You're talking about at the community, Wilmington. Or?

No, no the counselling, Relate[66]… last year. God, so recent!

What was the object of the exercise of the counselling?

Well, right from the beginning, at the end of the first session where we had counselling, we decided that our aim was to get back together, we would work out our 'stuff'. Something that shocked me with Maria is that even with all, supposedly with all the 'awareness' we have, it sometimes just bubbles up in my mind, "Well look, at least I know Ayesha, I know her baggage, I know how we work together…"

Yeah, better the devil you know.

Exactly! *We may be fucked up, we may lead each other to madness, but at least we know each other.* Why am I getting involved in a relationship with somebody else when I will probably just start repeating all my old patterns, blah blah blah fifteen years down the line? But I don't really have any expectations of Maria... Like there's no 'stuff'. No heaviness. No commitment.

Mmmm, No commitment. How long can it carry on like this? Something may change at some stage, you know a honeymoon period lasts, well what...?

That's what bothered me, is it genuinely this good, that we have a huge amount of awareness, we've 'worked on' ourselves...?

Dumping of issues, and punishment and disconnection and abandonment... all sorts of shit. Yeah! If or when that all starts to come up! Like I was saying earlier, the bedroom became the only place, and sex the only way to connect, for Emma and I.

Are you saying that this is inevitable? Is that what you're saying?

I'm not saying diddly!!

Ha ha ha. What leave that to 'a book of answers?'

Ok. Would you say - consciously, or subconsciously - that you and Ayesha still imagine, hope, believe you will get back together?

I would say that, really deep down, I understand that it's all over, but you know. We were best friends, we had good sex, lots of common interests, we could talk, gave each other space... it's gutting in a way. A BIG way, because it's like - if that doesn't work, and I look at so many relationships, fuck! What's left? But she says she has no interest in getting back together at all. And she said to me, "Don't ask me again." and I said "I won't!"

Maybe you 'peaked' early?

Yeah.

Maybe you've outgrown each other?

Yeah. It's the wrong way around. At eighteen onwards we did all the long-term commitment, the settling down, bought a flat…'til I - or maybe we - began to realize we were turning into our parents.

Right! Then perhaps you just want to have fun? Or at least for now.

Yeah. For now…

How cool is that?

Well, I suppose the, yeah!

Do you think she's really over you? How do you think she feels? Does she really not want you to ask her again?

I don't; well I suppose I feel that some element is a facade to protect herself, to let herself move on. And also big thing, I don't, and didn't, want to lose the good relationship around Malaika.

And really though, what choice does she have? Apart from, she can either get over you, pretend to get over you, or follow you around with a big open wound and a large packet of Saxa[67] for more pain, more rejection.

Yeeesssssss… *(sighs, 'deflates')* I think it's just healing really, really slowly. And for me, just as the wound is healing, I see her when I drop off or pick up Mallie, and the scab gets knocked off again. But the other thing that fucked me off is that, well basically, we have got the worst of both worlds in some ways. Like before, I said to her, *"I want a relationship with you, like you, fancy you, want to have sex with you, commit to you, but I just don't want to live with you…"*

Commit? "I want to commit but I don't want to live with you?" What kind of a relationship is that?

Well why not? Why the hell not?

"I don't want to live with you... ever?"

"I don't want to live with you at the moment" And maybe ever; I don't know. I don't want to be around my partner all the time. Or even most of the time!

So. Different levels, or definitions of 'commitment', different understandings of what a 'partner' means. You will always have a relationship basically, because you have a daughter together. So are you just being childish and playing games?

Childish? Is it inevitable and desirable to live together? Or is it like we've talked about, is it just economic or emotional convenience? Or is it that, as we get older, that relationships are about companionship, friendship, I don't know.

So something that we have in common is being adult too young. And look at it this way - for 'better' or for 'worse' you've got both worlds. Don't know if you've got the 'best' of, but you've got them both.

Yeah. Hmmm.

And good-on-yer!

But you know, the thing that bugged the hell out of me is that she wasn't going to, well she only told me about her and this new bloke once I had 'confessed'. Now that was always a pattern in our relationship from emotional honesty throughout, well similar, shagging other people and coming clean while she was working abroad. We both did it. But for some reason, I always told her first!

So... what a snake! Holier-than-thou Mummy's-girl! *I'll let you feel guilty, meanwhile I'm doing the same but not owning it.*

But also her being at her parents' place. She can't or won't move out, I

can't, yet, provide her with the means to move out. So still more guilt! I just want... God! I...

And it's not about being together, it's about being comfortable together?

Well, yeah, which is what I suppose it always was...

Really?

So why stir it all up? Jesus this 'crusade' for truth tires me out sometimes, but I have to get to the bottom; it's like an obsession. And also I guess because of all the stuff going on with Margaret, the sex, telling her husband. Jesus I sound like I'm just some sort of a crazed, sex...

You've rediscovered fanny again. Can't get enough!

Ha ha ha!

And good on you!

Fucking Margaret, and then her telling Adam, and him wanting to beat me up pheeooooowww!

And you thought, did you, 'Oh she and Adam are breaking up, he won't mind, he will understand...' Heh heh heh.

Ha ha ha! I feel like, I must, we were so naïve I mean, do all other men know this already? *You can't just go around fucking other people's wives, and expect to get away with it.* And, we agreed to tell him. It felt right, clean.

But there are huge amounts of men who spend their lives fucking other men's wives.

I know, but the ludicrous honesty! We both said to each other, again literally almost like, in-sync, I said to her, "I think we should tell Adam". I say ludicrous, but, here's a relationship where she's totally devoted to spirituality, while he was 'Mr Track & Field'. Sporty, but she's said, since he's known, he's been in grief, says his heart is broken; and to her astonishment wants to be involved in her healing, her therapy work. And, she said his Mother told her once, that as a little boy, he would cry when the petals fell off a flower!

Eh? I thought he was macho!

Totally. But with this big, apparently total, emotional cut-off. Until now. Her sleeping with me has changed everything for them! So something must have happened to him at that point, as a kid, someone must have said that only 'little sissies' cry when the petals fall off a flower, or whatever.

And so maybe his Mum bought him plastic flowers to help him out. Heh heh heh

Ha ha ha. But then isn't that what; children are just so emotional. Every child, whether it's a boy or a girl.

And they need to discover their emotions, not become like their parents.

Yeah.

And not have to, not have to avoid 'going there', because the parents haven't got the depth to 'go there', or witness their kids going where they won't go themselves.

Go where? To the emotion?

To their emotions. They need to discover, boys and girls need to discover their 'masculine' emotions, their 'feminine' emotions, their 'angry' emotions, their 'appropriate' emotions, their totally 'inappropriate' emotions. *How else does anyone find anything out, apart from 'going there' in order to find out where not to go.* Obviously, learn from other people's mistakes, if you can, but also claim 'their own'.

What friends, contemporaries?

TV, whatever, but there are certain times when you can only find out about yourself by 'going there' to know where not to go, rather than listening to your parents and never going anywhere, because it would make them uncomfortable, and you don't even know what's right for you, or wrong or what you do and don't like. It's more what's appropriate and inappropriate. Meanwhile, somewhere in there is a dead person with your facial expression. Do you know what I mean?

Yeah!

Grey! Heh heh heh

What, hair?

No!

Grey face? Grey everything.

'Fade to Grey'[68]

> 64. Passive-aggression. Manipulative disguised aggression, coming from the perspective of a victim / martyr, rather than an active-aggressive perpetrator.

> 65. Pia Mellody, 'Facing Love Addiction' (Harper SanFrancisco) 1992. www.piamellody.com

> 66. Relate. UK relationship counselling organisation. www.relate.org

> 67. Saxa. A brand of table salt.

> 68. 'Fade To Grey' (1980) Visage, from the album 'Visage'.

Paedophile

Here's one! Watching Michael Jackson[69], I thought, "Yeah, me too!" I'm not by any means saying... I don't come from wherever Michael Jackson has come from, but I can relate to him, in that he wasn't, and isn't, 'sexual'. I'd say I spent most of my life not being sexual. I mean sure, I've had sex - a reasonable amount - but I haven't been... dickled, where with Michael Jackson, I would say he's still pre-pubescent. Like being stuck in Maurice Sendak's *"Where the Wild Things Are"*[70]. Do you know what I mean? Let's go and play with the monsters and say "Now Stop" and "Be Still" and wear those costumes, or similar clothes with designer labels, and for no-one to say "Stop, with that spending!". His childhood was so stolen from him, big-time! So the poor guy. He hasn't got that to build on. That's where his pause button[71] is so down. And the bottom line is, he would want the sort of thing you were having with Ayesha. Blagging, or avoiding, but not having mates, and then suddenly supposed to be a man with a woman, and supposed to know exactly what to do, and 'how to do it', without any mates to check in on, or anyone to tell him what's cool, or 'normal' and what's not. And all you've got is what, porn? What other people have said or hinted at? But yeah, I so relate to him. It's like with Australian Bruce, um, we would sleep in the same bed when he stayed over at my house-share. Not naked, but I'd wake up to find his legs draped across my stomach. Same with a couple of mates – my age. Share a bed. Clean, innocent, safe guys - not dodgy at all.

But it's still taboo... I mean, remember all that fuss about some Tory MPs 'sharing a bed with each other' on a business trip, back in the 90's or 80's? The press had a field day!

Yeah. But look at it this way. Poor old Michael Jackson. If he's got the mind of a pre-pubescent, and he happens to be in this early 40's, or late 30's body, hanging out with these kids... *It would be okay if it was two kids the same age, measured in years.*

But people are...

I'm not saying it's good or it's bad. The poor guy is stuck in the image of his sexless 'purity' and there are a lot of people that are stuck, and it's like with this book. 'As soon as I have the awareness of where I am stuck, I can change the pattern, and it's no longer ruling me. I've automatically upgraded, or downloaded, or whatever'. So, maybe it's a time thing.

But you know, all the other stuff that's happening at the moment, the paedophilia, witch-hunts...

Well that's it. How easy it is to point the finger at someone else when people haven't explored their own shit!

Is it because the people haven't been given, or allowed, their own boundaries? They're still children themselves?

For me, in my life, I was scared shitless of children. I was, I didn't know how to be one, deal with one, and I didn't know how to go there...

Were you still a child in your own mind?

No! I stopped being a child when I was very, very young. But there's still a very, very childish part in me, which is why I'm 'inappropriate' quite often, because I don't know what's what. So I was suddenly a man, or blagging being a man, and there's a child lost in there somewhere. Put 'on hold'. The man built on abandonment by men, and pain from women, who were all I had left without the men.

So in a way, what we've talked about is. It's not sexual...

Yeah, but it...

It's acted out on the genitals, so...

No, no, no not necessarily. It's not even necessarily genital, unless you're really scared.

You know, like with Pete Townshend. I haven't read all the papers, but it was internet wasn't it? Pictures of children. And the media make the public fixate on fucking genitals. I mean that's what it's basically about...

Yeah that's what it's made to be all about, because sex is equated with the genitals, 'perv, perv, perv'. But is there any understanding? No. Point the finger and then run away, "cos I've got stuff too.' Who hasn't got stuff? So, I have friends that are very, very young. Young boys, hanging out. Didn't cross my mind, sexual stuff. Why would it? Kids. I mean, what is sexy? Children, they are barely male or female. Asexual, or bisexual… not even sexual. Same as me. If I was sexual, then maybe I would have thought about something sexual with these boys. But no way! So I was having 'normal' sex with women and stuff like that, and that was fine; it was like another part of me that had to catch up, subconsciously. Missing parts of my foundation. Not a 'sex-fix' to steal someone else's pure, innocent childlike essence. And recently, before this book, because I had not been able to carry on with my life at all. When I went out with Becky, being touched hurt my skin, even if it's 'normal' and important to be touched. And before going out with her, I hadn't been touched softly for months! My 'touch' was 'violent' male stuff. Playfighting was the best we could do. So many people, these so-called pervert-paedophiles are lost. They need somewhere safe to let them name their lost parts, go there, wherever 'there' is, find it and sort it out. Call it initiation - look at you and your sex life. You didn't have the 'lad' thing to 'graduate' from to move on to the 'girl' thing. For me, I didn't have the child thing, with mates, so I've hung out with kids and had a great time. Perverted? I don't think so. Once I've done that, okay to go to the 'girl thing'… stages, evolution. I was scared of 'alien' kids and teenagers, and having to interact with them, until my late 20's. Safety. I think I've almost caught up. I'm 'working through' my missed out teen years. Just a few years 'older' than Michael Jackson. Don't get me wrong – the 'kid thing' is the minority in my life. Most of my friends are young or older adults.

Yeah. Yeah.

Now we could totally talk about the paedophile thing for other people, but for myself, let's name it! The 'inner-child'. Old people dressed like kids, 'carrying around their teddy bear'. Please! It might work if I was a 'normal' middle-class white basket case! But my 'inner child', where I stopped being a child, *still reacting like a stuck little refugee child,* wanting to serve, *be like a little servant girl.* I had no idea! Just be harmless, have no genitals. Etc, etc, etc. So I need to get myself back. You could liken that to a paedophile, you could liken that to loads of people. People express where their pause buttons are down, and whatever it is in their darkside that they're stuck in, in ways that are inappropriate socially.

So why are so many people so fascinated by it all? Supposedly about seventeen million people watched the Michael Jackson interview!

Titillation! How many people have lives that 'they' lead? They just live the lives that they see on the soaps, newspaper gossip and yadda yadda yadda. Crap! There's no risk-taking. They are governed by 'what do people think?'

Or 'let's go to the pub'. Numb ourselves.

'I hate myself and my job, so let's be furious with everyone, and say how crap they are so that I can feel slightly better about myself for ten minutes, and gossip and celebrity-gaze or get totally rat-arsed, so I can't feel; or stoned; fuck my life away, so that everybody at least knows that I am good in bed if nothing else. Or so I get a fix from bed. The 'secret' undiscovered place.'

69. 'Living With Michael Jackson' Michael Bashir interview, November 2002

70. 'Where The Wild Things Are' Maurice Sendak. (Harper Childrens' Books) 1963. www.northern.edu/hastingw/wildthings.html

71. Pause button. (Mick-ism) Where / when the psyche is stuck in the past, though still (unconsciously) dominating the present.

Breaking the family curse

But our lives have changed! God, my life has changed! Your life has changed! You know, my friends, your friends, your family! Since transcribing all this, it's amazing how everything has shifted. And everyone has moved forward. Very basically, just talking about all this and gaining awareness, has brought it into reality. It brings it into the physical world here and now. And I have seen the way that men, women, boys, girls, 'hot-stuff people' who wouldn't look at me with any ease or acceptance, who I wouldn't look at. Now we're just hanging out. People want to speak to me. *My whole relationship to life has changed.* And that's one big thing, actually... my parents, my best friends, intimate relationships, it's been up, big-time!

What do you mean?

It's been up! It's going through change. I'm no longer who these people thought I am, or wanted or needed to be. Or who I thought I was. I want to have purity. I'm not sure that I want years and years of therapy. I mean, if I have to then I will. Recording our thoughts; with that, I want to just check things out that will get things done faster. Get it out of my system. I know people who have been going through therapy for years, just for the self-justification. They can get really stuck. Hiding, and 'treading water' and playing the victim.

Now, do you think it's possible, really possible to 'get over it'? I mean, like with my sister. That angry letter she sent me, she was basically saying, "Stop looking for 'the answers'. Life is rough and smooth, up and down." Yeah yeah yeah.

I think I know what you're getting at, but I mean the bottom line, for me, is. I've got over so much already. I am getting over more. Even though it's scary and 'out-of-control'. Embarrassing stuff.

I guess it's more, what we were saying about speeding things up. There seem to be a lot more processes designed to help you really 'get over it', whether it's The Journey[72], or any of those fast-track self-help programmes.

This is a really powerful generation!

Yeah, yeah. I think I know what you mean. Young people aren't content to spend the rest of their lives 'on the couch'. So this is where the Holy Grail[73] thing comes in. Searching for something, regardless of the personal cost. Something higher than, or bigger than us, than me. Oh, I don't know!

What do we seek? Happiness. Joy. Connection. Well you could say, it's an 'orgasm'. I suppose you could say if you could have a proper 'life' orgasm, rather than just ejaculating by yourself, or with, or in, other people. Nice bit of collective consciousness, big-time 'head-jobs'!

Just thinking again about that massage with Angus and Elizabeth. It was an amazing evening. I watched them at one point. They were dancing, she was topless, he didn't have… he was wearing these little pants that he had had to borrow off her. And they looked really good on him. We all said he looked like an Italian beach poseur! They were dancing together. It was all so warm and lovely, and loving and accepting, sexy and yet safe. Towards the end of the evening, Elizabeth mentioned that *they had been talking about the idea of threesomes!* In the past the idea of a threesome would have excited me, sexually. My first reaction would have been, 'Oh yeah, who'll touch who, what will I do'. But with this, with them, it wasn't. Because we - we - had so opened our hearts and ourselves. And Elizabeth started to say something, and she couldn't quite express it, and this Buddhist phrase - 'spaciousness' came to mind. With these people, there is this possibility… it would feel like a soul not just sexual connection. And it's like we said about 'be'ing, there comes a point with someone, whether it's two men, like you and Lui. Or me and Elizabeth and Angus that night. Or whoever. It's talked about, but it's not really talked about. You know, you get to a point with somebody, regardless of sex, men, women, where, the boundaries just, wanting to kind of 'merge' with this person. So, well, what do you 'do' with it. Where do you go with that. It's 'holy', it's union, and it's totally scary, because what do you say to one another after you have 'come down'? Getting into that person, wanting to be part of, wanting to 'be' them. Yet all of that is lumped together and labelled 'sex'!

One-ness.

Yeah!

With the other person; and at that level, that frequency, that vibration, with every other molecule in the universe. Now that is what I call a good shag! The bottom line is... what am I doing here?

Here? On earth?

Yeah. *There's only one option. And that's 'enlightenment'.* Otherwise, what am I doing here? And enlightenment is by no means a purely spiritual thing. I've got to go through the earthly, physical 'curriculum', and that is physical, mental and emotional and spiritual. Getting rejected, down and dirty. Having aches and pains. Done that. Or I have done that? Umm. But I've done it 'appropriately'. And now we have recorded this, these 'golden' passing moments, my exploits, in order to set myself free. The final dump. I just hope I'm not childishly getting 'victim-revenge'!

But it would have been very easy to get stuck somewhere in your explorations. Say, going to the sauna. You know, 'Wow this is great, I like this - I'll 'have another biscuit from the biscuit tin'. And another. And another. And another. Until there's no more biscuits, and I'll quietly get addicted to my fix.' Isn't it about taking 'something' and integrating it into your life?

Right-on!

But I think that's what happens to people... *That's what happened to me, with 'men fucking'. It fills a hole – but it creates another hole inside.*

HA HA HA HA HA. You didn't even get that – did you!!! Yup. They find something to identify with, and it's safe, it has 'status' within their community. Like, have you read *'The Autobiography of a Yogi*[74]? Bloody brilliant! He says, heaven is where you are. For arguments' sake, maybe, everything is crossed off my list on earth in this lifetime, apart from, say, I didn't experience having abs and thus being drop-dead gorgeous. In 'heaven', I can manifest these things, experience them and cross them off my list, get over it, and move on to the next stage. But it's so easy to be lost in 'earthly fixes'. More, more, more, and so it goes on, and you forget to 'come back' to where you are, or where it's happening, or where the pathway is, or whatever. Like the 'astral' plane. It's like here, the earth plane, only much, much faster - for manifesting things. Like the internet, in a way. God I feel dumb talking like this. *The way I really like to look at the internet, is that it's preparing us to be able to tap into the collective consciousness.* Without having a computer, or having it crash on you...

Or like riding a bike without stabilizers

For me, the object of the exercise is to remember to get over things, and to have as much sex, and as much of the things that bring me pleasure, as long as I'm not harming anyone, not stealing from anyone, and as long as I'm vulnerable enough to enjoy it and be fed by it. If I'm unconscious, then I can only treat them like my childhood script, or wherever it was that my 'inner child' was lost. Yuk! I hate that phrase, man! 'Inner child'!

Connection, compassion. If people around me are suffering, like the prayers all say, then I am suffering. The accusations I've had recently, that I'm too self-centred. But how can I heal or help anybody or be any bloody use, unless I have looked at my own 'shit'? Or know my own boundaries? Or if I'm not capable of protecting myself, of looking after myself?

And this book. I want it published mainstream! Not filed away for 'seekers of wisdom' only. No, I want this to stimulate people. Doing this book has lifted the 'depressed pause buttons' in my life, and helped me say what needed to be said, for me to be allowed to be me, and to get over my shit. I've got my life back. But yet we've both chosen to 'go anonymous'. I don't need anyone tracking my family, my friends. Or me. But this is life-purpose stuff. *All the money that's spent on rehabilitation, court-room stuff, dealing with picking up the pieces, punishing people, locking people up, all the admin, and all the 'tax-payers' money' and effort. Not to mention the suicides!* Time to stop it. 'Name' but not 'blame' or 'shame'. What's gonna come up next for us? Male education, initiations, more books, workshops, some sort of a 'clean' retreat place to be with other men. This needs to be turned around, eh!

Not to mention the conspiracy of silence on so many issues. And 'perversions' that could be dealt with if they weren't so shrouded in shame, and seriousness. Like when I was a child, our pet dog would roll 'round and get a spontaneous hard-on. Just like blokes do. I remember thinking, 'When does that poor dog ever get a shag?' And it occurred to me to give him a handjob! Ha ha ha! Never would have done it. Ugh! But to even have thoughts like that, let alone admit to it. The only time I've said this before was to my brother, and at a 'confessions' game I once played.

Well that's reason enough to remain anonymous! The RSPCA[75] would have your arse! Ha ha ha

Yeah, but we don't need Big Brother[76] to watch us. We watch ourselves!

We 'play dead', just like your dog, even though we're aching with life and bursting to let it show.

So, yeah, I 'pretend' that I didn't even have that thought. And like Martin Luther King said, something like, 'Love and fear cannot live together'. So no wonder people can't empathise with Michael Jackson, or Pete Townshend. It's like all the so called 'right wing' or any side, when it's extreme or in power or in control. 'They' would rather these thoughts and those who dare to think them, are erased, or locked away, or lynched, or burned, or whatever. It's much easier. *'That's really bad. Destroy it! Let's bomb the evil!'* Let's not try to understand anything.

72. 'The Journey' Brandon Bays (Harper Collins) 1999 www.thejourney.com

73. The Holy Grail. The 'sacred vessel' from which Jesus drank at The Last Supper, taken to Glastonbury by his grand uncle Joseph of Arimathea, after he used it to collect Christ's blood and sweat while he was on the cross. King Arthur is said to have used it to heal the mortally wounded. It's now, apparently, safely in the hands of the Welsh! - Or perhaps our physical bodies are the 'sacred vessels' housing us on our quests to enlightenment?

74. 'Autobiography of a Yogi' Paramahansa Yogananda (Self Realisation Fellowship) 1946. www.yogananda-srf.org

75. RSPCA. Royal Society for the Prevention of Cruelty to Animals.

76. Big Brother. Totalitarian watchdog in George Orwell's classic '1984' (Penguin) 1948

77. Pete Townshend has never been charged with anything other than investigating paedophilia web sites and apparently states that he was researching his way out of his own possible childhood abuse.

Please help me!

Are we just mulling over the same ground?

We're just talking about talking about it, wasting time and…

More stuff to wade through!

Exactly! Bottom line for me, is like, when something is named, it's no longer… I can get over trying to name it. And this is where I'm asking for help. From my parents, from my family, my friends, my - 'what is it that needs naming, that I don't know' - that people previously think I do? Blaming doesn't come into it! I'm not blaming anyone, I'm not being anyone's victim.

Exactly!

There's no blame at all. Almost maybe, on one hand, begging - for information. I've got my life back already. We've already finished taping, which was, apart from this evening, we've been starting to transcribe since Boxing Day, and thinking 'Fuck!!' with every syllable that comes out, because neither of us remembers saying any of this, leave alone that it actually makes good, simple sense.

Hmmm.

So, yeah! Name, not blame. And really, rather than being bullied or, um, some alternative. But to love my parents, my friends, the way my life is. Thinking, 'Nah! Some of that was actually toss!' And choosing to love, because I want to love. *I have never felt so much love for my parents, and my family, and people that I've been angry with.*

Hmmm

...and I want to make peace before I die. Because life's too short. But thankfully, it is maybe, the death of my past, and the birth of my life!

Hmmm!

The birth of my freedom. The birth of my honest expression. Rather than suppressed nonsense. Life's changed, and life is fucking good and I'm getting more and more; mad things, like, this might be my ego, but I want people to be able to tell the truth to each other... and me! I want people to be able to get over things. You know, people to be able to understand the way things work. With pause buttons being down. With drinking, and sex, and whatever. It's only when people understand, and they get over it, and then we're not going around punishing and hurting and lying and hiding and perving and stealing. But, getting over it. Understanding and getting over it. Understanding and not causing those issues, so that when we parent our children, we don't pass on the shit! Changing the way that we relate to each other, and tell the truth. Changing the way that we share and trust, rather than compete and steal. Ha ha ha ha ha... And the whole 'death thing' is really; most of my life, *I have been petrified to fuck about my parents dying*, and how I'll cope, and how I'll look after one when the other is gone. What's expected, you know, all these things that have never been talked about, or that are taboo. Find out and move on. And Rob is suddenly back from America, because his Father has died. And initially I thought, why didn't he really cry at his Father's funeral? I realized that, just because you cry, doesn't mean that you are hurting more or less. Everyone needs to deal with it in their own way and he has been an amazing inspiration for me. Selfishly speaking, we have been able to hang out and spend time, be men together. And I think I've said before, so many of my friends, my clients, they become their own man when their parents, or when their Fathers die. I want that now. And I want to be able to be a man with my Father. And embarrassing as it may be in the beginning, and what we need to go through to get over it, I'd rather share it with them, than wait for them to 'go', and do it 'behind their backs'. That's pathetic! Bruce's Mother dying. You know, he and I had a really good chat, and 'old me' wanted to catch the next flight out to Australia to make sure he's cool and look after him and save the day, and stick my knickers over my tights, and be the dutiful hero, do you know what I mean? Didn't need to. I've grown, he's grown, and we're men together. We're not sissies that need to huddle up and whimper. It's changed. Fuck, I've changed in that way. Yuh, I do feel like I have died. I have so finally died. Ummm, or the boy has died, and the man is emerging. And at least the bits that I don't have, or the bits that were lost, I'm not running away from, or pretending that I have, or avoiding. Or I am looking at them, or I am getting over them. Fucking amazing! I just wish, I so wish, that I felt safe enough in myself, and in the people that I, that I could stand up and say "This is my story and all that embarrassment and everything that probably all of you knew all along, and you can probably read me like a book. Well, yup, it's me." But I can't, because I don't trust that it's going to be safe for me, or my parents, or your child. I am not, I don't have the right to drag anyone else through anything, or tell anyone how to live. ***So I have to hide, and I hate that.*** So God knows what chances I have blown in writing this with my career, or Australia, or what I've blown. Or what's going to come out of it, but I don't know. I suppose I'd rather fuck up and lose things and make a true honest life and make something of it, than be 'fearful of fucking up' and 'play dead' for the rest of my life (nervous 'canned' laughter). My relationships have so been up in the last, what, week. It's been scary, in a way. Scary, and out of control. It's fucked me up!! I have spent my whole life following the same old patterns and just having enough, or maybe having lots and sharing it. I want to go up a grade - or several grades - and stay up there. Um, time for me to have what's mine! And this whole fucking dole thing. What an arse. Such a - how a normal - or 'not that many O-levels working-class-person' is meant to fill in all that paper work, and jump through hoops. First they send me the wrong forms, and then there was Christmas, then there was this, then there was that. It' just more of a battle than it's worth. And now I'm just thinking, I don't want that money, I don't need that money, humiliate myself, beg for that money. Easy enough when they take taxes, and waste our money on this, that and the other. War and expense accounts, all those, what do you call them? Businesses, public businesses that lose billions. The fuck ups that they make! And their huge wages. Do you know what I mean? It's dirty, it's just plain bullying. In a way this whole thing has been a communication to my parents, and I suppose…

The thing I liked about Lui's intro was that I felt I could use it to inspire my Dad to write my intro. And telling Lui, when he'd obviously just been 'on one' how superb I thought it was, what he'd written. It wasn't like I was saying it to make him like me. And then phoning my Dad to ask him if he would write the intro. It's not about "Hey son, I'm really proud of you for being a solicitor or for all your 'achievements' and certificates." But, imagine if my Dad could actually say, "This is what pisses me off about you Ed." "This is what I really value in you". Like an honest, clear, open exchange, evaluation…

You know what just struck me? "Don't talk to me like you're my Mother". Heh heh heh…

What, me saying that?

No, no. no. All that 'nicey nicey' stuff that is what your Mum would say, because she wants to protect you. That is not what you want your Father to say. You want the truth from your Father.

Again, if he could say "Yeah I wasn't that happy when Ed told me was giving up the law, or that he thought he was gay, but…"

Abandoned you instead, turned away to let your Mum and the women take you over.

Because it was what his Father did and, incredibly powerful stuff. And you know, we were talking about initiations. Do you know what? It kind of doesn't matter to me now what he says in the intro, whether it's good, bad or indifferent, or whether I even use it. It's actually the process of asking him to.

Yeah

Like, *"I dare you to be honest about your feelings towards me!"*

Or are you even 'daring' him, or are you extending a hand?

Yeah, it's not angry, like 'Come on Dad - let's have a fight.' Like it was for years when I was growing up. 'I really want to know you.' Like when I suggested he took me to Paris a couple of weeks ago, it's not about how emotional I was, it was something he said. He was talking about the Catholic Mass at the Sacré Coeur. It was something I'd said I wanted to do, because I like big church buildings and masses of nuns singing. So there we were, sitting in our twin beds in this hotel room, sharing a whisky or a glass of red wine or whatever it was. He's had a couple of drinks already, was quite mellow; I almost felt like he was talking to himself, and he just said " Yes, there's something very powerful, very moving about those services in the Sacré Coeur." And I was amazed. It wasn't said 'for effect' or 'for drama', or to impress my Mother, or... I mean for him to say that, let alone, you know, I didn't even know he had thoughts like that. I felt like...

Is that what mates are then?

Maybe, an extension, a tribe...

Yeah, part of the tribe. *Because I don't want my Father to be someone that threatens me and fucks me up.* I want to know him, hang out with him, and be mates...

It was like when I got back to the flat last night, Bob was in a right state. He'd had a - he'd basically ended up shouting at his step-Mum down the phone and had written an Email to his parents, or to his step-Mum? Wanted me to look it over with him before he sent it out, but it was excellent, because we just talked and talked and we had the same stuff going on. It's not like we hate our Mothers now, but we are taking space from their love, their mollycoddling[78], whatever. It's like they don't know how to release us, let us go on. And fuck me; when he told me, when we found out that this was happening to both of us! We both remarked that what used to happen, if we, when we phoned home, if our Dads answered there'd be a slightly awkward, embarrassed, erm, "How are things" brief conversation before "Oh, I'll hand you over to your Mother..." Now, with both of us, it's switched! I would never, in a million years have dreamed of this. The last time I spoke to my Mother, we had a fairly short conversation, and she said "Oh, your Dad's just here. I'll get him for you." Unbelievable. Absolutely umm... I mean, like you say, talk about radical change. If I had asked for one thing from this process, it's yeah, it's dealing with Fathers.

I thought my Father hated me for most of my life.

Hmmm. Ditto.

I mean he would always talk to me like I was a pile of shit. Look at me like I was a pile of shit. And same, on the phone, as soon as he heard my voice, "Here's your Mother!" Wouldn't even bother saying hello. And I could never figure out exactly what I'd done. And to ask him, or anyone, would be confrontation. Meanwhile, it's almost as if my Mother fed off it...

Yeah, oh definitely. And we were... I was complicit all those years. Like, 'phew what a relief!' because he and I have nothing to say to each other. Meanwhile my Mum and I will talk about him, how I don't have a relationship with him, or how pissed off he seems, or how angry I am with him; and she wrings her hands, but like you said, gives her something, power, control, safety, attention, love. I act like it, or he, or my relationship with him, doesn't really matter anyway. We stop talking the minute he comes in the room. Like a couple of gossips!

And acting guilty too!! What a script! What a trip! But everywhere… it just goes on for so many people.

It was us against 'him'. So, it didn't make sense. So much for a 'united front'. So much for 'parenting'. We didn't even have 'family' rules. As soon as someone walked in the house, we were 'moulded' around other peoples rules.

Hmmmm

So, no boundaries. There was nowhere that anyone could meet. We couldn't meet each other. We couldn't meet other people. We were so busy smiling and grinning and making everything okay…

Good 'coloured' people, like on the 'Black & White Minstrel Show'[79]; I assume you are talking about white people?

…that no-one was ever home. Fucked up. Totally fucked up. So, same happens throughout life. Because that's what we're taught. And to an extent, maybe I can't blame my parents. I know my great, my grandparents… um, my Mother's side anyway, um, their, their parents died, they were orphans, so my grand Father and my grand Mother had to bring up their brothers and sisters. What do they know about parenting? So what have they got to pass down to my parents? And my grand Father, apparently was an alcoholic, and he must have fucked everyone up, on my Mother's side. And my grand, my great-grand Mother on my Father's side. So, you know, generations, it takes generations, if ever, for this fucked up shit to work out.

Hmm…

Meanwhile, what rosy pictures do we hear? About our wonderful family. Never get 'the truth'. Nothing quite makes sense, and so 'normal' behaviour is this 'fucked up shit!' And no-one knows where it's come from, but it's normal, and what's not normal are the families that aren't fucked up.

Hmmm

Doesn't make sense. Simply doesn't make sense. So no wonder my, you know so we could... I would choose, erm, someone like my Mother, as my Mother probably chose my Father, to replace her angry Father who was an alcoholic, who she pretends, or 'remembers', was wonderful!

Hmmm

Oh, I don't know!

But isn't there, there's almost a simple 'pay-off', if you like, that, my thought is this: watching you and Lui today, having that very simple, straightforward hug. It's like, I don't know, I don't want to go on long, foreign holidays with my Father, and sit staring into his eyes, and say how much I value him.

Ha ha ha ha ha ha

...how wonderful it is to be emotional with him, it's just to have those simple everyday things, those moments that happen 'just like that'. You know, it's natural to embrace somebody like that, or, I don't know, without having to engineer...

Get 'all wet' and 'girly'

Yeah!

Yup. Honest expression. Honest and open communication.

Exactly! I mean, I wrote something, you know which I wasn't sure whether it was just for myself, 'therapy' or whatever, but I suddenly realized that so much of my sense of my Father was filtered through my Mother's opinion, and my sister's...

Same!

...opinion, and most of it, I didn't even realize was being filtered...

Yup!

I didn't even realize that the picture was distorted.

Because *our Fathers abandoned, and they didn't stick up for themselves,* or they didn't know because it was happening behind their backs. So how do we know any different? They're 'admitting' it...

And I mean...

...demonstrating it.

And that's not to blame my Mother or sister, because they're presumably just acting out some unconscious thing as well.

Mmhmm!

But I mean, my sister and I would talk about my Mother, my Mother and I would talk about my sister, we'd all talk about my Father, and it was just like this ridiculous game! I was absolutely terrified. The very idea of sitting down and talking, and being honest with my Father. I mean today, when I, I was on the phone to him about writing an intro for the book, terrified of somehow fucking up, or giving myself away, or saying the wrong thing, revealing too much, upsetting or angering him somehow...

Yup.

Revealing that there's things in this book about; but like you said, finally, finally, finally. Okay I'm going to show him the book at some point, in the not too distant future, maybe this weekend. What's the worst thing that can happen? You get disowned? Cast out?

Respected?!

Yeah!!

Heh heh. Change the dynamics. Ohhh!!... I know what the worst thing that might happen is... the Mother might... FROWN! Leave alone cry, or get upset or angry. But we're not even allowed to make them frown.

Hmmm

Don't want to hurt the little darlings.

And yet, I mean, we've been concerned - or it seems to me we've been concerned - about what our Fathers will think, when actually, it sometimes feels like it's our Mothers who have had a pasting in the book.

But...

I really relate to something I; God, I've been 'reading' that bloody Robert Bly book for, oh the last six months, it feels like, slowly and painfully.

Heh heh heh

Ha ha ha

Is it a crap book?

No, no not at all. I think it's very good. Maybe slowly, because I have been absorbing it and trying to live it by my own lights, but there are moments, it's like you're in a storm, I'm in a storm reading it, and then a great shaft of light comes through the cloud and I finally understand what he means, or his quotes or poetry, and he talks about, in the 'fairy' tales, with the step-Mother, the 'wicked' poisoned Mother or whatever. But it's, he talks about how Mothers are not consciously 'doing it', um, like our Mothers are not 'bad people'. They are not evil witches or whatever, but they are being driven by something much deeper. Yeah, like you said with your Mother, you know, she's looking for her abusive alcoholic Father...

Mmmm. Or the 'hero' brother that abandoned her and eloped with her best friend. Lots to punish Pa for:..

My Mother is 'looking for' this idealized Father who died when she was, what, only twenty-something, who used to take her on lovely long nature walks, was a gentle earth-loving man, in her recollection.

Mmmm. Yeah. And from what I remember, my Father, um... my grand

Father, would rarely get drunk and abusive, but when he did, it was bad. And when he didn't, it was great. Um, everyone was scared of him - I don't remember being that scared of him, but I loved it when he played his violin. I absolutely loved it! And I've always loved Strauss. And if it wasn't for my grand Father, I would probably think Strauss was boring as fuck, and Vivaldi's where it's at! Heh heh heh But I think it's my grand Father I loved, not Strauss.

Yeah! What's funny about you saying, it strikes me, again with music - the thread of our grand Fathers again. I was amazed by something my Dad said in Paris. Um, I forget even the context, but he said to me, **"Whatever you want to know about the family, I'm happy to tell you".**

I pray to God I get a little bit of that from mine.

But I didn't even know that was available! Because, I suppose my Mum's always been 'protecting' me, and I've heard all sorts of edited things, but like, he was telling me about - his Father was teetotal because his Father's Mother was a gin-soak[80], and his Father's oldest brother was a very talented pianist, and he, Ernest, the older brother, would be plied with beer as a child, to entertain the family, drunk enough not to be self-conscious and play. So as a result, my Father's Father would not allow him and his brother to have piano lessons, because he associated it with...

(Loud whistle of surprise from Mickey)

...so creativity, expression swept out of the window by alcoholism, and...

Yeah.

...family nonsense!

Yeah.

But he was so truthful. Simple, undramatic, unsentimental about it. It wasn't like he was saying 'I'm a victim' or anything. 'My Mother and Father didn't love me'. I was just blown away by his integrity. Which is how, I hope we come across here. Because I don't feel like either of us is, or maybe we've played the victim, or had a default victim script, to some extent, all our lives so far. It's just, it just won't work anymore.

78. *Mollycoddle. To treat with indulgent care, to pamper. Originally, 'an effeminate man'. Previous to that, 'a man who performs a woman's domestic duties'.*

79. *'Black And White Minstrel Show' (1958-1978) BBC television show.*
80. *Gin-soak. An alcoholic, who drinks (mostly) gin!*

Breaking through

Well... changes. Just thinking of changes. They've been so thick and fast, so quick. I no longer smoke dope or want to smoke dope. I no longer have problems shitting...

Hmmm!

...where I'd always need to smoke, a cigarette, or something. You know, I'd go for a shit without and within half an hour I'd need to go again. With a cigarette, just to get all the rest out. I wear different clothes, unconsciously. In the past, I would wear clothes that, unconsciously, made me feel like a cute little boy, at times.

Hmmm

And other people would think it's all quite trendy, and it looks very good, but now! I wear different clothes, I move differently, I attract different people, I have a totally different attitude about myself. It's just all coming my way. I don't take shit. It doesn't mean I'm out for a fight, but it means I am my own person. I have dignity, rather than the fear that I'm harming someone. *I have balls, rather than Elastoplast*[81]*...* And I can use 'my balls' to show my clients how to claim and 'appropriately' transform their apron-strings and footballs boots into something more real, here and now. I have worked with more men since writing this, then in the past five years put together. Huge results!

(Deep intake of breath) For me, it's, I think the biggest shift... I now would, if I'm upset about something, I'd ring you up, or I'd ring Bob, one of my mates rather than phoning Mum or sister. And so they no longer have strict ownership of me, and they have been upset about

that. But at the same time, what astonishes me, is, it's that thing... My fear of a reaction is much worse than the actual event. Last weekend, when I took Mallie to see her grand Parents, hardly spoke to my Mum at all. She occasionally tried to initiate the 'old' type of conversation. She didn't quite say, 'Tell me about your new girlfriend' or whatever. And this is like what Bob was saying. His Mother was exactly the same. He'd 'have to' tell everything...

Yup. Yeah. All the details so that they can be in control. I have recently grown out of having to de-brief with everyone like Ma's nice little boy. Felt strange at first. Now, space to play!

...and yet, the thing that surprised me was, as we were waiting at the station, leaving. Me and my Mum and Malaika - Dad was parking the car - my Mum said something like, "Oh I don't really feel like we've talked, apart from superficially, this weekend." And I felt like saying, 'Yeah, that's quite deliberate actually - I have to distance myself, to claim me and find out who I am...'

Heh heh heh

'...in order to have a better relationship with you in the future, if that's what's meant to happen...'

Yeah.

'...because I don't think we had a healthy, wholesome relationship to each other; through nobody's 'fault'." Blah blah blah. But, then I could still feel the urge to protect her. And I had read, in 'Iron John', Robert Bly said something like, *the man who has broken the unconscious ties with his family can see his Mother's neediness without having to move to fill it, or protect her, or look after her.* And I could see, in that moment, how I could easily have said to her, 'I'm really sorry, yeah we should talk'. The 'auto-prompt' script. I was about to say something, or my mind was processing it, when she said,

without any pathetic-ness or sadness really, "Well I suppose you've got other people to talk to now." It was like 'Phew, I have succeeded in claiming this. Thank you Mother!'

Yup.

You have set me free, or I've set myself free.

Exactly!

I'm not sure what it is.

Exactly!

And that was the surprise. Not the drama, of her 'lying on the station floor sobbing'.

Having a tantrum!

Yeah, maybe even wanting it, 'cos 'that's all I know, or I expect'.

Yeah, because if she doesn't - then she doesn't love you.

Oh blimey!

But it's almost like saying 'Let's 'meet' somewhere else, and then 'check in'

Yes. Yes. Through choice.

I've got my 'self' back. I have a need to make a difference. Where before, I would go into families, individuals, couples or even businesses, communities, and er, make a difference with my work using Feng Shui as a 'front'. It's not about that now. It's more about deeper, simpler issues, one way or another. As we were saying, um, claiming back the bits that are missing from people without them having addictions, perversions, the darkside. Um and it's actually even down to basic information, research, like the *'Hite Report'*[82] Shere Hite.

Mmmm!

And it doesn't necessarily have to be about sex. About 'life stuff'. So we know what's normal and what's not normal and don't need to hide. Even basic information like, *don't promote paedophiles by making 'sexy' clothes for children.*

Yeah.

To dress them up to show your friends and family how well they match your IKEA furniture.

Hmmm

That's just plain dumb! Don't dress girl pop stars up like schoolgirls, and get them snogging other girls in videos, if this isn't what you want to promote. Or if you are going to do it, then do it in a respectful way, not in a 'pervy' way. It's all about what? Power. Making money. What's gonna sell? What shall we get people addicted to? What are the fears we can get people to buy into, or buy, to avoid themselves?

Yeah!

Stay clean. Totally. And I suppose this is for both of us, our way of playing clean. And yup, maybe we are shooting ourselves in the foot, or in the head, or in the gonads, or whatever, but fuckinell, it feels okay.

Mmmm. Well also, making it accessible. Like with Marius, over Christmas. How extraordinary it was that we'd been talking, and then this amazing fifteen year old tells us what he needs to know, and it seems to be the sort of things that we've been talking about, and he's clear that there are things he wants to know about men, life, girls, bodies, etc.

Yeah.

Which we all wanted to know, from our Dads, and poor buggers didn't know how to tell us.

Hmmm. But I don't think it's all on our Dads.

No

But it's up to our families to provide us with community. I know nothing about the country I come from. All the countries I come from. Do my parents? Well, even if they don't, do they care? Do they want me to know? Or are they just going to watch TV and do puzzle games? How unfair is that? Just because I've turned out an 'okay kid', doesn't mean that I don't, that they could just abandon me and bury their heads in the sand because they're uncomfortable. Or they don't know how to deal with me, or they don't want to be adults yet, or they haven't got the depth.

Yeah, also, an 'okay kid'. Okay for what? Prepare you for a nice '9 to 5' office job for life?

Or so that I don't make waves for them. I am disgusted at the way children are treated. Um. Not only working class kids on the Underground who are shouted at and abused by their parents. But middle class, upper class, people I work with. It's just, it's sick. These are people. And just because they're young, just because you don't remember your own fucked up childhood because you were so young, don't think they're not going to. Or, they've got the right to remember. These are the things that run our lives. DON'T BLOODY DO IT!

Ummm

So, heh heh heh. Um, now I want lots of money and enlightenment now. Heh heh heh. And to go and live in a nice hot country, preferably in Sydney, heh heh heh.

That's not a country...

Okay, fucking Australia. But yeah, I want my life back now. I am not a running refugee. I'm not any of those things. I was. I'm over it now. But it's taken me being out of control, not being able to pay my rent, or do the right thing, having adolescent tantrums twenty five years late. Risking everyone dumping me and hating me; for me to claim my life back. And whatever's going to happen, let it happen. It's my life now. And, how can it possibly not work out?

I think, for me, the final thought is I want, *I'd like to think the next generation of children will be allowed to go into their darkside, embrace their shadow and come out the other side and live the 'clean stuff' in the light.* I mean I couldn't be where I am now if I hadn't had the thing with Steven; sex and, yeah, real love, with a man. To claim that, almost 'tick it off the list'.

But in another way, that would have been unnecessary, if we lived 'in community', if we were taught how to be, and be with, men. Like we said.

Yeah.

So we won't need to go into this paedophile shit and God knows what else. There won't be a need for the secrets and lies and hiding. And we'll be just like *'The Waltons'*[83].

Ha ha ha ha ha.....

81. *Elastoplast. Brand name for dressing for cuts or open wounds. Often 'skin coloured' (orange!)*

82. *'Hite Report' The Hite Reports on sexuality by Shere Hite. www.hite-research.com*

83. *'The Waltons' (1972-1981) classic US television family drama.*

Prayers for peace

Dear Mickey-boy...
(by Michael Elias)

Be gorgeous – you are!
...and you'll get yours, honestly
Cut the crap!
...addiction, ego, avoidance, laziness, victim.
Give energy (clean)
...not excuses (lazy)
Don't chase or hide – belong!
...from your own centre.
Be a good man
...and good folk will follow - then play!
Love
...unashamedly, unconditionally, no strings or chords.
Go to heaven...

Nature Boy
(eden ahbez) sung by Nat 'King' Cole

Unfortunately, permission had not been granted to reproduce the lyrics at the time of going to press, but check-out 'the first hippy''s magical words at www.fact-index.com/e/ed/eden_ahbez.html

Prayer of St Francis of Assisi
(Saint Francis of Assisi)

Lord, make me an instrument of thy peace
Where there is hatred, let me sow love
Where there is injury, pardon
Where there is doubt, faith
Where there is despair, hope
Where there is darkness, light
Where there is sadness, joy

Grant that I may not so much seek
To be consoled, as to console
To be understood, as to understand
To be loved, as to love

For it is in giving, that we receive
It is in pardoning, that we are pardoned
It is in dying (to ourselves)
That we are born (to eternal life)

Baha'i Prayer for Peace

Be generous in prosperity,
And thankful in adversity.
Be fair in judgement,
And guarded in thy speech,
Be a lamp unto those who walk in darkness,
And a home to the stranger.
Be eyes to the blind,
And a guiding light
Unto the feet of the erring.
Be a breath of life
To the body of humankind,
A dew to the soil of the human heart,
And a fruit upon the tree of humanity.

Buddhist Prayer for Peace

May all beings everywhere
Plagued with sufferings of body and mind
Quickly be freed from their illness.
May those frightened cease to be afraid,
And may those bound be free.
May the powerless find power,
And may people think of befriending one another.
May those who find themselves in trackless, fearful wilderness
The children, the aged, the unprotected
Be guarded by beneficial celestials,
And may they swiftly attain Buddhahood.

Christian Prayer for Peace

Blessed are the peacemakers,
For they shall be known as
The children of God.
But I say to you that hear,
Love your enemies,
Do good to those who hate you,
Bless those who curse you
Pray for those who abuse you.
To those that strike you on the cheek,
Offer the other one also,
And from those who take away your cloak,
Do not withhold your coat as well.
Give to everyone who begs from you,
And of those who take away your goods,
Do not ask for them again.
And as you wish that others would do to you,
Do so to them.

Hindu Prayer for Peace

Oh God,
Lead us from the unreal to the real.
Oh God, lead us from darkness to light.
Oh God, lead us from death to immortality.
Shanti, Shanti, Shanti unto all.
Oh Lord God almighty,
May there be peace in Celestial regions.
May there be peace on Earth.
May the waters be appeasing.
May herbs be wholesome,
And may trees and plants bring peace to all.
May all beneficent beings
Bring peace to us.
May thy Vedic Law propagate peace
All through the world.

Jainist Prayer for Peace

Peace and universal love
Is the essence of the gospel preached by all Enlightened ones.
The Lord has preached
That equanimity is the dharma.
Forgive do I creatures all,
And let all creatures forgive me.
Unto all have I amity,
And unto none enmity.
Know that violence
Is the root cause of
All miseries in the world.
Violence, in fact, is the knot of bondage.
"Do not injure any living being."
This is the eternal, perennial, and unalterable
Way of spiritual life.

A weapon, howsoever powerful it may be,
Can always be superseded by a superior one;
But no weapon can, however.

Jewish Prayer for Peace

Come let us go up the mountain of
The Lord, that we may walk the
Paths of the Most High.
And we shall beat our swords into ploughshares,
And our spears into pruning hooks.
Nation shall not lift up sword against nation –
Neither shall they learn war any more.
And none shall be afraid, for the mouth of the
Lord of Hosts has spoken.

Muslim Prayer for Peace

In the name of Allah,
The beneficent, the merciful.
Praise be to the
Lord of the Universe
Who has created us and made us into tribes and nations
That we may know each other,
not that we may despise each other.
If the enemy incline towards peace,
Do thou also incline towards peace,
And trust God,
For the Lord is the one that
Heareth and knoweth all things.
And the servants of God,
Most gracious are those
Who walk on the earth in humility,
And when we address them,
We say 'peace'.

Native American Prayer for Peace

Oh Great Spirit of our ancestors,
I raise my pipe to you.
To your messengers the four winds,
And to Mother Earth who provides for your children.
Give us the wisdom to teach our children to love.
To respect, and to be kind to each other
So that they may grow with peace of mind.
Let us learn to share all good things
That you provide for us on this earth.

Shinto Prayer for Peace

Although the people living across the ocean
Surrounding us, I believe
All are our brothers and sisters,
Why are there constant troubles in this world?
Why do winds and waves rise in the oceans surrounding us?
I only earnestly wish that the wind will
Soon puff away all the clouds which are
Hanging over the tops of mountains.

Sikh Prayer for Peace

God adjudges us according to our deeds,
Not the coat that we wear:
That truth is above everything,
But higher still is truthful living.
Know that we attaineth God
When we loveth,
And only victory endures in consequences
Of which no one is defeated.

Zoroastrian Prayer for Peace

We pray to God
To eradicate all the misery in the world:
That understanding triumph over ignorance,
That generosity triumph over indifference,
That trust triumph over contempt, and
That truth triumph over falsehood.

Contributions to this section would be gratefully accepted for use in future reprints.

Epilogue #1

(January 2003)

Last week was quite a week. In the midst of it all, I had my Tuesday night with my three year old, Malaika, when she stays over. We had an excellent evening, playing, eating, laughing, hanging out. I'd made a vow two days before, to have an evening when I didn't let my tiredness become anger or irritation and then take it out on her.

Bedtime for her. I was knackered. I could hardly keep my eyes open, and she was full of beans, looking gorgeous and bright eyed in her pyjamas. Suddenly, I lost it.

"Go to sLEEP!!!"

I half yelled - half-hissed through gritted teeth, and pushed her onto the pillow. Instantly her expression changed. Her eyes filled with tears, her lip jutted and she started slowly crying,

"Mummy… Muuummy…"

God, did I feel like an abuser! Tears welled up in my eyes. But out of nowhere, the process, the words, the feelings, the memories from this book, the lessons. It all came to me.

In the midst of that hot shame, I looked her in the eye and said, "I'm soo sorry, Mallie. I'm just really tired, and I really need some sleep. Please forgive me. Can you forgive me?"

" I am upset 'cos you were cwoss."

" And I'm really sorry. I'm tired. Is that okay? Do you forgive me?" To my amazement, she smiled, looked up and said,

"Yes". I didn't even sit there for long then. Job done. Let her drop off when she's ready.

If there's nothing else I've got from this book - and there's so much that's shifted - it's that gem. "Be real."

Be genuine. Don't be afraid to fuck up and admit it - but admit it.Be honest - with myself, with my kid, with my parents. Stop looking for approval and dig deeper.

In that moment with Malaika, I honoured her and myself. I am aware. I feel alive.

(February 2003)

Before this book, Mickey and I were suddenly on the phone to one another virtually every day. Both at incredible low ebbs in ourselves, our lives and careers. The only comfort I could take was from reading and sleeping. My light felt dimmed, yet I knew that I didn't want to put it out. He and I talked extremely frankly about this, and from somewhere within the sprawling mess, we started to talk about all the things that had lain neglected or untouched in our hearts. Funny, that Mickey used the term 'boulder' at the beginning. That same phrase had recurred for me in a conversation with my friend Elizabeth after the end of my marriage counselling.

Feeling as if we were fighting invisible obstacles, we didn't even resolve to change our lives. One day we found that we were sitting down tape-recording our most intimate thoughts and feelings, feeling driven by what we kept calling 'life-purpose'.

And it has been, to quote Mickey, "ridiculously easy" to tape, transcribe and edit. But most of all, to work together. As the 'book' began to emerge, we found we were already living it, and I am thrilled to say that I have a close mate like Mickey.

For me, the truest test of our friendship and of the 'truths' in this work came at the end of it. Our last session, to 'sum up', capture 'where we are now' as a result of the book, flowed well. Then, right at the end, I realized that a small button - the 'Voice Activated record' button on the Dictaphone - had been knocked 'on'. With a sinking feeling, I played the tape. Instead of our conversation, the dialogue jumped, jumbled frustratingly close to the point of confusion.

But, as I've described with myself and Malaika, Mickey personified what we had talked about in the book. A real mate. A good bloke. A compassionate 'Father'. He could have got angry at my incompetence ('angry Dad'), and I could have fed it with my guilt. The tape was, after all, 'my' responsibility. I hadn't noticed the button was down...

We could have got into all sorts of roles. Me playing the victim, dramatically accepting the blame, or hotly denying the 'unfairness' of it all (tick one or all of the above).

Instead, he was powerfully succinct, and 'no-nonsense'. "Here's what we can do, here's the challenge, can you make sense of it, Ed?"

He cut through all the sorry possibilities of how the situation could have played out. With steady compassion and strength he held the dramas at bay. And in so doing, broke the pattern for me. Amazingly, all my default behaviours from childhood, still lurking and ready to play: guilt, self-justification, wallowing in the problem, analysis and wanting to explain so that he wouldn't hate and abandon me - seemed to evaporate in the gentle heat of his calm and reasoned approach. My 'child' was allowed by his 'Dad'. Given recognition, but not over-indulged. And so I rose to the challenge, where I could so easily have 'pouted, flounced and lay sobbing on the bed' in despair.

If that's not living this book, then I don't know what is. If this isn't what I wanted, consciously, or subconsciously from this process, then I don't know what I did.

I want mates, buddies, blokes who will tell me to my face, from a place of loving, kind, but strong, criticism, "Stop your bullshit. You're better than that." Who can not just give it, but receive it, because otherwise it would be a bullying power-trip.

The Maoris[84] call this quality 'mana', which is virtually untranslatable. But Nelson Mandela[85] has it. Tony Robbins[86] has it. A strong, centred, compassionate, loving, real man.

And that's what I am turning into. I am.

84. *Maoris. Indigenous people of New Zealand, of Polynesian descent.*

85. *Nelson Mandela. Legendary former President of the African National Congress and Republic of South Africa.*

86. *Tony Robbins. Larger-than-life US motivational guru.* *www.anthonyrobbinsdc.com*

Girlfriends, Boyfriends...

So how's Malaika doing? I haven't seen her since you lived in the tent at the bottom of my garden...

Well, she changes all the time! Weekly. She's good at drawing...

So she's four?

She's four in December!

That means she's going to school and stuff?

No, she's going to be spared that for another year!

So, who looks after her? Her Mum; her grand parents?

Uuum, no – she's in nursery Tuesday and Wednesday. I have her on a Monday and Ayesha has her Thursday and Friday; and she has her every – well – we swap weekends. Every other weekend.

So at this age, what do kids get praise for? Drawing? Writing their name? Or...

Um...

She must have seen you draw all the time! D'ya know what I mean?

Yeah, I mean, it's not just praise, it's like genuine astonishment at the detail, or, you know, what she's able to draw. Yeah, writing, she's picked up her letters – I guess I try to; well I make an effort not to make that focus, 'cos that's all 'achieve, achieve' isn't it?

Yeah

What do I praise her for? Uum... well, yeah, politeness?

Manners...

Behaviour, yeah – being nice. One thing I really make a big thing of is getting her to be direct and ask for what she wants, rather than learning to get it by wheedling or hinting or...

Yeah – manipulation!

Yeah, trying to get me to work out whatever she wants.

But she is a good chatterer anyway!

Oh God yeah!

I'll bet you always know what's going on; not so much how she feels, and stuff, but what's going on at home, her Mother; if she sees her Mother's boyfriend and stuff...

Yes, she talks about Ray, actually!

So you get the truth about everything! Out of the mouths of babes...

Yes! And also because, I guess I'm not judging, like 'Don't tell me about 'him'...' Yes, I guess you're right – 'out of the mouths of babes' is spot-on, actually!

And surely, you share all aspects of your life really, when she's around. Nothing has to be hidden, or...

Well, there've been two really funny things; one of them was, umm, oh a few weeks ago, I was saying to her, "What do you think, should I have a boyfriend or a girlfriend?"

Naaahhhhhh...!

Yes!

How excellent!

And she said "Both!"

Ha ha ha ha ha ha ha!

And yesterday, she was saying, "Umm, Rychard" the Buddhist guy

Who's he?

This guy I met; oh, that's another story... I've met him several times over the years. I've been hanging out with him a lot; and she was saying "Maria is your girlfriend and Rychard is your boyfriend." Ha ha ha oh God, fucking hell! This child is...

That's so cool!

And also, I was telling her this story, the story I made up, for no particular reason, just introducing a character, a sort of side character who's a transvestite. And she just; I giggled that time she says the word 'twansvestite'!

Nah!

She said it so casually...

Hmmm.

'cos we were drawing...

Normal rather than sleazy.

...and she insisted that 'he' was a woman. She said "...draw him without a hairy chest this time!"

Ha ha ha ha ha - So what are you doing pushing hairy trannies on her already?

Well, we just had a story about a dress that ran away from a dress shop, which I made up, you know it's like, I'm so bored of all the 'stock' characters – so it's like an old woman, and a dog, and a magpie, and – 'Tony-the-transvestite', who just happens to be walking down the street, who can't catch the dress because his heels get caught in a drain...

Ha ha ha ha ha!!!

…and he falls over on his face.

Ha ha ha ha ha! Excellent. So go on then, spill the beans about Maria.

Blimey, the beans on Maria…

I thought it was just so excellent that the day before we moved out – the last day – she comes over, and hangs out, and it was good.

Yeah, that's true. That cleaned something out, didn't it?!

Since then; well, before then she wasn't around for quite a while, was she?

Yeah, about a month! But there was still contact.

Is that all?

Yeah!

Seems like a lot more.

God, I don't know what to say really. The old cliché about not feeling committed.

Who, you?

Well both of us really, I; you know relationships make me feel claustrophobic at the moment.

Aww Fuck-me! Same!!! Oh! Anyway…

Ha ha ha ha ha – how can I follow that! Umm, and the same with Rychard, there's been all this kind of moving towards some kind of a relationship and I've just been really clear. I don't want a sexual relationship!

So you haven't 'bonked' either of them then!

Yeah, well I did with her…

Yeah, but in the past, or since?

The amazing thing is that one of the weekends that I had Mallie, Maria and I had been; it was maybe a bit contrived, but Maria and I had decided we would explore 'physical intimacy' without 'fucking' basically... which worked for a while, but one thing just seems to kind of slide into another – so to speak, um, ha ha ha ha ha...

Ha ha ha

... and there was something very pure about this particular day, I think it was the last time Maria and I had sex.

A lot about exploring intimacy rather than just shagging.

Hmmm.

I mean with probably both of them – Rychard and Maria - it's about, you know, the kind of ego or whatever brings up stuff like 'am I playing games?' 'am I manipulating?'

Yeah

But, what it really feels like is 'What do I want?' You know? At the moment. I don't know what I'll want from the future, but for now, being able to, just; it's funny actually, Rychard said something which really touched me. He said "I'm really touched by the way that Mallie and you touch each other all the time. You know, the way you stroke her skin, stroke her hair and her face…

Hmmm

"…and you know, I guess, that's what I want from a man. Not necessarily child-like stuff, but to able to be very physical."

Yeah

In countries like; well I saw this exhibition, actually. There was a picture of these two old Turkish guys walking down the street arm-in-arm. You know, in Pakistan they hold hands, they sit on each others' laps – same for places like Nepal. I guess it's like, you know, we talked about before, the first tentative steps of physical same-sex contact beyond the family. You know, being able to lean up against each other and just normally touch each other.

Also - same for me - the name of the game has been intimacy. Getting over workaholism, drink, drugs, being too high, being too low, whatever. Avoidance of intimacy. Trying to blame childhood, parents, anything and everything. But, I think that's as far as I've got. The whole thing is avoidance of intimacy! Do you know what I mean?

Yeah!

And with that, it turns everything on its head, because it brings it clean, and here, and now. And it touches things. I realise that I don't necessarily want to touch as much as I thought I did; and sometimes when I do, before there is pleasure, it is almost like there is pain, or there's fear, or it's not… it's almost like remembering the reasons of why not to touch.

Say that again, so when you do touch it brings up all these…

Sometimes it can! It's not always necessarily pleasurable, or initially pleasurable, it could be fear first. It could almost be pain on the skin before my insides get over the panic, and the fear, and that kind of adrenaline[87] - and I get more into the mellow endorphin[88] thing. Do you know what I mean? Does this make sense?

Well, is it that touch brings up 'I've got to perform and have sex?'

Oh yes, there's that… but I'm kind of over that now – well I'm not over it, but; fucking hell, it's gone up to six pounds eighty eight! Seems like only yesterday this buffet thing was only a fiver! Still up for it?

I'm easy – well let's have a look…

(in the restaurant)

I was thinking about asking you about Gina.

Tell me about what's his face first...

Who?

There's Maria and...? What's his name?

Rychard. Hmmm. Very interesting! Still haven't quite got a handle on it. I think for him, it's more about being mates than having addictive sex, as in our pasts.

How long have you known him? Who is he?

Um, I met him, first of all about twelve years ago, on an art foundation course. Although I haven't known him for that long because he disappeared from the course. Um, and then I met him again when I went to meditation classes. I kind of met him briefly and then met him about three months ago, when I was down in Silchester. There was kind of like this, yeah – I fancied him. There was something attractive about him. Sexual. Then, ever since the first time we've been out, that was gone! It was like, um...

So you fancied him when you didn't really know him – now you know him you don't really fancy him?

It's funny, we talked quite a lot, because you came up in conversation, I was saying to him that Mickey and I were still processing and festering with a lot of the male/female stuff that we'd talked about. I was saying that I was sure that my mate Mickey would probably hate you because you are really feminine or whatever.

Oh, is he?

Well actually, he's not, in many ways. It's weird. All that's kind of been – I don't know! Not turned around, but I'm; it doesn't make much sense, it's not clear cut. Um...

And is he a practising Buddhist?

Umm! Twelve or thirteen years? And, most interestingly - well not most, but very interestingly – he lives in, they live in sex-segregated communities. Based on the idea that...

Wow!

...you need to have your relationships with women, whatever they are - whether they are friendships, or sexual - need to come out of an all-male environment. Which I find... most fascinating!

So where does he live and where does he work?

Well he lives in a, well it's a small community. They all, pretty much; people work outside, or in Buddhist businesses around town. He's a therapist, there are other therapists, one is a nurse, loads of different things. It's very communal. He even shares a room with another guy, which I would find quite challenging. And it's reasonably spacious, but...

How old is he?

Let's just say, he's oldest friend I've ever had!

So that's his life? He's lived there for a long time...

Pretty much. Umm, I mean, most of them spend a lot of time going off on retreat or whatever, but it's very much about being grounded in everyday life – and there's a really strong sense of community. I mean, going with him walking around the streets, he bumped into some ten or fifteen people – it must be what living in a village used to be like. Really nice.

How long has he lived there?

In this community, he's lived for about ten years.

Wow!

Which I find slightly unimaginable, living in one place for ten years. It's a bit like; I wouldn't mind trying it. I feel really drawn to it. It's like a community without being contrived.

So the men live in the men's house, and the women live in the women's house. Where do they get together then? Do they have sex and stuff? He he he

Well I don't think all of them shag all of them, but...

So it's not a 'no sex' type sect?

It's a what?

It's not a 'no sex' sect?

No! I mean, I don't know a lot about them. About the foundation of it. I think there's a lot of gay men there, but there's also a lot of straight men. It's lovely! ...to see such a range of men, in one community.

Is it open?

Well, yeah! Obviously gay people, there are obviously straight people, and some obviously who-knows-what... Um, I don't know about sex, because the women aren't allowed in the men's community and the men aren't allowed in the women's. So I'm not quite sure where the 'rumpy-pumpy' might take place.

So are you gonna move in there?

I'll probably try and get into a house-share around September and then get more involved in the community. Again it's the 'c' word, it brought up commitment. It's like, 'Oh my God... how could I become a Buddhist?' You know, what about my valuable time? I've got this thing about time and the scarcity of it.

So your relationship with him is non-sexual, it's really a first! Also he's older.

Yeah.

Which is nice.

You wouldn't particularly think it though! I mean I thought that he's in his early forties.

Really. And where does this boyfriend thing come into it? Do you know what I mean?

What, with what Malaika said?

No, with anyone! Why did the boyfriend thing come up if you were just mates?

Yeah, I think because of; it was like a time lag, you know, meeting him, when I had found him very attractive. I mean, I was a different person then. Even a year ago, when I last saw him, six or seven years ago. And it's challenging because he's a gay man. And, well, he said initially he really wanted to have a sexual relationship, and... it just doesn't figure. Well, we've explored the boundaries of physicality. We went on holiday to Cornwall. We slept together in the same bed, with no clothes on, but no, that sexual thing didn't seem to be there.

Powerful. Not to have to do it, eh... No clothes leads to a shag.

It's like circling though, isn't it?

Hmmm.

Circling the edge; talk about living on the edge...

Yeah.

Habit, it's just so strong. No, I think it brings up a lot of stuff. Well, both of us were sexually addicted. It feels like... I was going to say it feels like a very healing friendship. Sounds wanky.

Hmmm. But all the same, might be the best kind of relationship a man can have.

Ha ha ha ha ha

No not wanking! Healing. Friendship. And also with a Father-figure.

Hmmm.

A mentor, someone that has been there, someone that has been that age, or through that 'thing', had those worries; he'll tell you the truth rather than give you the appropriate answers depending on 'whatever politics'.

Hmmm. Also, there's an interesting kind of flow to it, like on holiday. I said to him about half way through, "Sometimes I feel really old, like I'm older than you, as if you're my son or my kid brother. Other times I feel like you're my big brother." It struck me, I never had a big brother. It's great, I think I said before that my younger brother used to kind of be really playful and just jump on me and...

Yeah

...I do that with Rychard. He just kind of – yeah great! – shrugs and fights back a bit and it's really cool!

So does he know your friends, or family or anyone?

He's met my parents; he loves Malaika! And this is the other weird thing – he's never had kids, obviously – we went out with his Mother and her Eastern European carer, and you could tell that this woman just fell in love with Mal. Women with kids is just extraordinary – the carer was almost in tears! Mallie came in the front door of this flat, literally this woman hugged her like she's never seen a child before, she had tears in her eyes.

Wooow...

Turns out she's got grand kids back home – so they doted on her all day! But what was really odd was – what was fascinating, because he told me this afterwards – we were down by the river in Henley, and Mallie – well, you know what kids are like – she climbed up on a bench, she climbed up on to someone's private boat and was playing with the wheel...

Aha ha ha ha

...and I just thought, 'fuck it, let her play'. You should have seen his Mother's face, everything was panic, fear, when she was saying "Be careful", "You'll fall off", "Be careful you'll fall in the river!" then Mallie brought a bunch of elderberries over, she was eating them, and his Mother said "Oh watch out my darling, you'll get stains on your dress!" and I must admit that there was a part of me that just wanted to strangle her and just say 'fucking hell, give the kid a break! She's three and a half! The stains will wash out!' – okay, the river, yeah! It may be slightly dangerous...

Fair enough, but not perpetual panic!

...no, and it was, it was perpetual panic. But what was interesting, we were driving back afterwards, after we had dropped Malaika off to her Mother, and Rychard said he had felt so angry because that's how he was brought up. Every other thing was "That's dangerous..."

'Precious, precious, precious.'

...you know, and again I've said to him, look, do you really think you're gay, or do you think you're just; and, you know, I kind of teased him a lot about being a Mummy's-boy, you know, as one ex-Mummy's-boy to another, whatever. You can see the way it moulds people. Totally!

Yeah.

87. *Adrenaline. Hormone from the adrenal glands, which increases heart rate and raises blood pressure. Triggered by stress in preparation for 'fight or flight'.*

88. *Endorphin. Substances produced by the brain and pituitary gland, with pain-killing and other properties. Similar to morphine.*

Approving Fathers

And, his Father – it seems a bit unfair to talk about Rychard so much – his Dad died when he was in his teens. It all fits together...

Yeah!

Very much.

It's been; if there's one thing I've achieved since leaving that house these last two months, is having a fucking excellent summer holiday. The one thing that has changed my life – I don't panic. I used to always panic. Panic about bills, or things that need to be done, or where I'm supposed to be, or what I'm supposed to do, or who I've upset, or who I should be pleasing, or whose – you know, second-guessing? Meanwhile, there's no life! Of course it's safe to be a workaholic, or an anything addict, because you've got to release the panic somehow, and that's straight into something else that you're addicted to and do it like crazy – so you get away from being under panic like crazy! But, well two things actually. With the panic; it wasn't just *my*

Mother, my Mother made me a Mummy's-boy, and she was precious, protective, over-caring, loving panic – where my Father's panic was threats.

Yeah...

Threats! 'This will happen', 'That will happen'...

Fear

Yeah, exactly, the fear of God! And I just don't hear 'my Father's voice' any more. And I used to hear it all the time – everywhere. No matter what I did, I just heard my Father's fear-panic; and he wouldn't even need to say anything. It was just a feeling – I would feel my pores close up, like the temperature had dropped, we used to call it 'cuckoo skin' in Africa – goose bumps. I do not hear him anymore, plus, I don't think he's that person anymore.

That's the key thing, changing your relationship to your Father.

Hmmm. And I'm not sure for how long he hasn't been that person. Plus, in the last two months communication has changed anyway, but - Fuck, what a relief. And it's just amazing not to have that; it's a bit of; it's almost; I think maybe there's a part of; no there wasn't even a phase of insecurity where without the panic voice there was no voice. It was just panic – to nothing! But then the other thing that's really weird, that's changed, is I used to always say I wanted to be like Lui and Lui used to say he wanted to be like me. I do things, I say things, I act things, whatever. And it's not his words or his anything, but after I've done that, with such confidence, ease, truth, honesty, purity and; not the nonsense pretty-boy egotistical shit, but the raw - right and wrong. I want – I don't want. Honesty, whatever it is. And once I've done it I think, fuck! That was like Lui. That's where I've learned this. And it's not like, it's not like being Lui, it's like being honest – ha ha ha – or… is that making sense?

Kind of.

I used to want to be like him. Now I find that all the bits that I wanted to be like Lui…

Surely what you are saying, or what you are getting, is that it's not really that you are being like Lui, but you are discovering those qualities in yourself, or how you do it, rather than how…

Permission to be honest!

Yeah!

Without the threats. Basically, which is the other side, I mean Lui is 'my

Father', again. Which is the other side of my Father — strong! When something is wrong, it's wrong. There's no haggling and that's fucking strong. *It's almost like dumping the panic side of my Father and picking up the fair, just, um, respectful, totally-cool-man part of my Father* that I forgot, because I was just so bullied by the 'cunt' for so long. Ha ha ha ha ha ha ha

Well, it's weird, isn't it! Being bullied by our Fathers who...

...is the person you love the most and the person you hate the most?

Yeah! Well also, who have they been bullied by?

Well, their Fathers, their family, their environment, blah blah blah... And it's the same old story of 'yeah, didn't they do well considering how fucked-up they were, blah blah blah...'

Yeah. Definitely! Tell you something, I've been going to this group, which is basically kind of 'sound healing', 'sound work', whatever. I mean, I didn't have any idea, really, that it would bring up all this 'stuff'! It delves out all these memories of childhood. I've been having one-to-one sessions with this amazing woman — incredible stuff. And about two weeks ago all this stuff came up about seeking my Dad's approval and going back to being about twelve, thirteen or fourteen. I was at this critical juncture where I felt like I either choose 'the real me' whoever I am, whatever my essence might be, or I seek my Father's approval. It was really clear, of course, what would you do? You want your Dad's approval. So I went on to do all this stuff to get his approval. In this process, with Lesley, this woman, and basically, she was saying *"You've been blaming him for your failures, for your not succeeding, for your inability to commit to things, and that's not doing anyone a service."* So she said that what I need to do when I next see him, is to say this to him. So to cut a long story short, coming back from holiday in Cornwall, Rychard and I stopped off at their house. Just as I was about to leave I remembered that I was supposed to say this to him and I thought 'fuck!'. So I shouted to him from the stairs and he came into the living room and just before I could say anything, my Mum appeared and said "Yes, what did you want?"

Ha ha ha ha ha – she what?

And I looked at her and said "No, I just want to speak to Dad." So she left, looking really quite pissed off. Then I thought, 'oh my God, how am I going to say this to him? Open your mouth and trust'. And I just said, "Look, I've been doing this work with sound and stuff's come up and I realise that I have been blaming you for a lot of the things that I have been unhappy about. All my personal fears and failures." And he just beamed... He actually said *"I forgive you."*

Faaking hell!

The point was that it didn't matter what his reaction was or anything, just for me to say that, for me to 'own' something and admit to it, which was just like; before I would say 'I'm not budging, he's to blame. It's all his fault!' Suddenly, with that space...

I remember that day that you, me and Billy hung out.

That was great!

Yeah. Yeah, the Men's Group[89], but 'the' thing is Billy saying...

Hmmm.....!

Ha ha ha ha ha! Okay, you may as well say it then, then you can switch the tape off and we can get some more fucking food – I'm hungry!

Yeah I really reflected on this, in fact when I got back afterwards I wrote a letter to my Dad, which I haven't shared or sent to him. He asked me a while ago what we actually did at our Men's Group. So I started the letter saying, 'Well, you wanted to know, this is what we talked about today...' So I said to him – it was funny – I described that moment in real vivid detail, I mean, when our jaws hit the floor.

Yeah! He he he he he he

I just thought it was amazing to be able to say to him, 'Yeah, well what do I admire about you?' What am I proud of in my Father...

Hmmm

...and...

The essence of what Billy said was, hmmm, us dedicating our lives to being, to getting our Fathers' approval and our Fathers being proud of us. *But how do they feel about how we feel about them?*

Exactly. Turn it around.

Yeah, totally! And all my life, my fears; I don't fix things, um, don't know how to play football, probably crap at catching and throwing – I haven't done it for so long and I was crap the last time I tried it – and you know, put myself down for sports, rather than the one or two things I may be good at, so I'd be a crap Father. And my whole, for how many years have I been scared of being a Father because he wouldn't approve of me?

Hmmm

I forgot.

Yes, that really was amazing! And...

A real turn-around!

Yeeees... Yes, funny for me 'cos as I say, I'm just going off to see my folks for a few days. It feels – something else that Billy said – you know, our parents want to be close to us! They want real love and they want real connection. There's, I mean, there's so much stuff going on anyway, but there's also this, 'cut the ties', 'be your own independent person', 'put 'em in an old people's home as soon as possible', I don't know, it just kind of melted my heart! A sort of sense of, bloody hell, you know, they want, they do want this connection but they don't know how to get it.

Yeah. Yeah. And we probably rejected them last. Over and over, a few times.

Yeah…

The one thing that's really going through my mind, is, what a fucking cunt I can be by stamping my feet and saying *how dare my parents not be enlightened - in every way - before they had me.* Ha ha ha ha ha ha ha… 'The sheer audacity! Huh! Like, don't they have any sense of responsibility?!' Do you know what I mean?

They know… whatever they know!

Otherwise I wouldn't have 'chosen' this family, or life situation to 'jump into this lifetime', to remind me what I'm supposed to learn, or unlearn, or what I'm supposed to contribute here 'this time around.' And, whatever it is that we're supposed to do with our karmic shit with each other, and all that. Do you know what I mean?

I know, what you just said about…

What, about Rychard – I didn't know he was so old, how cool that he's so old…

Hmmm

…and that it's so not an issue, that you'd even consider sex with him.

Hmmm. But what came up when you said that, was, I just thought about how nice it is to be with an older man who is so affirmative, you

know? He says things like "You are really good fun to be with!" and "You make me laugh!", you know, just kind of going on walks.

Hmmm

I was saying to my sister – she's been doing some life-coaching with this woman in Scotland and through that, she's met this older man who's also a life-coach, who is about the same age as my Dad, in his 50's or 60's. She's gone to see him a couple of times because he said, "Look, I felt that you are ahead of the others in the group and I wanted to work with you one-to-one", so it's like, 'Wow! Great!' She was saying the same, you know, people have gone 'oh he's after sex', or 'you know…'

Yeah.

And she said, "Well, I don't think, I don't feel like he is; and even if he was, I feel like I would be able to handle it." She said it… again it's having a positive older man. For her, the same issues, you know, whatever she may feel about my Mum. A lot of her stuff comes from negativity about my Dad.

Yeah. Do you know, when you said that, about what Rychard said to you, it reminded me of, um; Lui and I had a client, who actually 'won us' in a competition! The family won our feng shui services from a newspaper. And I spent good time with him, with her, spent time with the kids. There was one stage where after he and I went off and talked, we came back, we were in the house, we might have had something to eat – I don't remember – but he was doing something with the boy, the Father, with his son, and he said to him – I don't remember the son's name, but say Ben. He said *"Ben, I really like being with you…*

Waaaw

"…and do you know why I like being with you? I like being with you because you're

good fun!"

Hmmm!!!

And I choked up, Lui looked away, as soon as we were out of the house we were both just so on the verge of tears, because – we had never heard it before!

Hm

But imagine how that boy is going to grow up! And he got proper attention. And he was well behaved. He wasn't just another spoilt bastard from a rich family, or a poor family. But it was… honest.

Yeah

And if you get that, then surely they'll listen, and you can reason with them; oh I'd been thinking, Caetano reminded me of, um, the way my family – particularly my God Mother – but my grand Mother and my Mother – not so much my Mother – would just say weird things, scare us about weird things, like the 'gasia lorry man' - which is 'dustbin man' in Swahili - will come and take you away, because you are stupid. Well, my brother, he was dyslexic, no one knew. So he didn't know his b's from his d's – they treated him like he was being bad, like he was doing something wrong. And then there's all sorts of threats, I mean I can't think of many now, but really weird threats about what people are going to do to you, where they are going to throw us away, what's going to happen to us, and… we were kids!

Yeah.

…and so much of that, we believed! Because we were trying to make sense of this conversation that didn't make sense, because it was so full of lies anyway.

Yup.

How do we know?

It's funny you say that, because, um, with Mallie, she was walking

away from us and my friend said to her "Are you alright?" And she replied "I just need some space!"

Waaaw…!

And the friend looked at me, and I said, rather smugly, well just proudly, it's like 'be proud of it…', "It's a concept that I've introduced." 'cos there are times when, however much you love your kids, you know, they're wriggling around on your lap, sticking their hand down your trousers, constant for five hours, just like…

He he he he he he

…I don't want to get to the stage where I turn around to her and tell her to fuck off!

Hmm.

So, the concept of, yeah, right… 'five minutes space, I'm going over here, you stay over here, draw, play, whatever, but I really don't want any disturbance, so I'm going to sit for ten minutes or something, by myself' - it seems to have been introduced really effortlessly.

Cool.

But what I didn't expect was for her to do it herself - ha ha ha ha ha - it's like, 'it's good enough for Daddy…'

Hmmm.

'… so it's good enough for Mallie!'

Hmmm!

89. *Men's group. A group of men, usually supportive in some form, to relieve isolation from / gain the company of other men, for therapy and growth, or masculine exploration.*

Parenting vs abuse

And you have to honour that, really. But, coming back to what you were saying, what sparked it was, our parents really didn't have the resources. They didn't know that... *my God it's exhausting being around children all the time. You're going to want to knock their heads off.*

Yeah! But still perform differently in front of other people.

Definitely! I mean that's what so much of 'public embarrassment' is about.

Two rules, very often, isn't it?

Yeah!

One for home and one for 'out'.

Yeah. Yeah, and it is tricky sometimes. I don't want to discourage Mallie from making noise in public. But it is partly socialising and sometimes it feels like a tragedy. You know, to have to be the one who...

'Birch your child, flog them over the desk...'

...exactly!

But if the child understands why, perfect! But rather than telling them why; I mean, generally, the threats that my brother and I, and our whole family went through, no explanation. But, my Father... *"Do you want to feel the back of my hand?!"* "Don't answer back!" "Don't ask questions all the time!" so what… what are we supposed to learn from that?

I sometimes wonder if I do take it a bit too far, and I know if I don't; I mean we were on the train coming back from my folks', I think it was that really hot Monday a couple of weeks ago, might have been a bank holiday, quite a crowded train back from Waterloo to Ayesha's and Mallie had actually taken off all her clothes except her under pants. She was climbing up this pole between the seats and, you know, just kinda shouting and making noise. Most of the people were either indifferent or doing that kind of slight shy, benign smile that people on trains do in this country when they are obviously really thrilled, but… 'better not show it', huh…

Or don't know how to join in.

'Mustn't engage'. I noticed this, kind of, 'suit' sitting behind her and slightly kind of twitching, a couple of times, and then she made quite a loud noise and he went 'like that' *(wordlessly snarled around)* he turned really fast but didn't say anything. He just, like, opened his mouth like a Rottweiller, and I picked her up and said "OK, you'd better be quiet now." And this was just before we got to our stop. Afterwards, we were walking away from the station, she was in the pushchair, and it just came over me. I stopped the pushchair and I knelt down and looked her in the eye at head height and I said to her,

"Mallie, I just want to apologise to you because I told you to be quiet when that man; he should have asked us for what he wanted." And I said "It wasn't fair of me to make you be quiet when he hadn't asked for it." It was like, I was thinking, is this really complicated? But I got a sense that…

She got something.

…Yes! She understood.

Well, at least you didn't confuse her by, you know, this new unspoken rule that 'I will abandon you, if you get it wrong…'

Yeah

'…or punish you.'

Exactly. Like you were saying, you don't know what it was about. But at least if your parents are making an effort to acknowledge that; why should we be the ones to make them shut up…

Rather than, 'wait 'til your Father gets home', or 'you're going to be sent to boarding school!'

But I wanted to say to that bloke, like 'look, if you've got something to say, I'd really like you to say it.' But that would sound very confrontational.

But also, you have to protect her because you don't want an explosion.

Hmm. But you're right, you know, about our parents learning. God, kinda corny, but definitely forgiveness and understanding. The more we understand about how they got it wrong, or even not got it wrong, but how *they just didn't have the tools…*

…hmmm, *or the knowledge, or the resources.*

Hmmm. But for me, I'd say that working on myself is important just to get over the crap that bothers me sometimes; but maybe I'm doing it more for my kid…

Lui and I were on the Underground – not the first time this has happened, either – and this huge, beast-of-a-woman with a gorgeous little child – don't remember if was a boy or a girl, think it was a little boy – time to get off. The ugly bitch was obviously in a panic about her crap life and everything, and she started shouting at him, and threatening him, you know, all they were doing was getting off the Tube. And I turned around and said something, but she didn't hear. And then Lui sort of shouted at her, and then I shouted after Lui did, but not overly aggressive, but just that she'd - actually, no, it was quite aggressive - because the way she was going at the child; to stop her, to draw attention to her behaviour and try to bring her sharply to her senses. So she got off the Tube – and total respect to Lui, he's the man! I'm not good at that kind of stuff. And I kind of think - I think too much. Confrontation and trying to look, you know, whatever…

Up your own arse.

…Blatant fear, basically. Fuck knows what else! So, she goes off after hearing the both of us, and then she comes to the window, you know, really looking for a fight – huge thing! – and she starts, banging on the window, flicking the V's[90], shouting "Come out here and say that!" and "If you got a problem…" and I said something about treating the child like a dog, or whatever, but mine was crap. Lui was spot-on! Ha ha ha ha ha ha

So you were both in another Tube?

No, she was leaving the Tube.

Oh, I'm with you…

But, it hurts. Especially in buses, Tubes… women that shouldn't have had kids in the first place!

That's interesting that that happened, because down in Cornwall, Rychard and I were, totally different scenario, certainly not the stresses of the Tube. We'd gone to a National Trust house, literally, just having a picnic – it sounds terrible, but in the car park, on the grass verge.

He he he he he

It was a nice house – and we were in the car park. There were picnic tables around, and we sat down and just behind us - I didn't even notice them particularly - but you know how you kind of catch a flare-up in a family group? I looked over and this guy was sitting across the table from a teenaged boy, must have been about twelve or thirteen,

something like that - and what I caught, in the middle of this family group of Mother and older boy and younger daughter. The Father was leaning across the table and he had the son by the lapels of his shirt, the collar of his shirt, and I was like 'whoa, what the hell's going on there?' I could kind of feel the vibe coming off, the violence, or something, confusion. At first it was hard to tell if it was a jokey situation, and then *the boy slapped his Father across his face* like backhand, forehand, backhand, about ten times. I didn't hear what the Father said, but he slapped, he kind of whacked his son around the face, and he got up and the older son walked off with him, put his arm around him and they were walking away really furiously. The Father looked back, saying something like "You should be ashamed of yourself." It just went right into my heart. My whole body just started quivering. The boy who had been hit was howling. The Mother was just sitting there, don't know what she was – she wasn't doing anything. Anyway, they walked off and I just said "Aah fucking hell..." to Rychard. "God, that was really hard to watch and not take part in it." Then we went off into this talk about, I don't know...

What do you do, though?

I said to him, without being melodramatic, that's how fascism[91] starts, because people stop taking part. They stop being involved, or they feel embarrassed, or fearful, or whatever. You know, I was saying that I really felt like I needed to do something – but I don't know what. So I was saying, "Gosh, maybe... maybe I could go off and talk to him about Steven Biddulph[92] or something, you know, 'Raising Boys'[93]."

Ha ha ha ha ha ha

So they walked off, they disappeared, you know, they went into the house, we went around the house and it took me a long time to recover from it, because it really just struck something. Deep. Anyway, about an hour later we were walking around the grounds near the sea and first I saw the Mother and the older boy, and then down at the

253

bottom of the hill was Father and younger boy - who had been hit - and the girl. It's like I was saying to John in the Men's Group, you know when your heart pounds, it's like your heart's saying 'you've got to say something or this will just get stuck somewhere in your body and you'll get cancer, or whatever. 'You know - because you know you have to speak from your 'higher-self', or whatever – and I said to Rychard, "Look, I've really got to say something…" and he gave me this look, as if to say 'Are you serious?' and he hung back, and he said "I'll leave you to it…" and I thought, 'I've no idea what will happen, he might be a psycho!' 'cos I almost, in 'the gap', decided he was mad and that's why he was doing it. I just went up to him and said, you know, very English "I'm sorry to disturb you, but I just wanted to check that everything was alright. I was really affected by what happened earlier." And he gave me this look of 'what happened earlier?' And I said, "When you and your son were obviously having something happening between the two of you." And he kind of went, "Ah yeah!" And the kids at that stage started saying "Come on Dad, come on Dad…" pulling him away, and he said to them "No, you go and play somewhere." Because he realised it's obviously like a man-to-man talk. And, we just had this incredibly interesting conversation. He just – oh no, I said to him, because I couldn't work out what's happening… I asked him if he'd heard of Steven Biddulph. "You know, he's written books about raising boys and families." And he said, "Oh yes, I know Steven Biddulph, I've met him!" And it turned out he'd done this workshop…

Really!

Blah blah blah… But what was so extraordinary was, the way it, for me, it completely cleared anything I was feeling, any sort of anxiety. What we basically said, or our conclusion to the conversation was that kids are everyone's responsibility, you know, it's like all the papers bang on about society falling apart, no respect, none of this, it's like, well, we're encouraged not to be involved in things and it's none of our business; but these things are happening in public. What are we supposed to do? Turn our backs on it? Cry into our beer?

Hmmm!

And this guy was completely open. Turned out that - and again interesting seeing his side of the story! Because we only got a little snap-shot. - Apparently his son had told him to "Fuck off!" and he said he was really pushing it. This guy was German. He said it didn't mean as much to him as swearing in German. But you know, of course, he realised what it meant. He said he had started off joking with him. But then, when your son hits you across the face, what do you do? He didn't know quite how to handle it. But his instinct was, it hurt…

Yeah, yeah.

…if someone hits you on the face, it hurts and this is what it feels like. Which is definitely pushing political correctness.

Wow! Fine line. Very fine; but how cool that you found out!

Yeah! That's, actually, you're right, that's the key! You know, there is a column in *'The Guardian'*⁹⁴, parents sharing information. 'My four year old, or whatever, keeps biting other kids. She's bitten me sometimes. I've heard that biting a child shows them what it feels like. What do other parents think?' And about half the parents who responded said the same. 'I bit my child' - ha ha ha *(nervously)* - 'to stop…'

Really?

'And they've never done it again, because…'

But they'd probably never admit it to their friends. These are the things, the information, we all need to know what other people are doing and what works.

Definitely.

I mean, what do you do? Either allow the kids; they could bring them up quite well, but the best friend, the neighbour, their cousins; could be brought up like an absolute 'junglie', what do you call them, an imbecile, so what do you do? Do you keep yours away from those kids? Do you explain to them later? Different rules for your kids? Does that make your kids less 'cool' to the other kids who are allowed to do what they want?

I don't know, actually. I mean, I suppose, to me, when I see Mallie, it doesn't tend to be with other kids that often. She has a lot of her time with Ayesha with other kids, and at nursery. God knows what they get up to at nursery. I'd like to be a fly on the wall! Um, we don't know a lot about what goes on while we're not there. Ah, but then they'd change their behaviour when the parents are around - I'd have to be a spy! - Um, I mean peer pressure. A lot of parents buy ice creams, sugary things for her, and of course she loves it...

Hmmm

...and mostly I think, well, from time to time it doesn't hurt. I know it's not the same behaviour, but, getting that balance between the child feeling like they are a freak, because they don't get to do anything that other kids do.

Yeah.

But again, I think that if you explain why and let them know that they are not being punished, like 'I don't want to show you love by giving you stuff that's going to rot your teeth!'

Hmmm

'Give you hyperactivity, or...'

Something weird just crossed my mind. You and Maria making love. I wonder, when I was a kid, in Africa, I shared a room with my parents, and then my brother did too. 'Cos my grandparents had another room, but after they left for Goa their room was just a spare room. *So where did my brother come from? They must have been 'at it' while I was in the room.* So, did I see them? Did I hear them? Did I pretend to be asleep? Was I freaking out? Did I sleep through the whole thing all those years?

Because you didn't know what they were doing...

Then I imagine it would have seemed quite scary and painful. And that must have been the case for many people in Third World countries, that they have sex in front of their kids. Have you ever heard of anyone referring to how they deal with a kid catching them 'at it'?

There is a book called 'Three In A Bed'[95]**, which is about – not what the title suggests – about sharing your bed with your kids. And there are some good stories in there. Um, apparently, one little kid piped up in front of his grandparents, that he woke up one night and his Mummy and Daddy were playing – what was it? Something like – horsey riding next to him. The grandparents went "Oooh, how embarrassing..."**

Ha ha ha

Obviously the parents had explained, maybe in slightly naff terms, that this was their way of having fun and it's better than that 'freezing'... 'Oh shit, they've seen us at it!' 'They've caught us!'

I heard of a guy with a foot fetish. Have I told you about this? It started when he was playing with his train, or whatever in the passageway outside his parents' bedroom. His parents were dressing to go out for the evening, she was putting her stockings on, reaches her leg out, rolling it up her leg and as she does this the kid caught her playfully brushing Daddy's crotch with her foot. In a split second the Father saw the son, kind of panicked, cast a dirty look, maybe shouted – I don't think he even shouted – but there was a 'funny vibe'. Panicked look, closed the door *and that's where the fetish started.*

Hmmm. And even not to do with sex. I mean I told you and Billy about that scene on the train with the American family - do you remember? - the Father and the three sons and the Mother.

No...

Well they got on the train, at Vauxhall. The Mother and the two older sons, who were teenagers, say fourteen and twelve, something like that, were all having a laugh. The oldest was standing next to the Mother, the middle son was kind of, I suppose if you had to categorise him, the older son seemed kind of boy-ish turning into a man. The middle one was still, probably hormones all over the place. Quite hysterical, giggly, really laughing, madly. And the older son sort of linking between the two of them. He'd laugh a lot with the younger son, then say to his Mom "Aw Mawm, he's just crazy isn't he?" But what was really striking was that the Father, who looked like an 'all-American-beefcake' or whatever, stood with his back to the group, completely ignoring them all, holding the youngest kid's hand really tightly. And there was like this kind of weird 'transference' because the Father's face was really grim and the little boy looked like he was going to burst into tears. You know, they were completely separated from the rest of the family. You could tell that there was something going on. And again, it's nothing massively dramatic, or violent, involving fists or hands or anything. After a while, the Father just turned around and really hissed at the middle son to be quiet. It just really reminded me about my past. It's like 'don't be exuberant', 'shut up', 'girls…'

Play dead! No expression! Not that there are good expressions or bad expressions, this is appropriate or this is inappropriate… die.

Yeah, exactly. Like having a blanket thrown over you.

With all my most embarrassing problems, twitching and grunting, obsessive-compulsive and God knows what…

Hmmm

…my brother reminded me about this. He said that, um, especially with my Father, I was treated as if I was doing something against the family, something bad, embarrassing, rather than my dysfunction being some sort of a reaction or unconscious cry for help, or, maybe 'there's something up here'!

Yeah. So I guess what I am starting to get from this, for a start, we should all summon the courage to be involved. It's not like become a kind of 'thought police', but when something really feels wrong like you were describing or I was describing, just to go in with the right attitude, that's not kind of 'right, I'm going to sort you out...'

Exactly, not looking for a fight.

Yeah, just like 'what is this all about?' People need to be taught how to ask for help, to parent...

There aren't so many teachers around, but we're not short on critics! Everyone is like 'that's wrong, so I need to put it right, I'm out for a fight'. But, you know, if someone half my age approached me and was on the same side and said something to me, I'd be so grateful! But, if someone did it, not even in a confrontational way but in a way that I didn't feel was on the same side, I'd be too scared and freaked out and I'd react like a wuss! And I'd probably fight back, for the sake of – panic, I suppose. It comes back to panic, doesn't it! Fear, panic...

90. *Flicking the V's. Telling somebody to fuck off, using two fingers of the right hand.*

91. *Fascism. Started by Benito Mussolini in Italy, after World War I. Like a colony of ants, every individual works for the 'collective' (invisible queen).*

92. *Steven Biddulph. Australian author on parenting, families and social change. www.stevebiddulph.com*

93. *'Raising Boys' Steven Biddulph (Harper-Collins) 1997.*

94. *'The Guardian' UK left-ish broadsheet newspaper. www.guardian.co.uk*

95. *'Three In A Bed' Deborah Jackson & Tom Newton (Bloomsbury) 1990.*

Wild Man of Box Hill

Where have you been living?

In my tent.

Where?

Box Hill.

Where's that?

Surrey.

Where about?

The National Trust[96] wood in Box Hill.

Oh, it's illegal?

Hmmm.

You're not supposed to be there?

Dunno.

Is it quite well known? Because I can never remember its name.

Ummm, it's a big biking place. They just go there.

Ummm, ley lines[97] or something?

There's something there. It is definitely a powerful magic place.

And what's it near?

Errr, Dorking...

How did you end up there?

Well *after I moved out of the tent in your back garden*, umm; I can still remember, actually, having a day, well, of panic actually! I just thought, I don't want to go back indoors, and I don't want to end up in just any old house share, I remember I was working - massaging somebody - and it was suddenly, just like the idea, I'd had a really desperate half a day but I'd given up being desperate and I'd finally 'got out of my own way'. This idea just popped 'fully formed' into my head – 'go and camp in the woods'. Come into town, wash in the river; it's kind of weird how modern technology – because I need a phone for my work – makes it all so possible.

So didn't you ever get freaked out by the Bogie Man? The *'Blair Witch Project'*[98]? Things that creep about in the dead of night and wanna come get ya?

While I was living there it felt like a breakthrough. What is there to be scared of? And wouldn't it be great to take your kids, boys... no girls! Why should girls be afraid of the dark? I don't want my daughter being...

Yeah, exactly!

...learned helplessness. Increasingly I can see how much we're controlled by fear – and so much of it is so, so subtle. And it comes from so early on, yeah? Relentlessly.

So you've been staying in the woods, in the same space, for the last six weeks – is it six weeks since we moved out of Muswell Hill?

Yeah! I had the odd night here and there, with Rychard or Maria...

Oh, is it cool to stay there?

Yeah! He's in a great community. They are such nice guys. Really friendly! It just feels really grounded and, dunno, just a good place. Um, and I had about a week, where, I dunno, it was quite timely, some friends were away for a week and they just said "Do you wanna stay in our house?" I felt like I'd be able to do a lot of artwork or – sort of – artwork or creative stuff at night there and I wasn't doing that at the tent because it was dark.

Yeah.

There was a bit, yeah, I suppose it's a weird thing actually, having the light - that was when I became afraid. When I was in total dark, I felt secure...

Yeah?

...like there was no way that you could attract anyone's attention. But if I had been sat there with a torch...

Ahhh

...in a tent...

Yeah

...what if someone sees that!

Yeah, yeah, seems very visible! What is it, comfortable to be invisible or was it safe to be invisible? Or both?

Aaaah...!

Were you hiding? Do you know what I mean?

Good question... I suppose there is definitely an element of distancing myself from what seems like a mad society. But, no I think a lot of it was, just, almost beyond a conscious decision. It was just like 'I have to be there'. Um, as you say, getting over all these fears! And I feel much happier about the thought of living in a house again. You know? It's like; and partly it was so that I could take away the, the outgoings required for rent...

Council tax and bills and

...all the usual.

How much was I paying?

£600 in rent, weren't you?

Yup, plus £100 for council tax and bills - £700 per month. That's before I've even eaten. Plus travel obviously! And self-employed tax... and so it goes on...

Do you remember that network marketing company I was part of? It was part of their 'sales pitch' to get people to join, but there was this really convincing internet site called *'Work Versus Prison – What's The Difference?'* but it's absolutely true for a lot of people. Somebody else sets the rules.

I feel like I've been really lucky that with work I've been able to go into so many people's lives and see that if you 'do this', 'this will happen' – if you 'act like this', 'that will happen', blah blah blah...

Hmmm

...but one thing that struck me is, going through people's history, what happened at this age, or that age, blah blah blah, so many people say that "Between the ages of, say, twenty three and twenty nine I worked for 'MEES Ltd'," or, "Between the ages of twenty and twenty six I was with 'The HAL Corp'"; so I say, "Okay, what happened in your life?" And they say, "I went to Mexico one year; or a couple of little trips abroad every year", but it's *all these huge big chunks of lives that they gave away to the company which they sold their souls to.* Sure it's justified with workaholism, the addiction to adding value to property or moving and moving, high expenses and paying bills and debts and all that. Absolute toss! It's just 'lets play dead for all those years' while waiting to die. Just avoidance – absolute avoidance. Justified, maybe even mostly encouraged, because that's what the family has done for generations. Maybe it's the path of the poor family that has done well. The other one that people talk about is drugs. "Oh, between 1997 and 2001 I was a drug addict…"

Hmmm

96. *The National Trust. UK organisation holding parks and houses 'in trust for the nation'.*

97. *Ley lines. Channels of energy that run through the earth (invisible to the eye).*

98. *'The Blair Witch Project' (1999) Eduardo Sanchez & Daniel Myrick, USA.*

Imaginary friends

...and then they go into their glamorous stories of "I should be dead because I took this this this this this, and I did that that that that and that drug..." and to glamorise it even more, "I was a dealer, and I..." – you know, it just goes on. But it's a load of toss! Over the festival I had the most brilliant time recently.

Which festival was it?

'Nirvana', which they don't advertise, and - you know - there was only one and a half thousand people there. It was just the best! There was a 'secret area', fires everywhere, really good music, good people, healing stuff, food, you know whatever.

Hmmm

Um, there was... you know the way people sell things at festivals, food, drink, whatever it is. This guy was going around when it was quite dark and he started shouting "Imaginary friends! Imaginary friends...

Ha ha ha

"Three for a pound! Guaranteed to like you!"

Ha ha!

These people just doing things, saying things; one night it was fancy dress, and the blokes there – bloke blokes! Proper bodies, they work outside, big hands, not wusses, not gentle professional little people who earn lots of money...

Yeah, yeah

...blokes! And, fancy dress, probably a third – if not a half – of the whole of the festival, without saying a thing, everyone went trannie!

Really? My God!

It was unbelievable! And some of them wore their dresses for about two or three days.

How amazing...

Hilarious! And they were just acting normal.

Yeah.

And a lot of them were doing drink, drugs, whatever. So it wasn't such a big deal like 'ooo-hoo let's talk about it...' Everyone was just – chilling. It was fucking amazing. It was absolutely amazing! We were right near the main path. Perfect for people-watching – saw so much.

Hmmm

There was this guy, just wearing jeans or shorts or something, and a dog's head, and a big kind-of water bazooka – what do you call it a rifle, or gun with a big pump in it. And he was just – 'doof!' 'doof!' everyone that he was passing got shot with water. But not aggressively! Playfully. You know, playing a little bit more with some, men, women, kids, whatever. And then about an hour later we heard this little girl shouting "Stop that dog! Stop that dog!" and I thought 'ahhh, she's lost a puppy!' It was that guy, with the water bazooka walking ahead of her, and she had a basin, trying not to spill the water and catch up with him and he was just walking at the right pace so she couldn't catch up – she obviously wanted to soak him back...

Ha ha ha

...the little things that people do... just to play! There was, we were just sitting before the bands came on and there was this kid, watching a guy – what do you call it, those two sticks with a round thing in the middle?

Oh God, I don't know, um…

I don't remember what it's called! So anyway, the kid was just watching for a while, and then the guy showed the kid how to do it, gave him the sticks, showed him, helped him, held it – total strangers – and that was it!

Hmmm

All the kids, all the time, had attention. If they wanted it from kids, they had it from other kids. If they wanted it from adults, they had it from adults. And Felicity and I went in the sauna and there were a couple little boys there just hanging out. And we were all just chatting. It was just fucking excellent! It was good safe community!

Hmmm

I don't know how it works with education, I'm not sure how it works with money or anything like that, but the essence of that; it's like Freya was saying about Dennis that it would be great for him to just be there, to be with the kids and hang out, even just for the festival. But the kids have to know that way of life. You can't just throw a kid in and wrench the kid out again.

Yeah

And they were such intelligent, confident, kids with boundaries, they were proper decent kids. They weren't fucked up or manipulated. And it's the kind of situation where the kids could all be together because they all had the same rules. And it's very basic right and wrong. Simple as that! So anyone could tell any kid, but wouldn't need to tell the kid off, but it's like everything's for everyone's welfare.

Yeah. It's weird you say that because a lot of things came to mind as you were talking. I remember being with Mallie in Highgate Wood in the kids' play park and these two girls came up and they were both dressed in - they must have been seven or eight - dressed in designer

tracksuits. - Quite naff! - Anyway, that's another story... My snobberies or whatever. And I don't know, she went through this phase where she was just trying lots of things, and she was chewing grass. And this one little girl came up to her and looked at her with complete disgust and said to her "Why are you eating grass?" And Mallie looked at her and didn't quite know what to say...

Hmmm

...and, um, the girls went off and she said to me - almost tearfully - *"Is it wrong to eat gwass?"* And I said, "No, I don't think so... you know, if you enjoy it!" (As long as a dog hadn't peed on it!)

Ha ha ha ha ha ha ha

And I said "Well I don't particularly like the taste of it, but it's absolutely fine!" But kind of, like you say, having different rules... That's my biggest fear that, you know, if you bring up a child and when they are not in that festival kind-of environment, they will be branded freaks, if they behave 'inappropriately'.

Yeah. Hmmm.

Two other things as well. You know, Rychard went to the Buddhafield Festival and he said he was really moved because the children had such freedom.

Hmmm

You know, they were – more or less what you've just said. They clearly knew what they could and couldn't do within broad boundaries...

And they wouldn't need to break the boundaries because they are being entertained, they are not trying to challenge anyone, they are not trapped wild animals, they are not being threatened, no TV, they were singing, they were always doing stuff. They were normal natural kids having a fucking ball!

Yeah

It was excellent!

Yeah. And the other thing, actually. You were saying about that guy showing the kid that game of balancing the reel on the string with sticks[99]. It reminded me of what we said before about mending the bike, do you remember that?

YEAH...

But also, I never thought I would break through, but it never occurred to me that I was quite a weak swimmer, but in Cornwall, Rychard and I were swimming in the sea and I was just like, cold. You know, keeping moving. And Rychard, it turns out, used to be a championship swimmer. You know, very fit. And he said to me, "What strokes do you know?" And I just sort of giggled and went, "Well, I don't know, I can do the breast stroke, and um..." I couldn't think of any others! Ha ha ha ha ha

Ha ha ha ha ha

'Doggie paddle?'

Ha ha ha ha ha

And he laughed and said, "What you don't know how to do the crawl?" And I was like, not exactly ashamed, but I said "Show me what it looks like and I'll tell you."

Ha ha ha

So he did the crawl and I was like, 'oh no, I couldn't do that!' But, I'm not quite sure what happened, but he just was really encouraging. He said "It is really easy and it gets you through the water fast!" and so he gave me, like a swimming lesson. And it; I don't know, about ten minutes. And I felt very clear with him when I was tired or I had had enough, because, I don't know if you have done it, but it seems to take a lot of synchronising and I ended up with a lot of salt in my face and down my throat. There was that thing of just having somebody who was just prepared to, I don't know – make it safe; and make it fun as well!

Yeah!

And be really encouraging and not kind of going 'well, you need to do… or you're taking a long time to do that, aren't you?' Be sarcastic and a bit like impatient. "You're picking this up really fast!" What a difference! It's like my so-called 'inner child' or you know, the unconfident part of me was really really encouraged.

Hmmm. Hmmm. I remember that, talking about the festival, I noticed, the alcohol was not nice, I never liked it. But what I noticed was that that's where the aggression comes in, that's where the sexual stuff comes in, but it's like seedy…

Hmmm

Not nice. Darkside stuff. What was great is when we take drugs - no matter what the drug is, generally and very brashly speaking - it's like skipping over whatever pain and conditioning and 'pause-buttons'. Everyone is everyone else's best friend in nursery school again, or primary school. Everyone talks, everyone's trusting, everyone shares, people are cool to touch each other and it's not all sexual. You know, lean on each other, it's just normal! We just… hang out! Everyone's on the same side! And it's magical. It can get a little, you know; and then people get into the sexual stuff a bit later, which is fair enough! Depending on where you are coming from. But you know, it can be really good fun until the darkside kicks in, sometimes a lot later or when you're beginning to 'come down'.

Yeah

And then it can get quite ugly on the 'come down'. People get messy or they don't feel good any more, or you know, they're 'gurning' which is quite an unattractive thing, you know, chewing like a camel when you are on ecstasy or whatever. But, it was really magical. The people that I met, chatted to, hung out with, blokes, women, everyone, just because we were next to each other. Fucking excellent. And that, I think, is *the good part of drugs that everyone likes.* Freedom to be.

Yes.

Until it becomes too much, and it's a medicine, and its not fun anymore, it's just for them to take.

Yes, so you have to keep increasing the dosage? Reality starts seeping through again.

Meanwhile, all play and no work makes…

Yes

…for a failure and embarrassment to your parents, when they can't talk or brag about you.

What you said was interesting about Dennis, the kind of, how you can't just put a child in there and wrench them out again. It's too, too different. I don't know, I'm trying to get my head around what I'm thinking. I'm not…

Maybe, unless the child has been going to festivals once a year for the last two or three years…

Yeah. Introduce them quite early, as well – around Dennis and Mallie's age. Well, I took Mallie to Buddhafield a couple of years ago and there was also some shit happening with Steven and Cynthia – all sorts of shit! Mallie loved it! I mean, she was naked most of the time and she just ran around, from tent to tent. I mean I think that literally what I did was just chase after her the entire time and I didn't have time to do anything.

Ha ha ha ha ha

I know, I think, yeah! Now, it would be great because she can sit, she can take part in the activities, you know, she can be much more

engaged. And growing up with that…

Yeah!

…and then they can reintegrate, 'cos, let's face it, this friend of mine who has converted to Islam because he's married into a Muslim family, we were just talking about, what is there now, you know. Socialism is dead. It seems, all the 'isms'.

Hmmm

So it's like, everybody has had to accept what we have now, you know, society as it is. But somehow not be too sucked into it.

Hmmm. One really upsetting thing that happened while we were watching a band, right at the end of the festival, is a guy leapt up, he seemed really enraged, with his baby under his arm like a barrel of beer or something. Rushed to the, um, security guards or whatever, very little was going on as the bands had just finished and there was an announcement and it turned out that he had lost his child. *He'd lost his little girl!* I don't remember how old, I think about four, dressed in a pink dress or pink top or pink fairy costume like every other girl there. And, he was absolutely in a mess. Obviously! They were radio-ing everywhere – it just went on and on. It obviously changed things. It was really really really upsetting.

Hmmm. Why, because he was worried about…

Because he had lost his girl!

No, I mean, I understand that. Were there boundaries around the camp?

Yeah, but the kid could have wandered anywhere, got knocked out, been abducted, been sexually abused, been murdered, been anything. Been 'nicked' and driven off in someone's car. Anything, really. Ummm, and it was fucked. They radio-ed around; and then, quite a little while later – I was really astounded at this – he was obviously on drugs, or drink, or something or other, he wasn't quite there! Or he had been, err, I'd imagine, because everyone else had. Ha ha ha ha I know I had! But late late late late that night, we find out through the grapevine that the little girl was found and was with the Mother all the time! So what probably happened was that he misheard, or it wasn't clear, you know, stoned or whatever he was; but how fucked that they don't make an announcement that they found the child and she was with her Mother all the time and everything's cool!

So it's, just tell the parents and everyone else can just assume…

Fuck themselves! Never go to festivals again and feel upset that somebody did whatever it is that's in their worst imagination.

Hmmm

Do you know what I mean? Stupid.

Yeah. It is stupid. Yeah, it's a shame that they didn't see that the community extended that far and that people would be concerned.

Exactly! Exactly. Little things like that are what makes and breaks it. I so felt – the whole festival apparently is by this one guy who owns a couple of restaurants or something or other. A nice enough young guy. Man did I feel for him! You can have every, every success, make a fortune, millions of happy people, thousands or whatever – one child, once in your career…

Yeah

…how do you live with yourself?

Yes

My jealousy went out of the window in a second, thinking 'you take it!' Ha ha ha ha ha

Well, I suppose as you say, it goes with the territory.

Yeah!

But also, I mean, I don't know, I guess from the time from when people were living in caves, your kids – 'have they been eaten by a Sabretoothed tiger?' You know, or whatever. I do think, coming back to that fear thing, fear becomes paranoia.

Yup.

Collective paranoia.

99. *Diablo!*

"You be noodie too!"

My Father used to hassle us, shout at us not to whistle at night. In Africa, he scared us because he said snakes would come.

Really?

I don't think it works that way.

Ha ha ha ha ha – 'Heel Rover!' *(whistles…!)*

In Wales, we didn't quite buy it! Ha ha ha ha ha – but, um, my brother and I were talking. And it's like, I wonder where that comes from! Because maybe, way back, in Africa, or Goa, or maybe even Portugal, way way back if you whistled, then maybe the neighbouring tribesmen where there, or *a Sabre-toothed tiger that was trained by someone to turn up and bite your bollocks* or whatever. So it's these fears that don't mean anything that are passed down and curse us – do you know what I mean?

As you said, fear of fear… I mean, walking through the woods, not Box Hill, I mean back in Muswell Hill, before. Is it Cherry Tree Woods? You know the one, between East Finchley Tube and your old house. Occasionally; all those films you see when you are a teenager, where a hand appears out of the dark and snatches you into the woods. It's like 'Fuck!' In Box Hill I'd know that I've got to walk through that darkness, through all that, because I've got to find my tent.

Yeah.

You know, there's no way, there's no where to turn back.

So you've been living there until you move to the flat-sit now?

Yup, pretty much.

For two weeks?

Yes.

And then?

Then hopefully round the, well hopefully my aim is to probably go to the Buddhist Centre, until I don't know when.

I think when I come back, um, maybe even before I go to Vipassana[100] I'll phone the press and say hey, here's a story!

What, about living in the woods?

Yeah! 'Strange man living in tent in Box Hill...'

Really?

Unless you want to call them! But it's a story and it gets the fucking book out...

Hmmm... Funny you should mention that, because when I first moved there I religiously kept a diary 'cos I thought it would make such a good story. Yeah! I mean, I didn't keep it up for more than a couple of weeks, but enough! I mean it's similar to a lot of the stuff we talked about, um, and I even actually Emailed *'The Guardian'* with a little summary of what I was doing. But funnily enough, I mean, it's weird, this whole life-influencing art - or whatever you want to call it - I was aware, when I was writing, that it might be read. It subtly started...

Really!

...yeah yeah, so what I was writing...

Not expressing the truth – performing!

Umm, coming back to 'the fear thing'. I was down in Silchester with my Dad and Mallie at these sort of fountains. It was very hot weather,

and, we were driving down there and my Dad said "Has Mallie got a spare pair of pants?" and I said "What for?" And he said "Well if she went into the fountain she'd get her pants wet." And I said "Well she can get those ones wet... and whatever..." So we got down there and she took all her clothes off, which was fine by me. My Dad had been photographing her, but as soon as she took her clothes off - he put his camera away. And I said "Are you not taking any more photos?" And he said "I'm not taking any pictures of her without any clothes on." He said "Your Mother and I have been talking about this, and, you know, the process lab might call the police...

Yeah...!

"...because of these photos." And, you know, there was a divided reaction. Part of me was like 'Oh, for God's sake!' And another part of me was, 'Oh God, you know, the level of paranoia we have to live with – it's ludicrous.'

And for parents, some of it is justified, because – where do you draw the line? How do you know what's; I mean, I haven't got a kid!

Well, it was funny 'cos, I mean, it might have just been since he said that, or when we were there, that I saw what felt like a couple of the Mothers looking disapproving. You know, frowning. *(whispers)* 'You can see her vagina...' um, and I don't know, maybe, maybe people do – even though they wouldn't even express it – does this mean even being 'looked at' by somebody that might be a paedophile, or 'not quite right' in their sexuality, or whatever you want to call it. Would that affect a child? Like, do they pick up this vibe?

I'd say!

Hmmm...

Definitely, I'd say!

I mean, I did feel a bit weird about it, to an extent. I don't know, this is a tough one...

I feel for me, personally, umm, not that long ago I didn't know 'sex vibes'. And now that I do, *I can recognise them as sex vibes rather than someone just being nice.*

Hmmm

Or someone that I've got something in common with. Like on the Underground I can acknowledge people for so many different things that I might have in common. Maybe – I don't know what... smokers - dope smokers - people who have taken ecstasy, acid, the 'abused', people with the same story, people with the same attitude, people who are just on the same level, that isn't too high or too low, but just that, you know, I don't know what it is. But I make a lot of eye contact and acknowledge people. I remember, within the last... year, suddenly getting a shock and realising that with some of these people, it was sex vibes that they are giving to me, not a 'same-same' recognition acknowledgement. And that is not where I was coming from. And I got into, 'Oh my God! All this time... have I been getting a sex vibe while I've been thinking that 'they recognise the God in me like I recognise the God in them'.' You know? Ha ha ha ha ha ha ha! And what they're really saying is 'fuck that – I want yer sex!' Ha ha ha ha

It's weird, isn't it?

Weird.

I mean, that bloke, who I shared with for a while, in Ashbury. He said he felt uncomfortable with Malaika with no clothes on. He said, "Well, no, it's okay in the house, it's okay in front of your family, but I don't feel comfortable with it. And also, what if she talks about this at nursery? You know, 'I live in a house with two men and I run around with no clothes.'" And I thought, 'what if she does talk about that? I'm sure we can defend ourselves'. But already there was an assumption that we'd have to defend ourselves against the accusation that there was something weird going on. I suppose kids don't understand...

The name of the game is 'abandon their childhood - or you, the parent, will be called a paedophile'.

But I mean, she doesn't understand... When she takes her clothes off, in the garden or outside, she always says to me – 'cos she's picked this up from her granny – "You be noodie too!"

Hmmm

And it's really struck me, because how can I explain that 'It's alright for you...'

That I'll have to 'sell out' on my truth of getting naked now, like you'll have to 'sell out' later.

...well exactly! I've already learned that I can't be naked...

And at some stage, you're going to have to sell out and be broken into society.

Exactly. When we were playing in the garden at Ayesha's parents' house earlier in the summer, we had a hose and she was soaked. Naked. And it would have made total sense for me to be naked. And I said, well, all I could say was "I don't want to be naked in front of Ayesha's parents!"

Yeah

But it's like, 'Oh for God's sake! That sounds so lame!'

Yeah

What the fuck are they going to say, 'Oh Ed's got his dick out!' You know? It's kind of ridiculous, really, to...

It's a weird one. Very very weird. Because, um, this is as close as I've got to any issues around it. If I live at Freya's, I'm going to get close with Dennis.

Hmmm

Because we're cool together.

Hmmm

I don't know how I'm going to deal with him wanting to come into the loo - you know the way that kids always want to? - when I'm peeing.

Because I let Mallie in.

Dennis is someone else's child...

True.

...plus, say I'm in the bath, or pooing, or whatever, he won't understand, especially if we're laughing, or talking, or something 'normal', why his Mother can't come in as well.

To see you, yes. Hmmm

Just to chat. Because we're chatting. Because, you know 'your wife'; my wife and my child – no problem!

The difference is quite inexplicable to a child.

He'll um, he'll ask about dicks. I mean - what's his name - Marius is sixteen now and we still talk about stuff, because he's starting to experiment with sex and he needs to know about fannies and the whole thing.

But it's funny, um, 'cos I have to explain to Mallie, because she likes, you know, if I'm lying down she'll jump on my stomach, and she'll jump anywhere. And I said to her, "I don't want you to jump there, because those are my balls, and they'd hurt..."

Yeah

...and then she went through this phase of being really interested in them. "Are these your balls?" She was kind of obsessed...

Ha ha ha ha ha

...and she went up to my Dad, one time...

Ha ha ha ha ha HA HA HA HA HA

...and said *"Gwand Pa, are these your balls?"*

HA HA HA HA HA HA HA

...And then she started saying "I've got balls!"

HA HA HA HA HA

...And now it's like "Do women have balls?" 'No...' "Do boys have balls?" 'Yes...' "Do little girls have balls?" 'No...' You know, it's like this kind of weird obsession, and with Rychard she said "Let me see your balls!"

HA HA HA HA HA HA HA HA I can't believe you haven't been locked up!

I know, I – extraordinary...

Fucking hell. What about just sitting her down with a book, a picture book, and... 'What are those? What are those for? What are those? Why that?'

Yeah, I think that – well, that's next. Really, because it's getting to the point – and it's time, well, even like you say, well, is it appropriate for her to come in while I'm having a pee?

Yeah.

Because you know what kids do. She'll stick her finger in the stream of pee, and laugh, and try and touch my dick or whatever...

The same as if it was your nose or your elbow?

Yeah! And I suppose, yeah, the best thing to do is to gradually start to explain.

It's the 'space thing' again. I mean it's easy for me to say, but you know the 'five minutes, I need some space...' that you were talking about? '...when I'm doing 'this'.'

Yeah. I think the other thing may be that children do understand a hell

of a lot more than we realise. I mean, like with Dennis, as you were saying, I sometimes think I over-complicate it because I have to give a full explanation, but it's not, you know, it's just not always necessary to.

Yeah. Yeah.

Or, I mean with Mallie, I said to her, "Look, I don't mind you coming up – I think it's funny – and saying 'Are these your balls.' Or to your Grand Pa. But don't go up to just anybody in the street…

To the Vicar - Ha ha ha

"…and grab their balls."

He he he he

She did something that, that wasn't to do with balls, but um, while we're out kids do say things like "Look at that man who's got a fat tummy!" You know, the way kids do. 'Oh my God, how embarrassing.' But it's usually true, that's the other thing. Because he usually has got a fat tummy.

Or he is ugly, or… but again, your kids, other people's kids, do you know what I mean? Because I know now, thinking back, that my family were really fucked up. Physically and sexually. My cousins, from Liverpool, were 'normal'. They did sports, they changed, I mean, they had a different situation – but they're only half Goan, in Liverpool, no big deal!

Exactly, a big cosmopolitan city.

In my stupid little town, I may as well have had three dicks – all on my forehead! Ha ha ha ha ha

But you have – has no one ever told you?

Ha ha ha – but yeah. It was fucked up. But we got on great! Especially my Uncle and I were quite similar and got on really well. My cousin Alice and I got on really well. Curt – who was bullied by his Father – and, um, he was just bullied, basically. I remember one day she was sitting on my lap - I must have been about eleven-ish - as we listened to music, my uncle and Father were around and she was swinging her legs or whatever and I had a stiffie — whatever that was! And every now and again, it throbbed, and *it kind of like swung up and whacked her in the 'tusch'*. - Ha ha ha ha ha - and she went "Oooh, Mickey, that feels really funny! Yer 'widgie's' tickling me bum!"

Ha ha ha ha ha - And how old was she?

Nine-ish - and you know, all that sort of stuff, and we were just having a good time and there was no problem; but now, looking back - and I remembered this, only a few months ago - my Father and uncle looked at each other, didn't know where to look, didn't know what to do, didn't know what to say, didn't stop us, didn't not stop us; and I remember another time where I promised to show Alice my dick, if she did this and this and this, and it was just stuff you're supposed to do like you know clear up and whatever whatever. So she did all these things and I didn't show Alice my dick because I was, you know, fucked up! Wish I had! But, I went and triumphantly told my Mother what happened, and that I didn't show Alice my dick, but not that I did or didn't, but that Alice did these things, and my Mother was... not livid, but there was a huge disgust - abandonment!

Hmmm

A lot of it was just without words, but it was nasty! It was really nasty! And she probably didn't even realise she was doing it.

No, just a knee-jerk reaction.

Really fucked-up! So — they were really normal; now, they have normal, healthy, strong relationships, sexual relationships; and I don't even take my shirt off in front of my parents!

It's funny, my friend Shane is like that. I mean, I never realised what a taboo it was! But then he was saying it was because he was hairy,

and *his family was all women, and to be hairy was quite disgusting!*

Exactly! So my Mother used to say about; she'd laugh childishly at men! "Look at his hairy back!" "Look at his fat!" 'Look at this... look at that!' ...well, he's a man!

Yeah, that's what we're like...

Yeah. And where does that leave my Father? Put down for being male? Where does that leave us? Shouldn't grow into being a man? Shaved? But, um, no one bought me a razor or anything. I was hairy and sweaty and nasty! And I had to ask for deodorant – didn't really know what it was, and I felt bad because it cost money. And shaving, well I remember for a long time having to pluck them out with my Mother's tweezers because they were getting too long and it just looked messy!

What your face hair?

Yeah!

It must have taken a long time...

Yeah. Ha ha ha ha ha. But it was just sheer desperation. Until I ordered an electric shaver from the catalogue and paid for it, or whatever. And they were probably just too embarrassed - my Mother was just a giggly little girl - and then, I'd be teased when I shaved.

Hmmm

Fucked up!

Hmmm

Meanwhile, where's my Father?

So, it seems like we're looking for the answers again. It's like we were talking about getting over all this. What could we do? What could we offer people? I mean what...

Well, I'd say, first and foremost, name it – not blame it. Because, yeah, they fucked up.

Yeah.

So?

They didn't know what they were afraid of.

Exactly! They didn't know any better, they couldn't do any better, they didn't have any better, they didn't teach; and even if they did know better, poor fuckers were scared shitless themselves, you know, maybe my Father was scared to say to me "You need a shave" in case I bit his head off and said "No I don't – leave me alone!" through sheer embarrassment.

Yeah!

We were all 'killed' by embarrassment – big time. Still am, to an extent! *Embarrassment rules…*

What we're saying is that our parents were given the job of 'shutting us down…'

Yup!

'…or shutting us up'.

Hmmm. And they were so desperate, probably, yes. My Father, just, you know, got over his parents, his family, because they fucked him up so badly, and I think that, I realise quite recently when he said something about listening to Goan music, or Goan stuff upset him. Because it reminded him of his fucked-up childhood. I didn't know that. I'm thirty nine next week and I didn't know that, and now have a vague idea – that I can totally forgive – of why my culture was kept from me. Everything about it. If I'd known that, 'whenever', I could have forgiven – 'whenever'. Rather than just being livid and venomous about it.

Well maybe when you were a teenager, or something.

100. Vipassana. Ancient meditation technique revived by the Buddha. www.dhamma.org

RIP Idi Amin (and other bullies)

Hm! Or done it myself. But, it was also confusing for them. They didn't know whether we were supposed to be Goan, African - like Swahili-ites - or something Welsh, or something English, or which class, or who, or… none of it worked! Which bits do we suppress? Which bits do we show? They didn't have a clue! And, like I said, they were kids! Far more kiddie than we ever were, I'm sure. They didn't have a clue – the poor fuckers – they simply didn't have a clue. But for me - I think I just said earlier - finally, thank God, *I think I'm over blaming my parents, blaming my environment, blaming bloody Idi Amin* – who died last week – and I was astounded that my parents didn't even phone me. All those years of "We hate Idi, he ruined our lives" and he dies and there's nothing? *(kisses teeth!)* And I thought I was supposed to hate him too, and everything else that they loved I was supposed to love – and everything they hate I was supposed to hate. No one told me that… the fashion had changed, that I had based my life on… Ha ha ha ha ha… Fuck! Yeah! Just get over it! I've got to take responsibility – and do it. Nah, I'm just; I'm over blaming them. And it's weird. Being thirty nine next week. That's forty, basically. And, I think 'it' is just beginning, somehow. A year ago, or two years ago, Lui and I had that really really really really really bad fight where it felt like we wanted to kill each other, and stuff, and he left that message on my answerphone "You're nearly forty and you've got nothing!" Fuck that really had me fucked off, but I am nearly forty and I feel that I've got more than most people. But rather than feeling – I know a few people could feel it's a failure, not having a home – like my own house – or a wife, or kids, or whatever, but right now, right here, I'm thinking 'thank God I haven't!' Because otherwise, I wouldn't be able to just stop my life, get some space… I mean, since leaving the Muswell Hill house, it's been fucking amazing. Just like, those two months in Hampstead in that beautiful flat, coming and going out of London when I have to be here, checking in with friends all over the country, places I wanna; everything I wanna do, all my dreams come true – this is the best summer of my life!

Hmmm…

More than anything, this summer, this year – I'm sure a lot of it's to do with, um, not wearing glasses any more, too! Like I've – taken part. I've so taken part this year. And it's been the best!

Also, it feels like you have to use gained awareness, and whatever, as a means to get over it. You have to dig around, get upset, get angry…

Yeah

…instead of it being suppressed, release it.

To get over it, get all these things out, rather than buying into one of them and hiding behind them – really.

I mean last time, I must admit, the Men's Group that we put together, although it's only been three sessions – it's just that being able to be with men…

Check in!

…it's great! It doesn't have to be a lecture, or workshop – we just talk about how we're feeling.

Yeah.

Whatever…

I remember that big party after a Men's Group, that you didn't stay for?

Hmmm

That one! That was *the first time where I wasn't a plaything for the women*, so they can flirt and I can, you know, blah blah blah... do their thing with boys; and I was with the men. I had to really shout at Emma. And I said to her – because she was desperate for attention and she must have needed to show everyone that she's 'the ex-girlfriend', and she rules, and everyone else hasn't got...

Was that the one where, um, we were with the men more and – what were those guys from Brighton called?

Yeah! That was the one.

Yeah! I missed the other party.

Oh yeah, yeah. It was that one. I was with the men and then, what, a week or two later, my family, my God daughter's First Communion. And even though I'd been told to 'wear this, wear that, wear a tie, wear long trousers, be here early...' Fuck all that! I did my thing, turned up and I was with the men, the kids, or the outcasts. But I wasn't trying to; be with the women, serving the women, looking after the women, being owned, manipulated and God knows what else by the women. I chose to allow myself to be; to accept the men and be accepted by the men. And it's changed, and changed. Like, wherever I go out now, generally I'm with either Gina or Felicity...

Hmmm

...but – but we'll come to that later! – uum, or with 'a girl' or something. Ummm, I'm with blokes. I love chatting with the blokes! The girls generally, just want to be stupid girls flirting around because they want a shag, or a boyfriend or something – that I'm not really interested in – so there's nothing to talk about, because I've got mine! Ha ha ha ha ha

Oh.

So there's nothing to talk about. But it's been fucking amazing, hanging out, having a laugh, but really having good good conversations with blokes. Really good. And then for them to introduce me to their mates, because they want to talk about the same stuff. It's fucking excellent! It's absolutely; because before, I'd hang out with Mummy's-boys. Now...

now it's almost like crossing over, where I don't feel, I'm part of it. Not only do I not want to 'be like them', or 'I'm not like them any more' but I don't really want them near me, because I don't want to express that side of me, because I've done it, and I'm over with it! Or at least for the time being.

Hmmm.

But *I'm enjoying expressing my masculine side with the men.* Rather than my feminine side with the feminine. Does that make sense? Something like that, anyway! It's so different. And I, you know, I would have, I suppose on the other side, prayed for some guy to say look, this is what's going on. "This is how to be the man that you really are…" or whatever it is, and not be like that. But I can't imagine sitting any Mummy's-boy down and saying…

Yeah

"…Look!" I don't know why… I don't know whether there's a language for it, or whether it's something that; it just, it's just languages. It's just like riding a bike, I suppose. Once you've ridden it, you can always ride a bike. You're there. But until you have got there yourself, or until that part of you is brought alive, or you are not scared, or something…; it's so… so. And the stuff that we talk about is not necessarily deep or heavy, or not necessarily stupid. It's different, with different people, at different times. It's not necessarily football, or tits, or fixing things, or cars, or something like that. It's whatever. It's being there quietly together. Do you know what I mean?

Hmmm

Like Lui said something about, this guy who phoned his mate and said "Wassup?" "I'm feeling down." His mate said "Okay, I'll be around in a while." He goes around with a couple of tinnies, they sit, watch football, the football's over, they say two words to each other and then the guy says "Hey, it's getting late, I'm gonna go home!" and the other guy says "Totally excellent you came over!" But meanwhile, they shared space. Do you know what I mean? And that's all he wanted. To share space! I wouldn't have got that. We would have done the Mummy's-boy 'Oh, let's talk about it. Oh it's this, it's that, where does that come from, let's process or therapy it'. Fucking hell! But just learning to have; and maybe that's down to intimacy again. It's easier to babble and cluck around than to just be there together.

Fuck!

And that's another thing about the summer; well since the first half of the book, ummm, I can tell the truth! Which means, I have opened the doors to intimacy. And other people can meet me there. If that makes sense. Where before, I, I, I'd feel like a fraud, because they don't know my secrets. Now they don't need to know my secrets. Uuuuum, I kind of dealt with all my backlogs of being a liar with this book.

Hmmm

Something's changed since being authentic, telling the truth, joining in. It's so changed. With everyone. The book has changed everything.

Just like we said this evening, we don't have to do this de-briefing with a particular aim in mind. But how does what you're saying fit in with, say, like the Men's Group, where we... everyone talks? Well, not everyone, but we all... exchange, a lot.

I suppose the Men's Group's a place where we can go with specific, maybe personal or sensitive issues in mind, that we wouldn't want to take to our own communities, who would have a vested interest or a pattern of beliefs. Where the group is – I don't know – more neutral than that.

Hmmm

But I wish that most things, if not everything from the Men's Group, could go into my daily life.

Hmmm

But then there are certain things and a certain energy when you are around with men.

Yeah. It's an interesting one that, 'cos also, when you were describing that 'thing', you know, those two guys that got together with a couple of cans of beer, or whatever. To me, I can see what you mean about them 'sharing space', but also it seems to hark back to…

You need alcohol

…well, you need, yeah, you need alcohol – but also that *men don't talk about things'*. It's like, well, suppress it because it's wrong, less girlie.

Is that only because no one has given them permission? Because with all the men; I have never come across a bloke that blatantly said "I don't want to talk about that…"

So what you are saying about those two guys is that they don't have permission to…

No! They just needed to share the space. Which is something I forgot that I could do. I felt that I needed to come up with a solution, take sides…

Yeah

…fix it…

Ah, now I see what you mean, yeah.

…process, which is a new thing for me really, isn't it?

Yeah, interesting actually, because a word I have been hearing a lot of recently is 'witnessing'.

Yeah

In the Buddhist Centre, Rychard was saying that they talk about this a lot. You know, that you're not there to hold someone's hand, or, like you say, to give them the answers, but you 'witness them in pain', or you can sit and 'witness somebody as they cry', or maybe even be physical with them as necessary, but it's not like you're trying to rub

their noses in it or anything.

Yeah, or steal their power.

Yeah, yeah.

Or dump yours on them.

Yeah, hmmm.

Hmmm. It is, it's like being there, and being on the same side.

Hmmm.

Because it's very easy, I mean, how many marriages, friends, how many people in my life in the past, that I've had very very strong relationships with, but it was all I knew. A battle. Same as home. We are now being peacefully on the same side.

Yeahhhhh…

Yeah. I was saying to Rob that the way I spoke to him and the way I treated him when we first knew each other was, just, the way that I knew. The way that my Father shouted at me, spoke at me, treated me – it wasn't 'bad', it was 'normal'. Much better than my Father had. But, not the way I'd see people treat each other 'out in the world'. Much worse than the way people treat each other in the world. But isn't that most families? *There's family behaviour 'in front of company' and family behaviour 'behind closed doors'.*

Hmmm

Lui is the big one. Lui is definitely the big one. Because with everyone else, I love myself, I like myself, I am comfortable with myself, I accept myself or whatever. But with Lui, I just don't!

No.

Or haven't. Or I'm criticised. Or there's a drama. Or there's a panic.

Or there's something something something. And to me, it's Lui avoiding intimacy.

Hmmm

Or being calm, or being okay, or you know, whatever it is. But, I'm so chuffed that he's been away for what – a month.

Yeah

Then he's back for two days. And I'm gonna bite my lip in those two days, because I want him to go feeling strong, and happy, and loved and everything. But it might not be easy. Because I don't know what the cost - to me - will be.

Yeah.

And then he's gone for two months. And when he comes back, I'll be so much more stable and knowing myself - or whatever - that it's like 'the final beast to slay'. Which is nothing against Lui. It's me, it's my stuff, it's my path, and he is just the perfect bully to teach me.

Yeah. Yeah, yeah. The mirror.

But for you it's been different because you've got all these men that you want to be with, where I've had a lot of mates that I've been with, that I've wanted to be like, but at the cost of having to drink, drugs, play small, play big, be stupid. You know all that kind of stuff a lot of the time.

Hmmm

And, had fuck loads of fun! Because I've really had the best time with them. But, I'm not an adolescent any more. Big time turning into a man, even if it's just because of my age, but something's shifted! I don't know. I'm a man now - or certainly getting there - and people treat me differently. I act differently. I don't – how can I put this? – walking down the street, I don't, I don't interact with younger boys like I'm on the same level checking out the pecking order, but I interact with them like I'm the authority. And 'you don't mess.'

Yeah.

I'm gagging to hear what you remembered, and I know it was ages ago that you left that message...

Well, it's probably not as exciting as you're imagining, and it's nothing specific, but again, its more to do with an atmosphere, a kind of abusiveness – I'm trying to think now. I was given; I was feeling ill and I was at a client-friend of mine's. He put me up for the night...

When was this?

...this was when I had this feeling come up and I rang you the next day.

Right.

And first of all it was kind of, to do with his hospitality. The shock of someone looking after me. But as I was lying there, because I was really feverish, the next morning, I just remembered this atmosphere from school. And kind of like something's been coming up. I saw a guy on the Tube, this really really big, fat bloke. I think he had, um, mental health problems. But, threatening. And I felt about five years old around him.

Yeah?

And a similar feeling, it was almost like something around the school I went to. It might just have been not feeling safe. You know, feeling unprotected. And that was what really came up with men. In a way with what you have just been saying about Lui. The feeling of... being very vulnerable around men. Feeling that they are threatening.

So you stayed at this guy's house because you weren't feeling very well.

Hmmm. I had a temperature and...

And then when you woke up in the morning, you felt vulnerable.

...yeah! Yes, it was very strange. Well, there was also a sense of, when I first met him – 'cos, like a lot of my clients, he's gay – I couldn't, quite read the energy. Because I wasn't sure how I felt. 'cos part of me was thinking, 'Well, am I over all that? Is there some sort of a sexual thing?' But what it feels like, with most men, it's this longing for friendship as well as the physicality.

Yeah.

And, you know, he's just a really really nice guy. Very hospitable. Very wealthy. And that's new to me as well. Because my impression of the wealthy is that they were very stingy...

Yeah

...and that they didn't really share anything. And I kept saying to him that I felt really grateful, and he was saying "Well, I just share. I have things, so I share them." Which is great! So yeah, all this weird stuff going on.

In a way, did you feel that it reminded you of being an unprotected child?

Hmmm. Somebody being nice to me. Brings up this sort of, brings up this, 'it's not safe. There's something... Something, somebody wants.' Which kind of made me think, 'Well, was it sexual?'

Because he was nice, you thought maybe he wanted something. You thought maybe he wanted a shag.

Yeah.

But he didn't make any moves. But there might have been something in the air, but you're not sure.

Yeah, and I don't know whether it was something I was generating, or something he was generating.

So how did you go to bed, and how did you split in the morning?

Well, I slept in his bed, which was very very comfortable. And he went downstairs to the, like a basement, with a pull-down bed. So I felt that I was getting the best deal. But it also reminded me of being in hospital at the age of six having my tonsils removed.

I had mine out as well.

Did you? Yeah. But it's such a weird thing. I don't remember anyone explaining. It feels like, I'm sure my parents tried to be loving and whatever, but here you are, you're shunted into this, quite scary atmosphere...

'Better not tell you, because otherwise you might be scared.'

Hmmm!

Ahumph!

I can still remember them putting that mask on. You know, the anaesthetic. And they must have explained that I'd feel sleepy, but it was still a surprise and I thought, 'My God what's happening.'

Hmmm.

Actually, that's the other thing. This sore throat I had was where my tonsils were. Agony! And I've since learned, in anatomy – in the massage course – that they're actually part of your immune system.

Nooo!

And they've stopped taking them out now, because basically when they swell up, it's that they're fighting infection. So they cut the fucking things out!

Faaking 'ell I don't believe it!

But again it's like a wound, you know. People talk about how your body knows where something's missing...

Yeah.

...so somehow, as I say - I don't want to sound all dramatic, like I don't remember a person fucking or abusing me - but it was something around a particular teacher at school. He liked 'slippering' kids, you know, like kind of whacking them.

Right. Hmmm.

And so, just again, the whole thing around men.

So, off the top of your head, *who didn't protect you*, would you say?

My parents? School teachers? Friends? It's got to be a mixture of – I'm not feeling like I didn't have enough guidance from my Dad, but it's as though, who are these male role models/teachers? There was nobody really.

Hmm.

Hmmm, strange.

And *who weren't you protected from?* The rough kids? Working class bullies?

I can honestly say it's just not feeling completely safe in the world. No specific bullying or person.

Hmmm.

And maybe again, not kind of being initiated in a world of rough and tumble in the playground.

Family shit

Exactly. How the fuck do I do this? Yeaah. Because I never had... I'm reading a book on obsessive-compulsive disorder. It took me fucking ages to get a book that's not too – what do you call it – intellectual.

Not a medical text book.

Exactly. But I found a nice little *'Obsessive Compulsive Disorder – The Facts'*[101]. Ha ha ha. Simple book, and I've got, I've got my secrets. And I've grown out of them. And, um, I remembered that throughout school, in Africa, in this country and at college, having a problem going to the toilet and I avoided changing rooms. I couldn't deal with them. And with obsessive-compulsive, it's all dirty and everything's contaminated.

But didn't you have those memories before?

I didn't remember that I didn't go to the toilet. At all. And even the fear of toilets, because of all the contamination, I didn't remember how much I used to check my pockets. Over check and check and check and check. Check everything. I didn't remember the way that I ruled my family and shouted "HAND!" really loud, just before anyone was going to sneeze, and they would automatically put their hand over their mouths. Everyone had to deal with it. If anyone coughed or sneezed in the room when I was eating, I couldn't eat my food. But no one would even have noticed the way that I'd deal with it, but no one would know that anything was going on. I'd count everything, I'd touch everything, I'd put everything in order, I couldn't clean a lot of the time - though there were some things I could clean - because I'd be contaminated. On the one hand everything needs to be cleaned. On the other hand, I couldn't deal with so many things because I was sure that I'd be contaminated. So I was feeling quite fucked up. And it was a lot easier in Africa. I'm not totally sure when it started. It may have properly started when we came to this country, but I'm not sure. I need to remember that. I'm sure I'll remember it soon. I remember when I was a kid – and I keep having this memory – I was really young, I had my special little 'throne' that was put over the toilet, a really nice little chair, and I'd sit on there, and 'make ca-ca', and I just came out screaming my head off from the toilet because I thought it had bounced and come back and touched me, so I had shit on me. But it wasn't. It was a splash or something. But I was hysterical! And I'll never forget that. I don't know why. I don't know why I didn't remember that. Because it was big, and, umm, I think it might have been around that time – but then going back to my 'family block stuff'; well my Mother, her brother and sister, totally obsessive-compulsive. Totally needy and, you know, passive-aggressive manipulation. Need to 'sell' themselves, what they have given all the time and 'I did this' and 'I did that' self justifications. I said to my uncle 'So, how was the trip to so-and-so…?' "Well, I fixed this, and I fixed that, and I did this, and I did that, and so and so said blah blah blah about me…" and that's what they're all like – and that's what I became like. It's just crazy, ridiculous.

What triggered it? I mean, what do you think…

I think they're all competing for the love or approval of their parents, basically. And it seems that my grand Father had a really shit relationship with his Father, like my uncle had a really shit relationship with him. So obviously, his son, my cousin, who I'm going to see next week or the week after… but, going back to Swindon, I so got that, those people – nothing wrong or bad about them – but I don't want them around my kids, and I'm not sure that I could deal with them around me.

Hmmm

Everyone screaming and shouting at the same time. Hysterically. And through sheer – that's not the way to communicate! Everything's a panic. Everyone's fighting for attention and fighting to sell themselves to each other. Or to show, whatever it is, that they love each other.

Do you think that's all it boils down to then? Competing with parents or for somebody's attention? Because when you were talking – and I don't know if I've talked about this already – fuck! It is one of the most embarrassing things I can – and I'm not just saying – I think I might have told you this. A phase, when I must have been about seven, eight, nine, ten? I don't know exactly the mechanics of how I did it, but

I used to eat my own shit.

Really?

It's fucking awful! Looking back I think, 'well, what the hell provoked - that?' Because, my sister – well, everyone must have known. I remember my sister saying, years later, "Yes, your breath stank." It's like, how embarrassing!

But no one said anything.

No, and I don't know what was going on! There must have been some major trauma.

Yup!

'cos kids don't just do that, do they? With that, I'd kind of linked it to this kind of memory I had. I thought maybe it's connected to school.

Oh, you ate your own shit, just at home, in the bathroom?

Yeah! Well I don't know, it's just, but talking about 'blank', I can't remember how I did it. I don't think I fished - and this is really gross, isn't it? - I don't think I fished in the toilet and ate it. It's more, okay, horrendous, disgusting – but why? And the same with you, why become obsessive-compulsive?

Yeah. And there's something, you know, flicking through the book, that says, you know, all these different reasons. And the only one that really rang true was something about the anal stage and potty training and that's where it all began. And that's where it all… and that was kind-of me and my…

Yeah

I was basically locked in the toilet. "You're not allowed out until you've done!"

Aah!

Meanwhile, I couldn't shit, like no one in my family can shit. You know, even the kitten had problems. *'course you can't shit with that much panic going around.* Huge amount of panic.

It's good that; it's amazing to be able to talk about these things, without necessarily – I mean, maybe it would be useful to talk to a therapist. It may help retrieve memories. Yeah, these memories… appear. Maybe, maybe it's just layers and layers…

Something like that. It's got to be, maybe, surely you could find it on the internet or ask someone.

Yeah.

So many, isn't it where kids eat mud they're deficient in certain nutrients – same as people who do that.

Yeah.

And Billy was saying something about, um, in India, your piss is not only, like, you drink your own piss – it has everything in it that you need to get your body back to balance…

Yeah

…but, they wash their faces in it…

Yeah!

…they deal with their wounds, it's good for your skin, it's good for this, that and the other, it's the best thing, apparentlynotthatI – last thing I'd imagine doing!

Well that's it.

I'm still quite obsessive-compulsive.

Yeah. Well I had eczema on the side of my leg.

It's supposed to be the best thing for eczema!

And it's great!

One of the first things we were told in this country, when we discovered what chilblains are and why our feet were fucked up, they said "Piss on them." That's what deals with it. Piss and snow.

Yeah

Meanwhile, you know, obsessive-compulsive family is covered in chilblains and cold for the first time...

They're really not going to piss on themselves!

Ha ha ha ha ha – or to go out stomping in the snow. Ha ha ha ha ha. But, so far, it does boil down to the fact that *we all just want love from our parents.* Or attention from our parents. Or if not parents, whoever the substitute was. So far, it seems to be, with everyone I can think of.

The biggest challenge is – and I've been realising this since showing the first part of this book to my parents – realising how hard it is for them to accept criticism. Like the other day, well, it's a little story, but without going into all the detail, I'd basically been really pissed off with Angus, a friend of mine, and I told him to his face, which is quite unusual for me, because I normally laugh things off. And that's it. Fine. And I was talking to my Mum about this and she said "Oh yes, I think it's really important for children to be able to, you know, express their anger. You know, we were like that with the three of you growing up." And I just said to her "Well I remember you sulking a lot."

Ah! Excellent.

And she got really upset. "Well I didn't sulk all the time... and anyway, I've stopped now!" 'Ah! That's not the point.' And later on she, when we were out shopping with Malaika and she said, um, "Oh, um, I get so worried. *All you seem to remember are the negative things from your childhood.*" And I said, "Well basically I'm working through them and trying to make sense of things. And I'd much rather do that with you, rather than feeling that there's this defensiveness."

Yup.

So you can say things to me like "Well I didn't sulk all the time. All you think about is terrible negative stuff..." You know, I feel like, actually think that showing them the book has changed our relationship hugely, but there's still a certain resistance and I can see where I got that from. My brother and sister and I have always said how bad we are at accepting criticism. But yeah, ultimately it is parental approval.

I know that my parents, they didn't treat us like we were kids and they were parents. They treated us like we were their brothers and sisters that they were competing with. My Father competing with me to have a childhood.

Yes.

And an adolescence, you know, rather than... being the Father. He could bully, thus he had the childhood and adolescence - and I got whatever was left over.

Hmmm

And it was easy for me, being the oldest and the Mummy's-boy. I took the role of being the Father and the husband, and where did that leave my brother? He hadn't got a role. He had no place in the family. End of story. I mean, I'd rather have none, looking at it from here and now – but from then, my brother would probably, rather be, who I was, for a while. Do you know what I mean?

Hmmm

And the same with my sister, yes, my my Mother.

Sister! Ha ha ha…

Oh fucking hell! Sister, daughter, Mother, fucking ha ha ha… But yeah, she she was, she'd act hurt – and that's how we've been manipulated. She'd act like the helpless princess that everyone has to save, because she's so – cute. Where's the parenting in that? But then, you see, I don't know whether this is true, but, my grandparents - I think both of their parents died early and they were both, um, adult brother and sister in the role of parents. So they didn't have proper parenting, they had their childhoods stolen and they had to bring up their brothers and sisters. So my grand Father became an alcoholic, my grand Mother was probably quite needy and seems to have been the key manipulator that no one really knew what to do with. But they didn't know. And then there were these huge cultural differences as well. When they went back to Goa from Uganda, and they probably didn't quite know what was going on – and what was Goa like for both of them? My grand Father – who was he? And how did he bring up all his brothers and sisters and put his brother through Seminary[102], sending money back to Goa while working in Africa. How did he end up in Angola, then Uganda, then back in Goa once the Indians took it over from the Portuguese, to find out that Goa no longer existed and neither did the house he owned that had been stolen by his own priestly brother? All that aside, I don't really get it. I don't know. How could any of them have any idea about parenting? I can't blame my parents, or my grandparents, or *Kunta Kinte*[103] himself! Ha ha ha ha ha… So, fuck! No one to blame! Better just get on with it I suppose.

It's odd, that reluctance they have to actually share their family histories, apart from the odd, kind of memory here and there. Strange.

And they don't want to tell us.

Yeah, or they can't remember it.

101. 'Obsessive Compulsive Disorder – The Facts' Padmal da Silva & Stanley Rachman (1998) Oxford University Press.

102. Seminary. Training college for priests.

103. Kunta Kinte. Key character in 'Roots' (1977) groundbreaking US television drama about a West African enslaved in America and his descendants.

Stags

I think for me, the book, and talking about it, and actually – as we've said before – making it important enough to transcribe and edit, it's our lives, rather than having to read someone else's book about someone else's life. That's really changed my sense of myself really. I mean, I've done a lot of things recently – all sorts of therapy-type things. And they've brought up a lot of really amazing memories, like yesterday, I was doing this really amazing singing therapy with this woman Lesley, and one of the things was a confusion about sexuality, still. Still, still yearning for men, but not just any old men – do you know what I mean? It's like… I'm still not clear what that's all about. So I sort of sang and moved through this process and I got this incredibly strong image of standing in the middle of a, being in a big circle of men, just being approved of, or just being seen and witnessed just as who I am, rather than having to put on any kind of show, and it was about acceptance. Fuck, I had the most amazing dream last night! Very bizarre. It was like, um, the first part was just sort of, err, like a sort of volunteer army in a desert and all these guys, who were absolutely terrified of something, it was like a really frightening enemy. And then – I can't remember all of it, but – it was a really weird memory. A train drawing up in a kind of makeshift station and this enemy had set traps for people and suddenly all these ropes pulled all of the soldiers out of the carriages and they were all hanging upside down by their legs…

Huh!

…and then being pushed on this conveyor belt, and this enemy had these curved sabres that were really really sharp. And they were cutting one arm off everybody. And it was fucking awful! I mean I woke up in a sweat about five o'clock because I was vividly watching these men's faces as they screamed and have their, you know, watching the sword cut through the muscle and the arm just falling off. Ah cooowr…! So vivid. I don't know what that was all about, but… male wounding or something. Holy shit!

I found out, years later, that the blokes I used to hang out with in school, um, have mainly turned gay…

Hmmm.

…and I had no idea. But now looking back, um, they were the harmless blokes. They weren't dirty, they weren't shitting and farting and picking their noses and flicking and fuck knows what, d'ya know? Some of the others *(kisses teeth)* just nasty dirty things. I couldn't deal with the dirty and I couldn't deal with the aggressive.

Hmmm

They were clean and non-aggressive. Nothing else came into it. Ummm, and now, like listening to what you're saying about approval with men and stuff, now it's different. Now my friends are totally across the board, and; you know, look at Lui. Lui can be really quite filthy with some of his habits, and, I haven't got the issues that I used to have with my friends or with anyone, about um, dirt and the obsessive-compulsive. I mean I couldn't be in a house where there were bare feet…

Hmmm

…or touch anything that a bare foot might have been near, or anything like that. Now, whatever! I generally have… bare feet! And so does everyone else, blah blah blah. But, is that, are those the men that – I was just thinking about what you were just saying about wanting approval – *is it those 'boys', the 'dirty cunts' that you want approval from* because now you're over all that, and now that we're 'out of school', the rules are different.

Hmmm

When I started working; in college I remember going to the loo maybe… once. Generally, I'd dash in if I really needed to, lock myself in a cubicle – so I could clean myself and I wouldn't have to smell the piss of the urinal and be next to someone. Go out, wash my hands, and – if there was anyone in, I'd stay in the cubicle until the coast was clear, then I'd dart out, wash my hands and leave. I just didn't even want anyone to know I was in there. Um, but now the rules are different. After school, college was better, work was not a problem – with work you are generally obliged to treat everyone relatively well. And as far as acceptance with men is concerned, I know we were saying something a long time ago about 'the buggery thing' and what that might be about for you and…

Hmmm

…acceptance from men and that's all you're worthy of.

Hmmm

Is that a similar thing, that the acceptance that you now want; because it seems that you are well over all that, is, those types of blokes, but you don't know how to be one of them or accepted by them; and maybe you don't want to be like them.

Well I don't. I mean, if it involves getting completely pissed or stoned all the time, which is what it seems to for a lot of men, forget it! I'm not interested! But, it's almost like trying to create something new; because the gay scene is not interesting, in terms of people. Most of the people; I think there's a lot of people who just…

The gay scene, generally, is where the party is – whether you're gay or straight or what!

Yeah.

It's, the best quality, the best areas, the best style, the best music, the best party in every way – the best drugs even. In every way, that's where it's at. It certainly was in Sydney! I don't know about this country, so much, but, I mean, Anna and Simon have given me this place in

Hampstead for how long... I had no idea how gay it was around here!
It really is a lovely area, and it's just – I haven't seen so many gay
people outside Brighton...

No... also in places like Chelsea and...

...that's it. All the best places.

Yeah.

Near the river, quaint, clean, nice...

Yeah, rivers, heaths,

...and in my experience - someone told me differently, though - but in
my experience, there is no aggression around gay people.

**No, I think there's a kind of – there can be that... slight hysteria. Yeah,
I'm sure there's bullying and I know there's supposed to be, you know,
domestic violence, whatever. But, yeah, generally speaking, it's quite
different. But yeah it's, I know, it's almost like I don't want to fit in any
particular box or category. But at the same time, there's a need for
some kind of social group. Do you know what I mean?**

Hmmm, hmm.

I mean that was the thing...

Yeah,

...that I was saying to you...

a sense of belonging you mean?

**...well kind of. But yeah, just an ease. I mean that's what I found at
Chariots. A sense of ease...**

Well there you go – it's gay, again! The best 'e's!

Ohhh...!

Sorry!

I-don't'-mean-those-kind-of-'e's...

Ha ha ha ha ha

No but at Chariots, you know, I popped there...

TELL ME ABOUT ALL THAT! Ha ha ha ha ha ha...

Well, it just felt like the right place to go. I wasn't particularly cold, but I just thought, well, it's an area I haven't really explored. Loads of people have said that they are quite friendly, interesting places and; I was feeling quite horny, but I didn't... have any sense of wanting to have sex particularly, if that makes sense. Um, but no just the experience of it was a bit surreal, with all these naked men wandering around and some really checking each other out...

But they're not

...no

But most of the time they are wearing towels.

Yeah. Well that's it, I mean they kind of insist you wear a towel. It's the rule. But the thing I enjoyed was just hanging out in an all-male space, just relaxing. You know, it's like the pool, the sauna, the steam room, chatting to a couple of guys. One guy I did speak to was an Indian guy who was married. I couldn't stop laughing! I found the whole experience so funny.

Why?

Well I just felt really – just at ease, you know, comfortable. And everyone else was looking so serious.

Ah, because they were trying to pull, or something.

Well they thought they were trying to pull, I don't know. It's like you have to look really po-faced. And if you were laughing or smiling you wouldn't be attractive. It's like, to me that's the most attractive quality in somebody. If they're happy...

Maybe they're paranoid that, you know, they might bump into their brother-in-law.

…may-be.

Ha ha ha

Yeah, but anyway, that's what – I smiled at this guy a couple of times, but it was obvious to me that it was like just laughter, rather than trying to sort of… smile and catch his attention. And he came over and was just chatting in the jacuzzi. I jokingly said to him "So, can you spot the married ones?" and he said "Why, can you?" and I said "Well, no, I mean, I'm divorced!" and he said "Oh well, 'cos I'm one of the married ones!" Ha ha ha – and, it's strange. I was talking to Maria about it afterwards and she said, *"Gosh, it must be weird to live a lie."* Because his wife doesn't know he's there. But it's that thing again, isn't it. Why can't people just be honest about it? What is so criminal? I mean, I don't know if he goes and; I saw him later on in the other jacuzzi with his arm around a guy and they were obviously just being affectionate. It was like, how nice! Rather than, why can't he just say to his wife, "…this is what I like to do – and probably you'd enjoy going to an all women's environment." Anyway, he told me that he told his wife that he was having a night out with the boys! Ha ha ha ha ha

Ha ha ha… And in other cultures, it's okay to put your arm around another person of the same sex.

Yeah! Absolutely! And then, do you want emotional detachment? You know, you want the physicality, sometimes, I mean I'm not saying always!

Hmmm

Sometimes you just, you might want a shag, or you just might want a hug, or to sit with somebody, not even making physical contact but just being comfortable with other people.

Or a massage...

Yes.

...men are stronger than women and they can get to where it hurts better.

Definitely. Yeah.

It is a funny one. And I'm not sure if it's out and open and normal in the Third World countries any more, because of the Western influence. Do you know what I mean?

Hmmm

Where it was normal to wash together and whatever. Maybe now it's frowned on. I heard - I can't remember the countries and I don't know the details - but there are certain countries where, um, you don't have sex until you're married and stuff like that, with the opposite sex, but it's cool to do stuff with your own sex.

Yeah, I've heard about that too, actually.

Where was it...

Just to find out

...but it's not boasted about, or anything. It's just 'normal'. Do you know what I mean?

Hmmm.

But then again, community - these issues won't be there.

Well it depends on your community. I mean, as we've said before, in the 'artificial communities' these issues do arise...

Yeah

...where do you find a 'natural community'? But it's that desire for physical contact, because my brother was back again recently and we were up on Box Hill, showing him my tent, and, um, we were chatting and I just got to a point where I felt that my head was going to explode because we were just talking, talking, talking. I then threw myself at him and we started wrestling and fighting with big sticks and it was fantastic! Because we haven't done that since we were kids and probably not, it felt like we didn't even do that properly...

Yeah.

...like I said earlier,

As kids?

Yeah, I would just kind of surrender and he'd kind of jump on me and; this time it was really equal. I'm not - I didn't want to hurt him - I really, we were going for it with these chunky sticks. It was so funny, but it was a sense of wanting to have some physical contact with him. You know, somebody of equal strength and...

Like two stags and their antlers.

...yeah! I mean I don't know what we've concluded before, whether we're trying to find 'the cure' for being gay. He he...

I don't think it's anything to do with that.

What do you think it is then? Because I'm... confused.

Permission to have normal relationships with men and women, older people, young people – do you know what I mean?

Hmmm.

Just normal, relationships.

Hmmm.

And, I've found that so many other people around me want that. And so many men are not great in the sack with their women...

Hmmm

…and, have no one to talk about it with, or ask questions with. And so many men want to have mates, want to have friends, but they don't know how, because they are so *busy bullying everyone that no one can come near; or they need to be the biggest, or the richest, or the one — you know, the candy-man with the drugs…*

U-hum

…or they need to be saved, or they need to be a victim, or you know — they are so into their roles that no one gets to hang out!

Hmmm

'cos everyone's putting some sort of control trip over each other and everyone is so scared of being abandoned or humiliated or something.

It's funny though, I'm starting to realise that being, being myself — whatever that means — in terms of sexuality or person — it's almost like beyond sexuality…

Yeah

…the friends, the male friends I have around the Silchester area, I don't know what it is. They're straight, quite vulnerable and they've all had their, quote, unquote, issues, what-have-you. But, they seem very up for physicality, like holding hands, sitting… you know, touching each other. Um, and, maybe there's no coincidence that there's a load of people who've done massage training or are into massage. But it gets you that opportunity to connect…

Yeah

…but with no funny-business. I mean, how funny because this guy was telling me, um, he'd had anal sex with his girlfriend for the first time, and I was massaging him at the time, he was lying on his front – and, I almost couldn't believe that I made this joke – I was, sort of kneeling over him and I jokingly said to him *"...and now it's your turn to find out what it feels like...!"*

HA HA HA HA HA HA HA HA

In the wrong circles, that could have gone down like a lead balloon. But, you know, we both thought it was really funny...

HA HA HA HA HA

...it's that sense of people who are, I don't know...

They're over it!

...yeah. They've got nothing to prove, so, like, 'oh no no I couldn't be buggered!' People who probably wouldn't, but they might think, 'Oh I wonder what it feels like!'

Hmmm

Which is different. It's almost like, oh I don't know, I wonder what it feels like to live in Australia, but you don't have to go and live there.

Hm.

You can muse about it. Actually, it's not like that at all, is it?

Haa. It's just not a big deal. It's the same with schools. Umm, there's a phase where everyone just goes 'that's gay', 'you're gay', 'it's gay', it all gay gay gay gay gay gay! It's boring. And, what type of rejection is that, generally? They don't even know what's going on. It's just that, maybe suddenly, they realise that they are at a stage that there are boys, and there are girls, and girls like boys, and boys like girls, and all this time they've been innocent, being bisexual, asexual, sex-less, and then suddenly it's a shock! Because they need to prove their, their status or something.

Hmmm

Fuck knows! But, I'm the same. I'm still not great at being touched. Or touching. Simple as that. And I wish my brother and I could have a stick fight or something, but, I wouldn't have the foggiest – you know, how to chase someone and catch them and then what do I do?

Yeah.

Ha ha

You just end up laughing!

Hmmm

And then eventually, it just stops. But maybe that's where sometimes, when people, it's like you said before. Sometimes the energy gets too much and you don't know what to do with it, so – I'm not suggesting it with my brother, but, with say a male friend, it could suddenly go 'ooh, what do we do?' Sex? Oh, I dunno!

Hmmm. But then, where does the label 'sex' come from?

Well exactly.

Maybe what you do is not sex. Maybe what you do is strip off and run around the woods, yelping.

Hmmm. Is that sex because you're naked? Or is it sex because one sucks the other one off, or gets tossed off or something like that?

Hmmm. Where does it; and surely it's more okay for something like that to happen when you are younger rather than older.

Yeah.

But if it's never happened all your life, then maybe you need for it to happen once so you can get over it and carry on with your life, rather than being scared of anything.

Yeahhh…

Hmmm. But it's it's interesting, now that I've, um, moved in with Billy. Ummm, came home, because we're doing this fast, or, what-do-you-call-it? Cleanse. So just drinking this shit, not eating, just drinking water and shitting like there's no tomorrow, pissing like there's no tomorrow. Came home – he finishes at three, four and then he's got paper work and stuff – and said right, "Let's go for a sauna". And Billy has got a great body. But, to me, it's a totally unattractive body. Um, it's, I don't know, your classic type everything-in-the-right-place in the right proportion and blah blah blah hairless type body, but it's like 'Aah, keep it away!' Not that it repulses me, but it's not something I'd want to touch, or get sexual with or anything like that…

Hmmm

…so Billy says "…so, let's go to the sauna…" and I thought 'FUCK!' Ha ha ha ha ha.

Well he doesn't have to be near you!

And it's just, still, there's that shock, I mean, sure I can go to the sauna with no one that I know, with strangers, but to go with someone that I know; the last time I remembered, the only time that I've been, I used to go swimming with two friends when I had my old marketing business, one was a printer who was a close friend of mine and another one was a designer who was working for me. And they were close friends, really great people. I probably went with the printer twice and with the designer, I don't know, twice, maybe… But, I would generally wait for them to go, they'd change, they'd be out and I'd have my own space to change, I wouldn't want to be in the changing rooms with them. I would be uncomfortable about it, I didn't know how to do it.

Hmmm

And with Billy, it's like, it's different for some reason. And we were cool changing, whatever, whatever… I was a bit, you know, I wasn't taking the lead role and being comfortable – it was his way. Umm, but still, I shat bricks! Like I was saying before, never go into a public toilet, never go into changing rooms, or very very few times in my life - to the other extreme… fucking cottaging!

Hmmm

Even though I didn't really wanna take part, because it still was dirty…

Because I suppose you haven't gone for the simple normality, that you had become attracted to the extremes.

Exactly! It's the other extreme! And even then, it's not really the place to have sex for me, or even to touch anyone or anything, because the bottom line is, it's contamination.

Hmmm. You know what I thought – I mean I wouldn't necessarily suggest it, because it was just a thought, but I thought it would be great for our Men's Group to go to a sauna together and just hang out. Talk there, as people do.

Hmmm

You know, get naked together.

Yeah.

Why not?

Yeah. That would be a stretch! I've got some stuff. Oh have I been writing stuff! I'm so up for just questions and things and things for the Men's Group.

Hmmm

Really looking forward to it.

Yeah. 'cos it's potentially…

People want it! But it could fizzle out.

And it could just become a kind of, moaning shop.

Yes.

Although so far it hasn't. But then we've only had, what, two or three sessions. Hmmm…

No, I don't think it will. But that's it. It's from one extreme to the other.

From the smothering Mother to, I haven't really got a problem with girls, they come-on to me…

Hmmm

…and I've never really chased girls in my life – to, an abandoning Father, then – I chase men. Be my best friend, um, or let's do this, or let's do that, or the mates thing, or smoking dope, or whatever.

Hmmm

Hanging out with mates comes before girls,
because they're just there. Do you know what I mean?

Hmmm.

Not doing changing rooms and toilets to cottaging and saunas!

Yeah. What is it? It's just that search for something that's missing, isn't it? I mean I've come to the very strong conclusion, recently, that – haaa – it's central, I mean, we should be taught, or it should be clear with kids that masturbation is fine, touching yourself is fine, enjoying your self is fine. And I realised, funnily enough, for the first time in ages, over the weekend - on Sunday, Monday, Tuesday - I could seriously have gone back and gone to the woods and had sex with somebody. And, but there was a real resistance. I thought, 'No, I don't really want to go back to that.' But at the same time, I thought, 'What's this all about?' And I've realised in yesterday's session with Lesley, all these people I find attractive are either aspects of myself that I really like and have somehow distanced myself from, or things that I really would like to be like, or things that I am like…

Hmm

…if that makes any sense, and it's like the mirror of somebody. And so learning to enjoy my self, you know in this session, this might sound a bit daft, but I was just 'Fathering' myself, touching my own skin - and this was being witnessed by Lesley - not sexually, but allowing myself to touch every part of my body. I wasn't naked, it was clothed, but it was so liberating, just that sense of 'Ah so this is what I have been looking for in other people. Finding the perfect body or the perfect person or the perfect personality'. Or whatever. I could just find it within myself, and then...

Share it!

...yeah, I can attract it, yeah exactly, rather than needy needy needy, 'fulfil a missing part of me that I don't even know I'm looking for'.

Yeah, exactly.

Endlessly, on this fucking hamster-wheel of pain and suffering.

Lack.

Hmmm. Well it's like I said to you, I mean, a couple of times this year I've recently rediscovered, I mean I've always been a wanker, huh-ha, but, um, the last six months to a year it's really stopped. Until recently again, discovering that I nearly always fantasise, rather than just being present with myself and enjoying my self sexually. It's gotta be, '...ooh, who can I think about?'

Yeah.

'Ooh, I'm being touched by somebody', or 'This person is tweaking my nipples', or whatever, it's like – yeah, just enjoy...

Well, *I wish I had been a wanker.* Because I feel like I've missed out, and, it was a bad-dirty-wrong-guilt-thing-to-do, uum, you know, the whole Catholicism, you know, all the saints were in the corners of the room just watching me...

Hmmm

...and, I didn't know how. You know, it's quite simple to wank I suppose, but it's only watching other people on the internet doing it, that I thought, fucking hell! And then I knew, there were options, they were different... it was liberating! There was permission.

Yes.

But, who does? Well, maybe a lot of people do. But I was…

Imagine if your Dad sat you down and showed you how to do it! I mean, it sounds, idealised – ha ha ha

…but then these kind of things; I'm not sure I'd want my parents to be involved or anything.

Well maybe not a Father, but like a sort of mentor figure. Well, or even just your peers, I dunno.

Exactly!

The permission to do it, rather than it being, behind closed doors.

Exactly! And if it's in a community, or a group or friends, whatever, whatever, you hear about it, you see it, it would be, it would be normal rather than an organised 'right it's your duty!'

Yeah.

Rather than it being someone's duty, why is it so hidden? Because if it's not hidden, then it would naturally come up! In normal conversation, like squeezing spots, piles, genital warts and – you know that thing that, there's some disease that some of my friends have had, 'social disease' where you push that needle thing up the, up your 'Jap-eye' up your dick, and you turn the end and it opens inside it and scrapes the inside of your…

Aaahhhh!!!

…ha ha ha.

What, for pleasure!

Are you kidding? It's to get the infection…

Ow ow ow…!

…it's some social disease, I forget what social disease. And I've heard lots of things, that people don't lie about. It's cool to have social diseases and for some men to talk about it, because it means, 'hey, we're having sex'.

Yeah!

But everyone denies wanking. Leave alone how, when, why it – do you know what I mean?

Cleaning out my (our) closet

Yeah. Hmmm. How are things with Gina?

Funny you should ask! Ha ha ha... It's fucking amazing! It's so, so, good. We've just had the best; we're still honeymoon period, big time, because we spent all summer just travelling around the country, seeing friends - my friends - and staying in Hampstead, at this fucking amazing plush place where we first got together.

Hmmm

And this place has just been 'our home'. It's been amazing. Ummm, and, everything's been great. I've never known a girl like her, in that, she's not addicted to me, or doesn't want to trap me, or doesn't want to have my kids, or – it's free! Whatever it was, like same as me, *'pathway'* [104] *first*. At least that's how it is now, still. But it is pathway first! And she's twelve years younger, which gets me off the hook, because girls of my age wanna have kids.

Yeah, definitely.

Quick!

Yes! Now!

And / or get married. And / or get pregnant. Then you're fucked! Huuuuuh! And, um, she wants to do a lot of things that I've already done in my life. Travel a bit. And make a change of career and stuff like that. But, fucking amazing! So, I took her to Liverpool to meet my cousins - got on brilliantly! Really liked them, loved the family, got on really well, had a bottle of wine from her Father's vineyard to bring to the table, and my aunt and uncle were there before flying off to Canada the next day, but my aunt made the most gorgeous food and we had a nice big meal with my cousin and her husband and baby, then my other cousin came down from Chester with his wife – who's pregnant – and the child they've already got, and it was great! And we stayed for a few days, looked around Liverpool, it was wonderful. Absolutely wonderful. And then it was Swindon time. Liverpool, that's the uncle who eloped with my Mother's best friend and no one knew anything was happening. And I asked in Swindon, "What's the story? What actually happened?" The story I got from them is that there was one friend, I think, that knew - but not any of them - and my aunt used to take her clothes and bits, every now and again, to a friend's house and leave them there. And apparently, ummm, she left with her Mother's jewellery (her share of the inheritance, anyway) – ha ha ha ha ha ha – and my uncle, and they just left.

Hmmm

And it's them that didn't keep in touch with the family, rather than the other way around. Apparently... Fuck knows if that's true. But, apparently, the shit flew big time! And that's when my grand Father started drinking – more! He drank before, but not hugely. But that's when he started the alcoholism.

I don't quite understand what the problem was because he'd just disappeared?

Yes, because they eloped. Because, I think it's basically because their side of the family wouldn't accept Goans, the Goan family wouldn't accept them and that's the way it went. Ummm, I don't know which was predominant or what the situation was exactly, but, you know, if my uncle was my grand Mother's Mummy's-boy, and my grand Father's enemy, then – you know he wasn't living at home anyway, so it was easier for him – and apparently, you know, he was, he had a successful band out there playing jazz and stuff. They went to some band member in Europe and then came here to live in Liverpool for some reason. Whatever. That's when my grand Father started drinking and that's, that's something that my family never talked about – or got over – meanwhile, we all suffer from that. And then there are other stories about them. But, the time that the bitchy stuff happened is the next weekend – Gina and I went to Swindon. Ummm, and, first night I stayed with my cousin and there was bitchiness straight away. My God daughter is only eight – going on eighteen – and acting as if she has already been left with a child and on her own, do you know what I mean?

Hmmm.

She - my God-daughter - apparently said to my cousin Mary-Ellen "So who is Uncle Mickey to you? Why is he going to..." and everyone was like, a bit nervous because I was going to stay with my cousin rather than my God Mother or whatever. This is political straight away. You can't fart! And the stories that are flying around, just for the sake of stories flying around. It's really boring. Cut a long story short, Gina turned up the second day – because she was working – and um, they went out and bought some food, plus we had some great left-overs because they did some cooking because I was coming over – some lovely lovely Goan food. And everyone was a bit excited, and the whole family, Liverpool, Swindon, everyone, cannot deal with couples...

Hmmm

...or affection...

Hmmm

...or touching, or girlfriend, or boyfriend, or...

So you kind of sat literally separate, the two of you?

In a way. In another way we just didn't bother.

Hmmm.

Aam, but in a way, yeah! It was weird. We didn't know how to do it. So, my cousin, Mary-Ellen; the kids 'ambushed' my girlfriend, they stole Gina because they loved her, and she loves kids, so that was fine, but it was time to come in and eat, so it was all served out, and Mary-Ellen said to me "Tell Gina what it all is." And again, everyone 'panic!' and shouting, and talking at the same time, and selling why they're okay and why they're good and what they've done for each other – it's just mass hysteria. I didn't know what the food was – I didn't cook it and I don't remember and – you know, why ask me to tell her, whoever cooked it will probably know quite well what it is. So I said, "I'm not really sure, I don't know what it is" and I don't remember at what stage, but Mary-Ellen came up to me and banged her glasses case against my head. And, without thinking, I just turned around - and I, I shout… less than half a dozen time a year! Properly.

Hmm

And I shouted! And it wasn't a big mad one, but it was a shout. And it was *"WHAT THE FUCK DO YOU THINK YOU'RE DOING hitting me!"* or something. Or, what the hell, something-or-other. Because it was a shock. And to me, you don't hit people, especially with something hard, and especially on the head. You know, a tap on the bum or whatever, or on the leg, or whatever, but – I don't know, maybe it's a cultural thing. But, the head is absolute disrespect and humiliation. In a lot of countries you just don't touch the head. I think even in this country, to touch someone's head, it's just, you know, it's not on. And maybe I'm wrong. But, to me, it was quite a shock and I was… I was not happy. And it was a reaction. So maybe I over-reacted, maybe I was totally wrong. As I shouted that - fuck knows how the family'd deal with that. As I shouted that, my eight year old God daughter shouts "Uncle Mickey, don't say bad words…" but, a child? She's supposed to be eight! Jumping into that!

But kids do that, I mean, I think they kind of assume a slightly adult role sometimes.

Yup. But the problem with these kids, is it's all the time! They have not been parented, there are no boundaries, it's just it's fucked up. And the kids are there for people to spoil, to run around and do things – it's manipulation, same as I had. If I do this, if I pull out my God Mother's or Mother's 'unsightly' grey hairs with tweezers, I'm good. If I get this, get that, run here, do that, I'm good. If I make noise, then I'm harming them and they'll abandon me and I'm bad. If I buy them things, or say the right thing, or whatever, then I'm good. If I do anything bad, then I'll be compared to someone – do you know what I mean?

Hmmm

Sheer manipulation. And the kids are just, you know, poor bastards. They're just meat thrown to the lions in my family. Same as all the kids have been. And, maybe they don't know any better – whatever. I'm not sure that they wanna know much better. It's convenient this way. Someone's got to look after the kids, and, so – I'm not sure how good relationships are generally in couples in my family, and same has happened to me. 'Fuck the couple, now we've got children we can hide between that!' Or avoid each other because of the the the kids, so the kids have to grow up - *the kids are pawns in an adult relationship,* and that's exactly my story, basically.

Hmmm

It's exactly what's happened to me. I've been pulled up where I shouldn't have been pulled up, and where's my childhood? Same as this girl, with the eight year old personality she's got, if it carries on this way, she's going to be pregnant before she's twenty. And, is the bloke going to be around? I don't think so. Not good! Meanwhile, what do I say? 'cos, I've so talked and talked about this with friends, saying, she is my God daughter. When I was asked to be God Father, I wanted to talk about it with my cousin. Because I rate my cousin – I think he's cool – he's just got his hands full with the family he's in, and now, before he knows it, he's got kids, and he's just in the thick of it. How does he get over or change anything? He probably knows better, but doesn't know how to change anything, because he's got his Mother, his wife, all his sisters, you know, he needs; he is part of the drama basically, whether he likes it or not. And all the men of the family are hen-pecked anyway, one way or another. So I wanted to talk to him about being the God Father and saying, well, does this mean that if I don't agree with the way the child is being brought up, I should say something, or does it mean that you just want me to send birthday cards once a year? And me just wanting to talk about it upset him. And it's like, 'Well, don't you want to be God Father?' And he was so upset.

Oh my God.

Exactly!

Mad...

And it's like, well, my brother and I were going to be God Fathers, it's, well, of course we will. But I want the best for the child. But talking with friends, it's like, 'Don't say anything. They don't wanna hear anything. All they want is a card a year. Send a card a year.'

A pointless token.

Exactly! Exactly! Meanwhile, I feel like shit because these kids – and I love her brother, even though he's not my God son, but how does that come into it? But, they're dysfunctional kids. They've got problems. Big problems. Obviously, they can't shit either, but then, you know, *not only do we not have genitals or emotions in the family, but our arse-holes are sewn up,* because we can't let go of all the hysteria.

Jesus...

So, in a way, thank God the child piped up and shouted 'Uncle Mickey blah blah blah', because then it's diffused between my cousin and I, because no one would know how to deal with that.

Hmmm

And then, I shouted at the child, something about teaching the child some manners. And from that time, it was quiet, for a good couple of minutes. And then, we chatted as usual as if nothing happened, but what really got chatted about, until the end of the day - probably bed time - they bitched like crazy about the Liverpool people, and what they did, and what they didn't do, and 'they didn't want us when we were refugees, and they didn't help us out, and uncle Frankie didn't want his

Mother here, and he didn't do this,' and blah blah blah, it was bitch bitch bitch. Whether it's right or wrong, whether it's information or not, how cheap that as soon as there's something up and we pretend that it didn't happen, typical in the family, a small thing like this. Imagine everything else. Then daggers to everyone else.

Hmmm

I could not believe it! And I so felt for Gina. 'cos I didn't know whether to just leave there and then. Take her with me? Or, um, say something about 'something's happened here...' or what or what or what. I just didn't have a clue. I didn't know what to do. But poor Gina was in the middle of it, and it seemed that they wanted to do all this bitching – and my God Mother, for example, revealed that she had been a 'drug addict', because in Africa you can go to – and I think in the early days in Goa, for all I know, the same now – you can buy certain things over the counter that you just could not buy here. And, in one way or another, it gives you a buzz, or it helps you to avoid your own life, or your emotions, and whatever it is. And that the nuns took her in and that she lived with the nuns for two years and they got her off the drugs, and whatever. I didn't know this, but there's stuff that they said about themselves, so easily – probably a lot of it was the stuff that they thought I knew anyway – umm, and they said it in front of Gina. The stuff that they said about the other side of the family, Liverpool, in front of Gina, I think that was just cheap sales! 'You think we're bad, well, this is what they're really like! You liked them did you? Well, check this out!'

Hmmm

In front of Gina.

Why? Why were they like that?

Um, it's the same old 'love me'.

Yeah.

'I'll tell you why everyone else is shit and I'll

tell you why I'm great.' Nothing more, nothing less. That's how we were all brought up. 'Sell yourselves, jump through the hoops of fire, never ask if any one's angry, because you should know why they're angry because you're the cause!'

Yes! Ha ha ha

But, fucked up! And what do you do? Like, thank God I went and checked all this out, and know that there's not a lot I can do for these people, they don't want me to do a lot, and, I won't want my kids around them. Much as they are lovely people and I love them and all that, I don't want my kids to be part of that!

Hmmm.

The trap was just guilt. But fuck it! It's been like permission to go – do you know what I mean? You know I said about my God Mother, and all that kind of stuff? And the way they were bitching? With Gina – Gina didn't know what to do either.

I wanted to know; that's what I was going to ask, actually.

Her side of it?

Yeah!

Yeah. Because for me; we did not have a problem with each other. We've tried to have a problem...

'The in-laws'

...yeah. I've even suggested that we...

Have a row!

...exactly, exactly!

Ha ha ha

So what happened with that; and I said to her, "Look, you're going to project your Father on me, how could you not? I'm a man. That's your thing." Blah blah blah...

Yes!

And, after I shouted at my cousin, Gina went quiet, she was stunned, she didn't know where to put herself, but more than anything, it was her Father. 'I was her Father, shouting.'

Aaahh.

And, she felt weird, and we didn't really communicate, and after a little while, she said "I need to go for a walk." It's quite dangerous out there these day.

Where, in Swindon?

Yup! And, um, we took the dog and went for a walk together, and we had a really good chat. And I didn't talk a lot. It was about her, not putting her shit on me. And me not putting my shit on her; and knowing that no matter what was going on with my family, she just brought it to herself and said to herself 'Okay, what is this all about for me? Why am I here? What's it all about?' And it was about her family, it was about her Father, me 'turning into her Father' and shouting, her being scared of me, blah blah blah blah blah, and I suppose the only one issue I can say that Gina and I have had with each other, is that, rather than withdrawing and saying 'this is not about Mickey, this is not even about the situation in hand. It's about me and my past.' Rather than withdrawing, it's like, sharing. Because, then, you know, there's like enough shit for everyone. Then I know what's going on, she knows what's going on, and same with when I've got shit with her. If we share it, then we both know what's going on.

Definitely.

'cos otherwise, I'd feel 'What the fuck's going on?' You know, my imagination would run wild and we'd react to each other's; we'd react to our paranoia of what the other person has going on — and the relationship would just not make sense. Do you know what I mean?

Yup.

She's just fucking excellent!

Well otherwise, everyone just starts making assumptions. 'It must have been something that I've done, something I've said…'

Exactly.

'I'm no good in bed…'

Yup.

'Something that I should have said…'

And she was just great! And we could not wait to get out of there. The next day people were around, had to say hello, had to say goodbye, had to get up early in the morning; "The kids would love it if you both took them to school", we were up very, very early, it was all charade, charade, charade, jump through hoops, do this, do that, and it wasn't 'real love'. It was jumping through hoops of fire. It was 'what drama do I have to do…'

Real love from what, from you to them?

There was no space for anyone to love anyone. There was too much hysteria, and 'sales pitches' and - is that some famous dude, because he's walking like he is, she's not that hot, who is he?

Dunno.

Jude Law or something? Fuck knows what these people look like. Ha ha ha ha ha – well that's Hampstead for you. - So, tell me about Malaika! Um, when's the last time I saw her?

> 104. Pathway. Spiritual / life path, that is 'grown into' and lived beyond the personality / ego.

"I'm your Daddy"

I don't know.

July.

Oh, really?

There are two children that I think about regularly. One of them's; well, one boy and one girl. Dennis and…

Dennis and Malaika.

Hmmm

They're almost exactly the same age, as well.

Really?

Hmmm

But Malaika, for me, is how children should be. And how children should; and the way you treat her is how children should be treated. Do you know what I mean?

Yeah. She has, yeah… there's a kind of innocence. Purity.

And because she hasn't had that beaten out of her, she's a gift to everyone! Do you know what I mean?

Yup.

So what, what's news?

No, just the touching-ness of our relationship. Um, when we were driving back from Silchester the other day, just about ten minutes from her Mum's place. Mallie just leaned over - and it was the sweetest

thing - she leaned over and put her little arm on mine, with her head on my shoulder, and said *"I'll really miss you, Daddy..."* she said "...and I'll get really upset later when you go." And... for me, even after all you and I have been through, talking, processing, whatever, I really still have to curb the urge to say to her "No no, come on now, be brave..." I even nearly said "be brave for Mummy." My God, wh-ha-ha-at the fuck! But that would have just shut her up.

Yeah.

Like 'don't be emotional.'

Yup.

'Don't tell me about this. Or be upset. I don't want to hear about it... because then everyone else gets upset'

Yeah!

And it's wow, 'I can deal with it.' Yeah, it upsets me, because it makes me sad. But I'd rather she said that, than pretended.

Yup.

And I've, yeah. I mean, I've found that... I've been - close.

Close. It was close, ummm, to almost say, 'suppress it'.

Hmmm

Do you know what I mean?

Yeah.

And I imagine, it just takes one person, in anyone's life to say 'it's okay to be honest about your emotions, it's okay to be honest about your fantasies, your thoughts, your dreams, whatever'. That one person's enough for that person, for the other person's dreams to come true.

I bloody hope so! Because the odds are stacked against most people, aren't they?

How are they with Malaika? Like her and her Mother, and grand folks, her Mother's boyfriend and all that.

Ummm, I imagine Ayesha's pretty good with her. There's a certain amount of fear from her. But Ayesha's Mother is the classic fearful grand Mother. 'I don't like her playing rough.' 'I don't like…' And she says things like "Oh, I expect your other granny and grand Pa really spoiled you again, haven't they?"

Hmmm. Do her other grand parents say that? Is there a grand parents competition-thing going on?

Probably, subtly.

Yeah…

But, actually, Mallie was great! She said "No they didn't." Ha ha

Cool. That's it! She tells the truth. But how many adults laugh at kids when they tell the truth or say something that's honest and pure – from their own embarrassment, they laugh at the child, humiliate it, then 'break it' – generally.

Yeah!

And what about the boyfriend. Does she still have the boyfriend?

Hmmm, yeah. It's going from strength to strength, really. And I'm, actually, having got over my upset that Malaika might spend more time with him than she does with me, ultimately…

Yur

Um, I really have come down on the; great! She'll have all the influences and role models. But, I see, Mallie's great as a mirror for me to see how… how unreasonable I can be with her sometimes.

Really?

Like I'm driving away on Sunday, went to pick her up from Ayesha and Ray, together on Sunday, and, um, Mallie's got this thing, oh, when it's like the 'hand-over' fresh from Ayesha, she always calls me 'Mummy'.

Say that again…?

Right, when I've just picked her up, it takes her a while to…

Riiight!

…like that's the word that's on her lips. And, um, so she's been with Ayesha and Ray, so she said "Ayesha, Ray, Daddy…" at the start of her sentence. Um, my God, for a moment I was like, 'Oh, so I'm third in the hierarchy' – it's like, ego.

Yeah, yeah.

Just ego. And I could so easily have said to her *'Look! I'm your Dad! I come first!'*

Yah

But instead, I just said to her "Oh, is that your new name for me?"

Ha ha ha ha ha

She just kinda giggled.

Brilliant!

And that's it! It's like, 'God why do we take ourselves so fucking seriously?!'

If you do this 'I come first' thing, then it's the same old; like I was saying about my folks. It's not parenting, it's competing with your brothers and sisters. It's sibling rivalry with your own kids – do you know what I mean? 'I'm your best friend!'

'Yeah, the new boyfriend's nothing. He can't buy you nice presents…'

Exactly!

…he's not that…

'He's bad!' He he… 'My Daddy can beat up his Daddy any way…'
Do you know what I mean?

**And there's no denying there is a bit of – I don't know, what is it?
Competitiveness? Ummm, something in… genetics, I think. That doesn't
want her to call him Daddy. It's almost like I can live with anything
else…**

Yeah, yup! And why would she? Why would anyone want him to? Do
you think that would come up as an issue?

**I don't think so. I think Ayesha and I are very very lucky. Having had
such a long relationship, no matter what went on between us…**

Yeah.

…there is no funny business around Mallie.

Yup. Lucky girl! Usually the kids are 'the' weapon.

Yup.

The pawns. And, you know, how many parents justify it by 'oh the kids
won't remember, the kids don't know what's going on, they only know
what they're told' or blah blah blah, yeah - bollocks!

Ha haaa

Rites of passage

What about the, the 'getting ill'. Is that about being in the tent? How long have you been in the tent now?

It's been a…

July!

Yeah, first week of July.

Well, in the tent in Box Hill, rather than the tent at the bottom of my garden. So that's July, August, September, October – that's four months!

Yeah. I think I'll be there until the end of October.

Good on ya…

More or less.

Isn't it wet, or damp, or…

It has got a little bit wet, sometimes. I mean, I did get ill, but everyone – all the clients I had – everyone was coming down with it. Like I've just said to you, I think, being outdoors actually really strengthens you. Your body's systems…

It toughens up the immune system…

Yeah. I think that I was just unlucky. Ummm, but it's been great! It's just been claiming that space. Like you said, a rite of passage. Which, um, my version of manhood, whatever the hell that is. It might not be everyone's version of manhood, or everyone's idea of it. How you get through it. Yes, it's been about just claiming a space for myself.

So, from obsessively drawing gay men coming out of tree bark…

They were not necessarily 'gay men' thank-you-very-much!

Ha ha ha ha ha ha ha ha…

But yes, from obsessively drawing gay men, or men, whatever,

'Tree men' ha ha ha

I've become one!

Yeah. Exactly! You claimed it. You are… Grizzly Adams[105.]

HA HA HA HA HA ha ha ha ha ha

Grizzly Adams-Smythe…!

Ha ha ha ha ha – it has been the most surreal experience! Though…

How many people pay so much money to spend a weekend, to be dropped somewhere remote, and – do you know what I mean?

I know…

Four months, and you've done the 'real thing'! Without light and fire? I mean, what the fuck's that all about? Are you gonna; we should have the Men's Group

…in the woods.

…and help you pack up and have a dirty great fire there.

That's a very good idea.

That would be f-u-c-k-I-n-g a-m-a-z-i-n-g… can you imagine that?!

Why don't we do it at the end of October? That's the, that's the kind of Samhain[106], Halloween, isn't it?

Yeah. Well let's do diaries before we split. We've got a couple of dates – but what a thing to do! Faaking hell!

It would be great. And anyone who wants can go naked, swimming in the river. Ha ha ha

Ha ha ha – step by step... As long as there's no... lights. Or incense.

That's another thing, everything at night is just amazing. Um, I've realised that there's so much fear around the dark....

Yup, yup.

...in our culture. Absolute terror. Everyone, so many people have said "Aren't you scared at night?"

Yeah

Quite the opposite. Actually, what made me feel, the only time I felt vulnerable was when I lit candles, or, um, and that's not... fire hazard. The tent becomes like a lantern.

Yeah

When I'm sitting in the dark, I have absolutely no fear what-so-ever.

The first time I got naked with Gina was in your – not the tent you've got now, but the other tent.

What the white one?

Yeah.

Ha ha

Remember that weekend you were away and Gina and I...

Yeah, yeah.

...spent the night...

You soiled... my tent!

...no we didn't shag or anything. We didn't shag! It was just really lovely to be out, on the ground, in the rain, and the sun going down, the sun rising and the leaves, with the wind, and it was just fucking excellent!

There's nothing like it!

But you've got to see, what... two seasons in it, basically!

Hmmm

Summer and Autumn.

The hottest Summer for years, and then a fantastic Autumn.

Yeah! I mean, look at it now. Look at today!

Yeah. What is it, the fifth of...

Half way through October and it's like this! It's fucking excellent! Global Warming is where it's at! If we get weather like this, I'm all for it.

As long as we don't have too many tornados!

Yup. And bisexual fish..

Bisexual fish?

Who was talking about fish changing sex from female to male, because of the stuff that's being pumped in the water...

Hmmm! That's not global warming, that's kind of pesticides.

And also, someone-or-other said yesterday – or was it you, earlier, that said about – Billy, said it this morning. *That some whale had been officially labelled global – what is it? – toxic waste.*

What?!

Because of all the shit that's inside it!

Oh, my God! That's convenient. Now they can slaughter them and sell them for cheap blubber.

Yeah, and tuna. But that is a fucking excellent idea, because Bob and I were looking at dates, so end of October / beginning of November will be the ceremony of not only the Men's Group, but then taking down the tent.

Exactly.

And FUCK what an inspiration to all of us. The respect that people have for you – I don't know whether they understand or can put it into words, and I'm not even sure that you've got a clue about, but there is a big respect because you haven't 'sold out' in any way. You've gone from sleeping with men, women and God knows whatever else you've slept with, and you've gone for not doing the drugs, not doing the drink, you haven't sold out, basically. *In any way, you haven't sold out.* You are a fucking good Father, you've been married, you've got divorced, blah blah blah – but you haven't sold out. True to yourself every step of the way, and there's something about that, the way that, yeah? Sometimes you move around like a man, sometimes you flounce around like a woman. But, it's honest! Do you know what I mean?

Yeah.

And people haven't got the guts to do that. But they can see it and respect it. You're gonna blow them away with your tent and your lifestyle and everything. Plus, we get… to all light the fire. Finally light a fire there – what a way to go! We could call the press in.

Ha ha

That is a great story, actually. Call the press in and launch the Men's Groups. Because I was thinking, maybe we could; because I'd love to stick something in *'Time Out'*[107] and say 'Men's Group, call this number for information…'

Hmmm, that's true. Really spread the word.

Yeah. But I'd love to start really doing the Men's Groups. Gagging for it!

Yeah. Actually that sounds like a good reason to get publicity. Not for

my own personal…

And maybe only tell *'Time Out'* or something. Or…

Yeah, no, that is a very good idea. And also the time of year – Halloween.

Yeah.

November fifth.

Yeah. Sacrifice a child.

Pagan? 'Not mah baby…'

Ha ha

We could go to some council estates – NO THAT'S NOT GOING IN THE BOOK!

Ha ha ha ha ha ha ha

But that's what the rich have always done, haven't they?

Totally!

Jack The Ripper and his friends…

Yeah, absolutely. Well everyone. I mean, look at the old days. The 'Lord of the Manor' had the right to de-flower the bride before the groom had a go!

That's true, isn't it? But there's some film where that happens.

Servants were for shagging. *'Braveheart'*[108].

But it's funny, it's actually very hard to, I find it very hard to receive that - kind of - praise that you were just giving me. Why not accept it? I suppose, because I think, 'well, I was married, but didn't ever really feel committed to the relationship, if I was completely honest…'

Yah

343

...it was just like, always looking for a way out, but never having the guts...

It's all the 'yeah buts'. But maybe, quite simply, the bottom line is – like you said with the book – it's about 'accepting yourself as one of the men', rather than 'being accepted by the men'.

Yeah, yeah, yeah.

And all the men could accept you to fuckery – it's down to you!

Yeah.

And *how could the men possibly accept you, unless you've accepted yourself?*

I think that has; that's what's changed for me. And I think, in as much as you were talking about how Bob has changed and he's accepted himself a lot more.

Yeah.

But yeah, I do feel more comfortable with myself. I almost feel like it doesn't matter if I'm straight or gay or married or single or shagging or not shagging.

Yeah. Do you know what Billy was saying today? And I thought 'fucking hell – spot-on!'

105. *Grizzly Adams. US (film 1975, television series 1977-1978) based on a true story.*

106. *Samhain. Summer's end / New Year in the Pagan / Celtic calendar.* www.celticspirit.org *and* www.witchvox.com

107. *'Time Out' Listings guides, originally London, now worldwide.* www.timeout.com

108. *'Braveheart' (1995) Mel Gibson, USA.*

Social skeletons

Hmm?

Any thing that seems – or one of the main things that's left, because now the paedophile thing's out and the gay thing's out, and, you know, everything's out.

In the book, you mean?

No...

In society.

...he was saying, 'mental health issues!' And how many people are on; well, in my therapy group. Three people in the group are not practising therapists. One of the main therapists, a psychiatrist, is 'on something' and has been on anti-depressants for years. Meanwhile he's dealing with mental health patients and prescribing God knows what! Ummm, and if he wasn't on this, then he would probably be drinking, gambling, fuck knows what he's doing, even more. And, you know, he's messy!

Yeah. Isn't it just an open secret? You know, it's almost like one in three people will have some mental health problem in their lifetime. Everyone knows it, but...

I didn't even know the statistic!

Yeah,

But also with that, what does that mean? How do you deal with this? What do you take? Where do you go? None of that's known. It's something to, to hide. To pretend. Or to have unprescribed drugs – you know – dope, alcohol, workaholism, ecstasy[109], whatever.

Shopping…

Exactly, shopping is a huge addiction. The credit card binge.

Yup

More costly than chocolate éclairs – what the fuck am I on about?

Ha ha ha… But that's the thing. In a way, what we've been describing, *the dysfunctional family is like a sort of mini-version of a dysfunctional society.*

Yup. Totally. Spot-on!

Yeah, in tribes; I mean, again, it's easy to sort-of idealise a bit 'these quaint people living in their mud huts', or Pagans running around painted blue in ancient Britain. But I'm sure, you know, that if there was a dysfunctional unit within the tribe, it was sorted out.

Yeah.

It wasn't just ignored. Or it was acknowledged in some way, but it wasn't just shoving everything under the carpet.

Exactly. And people would know what's going on, and they'd deal with it, because they're involved. They are one of the members, or one of the women, or their kids play with these kids, or there would be – you know – a caring relationship. In our society, we're not allowed to care.

No

Where is the space? We're not allowed to care for our own family, leave alone our next door neighbour or anyone else, because everyone runs off different rules, different secrets and lies and different competitions. Different, you know, 'it's forbidden'. And also, if society works, where do they get the workers from?

Yes. Well exactly, it's like you said, I saw a chart in a nursery school the other day. And it was a, I don't know, a menu chart. And it was 8.30am to 4.30pm, and I thought 'God! That's a long day for the under fives to be separated from their parents.' And that's five days a week!

Yeah. But there's huge money in child care.

I know, exactly, and what does that…

Prime them for?

…I wonder? Going to the office…

Exactly.

…or the factory. The…

Yeah

Whatever.

The whole thing with schools is a hoax as well. Getting into a good school. And the amount of money that you have to pay to even be considered, I had no idea! Just being with Anna and Simon, talking about Alex and schools, especially in London, it's fucking mad!

Well there's regular articles in the papers about how houses cost about, I don't know, twenty five per cent more near 'good schools'.

Really?

I mean, no wonder everyone's so exhausted. They're flogging their guts out to pay for their mortgages, then to pay extra for a school that educates them, but for what?

Yup. Yeah, exactly. To compete, fuck other people up in society and be a cunt. But who could blame them? People think they don't have choice and people don't know any better.

Well, it's what most people's parents do and that's – do what your parents do.

Yup, the curse is passed on and on and on, because of panic-survival.

Yeah.

I'm looking forward to having a place for the winter.

So do you think you'll stay at Billy's?

Yup.

But you're talking about living in a community?

Yeah. Or something – something needs to come up. I need my own place. At Billy's I'm still in the process of spending time with people who I want to spend my time with, where as if I was working and I had my home, I wouldn't have the time. It's huge. It's sad. The way I've spent my Summer, up until now has been a luxury. Of quality relationships, learning, sharing, you know enjoying love, space, whatever; rather than working my fucking arse off and playing hard for the three weeks holiday – *three weeks holiday in a year!*

Yeah.

That's theft! That's disgusting! That's ridiculous... and how much does it cost to go on holiday? You've still got to pay all your bills, and you know...

Your rent, your mortgage, whatever!

...standing orders galore!

> 109. Ecstasy. *Methylenedioxymethamphetamine, MDMA, XTC, Adam, Love Doves, New Yorkers, M25's, Disco Burgers, Dennis the Menace, 'e'.*

Home time

You saying that, I'm really enjoying seeing people at the moment. I feel like I've pared down my friendships to; well, my life, actually, to the minimum.

Quality rather than quantity.

Exactly!

Billy's really looking forward to seeing you on Sunday.

Hmmm. Yeah, well I'm really looking forward to it actually, whether there's the Press there or not. How fantastic!

Yeah. Well I haven't had the time or the chance to write a press release, but today I picked up Gina's lap top, so I will hopefully be able to do that later today.

Hmmm.

Otherwise, we've got a lap top for transcribing the book, anyway. Oh, I got a text from Emily yesterday.

Oh yeah...

She was saying that she forgot about my previous text and please send a press release as soon as possible because *'The Guardian'* seem to want to do a story on your 'Grizzly Adams' stint. Whether the Press comes or not, we need to take our own photos. Bob wanted to pick Billy and I up, Marius wanted to come, so maybe he could make his way up to Uxbridge. I don't think anyone else will come. I, I don't really want anyone else to come. Maybe the Press, I mean, who else is there... that we'd want — or that you'd want?

Well, I'm not really that bothered. Of course there's the superficial lure of the – whatever – fame! Notoriety. But no, I agree with you, it's all about… community.

…exactly! And now you've got a community – you don't need a workshop. Ha ha ha ha ha ha ha. And a bloody good community, too. Billy is so chuffed. It's funny that I'm the go-between, saying what you think, and then what he thinks. And he is so chuffed that you are ready to do his artwork for him, and you wanna do it.

Hmmm…

And he's still a bit scared to even ask, in case he gets a 'no'.

How strange.

Hmmm.

I was really surprised when he was saying about not having self-belief in his abilities. It's so often true of people with so many obvious talents. Well, obvious to other people.

Yup. Yeah… totally. And also things that we do naturally, we take for granted that they're just ordinary and no big deal. Because it's no effort.

Well, I don't know actually. I've had to really push myself sometimes to; the funniest thing I've found is once I've built the relationship with a client, say, repeat phoning them, there's always that moment of 'What if they've changed their mind?' or 'What if they're bored?' or 'What if they say, 'well, actually, I don't like you any more!' hmmm, so bugger off…'

Yeah. Or, you're a fraud.

Hmmm. It's been a very interesting couple of weeks for me, looking for somewhere to live. Because I've found, a lot of places I've found are wary about having a child, part time. Which I can understand, I suppose, if you've got a space and you're not used to having children. But for me, it's really underlined, this fact that I live a 'double life', in a way. And, I would really really like to meet other men in my situation. But I have also been wary of, like, starting a 'club'. Because it's like the 'bisexual club' or whatever. I remember going to some 'thing' years ago, down in Kings Cross. Some sort of a bisexual, social evening.

Yeah?

And it was only afterwards that I thought... actually it was really dull. They just sort of sat, literally whoever you happened to sit next to, you ended up chatting with. And I sat talking with this woman who I had nothing in common with, apart from the fact that she said she fancied men and women.

Ha ha ha ha

I thought afterwards, that's actually really interesting. Why go to something where that's the lynch-pin. That's all you have in common, because; it's not the way you really meet people.

Hmm, hmmm.

'I must find people who are exactly the same as me'.

And surely, places like these groups and clubs and whatever, where people take their wounds rather than celebrate their whatevers...

Yeah

...their wot-nots...

Yeah

And *if you've got a wot-not, then you may as well celebrate it!* Ha ha ha ha ha ha ha

And we've all got one!

I wish I had one on my forehead. I've always wanted a 'third eye clitoris'.

I thought you were going to say 'dick-head'.

Ha ha ha ha ha... Anyway, what kind of places have you seen?

Oh! I saw one place that you would not be-lieve! I didn't believe that places like this still existed. Bed-sits. I told you about it, didn't I? Wooooagh... I mean it just...

Oh, the one that smelt of

...gas, damp, cooking, it smelt of, sort of Britain in about 1946...

ha ha ha ha

...I don't know why, but literally like the war had just ended, very recently. It just felt, almost as you stepped in the front door, there was this feeling of being coated in this, sticky, s-t-uff. I don't know, like it was everywhere. The smell was horrible. The room was; it was bizarre, actually, because I can't believe I must have lost my mind, because I nearly took it.

You're kidding!

It was only talking to you and Maria about it...

Oh it's the one you told me... it was that one! Yeah! It sounds like as soon as you walked in, it was like a film of loneliness and other people's, coated with other people's dead skin...

UUUGgghhrrr...!

...sorry, while you're eating.

No no that's true. That's exactly it! Spot on!

Ha ha ha - I do know what you mean.

So I looked at that, I mean I've looked at some quite extreme places. A place for about £150 a week in – where was it – Stoke Newington / Islington, which is very nice, but, I don't know, it was almost the opposite. It felt really sterile.

Hmmm

I quite liked the idea of sharing. But having my own, quite separate space. Within that. Maybe with a couple, maybe with – maybe with people with kids.

Hmmm

Then I can have a relationship with them and their child. And then there would be someone for Mallie to see, or whatever.

Where are the types of places that you could put something up? I mean like that café we went to the other day. Like, community notice boards – in Brighton I'd know one or two places, but here... places around Stokie, or – I don't know, family group places? What's the place in Crouch End called? The up-market café full of trendy happening families? 'Banners!'

Crouch End is too far. Buses only!

Or even, what's the appropriate magazine? Well maybe, let's just see what comes up from the article, because that's – that will be out next week... fucking hell! I'm really looking forward to writing that later...

Hmmm. Well, we've got the bones of the press release, haven't we?

Yeah, it's been weird. Much as I've been living with Billy, I've hardly seen him for a while because I haven't been staying there.

You've been coming into London?

Yeah, I stayed with Gina for a little bit, like tonight we're staying with Carolyn and Will – just for the fun of it, I'm staying with my folks while they're at Joseph and Mary's, Friday night I was in Wellingborough, seeing a client. It was great! But I'm just hardly there. Which has been really; Billy's been going through lots of changes. He's really been through his own changes, and it's been great that I haven't been there all the time, that there's been 'us' time, with 'him' time alone without me, and 'me' time without him I suppose, but going through his changes so he can claim himself, rather than my falling into 'parenting' again, or something.

I remember you saying that he was going through something similar to me, in that he's – it sounds corny, but – the only way I can phrase it is learning to 'have more of a relationship with himself'?

Yeah

Rather than relying on other people.

I think he's learning to stop being 'okay' all the time, to stop having all the answers with everything to do with health, fitness and all that shit. Stop. He's aware of his obsessive-compulsive side, his passive-aggressive side, his controlling and his just not making any space for anyone else to 'meet him'.

Hum

He didn't know, because that was survival. He's getting his memory back about things and he's had really bad stomachs.

Why is this happening for all of us? It's interesting.

Because we wanna get over it. The more you wanna move forward, the more you've gotta – this is my life, the way I see it – it's like a pendulum swinging. *You want more of 'that', so you have to go the equal and opposite distance back, to dump your baggage so you can get more of a swing forward happening.* Do you know what I mean?

Yeah.

That's the way I see it, anyway.

Hmmm.

And he really seems to be. But people; same as me, I've been spending time with my folks - and my Mother wrote me that letter and stuff - I had no idea. Now I understand things. I can't live that anymore. I can't play that any more. I'm just – over it! Plus reading – I've got some notes, I'll show you. It's about obsessive-compulsive, it's about; I've started reading about the Oedipal Complex.

What, Freud?

Yup. And, it makes so much sense. And I can't blame it on my parents, or bitch, but – when was it? Now, I haven't told you about this!

Yeah. But then it's 'normal' too, to bitch and blame. What does everyone do? They dread going home, it's like Christmas is coming, you can almost feel people going 'Oh my God I'll have to go see my parents...'

Sell out, play small, lie, get drunk with them...

Um-hum!

...whatever, whatever – and it all comes back. Who we needed to be, or how we were hurt, or whatever it was.

Hmmm

Have I seen you since we saw the slides? I haven't – have I?

I saw you briefly on Friday, but we didn't really...

Talk about it. No, we were talking about other things.

We were going to do the press release then.

Yeah.

For the woodland escapade.

Money, lies, worth, hokey-cokey...

Fucking amazing. We were just, well, we spent the whole afternoon. My folks were a bit earlier than I thought they would be. Went into the flat, walked down the road – I was going to take them to a Mexican buffet place, because my Father has always wanted cheap! Or value. To know how much he's gonna pay. And you can't blame him – ex-refugee! We didn't have enough money for food!

And here we are in an 'all you can eat' buffet!

Ha ha – but...

Like Father – like son.

But it's healthy...

Ha ha ha – you're nailed, mate!

I'M GETTING BETTER! Ha ha – no we're all that way, it's gonna affect us all. And even now, I can't manage money – I can not manage money. And all the manipulations that go with it. It's a fucking hoax! All these credit cards and God knows what. I can't, it scares me. I haven't got a mortgage. The whole thing scares the shit out of me.

I know what you mean. It's like, we're retarded, almost.

Yup, absolutely.

The things that everyone else seems to; but that's the other thing, as we've said before. Everyone is in debt! I saw, I was travelling on the Tube and I saw some headline about, there's a 'debt bombshell', a time bomb waiting to explode. I thought, 'Oh my God, I'm so glad I'm

not part of that.'

Yeah

Panicking about whether my mortgage is going to be beyond my payments...

Well it has before, hasn't it?

Yeah. In '92.

Plus, wasn't there a time when people's – what do you call them, retirement – pension funds went down? So they've saved all their lives, think they've got a safe, secure – um – retirement, nothing!

But also, when I was home recently, I just glanced at something, and it was talking about this, you know this advert with a woman delightedly saying 'Ooh, they're going to buy my endowment policy back!' and I remember when Ayesha and I bought our flat, everyone was told to get endowment policies as part of their mortgage. Later there was this huge turn-around because they said they weren't going to reach their targets. You wouldn't get your money. You wouldn't get your payments. And now, we're supposed to be glad that the same - probably the very same companies - will buy them back! For a fraction of what they were worth! So I said to my Mum "THIS IS OUT-RAGE-OUS!"

What a fucking swizz.

As far as I know, no body's been...

And people were stupid enough to fall for it?! Over and over!

Well, people forget. Survival I suppose. People can't afford to get angry.

Yeah, yup! Because they're scared. Because of what will happen.

Well I said to a woman yesterday, as I was massaging her – she said that she lived in Beckenham, and I said that a friend of mine was going back to Beckenham last week and a train got stuck on the track for two hours. And I just said, kind-of semi-jokingly, with a very wry laugh, *"Maybe you should have all rioted.* Just, trash the train. To make a point."

Ha ha ha ha ha

She just went, "Ooh, ooh… That wouldn't do much good, would it?" I said to her, "If people did that occasionally, it would be really quite powerful." And I'm not suggesting…

It's like the bully, standing up. You stand up once to the bully, and that stops the bullying. Not only from the bully, but probably from everyone. I've heard that over and over and over and over…

Yeah.

…even my Father told me a story the other day, about him doing that. Yes – um-humm, so we were going to go down to the Mexican buffet place, we walked slowly, no problem, finally got there – it was a bit of a schlepp because Mary's got a bad back, they're all getting a bit 'wrinkly' – so we got to this Mexican buffet, finally, it was getting quite late anyway, rang the door bell – they'd just closed. Forever!

Really?

So it was, and for me, it was, 'oh my God, I've got to take care of these people, we're in an expensive area, what to do, what to do,' they closed, they were refurbishing and they were going to re-open as a Thai restaurant! And I kind of felt like shit. And Goans, Catholics, older people, ready to bitch, ready to 'Oh, well, we should have phoned, we should have this, we should have that, whatever…' and my Father – was sooo cool. And we ended up going next door to a relatively expensive Chinese restaurant, everyone ordering whatever they wanted, without a bat of an eye-lid…

Wow!

…totally; and in the past he'd be all bitchy, worried and up-tight, he has changed! And it wasn't – the whole thing was just a dream. We really enjoyed the food. And it was just fucking amazing. We all had a really nice time. It was wonderful.

It's so amazing having money, isn't it? Well, it's a freedom, isn't it? A tool. A means to an end.

Not having enough is a sign of lack of self worth...

Yeah.

...because if it's a tool, and you haven't got all the tools, then maybe you're in a 'victim thing', do you know what I mean? 'I'm a victim, I'm in control, you have to look after me, I'll just dribble here...' do you know what I mean?

Yeah. Oh, well my Mum said something to me recently. "Oh I really worry about you, you three. My biggest fear is that you'll all end up on the street." Which...

Ha ha ha ha ha – one down! HA HA HA

Exactly! And I said, "Well I suppose I came quite close, didn't I? Living in the woods." But, that has been so freeing, because I think to myself, 'well, I know I can do more. That was such a good... 'experiment' is the wrong word. To be able to...'

'Phase'

...yeah! To be able to come into the City and work in really respectable places and be clean, be 'respectable', 'normal'. While living in a tent in the middle of a forest; and nobody knows.

Probably skipped train fares every now and again!

Oh no I didn't, actually, again with the money thing, that's the easy option. It was like, *I have to be totally impeccable.* If I want money to come in, I need to make sure it's going out – I mean occasionally, I'd rush to get a train and there's no ticket office at Box Hill; but I even got to the point that if I was having a single journey and I had made a single journey the day before, without buying a ticket, I'd buy a return even if I wasn't going back.

Good on ya!

Which is totally in reverse.

That is 'working in-line' with energy, isn't it?

Exactly! In alignment.

Totally.

But, um, yeah, I mean the funny thing was for the first few weeks I almost thought that somebody would come up to me and say "You don't have a house – you live in a tent, don't you?" like, some commuter, for no reason.

"Your name is Wurzel[110]." Ha ha ha ha ha

Ha ha ha ha ha – but it was so real, this looking around, thinking, 'they must know!' 'I mean, have I got… trees, stumps, twigs in my hair or…'

Isn't it like after the first few times of having sex. You expect people to point as you're walking by. "You've been 'shagging'!"

Exactly!

"I can smell your fingers!"

Aww-ho don't! I wonder how many other people did actually think that, when we first… were 'active'! Anyway, what were you saying about you set up a cinema for your family, post-posh-non-'fugee-Chinese-family-meal?

Oh yeah yeah-yeah… Upstairs above Anna & Simon, the flat that they gave me in Hampstead. Set up the projector, and we just watched all these slides. And… it was just brilliant! We were chatting, we were laughing; great that Joseph & Mary were there, because they knew a lot of the people, they were in a lot of them, from the 60's and 70's – thirty-odd years ago. And with the four of us there, we could just talk about stuff. And my brother looked like he was always 'on something!' He was, he was so happy! And his eyes were bulging, and his face was exploding and smiling, and I was a much more serious child…

Hmmm

…and I was the Mummy's-boy, he was a kid.

It's partly being older, as well. I think.

Yeah!

The oldest or the older child.

I had a fucking great time! *We were just – fucking – happy!* All of us were just blissfully happy. I haven't seen that kind of stuff around. Maybe it's a time thing, maybe it's because we were rich and living in Africa. So many people have said that was paradise. That time and that place. It can't be replaced anywhere. But all this about 'it was tough and there were problems', you know, 'I was frowning because I had a tough time' – bollocks! It was plain and simple sunshine!

What do you mean, sunshine?

Shining in my eyes!

Aw yes.

…so that's why I was frowning and squinting and stuff. Stopping the – you know, we didn't have 'sunnies'! Heh heh heh… yeah, but it was a bit different when my aunt and uncle were there. Things like, my cousins, my God Mother's kids were there – then they weren't there. And to be able to talk about, well, why were they sent to convent? There's one story, that my Father told me, that he was blamed for them going to convent because he'd said that the eldest – Mary-Ellen – has been so spoiled by her grandparents, so spoiled by everyone, so the best thing would be send them to convent so they'll be okay. And he was guilty about that. - That wasn't the truth! Umm, there's a story, from Mary-Ellen, saying that in those days, umm, people were raping young Indian girls. People might want to fiddle with my cousins. So they were sent to convent because of that. Again – crap!

Fear!

That's what Mary-Ellen was fobbed off with. And then there's stories of the way; 'cos I remembered my cousin, the boy – three girls and a boy – the three girls went first, and then the boy went after. I remember the way my God Mother used to beat the fuck out of him - the lame one - for nothing. It seemed, it didn't make sense. And then I asked about it. And then, I was told that, well actually, she beat the fuck out of all the girls as well. She just beat and abused those kids! Treated the dog well... Treated the dog like a bloody kid! But that's the way; she was a bitter and twisted bitch, basically. And – I told you that story about when we went to Swindon and all that shenanigans, didn't I?

Oh yes!

We had a fucking excellent time seeing the slides, how happy we were, how healthy, holidays in Kenya, God knows everything... it was just bliss. It was wonderful. And to remember that that's what I come from, rather than just putting it in a cupboard and throwing the key away...

Hmmm

...because, before it was like, 'Don't talk about Africa, because then we had trouble,' and to talk about 'anything' would bring up the trouble...

And open up the skeletons in the cupboard.

...exactly! Meanwhile, we're supposed to be running and surviving. Well, since staying at Anna's and Simon's over the summer, no more panic, no more running, no more 'surviving', no more workaholism, no more drugs, no more drink, no more fucking shenanigans at all, it's like 'now I can stop!' THANK GOD... So, we finished upstairs, we were gonna go downstairs to, um, just say goodbye to Anna and Simon, and then, they said, "Well bring them down for a cup of tea or something." So I thought, 'Cool, I'd love to!' So, um...

Did that cause any kind of panic?

I thought it would have. The men were outside, putting the stuff back in the car. I was taking the chairs downstairs and the women were inside just washing their hands or having a pee or whatever, so I asked to the women and they said, "Hum... haa... yeah – lets! Let's ask the men." Everyone is 'ooooh my God!' But no one; and then everyone behaved so well. There wasn't the usual panic and 'shoulds', no shit! It was proper, proper quality; not only quality time - which didn't really happen in that way with all of us - but family time with the whole family. So, um, I – we were all waiting to see where they were. They weren't coming back in, so I opened the door and they were standing outside, the door had locked, they didn't know which buzzer to press...

Oooooh nooo!

...ah ha ha! So they came in and then they hummed and ha'd a bit and I said, "Look, let's do it, because this is my only chance. You will never meet Anna and Simon again and I would like you to all meet and for us to hang out, just for a cup of tea or something."

Yeah, why not?

So we were downstairs, the kids were there, and I said to my Father – Simon said to me "What do they want?" whatever; I said to my Father "What do you fancy? Tea, coffee?" Then I looked at him and said "Scotch?" so all the men had Scotch and all the women ended up having orange juice, and we just hung out, chatted and – uh! I remember. The first thing that was said, when everyone was sitting down... oh! The kids were playing around and Mary loves kids, and Alex hit his head and he was crying so she got frozen peas – it was proper family, community stuff...

Hmm, Hmm!

...it was wonderful! So we were all sitting down quietly, and um, *Simon looked my Father in the eye and said, very seriously,* "You must be very proud of Mickey."

Wow.

363

And…my Father looked at Simon, just as serious, no change in his facial expression, and he said, very very honestly, "…has it's ups and downs." And we were just – all of us – on the floor in fucking hysterics. We were just hysterically laughing. It was just like, what do you say to that? What is the polite thing to say, or do, or whatever?

Good for him! Yeah! It's so easy to go "Well, of course I am."

Exactly, exactly! It was just – and honest – and I think that's the thing with our family now, is we've learned to be honest.

Hmmm

And we're finding out what the truth is, rather than lying automatically, or carrying on building on that shit. It's stopping and thinking and 'What's the truth?' rather than 'What's the answer?' …and Anna asked exactly the same thing upstairs, when I was in the downstairs flat, apparently. I imagine my Mother gave the polite answer.

But, it's interesting that, well, the whole thing of opening old wounds. That seems, in my mind, to equate to when you are prepared to – well, maybe not have therapy, but to – go back and look at things. Or, everything is just completely shut. I think there's this fear that you're opening the can of worms and everything will be worse. And I think, actually, sometimes it does get worse – maybe before it…

…gets better!

But, people's tendency is, as things get worse, they want to stop, so then they are 'stuck' in worse! And then that confirms what they thought and that it will be worse…

Yeah

…instead of continuing through, wading through the shit. I mean, I know maybe there's an argument not to…

No, I think that is such a valid point! And I'd say that the only argument why not to, is when people will leave prematurely. Which is like Vipassana, when all my anger, rage and revenge 'came up' – so; but I stayed until the end when I had 'got into' peace and everything. Imagine if I had left at 'revenge'?

Yeah

Well, same as therapy. If you've committed for a year, or two years, or whatever – then you go to the end and don't leave when the going gets tough, because otherwise you leave fucked-up!

Hmmm

Same for any workshops.

Yeah

Anything - see it through!

But also, I don't know, there's this thing about – people are afraid to make mistakes. I don't know why this occurs to me now, but I was thinking about it yesterday. Thinking, how incredibly 'teenaged' I was. When was it? Last, only; it was nearly two years ago when Steven and I went, we were, it's a long story anyway, but we were together, we were driving back across the country from Camchester back to Silchester and I wasn't sure whether he could come back to my parents, because that was where I was living at the time. I didn't phone ahead or anything, to tell them what was happening, and we were driving back...

Did they know you were having a 'thing' then?

...yeah, yeah! They knew, and that was fine, and they could accept that there was this...

The theory.

...the theory, yes. Somewhere, somewhere is a man who has helped to cause the break up of – the marriage. That was...

Of course, I forgot, it's not only having 'a thing',

...nnooo...

but it's *the home-breaker!*

Well, but then, that's another story. I'm not sure that they were that upset about the marriage being broken down, anyway, that's another story!

Ha ha ha ha ha

You know, I can still remember, he said, "I think this is a really bad idea." And I said "No, no it'll be fine!" and we went back to the house, and I will never forget this moment. As we came down to the – well, you know, 'cos you've been to my parents' house.

Yeah

You go down the stairs into the living room. And my parents were sitting, they have these little tables, and they were watching television, eating, and as we came into the room – hha ha – and I just, very breezily said "Oh, I'm back! And I've brought Steven!" and they were just like - they were frozen!

Ah ha ha ha ha

They were just frozen with the knives and forks up near their faces!

Ah ha ha ha ha ha

And slowly their heads turned...

Ha ha ha ha ha ha ha ha ha ha ha

...and – it was like a cartoon, their eyes kind-of popping out of their heads – like, 'Ooh my God. What is our son... he's lost his mind!'

Ha ha ha ha ha

And it was such a horrible evening. I mean he basically fled. He kind of retreated, went up to have a bath, upstairs, and I just...

So he didn't run straight out.

...no I didn't, because I thought...

Neither of you?

...no. And I had this big big row with my parents and said "You are so unwelcoming. You're homophobic!"

Ah, phew, ha ha ha

And my Mum said "No, we're just surprised. We'd like to know when you're coming home." And I said "Would it have been the same if it had been a woman?" and she said "Well, yes it would!" and I was like 'Yeah, bollocks would it!'

Heh heh heh heh heh heh

And, in retrospect, I thought, 'my God, that really was a big mistake.' And the atmosphere was really tense for that whole evening.

What the; how'd they know how to deal with that?

Precisely. But! Coming back to what we were saying, 'Well, fuck up! You know, make mistakes! Make them in public, instead of just hiding all the time.' That's what I used to do, I mean, it was 'God! Talk about hiding...' But with your Father, I mean, I found the same, that a couple of weekends ago my sister was down, and not because of her, but because I think 'us together', and our parents – the dynamic in their home was just, very strange. The last weekend I was there – and I had made a conscious decision that I would spend time with him – and I was going to do the gushy-gushy thing with 'well I don't think we spend enough quality time with each other' and...

Ah ha ha ha ha ha

...in the end, it was just, let's do it. Like he said he was going to go to the supermarket. So I said to Malaika, "Oh, let's go with grand Pa!" and it was very nice, we just hung out, we went to a park, he came and joined us...

Be-ing together, rather than doing process.

...exactly!

Yeah…

But I do wish – I don't know. I wish – people could be just more spontaneous and just enjoy themselves.

More honest!

Yeah!

That's the bottom line, isn't it? Don't think – get on with it.

Yeaaaah.

And, good if we fuck up. You know where not to go!

Yeah.

Otherwise, it's playing small – no fuck-ups but, so small that nothing actually happens…

…and no one will notice. Humm. 'It's all going really well.' And then they would really notice if we fucked up.

And then avoid each other, because it's just so boring being together anyway, because everyone's being so small.

Exactly.

So the last thing we did, like we hung out, chatted, had a laugh, whatever – it was great! The last thing that we did is that everyone stood up, said goodbye, hugs, kisses, invite to each other's house, whatever – and we happened to be standing in a circle. And the kids were gorgeous, going around with the food, and you know the little plates and stuff…

You didn't join hands and sing *'Kumbaya'*[11] did you?

…*we did the Hokey-Cokey!*

Ah ha ha ha ha ha!

Spontaneously joined hands…

Ha ha ha ha ha

…and we did the Hokey-Cokey!

Ha ha ha ha ha

The adults loved it, the old people loved it, the children loved it…

Who started it? Was it you!

I think I started the… we all happened to hold; I don't know…

Ha ha ha ha ha

…how, but we all happened to be joining hands, and I think I looked at Alex – who's what, six, seven, something like that – and I just did "You put your left leg in…" HA HA HA Ha ha ha ha

That would make such a good scene in a film!

It was, absolutely, fucking hilarious. And then after that we stopped, and Alex spontaneously did 'Simon Says…' and we did it for two or three minutes or something – and they'd already gone, changed, ready for bed – and then Alex – you know, everyone was ready to go; no pressure, Alex says "Simon says… time to go to bed!" and that was it! It was amazing! It was poetry. No one was playing small, no one was showing off, no one was 'performing', it was living. It was fucking excellent. But how funny, it could have so been 'Kumbaya'.

Hmmmm

Heh he he he he – well maybe not, we're much too cool for that.

Ha ha ha ha ha

But then, so after that – that was just the slides, not the photos. Ummm, then a few days later I went to see my parents one short lunchtime at Mary and Joseph's – I didn't have a lot of time. Hung out, they turned these trousers up that my cousin in Liverpool gave me, nice new Cat jeans. We just hung out, checked in, you know – just normal. Nothing much to say or do. And at the end, they said, "What happened in

Liverpool? What happened in Swindon?" Because, you know, I went to see the family, I told you about all of that.

Hmmm Um-humm.

And I said, "I'll tell you tomorrow, I'll tell you when Tony's here." 'cos I was really quite rushing and the next time we had more time to hang out and I told them about Liverpool and it was cool, "Uncle Frankie was a bit sheepish, they made a good effort with food and they rushed off to Canada, blah blah blah nothing huge to report." Then when I told them about Swindon, and the incident with Mary-Ellen knocking her hard glasses-case on my head, the shouting and my God daughter acting like an angry young single parent – nothing against single parents, but you know there's angry ones that shout in dole queues. People like that. Hard-done-by-victim-girl. And, told them everything, and, you know, it was cool, we just understood what was going on. Then after I'd left, I remembered two or three fundamental things. Really important things. So we went back on Sunday, and Caetano was there – my brother – and his girlfriend, it was family again. And, one of the things I remembered that I said to them, and I - pretty much as soon as I came in 'cos Caetano was in a little bit after me - was that Aunty Valerie (my God Mother) said that my Mother and I had fallen out because of that, that's been going on in the last year, was because of money. Because I owed my Mother money – and I probably owe something piddly, like a grand, which I could get tomorrow, it's not an issue, you know, with credit cards. It would cost and everything, but it's not an issue for anyone. Ummm, and that Aunty Valerie had said that not only have we fallen out over money, but now my Mother hasn't got the money, which is – the money that my Mother loaned me was the money that her Mother had left her, my grand Mother left my Mother – but Aunty Valerie was saying that it's for my Mother's coffin. *Now*

she hasn't got money for her coffin.

Oh God!

That's what I thought. Fucking hell! But, you know, being stupid, and Catholic and guilty and everything else and family secrets and lies, people talking behind each other's backs rather than telling each other, I took it as truth. Or at least partly as truth. Either way, it hurt. It fucked me up.

Hmmm

When I said this; they were as flabbergasted as they were when I said about her saying that she was a drug addict for two years and the nuns looked after her. Lies! The whole thing's lies. And then we looked at how, throughout her life, it seems that's she's been lying – various lies to various people – and if it comes back, she'd say 'no I said it like this, or I said it to this one, or that was a misunderstanding'.

Hmmm

But getting everyone running around her, fucking everyone up, to being controlling, to being popular, and whatever, and it started when she was lame.

But I think...

She was just a baby.

...so that was your God Mother?

Yeah. Because the doctor gave her the wrong injection, plus two other children – one of which was his own son – and people said to my grand Father 'sue the doctor' and, you know, you didn't in those days, especially in Africa.

I've heard so many people, of our generation, men, women, talk about Mothers, their Mothers, Mothers-in-law, whatever, who do this. They're trying desperately to please every body.

Yeah.

So they...

Or to control everyone.

Well, yeah, I don't know which one it is. Pleasing through controlling,

controlling through pleasing – I'm not sure, but it's that sort of...
basically, insincerity. And you end up...

I'd say more than that!

...having stories...

'Fuck all of you, as long as I feel okay!' Sincerity

doesn't come into it.

...yeah.

I mean, when I told Gina – because Gina was there when they were
bitching – Gina said "God, that's a real shock! It reminds me of my
uncle so-and-so who's done the same to my family." So they fuck up
their own families, plus their brothers' and sisters' families, and their
brothers' and sisters' families' kids, and it just goes on... Rules the
whole branch of the family. And she was like 'queen bee' in a way.
But, no wonder... it's just disgusting! So what's news with Malaika? Ex-
wife? Ex-wife's boyfriend?

110. *Wurzel Gummage. Children's TV scarecrow character.*

111. *'Kumbaya' Traditional African-American spiritual song, synonymous
with 'happy clappy Christianity' and camp fires.*

Kids remember

Umm. Things are great with Mallie. Ummm, ex-wife – seems to be, well, we're basically distanced. Lots of distance at the moment, but, the future? But, very very civil. I don't mean civil in the kind of cool way, but fine. It's fine. I haven't seen the new bloke for a while. Um, but something interesting happened at the weekend. Again, I made a very conscious decision to not only hang out with my Dad and spend more time with him, but to be even more patient with Mallie. But I realised there's a sort of a guiltiness I have that; there's a part of me that's quite glad that I'm a part-time Father, because it allows me to do all the other things. And also, as we've said in the past, appreciate her more. But there's also a kind of slightly dangerous side to that which, on-um Monday, when we were leaving, my Dad drove us out to the railway station just outside Silchester. But Mallie had been fine – we hadn't had any ruckuses or anything – but – and this is nothing! It's indicative of my own, I think it's guilt. When you have a child, part-time, you want everything to be perfect...

Yeah

...I don't want there to be any rows, any harsh words, and, um, she was just moaning about having to put her coat on for a two minute walk from the car to the station. My Dad was kind-of fussing around her and I just said, really impatiently, "Oh, be quiet!" to her. And I felt awful. And then afterwards my Dad said "Oh leave her alone" as if I was abusing her...

Umm?

...and I, well I felt like saying to him 'Well you never said anything like that to any of us did you? I'm sure!'

A-ha ha ha ha ha

I didn't. But I thought, well this is the thing. Grandparents think they've got license to – do whatever and say whatever and almost kind of undermine the parents' authority. It's almost like, what they're there for. But yesterday and the day after I felt so bad and then I thought, 'hang on, put this in perspective'. Because all I said, once, was 'Be quiet!' But again, it's, I remember reading, um, Anne Robinson – of all people – you know the woman that does that TV quiz show. What's it called?

'The Weakest Link'.

Yes. Because she was separated from her daughter, I think. I think, unusually her husband, or whatever, had custody. And I read that she said the same, on, on these precious weekend visits anything like that, however good anything else has been, is sort of like a little bomb goes off. And I think to myself 'she's going to remember that. That's what she'll remember. Not all the nice stuff and the fun and the cuddles. Because it's like those moments are the daggers.' I mean, I always apologise. Then I think, is that enough? Am I just paranoid? Well, I think it's the 'single parents' syndrome'.

I remember feeling that when I split with folk! 'They won't remember anything good, they'll just remember the shit stuff!'

Hmmm. My Mum said that to me recently!

What's that?

It's what, nine months now, since they read the first half of this book. "So, don't you remember anything good about your childhood?" and I said "Well, I do, but…" and again I threw the question back at her. I said, well, "All I've been told about your childhood is threats from your step-Mother, about, you know, 'you've misbehaved and so she's gonna leave', your Father telling you off because you'd upset step-Ma…" packing her suitcase apparently was the thing in her family. The step-Mother would pack her bag, put it in the hallway…

What?!

…ummm.

Her own bag?

Her own bag. As in 'I'm leaving. I can't…'

Abandonment!

…yeah – 'I can't live with this daughter, this step-daughter is simply unbearable'.

Yeah. WoW…

Big shit.

Well of course, kids don't take; they blame themselves for everything that happens anyway.

And I sometimes think that maybe I'm just not very robust emotionally. Because, you know, something like that – just take in your stride like telling your child to be quiet.

Hm.

I suppose I don't want to get in the habit of shouting at her.

In a way, it's so difficult. I'm blown away by my parents, because all through my life I could hear them say "Wow, you remembered that. And you thought 'that' because of 'that'. You were listening!" The other day Freya phoned me, really upset, because she'd smacked Dennis…

Right.

…and she hadn't smacked Dennis for a long long long long time. And not only was she upset that she had smacked him, but after that he said to her "Are you going to take me back to the shop for, um, little boys and bring back a good one?" Because the last time she did it – and it was months ago, over a year ago maybe – that's what she said she'd do! And she wasn't aware…

God!

…about parenting or anything then. So, a part of him remembered all this time, but a smack triggered that all back up.

Hmmm…

How many of us have got things that were said, in our subconscious, that we, even now as adults build on?

Yup.

My poor Father was telling us about what a bad time he had in, um, boarding school. I'm sure, my memory says that, um, he used to threaten me with boarding school. Not only in this country, but in Africa, because it would make sense. I don't remember him threatening in Africa, but the girls were sent - they're you know, my cousins – then the boy was sent – my cousins - it would be the 'normal threat'. Especially when you're not thinking.

Ummm

And he says "No I didn't. I wouldn't! I had such a bad time and it fucked my life up, blah blah blah…" and in those days, they'd get beaten, they'd get bullied, they'd get all sorts of shit and they'd censor all the letters, they'd steal money and stuff that's been sent to them, and boarders who don't have money sent get treated like servants! And they have to be servants, not only to the staff that work in the school, but to other boarders whose parents would pay a lot of money. He was treated worse than a bloody deformed cockroach. Ahhh – he was really fucked up. And he got really ill before he was sent home again. But he had a… he had a really fucked up life the poor guy. Do you remember ages ago, I said something about my great grand Mother – his grand Mother – fucked the whole family up?

Hmmm

I found out yesterday that there are two branches to the family with different surnames, and I never quite got it, but she was divorced and in those days, in Africa, it was unheard of. She had her first child at – she was married and she had her first child, from a man much older, who must have had some money – at the age of twelve.

That's very; she was married?

Yes. *She had her first child at the age of twelve.*

Good God!

To an old man.

Is that clinically possible?

And the family must have backed – you know – it wasn't a... exactly! If that's not gonna twist someone up and fuck them up and make them... and then she plopped out babies like there's no tomorrow, and then she got, apparently she divorced – he didn't die – and then she went to another family... but what happened to the twelve-year-old body, and mind, and emotions. No wonder she was so fucked up! *You know, with the worst, nastiest people, you kind of understand it, once you hear their story!*

Hmm

It's no excuse, but if it can be named and, you know, somehow stopped... And no wonder there are such funny sex issues. And he was saying about, I think it was about her, that she had a radiogram or something – and don't forget, this is like way way way way back. This is my great grand Mother. In Africa. It must have been one of the first radios to come out, type thing! – in her bedroom,

To 'coloured people'.

Sorry?

To Coloured People.

Well, to anyone I imagine in those days, depending on where, yeah. Because it was, I think, a similar status or class or whatever, out there, as it was in some countries. Quite a lot of countries. I think it depends on, if it's a European country, then maybe 'coloureds' come second or third or whatever. But I don't; well, maybe you're right. I don't know. Umm. But she'd lock it up in her bedroom and my Father and his brother and sister and whoever would crawl into her bedroom through a tiny little window, put it on, listen to the music - you know, it doesn't break the radio - and have a good time dancing to the music before she came home, unplugged it, switched it off. And I thought, no wonder, as a child, in Wales, after refugee stuff, I always felt really guilty playing music. Playing the stereo. Playing my records or the radio, batteries for the radio, whatever. Because, I just felt it was money that I shouldn't be spending. But how could I...

And it was something else completely.

...it must have been. And how could I do that if we didn't have enough money for food? That I would have picked up sub-consciously. I was never told that we didn't have enough money for food, but we were obviously very poor.

Yeah, well as you say, you do; it's amazing how, I've noticed with children, with Mallie, how old is she now? She's nearly four! She will, we'll be having a conversation of no particular consequence. You know, there might be a phrase, or whatever, and five minutes later she'll ask me a question about what I've been saying. And I've been really amazed. Oh no no, I don't think I'm stupid, but there's a part of me inside that's like 'My God, she's been listening! She absorbed everything.' I mean, you notice it mostly when you swear. She said to me the other day – I'd dropped something and I said "Oh bugger!" and she said "Why you say 'Oh bugger'?" she didn't know what the word meant, but it's like, she wanted to know what it meant.

Humm.

But with your parents, or my parents, or anyone's parents. What I found is, it feels like we have to unlock them. We have to be the ones that; I mean, I was telling my Mum recently, that when I was at school, you know, trying to say 'I don't know what my sexuality...' or 'I don't know because I hadn't got any sexuality, not actively' and how all these memories of my so-called friends at Junior School, calling me 'sissy', 'ballet shoes', and I remember once, joyfully skipping in at the end of school and a friend of mine went "Aaah! Skipping in!" And there was utter horror.

Hmmm

And I was telling her this, and she didn't say anything, except "Well I used to get bullied at school. People used to come up to me and push me and say 'You havnae got a Mither'" and it's like, it's the cruelty, isn't it? Whatever it is. But what struck me was why didn't she ever say that? Why haven't we ever talked about these things? I don't mind being the one to bring it up. But sometimes it would be nice just to...

Share...

...yeah!

...your experience. Make it okay to be you, rather than 'how do they want to see me and *who do I need to pretend to be in order to gain some love?*'

Or somehow think that you've been; that you've been uniquely persecuted. It's like you find out that this is the – I don't know what you'd call it – solidarity of suffering? You know. Everyone's been teased in some way. Everyone's been fucked up some way, but the more we talk about it, the more it makes it seem normal and we can then deal with it.

Beatings

I was thinking about male violence and the differences between men. It's probably not about the gay or straight divide, but more about those who have been beaten – and therefore are okay to fight and beat – and those who haven't been beaten – and aren't okay to fight and beat.

Yes. Which is probably us.

Yup! We weren't beaten. Slapped a bit, but we weren't beaten by our parents. We weren't beaten up at school. And my dignity was important to me. I mean, anyone would want to beat me up, surely! Especially in Wales, being the coloured kid, whatever. But I just held my dignity. You know, even now, I do not get threatened. Not even when I behave badly and over-step the mark. Some thing, I don't know what it is, I couldn't fight, I don't know how to. And I've always been scared of fighting, because I'm sure that my hand would go through someone's skull if I hit them hard and I'd have their thoughts through my, between my fingers.

I bet you'd learn, I mean think of, think of *'Fight Club'*[12], that first scene where he says "Punch me!" and he really pulls his punch. But then he punches him really really hard. I think it's, it's a very hairline thing. Given the chance, if somebody said "Smack me as hard as you can…" I mean, I see it with Malaika and other children. They are so restraining themselves. When they get angry, their jaw tightens, their fists clench, their faces go bright red… Same with grown-ups, so-called grown-ups.

Well, *I'm scared of fighting.* I'm scared of getting locked up after killing someone.

There is that, especially after what you've been through with Lui.

Also, it's rare that I've lost my temper. But with Lui, with Rob, I lost my temper a few times. I really lost it! I am shit scared of killing someone, or damaging someone for life. Knowing that someone is brain damaged, or got scars or stuff like that.

But surely, the flip side is to allow healthy expressions of anger, because surely that's…

I don't know what the boundaries are. Without being beaten up, without fighting and stuff like that, playfighting and stuff, I'd still hold back a lot…

Yeah

…and also, I would know that I would go so far, and Lui would go so far, and he'd go further than me, because I wouldn't go any further, because I wouldn't know where to stop.

So he'd – 'win'.

Exactly!

Yeah.

And I wouldn't wanna take it any more seriously. One, you know, it takes one to say 'enough' and that one's supposed to be the loser. So that's the one that stops damage from…

The 'weak one'.

Yeah! Or so we're told. And, when it comes down to it, when you're really in a proper fight, do you remember what you; I was just thinking about, I've talked about my cousin, who was a martial artist. When it came to street-fighting, apparently he didn't do the martial arts. He just fought like everyone else. And it wasn't within a forum. Within a – what do you call it – a kind of, 'we're doing martial arts' thing. We're fighting. Forget about the rules and martial arts. I don't know. There seems to be a big split. Those who fight – those who don't fight. Those who fight – and they were beaten – they're probably, by far, the more paranoid, and in my experience, clients and friends, or into their booze and their coke![113]

Hmmm

But it's still working out, what is it? What's going on under there? It's not about sex and sexuality, it's not about looks, it's not about being able to fight and boast, it's like, in the last few months, a few of my very good-looking friends have been saying "It's not about looks, is it?" - from their girlfriends or other girls - they don't care about their looks. The girls are into their blokes, but their looks don't come into it. The looks seem to be something to make the blokes feel less; the same with the muscles. Probably same with the big dick in the changing rooms.

Hmmm

Whatever. *Is that for the girls? Or is it to compete with other blokes.* Do you know what I mean? It's been interesting doing this cleanse, and um Billy and I just drinking that stuff and not eating. Going to saunas and whatever. It's just been totally different in changing rooms.

Hmm. Changing rooms have changed!

Yeah. And it's not that the gay ones are safe, or anything. Maybe it's me that's changed. But, kids there. Before I couldn't deal with kids in a changing room. But then, kids in changing rooms in Wales were barbaric. Gobbing on ceilings, and — you know, just dirty stuff. Funny, stuff that they got up to. Whatever.

It's funny, thinking about things that have changed. I dropped Mallie off on Monday night and I was just, I always feel gutted when I leave her. You know, we've always had a good time, but there's usually been something that makes me feel guilty, just to add to the merry mix. And I was coming away and I just, actually thought, 'Pull yourself together. Just, take a breath,' whatever. Which is what Malaika says to me whenever I cry.

Does she?

She still says that! 'Take a deep bweath…' I mean, we've talked about it. But anyway, I was walking, I thought I'll just get some food – it was about six o'clock on Monday evening – and I went to the local shopping centre and it was shut. There were these two lads there, about twelve and nine, something like that. And the security guard told them that it was shut. And I was surprised, because it was so early. This guy, the younger boy said to me, "Um, have you got; do you live near by? Have you got a ladder we could borrow?" And I was thinking, 'What's this all about?' Anyway, it turned out he'd been kicking – I don't know – a ball and his trainer had flown off…

Ha ha ha

…onto the roof of the shopping centre. And, er, like you say, I used to, I remember being scared of boys. Almost like, it takes me back to childhood. Somehow I think that they'll go "Oh you poof"

Or fuck! They'll want me to kick the ball back…

Yes.

…and I know I'll kick it totally in the wrong direction, fall over!

But this was great. It's like joining-in. It's like getting into the tree house and them going *'You're our mate!'*

Yeah

So to cut a long story short, the taller one basically stood on my shoulders, climbed up, got up onto the roof, got his trainer, came back down again, and it was all so easy! There was a part of me that was thinking 'I know I'm strong but I'll probably fuck up!' and then they'll go 'You're a stupid - whatever - you couldn't even help us get our shoe back!' It's just like, preparing for humiliation. He climbed down and they were both; it was really simple. They were both really happy – and I felt… so chuffed. I was grinning from ear to ear!

Ha ha ha ha

You know, I thought to myself, do other people have this? Am I making a big deal of this because I never had it? Or is it just something that is like 'being part of'?

Any gang, every gang is different! And just because you're accepted in the elite gang, doesn't mean that the nerds are gonna accept you.

Hmm

It's still rejection if they don't.

Yeah.

Or, the, you know, not so elite gang, or the sporty gang, or the chess club gang or whatever.

Yeah. It is funny though, isn't it? How those things carry on.

Quite recently, didn't we say about, umm, how all the other men respect you and have respected you?

Oh, yes...

But it's up to you to accept yourself as...

Yes, exactly! Which is so perfect, because in the past I'd probably have - because Ashbury, Ashbury is pretty posh - but there is the, kind of 'gor blimey' accent as well. A sort of 'Saaf Laandan'. In the past I probably would have toned my accent down a bit, to...

Yah

...not stand out. But it didn't even occur to me. And thinking back, that's what felt like the difference. I was just totally myself.

Yup

And I said, "Oh, I'm surprised Waitrose is shut!"

Ha ha ha ha ha

It's like, 'Hellow, aim really posh!'

Wa ha ha ha ha ha

There was no, kind of funny stuff from them like 'Oi, posh bloke...'

Ha ha ha ha ha – 'Oi, upper case CUNT...' 'You're caps, ain't ya?' 'We're just lower case, us!' 'Naw serifs, neever!'

Ha ha ha ha ha ha ha – 'And you're a poof, too!'

112. *'Fight Club' (1999) David Fincher, USA.*

113. *Coke. Cocaine, Charlie, Snow.*

Nigger for a neighbour

Yeah… Anyway, check this! You know I was saying about remembering my childhood in Africa, how great it was, blah blah blah? What I realised – especially after I bought this book on obsessive-compulsive disorder, and it took me a lot of effort to get hold of a book on OCD; and then to get hold of a simple little book, rather than something too heavy. And I realised, reading this, that, my; well I'll read it through, and we can edit it, or whatever. Happy childhood… or was it? Ha ha ha ha ha Right! All I did was I underlined a few things.

By the way, I'd just like to point out that I will probably have decided that I am an obsessive-compulsive by the end of…

Oh yeah. You are! So's your Mother…

Really?

Ha ha ha ha ha ha ha

See how easily I'm; oh my God!

But also, I am, my Mother, her sister and her brother are, on that side of the family.

But I don't think of myself as…

Well no one does!

What are the symptoms?

Right. This is all me. The book I've got this from is called 'Obsessive-Compulsive Disorder – The Facts' by Padmal deSilva (male or female I don't know, seems to have written all the books on obsessive-compulsive, and there are very few) and Stanley Rachman. But it is, a horrendously huge thing. It's just people don't even – I've said to Billy, I asked him "Do you count? Do you count when you do this? Or that?" and he went "Nooo!" but then the next day, he said "Man I have been so aware of the times that I count. And I add numbers, and I – there are so many things that are common in our private worlds."

I didn't know that.

No no no, I don't imagine you do. There are a lot of things that you wouldn't know. Okay, this is all about me! Right... *'An unusual, but often inflexible type of compulsive behaviour consists of a powerful urge to put matters right. Typically, to place one's belongings in a particular place or order, in a rigidly prescribed manner, to ensure that one's appearance is exactly right.'* And so on. *'There are also covert forms of this compulsion'* – covert is inwards, isn't it?

Yeah.

And overt is outwards. And I know that, my family were all, my Mother, my Uncle, my Aunt, me, my staff, when my girlfriend – when Emma worked for me – I'd get her to put things in order of height, flush to the front, stuff like that – but I couldn't carry on until; generally it's me, needing to touch, needing to make matters work right in my... life. Or in my surroundings, or in my – I don't know – situation as a kid, after refugee times, or whatever. That I did it this way, inflated responsibility, this goes hand-in-hand. *'Many patients experienced an inflated sense of responsibility, even for events over which they have no control. This is particularly common amongst those whose main problem is excessive checking. This inflated responsibility commonly generates intense guilt.'* That's me!

Umm. And my Dad and my sister.

Really! Check the doors, check the gas taps, check the ordinary taps, check the lights, check the doors again, check the pockets, check the bag, check anything and everything all the time, um, check that my Mother's still breathing in the middle of the night. It was really fucked up! But also responsibility. If ever my parents went out and I was in control, I knew that I was gonna burn the house down. And then what? It was fucked up; and guilt. If I wasn't being guilty, I may as well be

dead. Good Catholic boy. *'Obsessive-compulsive personality disorder.*
Long standing personality traits such as obsessive rigidity and
perfectionism.' That's me! And it's almost like, well this is the way; and
if there's a better way, then I'd better not let that other way come,
because then I would be thrown away for not getting it right, type
thing. And everything having to be dead right, because otherwise -
criticism. So I get you and Lui - 'good Dad' and 'bad Dad', both born
in 'The week of Drama & Criticism'.

Umm-hmm.

'Undue preoccupation with details, indecisiveness and so on. And no
episodes of ill – and not episodes of illness. These features are well
established by the adulthood. In addition, these people will tend to
show a lack of, or limited ability to express warm and tender emotions.
They do not necessarily have, or develop true obsessions and
compulsions.' Impossible. I could be there for people, I could talk
through stuff, but they could cry and get all fucked up and I wouldn't – I
wouldn't feel...

Hmmm

...no emotion. And that's the thing. I wouldn't know how to express
emotion - apart from maybe anger, and apart from maybe passive-
aggressive - but to be properly, honestly, truly emotional...

Hmmm

...I'd love to. Dunno how. I simply don't know how. And it was such a
relief to read that thinking, maybe now I know this, I could do
something about it and become human again.

Hmmm

Do you know what I mean? *'Compulsive hoarders.'* Now, look at my
parents. Not only after refugee days, but also their childhoods. More
my Father's lack. And even if everyone else in his family had, he was
treated like shit, so he definitely had 'lack'.

But to some extent, from our Fathers' generation, isn't that partly kind

of how they grew up?

Yup. But that would be their 'normality'.

The Depression, the War…

And then there'd be the obsessive-compulsive, above and beyond the 'normality'.

Oh, okay.

Do you know what I mean?

Yeah.

'Compulsive hoarders. They fear that they might suffer from a sense of loss. This is particularly true of those items that are hoarded for sentimental reasons. Either because of their symbolic value, or because of the memories they evoke, in those instances where the person derives his emotional sense of comfort and safety from the collections, the fear of loss is readily understandable. Incidentally, in these cases they attach a particular importance to having the collection in view. They need to see the collection, or items from the collection. Common belief that compulsive hoarding is the direct result of a period of deprivation, especially in childhood, has not been confirmed by scientific research.'

So what I just said doesn't necessarily hold true?

And whenever I read that, I think of my Mother. And my aunt, people from that side of the family. Going to my uncle's house in Liverpool, I sent him – I really felt great that I found a couple of little Frank Sinatra books, a postcard with Frank Sinatra that I sent him from Sydney. And he kept them. And it really meant something to me. Maybe that's not hoarding, maybe it is. With my Mother, bits and pieces that she's got from when we were refugees, little kids, things that we gave, things that other people gave, it really means something. But, that is hoarding and it's displayed. And I used to have – you know, it started off as a trunk with my stuff, and then it became a room. All the things that I'd saved to remind me of good times, happy times, being cared for, to remind me how great things; how times were, and it's almost holding on. And I used to think as a kid that when I'm old and sad, that I can look through these things and remember all the good times I've had...

Ummm

...meanwhile I'd keep in the panic of moving on and having good times and doing things, rather than *stopping. And enjoy it in the present*, do you know what I mean?

Yup. But isn't? I mean surely, this is like a lot of; I mean my Dad was talking about – he must have heard it on the radio – this whole thing. And we were saying, surely like a lot of dysfunctions, it's, there's a continuum from; I mean, everybody keeps some things.

Yes.

I mean, I noticed I've started to keep things like Malaika's drawings...

Yeaaah.

...which, I suppose if it becomes out of balance, that's when it becomes a sort of dis-ease.

I find that – like I think I mentioned earlier on, a few years ago, just burning most of the things from that trunk that turned into a room.

Hmmm

But then, so many things that I've looked at, and even photographs, I don't remember. But I keep the two or three special ones, that are really special, and that I remember, rather than 'admin' stuff. Do you know what I mean?

Yeah. *'Those with obsessions...'*

'Those with obsessions unaccompanied by overt compulsions. For some time our patient had been assailed by the obsessions 'Am I going mad?' 'Will I end up insane?' 'Will I be locked up?' And so on.'

Sounds familiar.

I had that! And you did. I remember you talking about this.

Yeah, only last year. Definitely!

And for years I used to watch prison films. I was obsessed by prison. And it was 'will I be locked up?' But it was almost 'when it happens I'll write a book, I'll get a degree, I'll do this', you know, whatever. Or, it was almost taken for granted and that was my obsessive-compulsive something-or-other.

Well for me it's always been a question of 'how does everyone else manage to function' – which they don't.

Yeah. Well, you're not in debt. To people, or money, or anything. Who else can say that?

Well, to my family, but that's slightly different. Well, they're not charging me any interest!

'And carrying on from that, a man in his early 30's had a recurring thought that his Mother was going to die, although she's in good health. He found it very difficult to dismiss the idea from his mind and he was very upset by it.' I used to check, in the middle of the night - when we were in Africa, before coming to this country, before refugee stuff – that my Mother was still breathing. I'd be panicked in the middle of the night. Uuum, and stuff like that with both parents. I would be really obsessed that they were going to come to some harm.

Hmm

And I'm not even sure that it was, 'Who would look after me', but, 'How have I failed them?'

Hmmm

Or how is it my fault. Or…

Or did it even get that far, or was it just blind panic?

I'm not that sure that it did, actually. Yeah, I think it was blind panic. *'Mental Rituals - a patient's account. The thought is that something awful is going to happen, not to me, to my family'.* Well, we just talked about that.

That's weird, because I remember finding an old diary not so long ago. My brother had the same, but I wrote in this diary – this is really embarrassing, actually – on, I don't know? Every other page I'd have something or other. And this kind of panic about my Mother and it says 'Mummy is going to live forever'.

Yeah.

Jesus! Exactly.

But it's so 'normal'. Can you imagine, like, probably most people have something like this? At some stage? As a normal part of them. And then they feel guilty, they feel weird, they feel, um, as if they're going to cause harm, or they have to protect their parents, or... do you know what I mean? All these things?

Hmmm

I've had two or three young boys who used to get voices in their heads saying "Kill Mum!" "Kill Mum!"

Really?

Yeah, and then their parents called me in to say "You need to speak to our kid and somehow deal with this because we don't know how to reach him or what's going on!" Common. And you know how, well, with counselling and stuff like that, uum, I've always been told that clients come in batches. Same with me. A batch of drug abuse, sex abuse, 'kill Mums', rape, people who know that they're products of rape, you know, amputees – he he he he he. Not a big batch of amputees, there were three!

Three in a row, just like buses.

He he he he he – and these are my notes. Check this out! Something's going to happen to my family. When we first moved to Wales, there was a petition, apparently, and I think there was a big thing in this country around the refugees who are going to take all the council houses…

Ah, yes.

…and there was one against us. Coming to Wales and that we weren't wanted.

Oh, yes.

And we, um, in a council house. And I didn't even know what a council house was, but I heard 'things' and I had to work out what it all meant. I just felt unwanted. And then when I was a bit older, I remember the guy next door - who was, who wanted to be with my family, you know, a relatively close friend — apologised to my family, saying that *he was one of the people that signed the petition that didn't want us to come here,* because blah blah blah blah. And it's not like, they were hard done by, or anything, but it's, I suppose, mass hysteria.

A knee-jerk reaction. Yeah.

Hmmm. And then, my wallpaper. Ummm. On one wall — I had a small room — because of my OCD I couldn't deal with a big room. I had a small, manageable room… and, on three walls, I had a black and white textured paper that was quite nice. On the fourth wall was 'slavery posters' wallpaper.

Sla… what, like

Yup

for sales.

Yup

Slaves?

Yup — and other things for sale, like coffee and boats coming in. It was un-be… I have always… typography makes me weak at the knees.

So it was the typography rather than the subject matter?

I don't know. Thinking about it, the subject matter, surely. And also my parents having this thing about 'We're not black, we're not Indian, we're not this, we're not that' I must have been proving to myself that I'm not, and it's not an issue, and....

Hmmm

...but there must have been something going on there. The typography, really, just — I wish I could design like that today.

Hmmm

But, there must have been something. I mean, it's a bit much. The only coloured family in the area.

And their son's got slavery sales posters all over!

And it was relatively expensive, if I remember. Huh

Very strange...

Some guy gave us loads and loads of furniture, books, toys, old stuff. It was interesting. It was almost like a house-clearance. Suddenly we had all these things. Old things, and even — you know — now, or until the last house in Muswell Hill, I'd go into charity shops to see, very interesting things to buy. Crystal bowls that I would 'ting' and sell to clients....

Well you still do that!

...nice mirrors, yeah I loved it! But then I'd buy things like things an aunt or grand Mother would hand down. Like vases, and — you know — you've seen my vases and some of my strange things. And I think wacky, and cool, and nice but; this guy. It's almost like buying a history. With this guy who gave us this furniture and toys and everything. And he gave us some old encyclopaedias, um - Children's Encyclopaedias - and I remember flipping through, and there was this whole chapter, or whole section on why coloured people are different to white people — and why they're more like animals. And why it's good for them, or right for them to be slaves and workers.   •

Who wrote this?

It was in a children's encyclopaedia.

Jeesus.

And at that age, with my paranoias, coming into this country, unwanted, with people who are very different to us, that play in the street and – I remember one of our neighbours whose kids were playing at the top of the stairs and one brother said to the other "Let's see who can piss further down the stairs!" so they both pissed from the top step, right down the flight of stairs to the bottom. For me, I was dying. Meanwhile, their Mother goes "Ha ha ha ha boys will be boys!" While they pissed down her stairway!!!

It's true. Boys will be boys. 'Peerticarly n Weerles…'

Then, suddenly I'm in this barbaric situation; waiting for something to happen, like the law to change, or someone to notice something and then suddenly, all black people will be re-made slaves like on my wallpaper. And because the people in my area didn't know, you know, Wales. When we first went there they didn't know whether we were cannibals, or some children looked under the furniture to see where we hid bows and arrows because they were told we were Indian so we must have bows and arrows. We were everything 'foreign' that they'd ever heard of. So *we would become slaves at some stage*. And this was like 'something awful is gonna happen to my family'.

Hmmm

Do you know what I mean?

Hmmm. Well, yeah. The 70's. Enoch Powell[114] and 'rivers of blood' and 'If you want a nigger for a neighbour, vote Labour.' Nice little slogan…

Fuck! I don't remember any of that. All I know is that I had a 'busy' childhood. Meanwhile, everything was fine on the outside. It's the mind of a child. Anyway… ha ha ha ha ha. God these things have just made so much sense. But yes, I did have a good family, a good childhood, my parents did their BEST, considering their fucked up lives they did fucking excellently. Seeing them recently, I've never seen them so great together. And so cool together. And realised what wonderful people they are. And what they've been through, and what they've had to suppress. They did fucking excellently. They weren't to know what was going on with me. And even if they, you know, if my cousin – when I was in school – said something about Mickey's an obsessive-compulsive… what would that mean? And what do they do with it? We weren't brought up to go to doctors and say…

'You need therapy'

…exactly. Therapy! There was no such thing. It was for Hollywood film stars.

Yes. Or 'mad' people.

This was fucking Welshpool!

Which was probably the same thing.

Heh heh *'Effects on work and social life. If the disorder was severe, many will become restricted in their social lives. Avoidance of certain places or certain behaviour, for example, hand shaking…'* For example toilets, changing rooms, even the playground. I didn't go out. Not only was it cold, but it was dirty, the people were dirty, they were doing dirty things, so I stayed inside. I asked the dinner ladies if I could help them put the chairs on the tables. I didn't want to go out and – attacked by the dirt and surrounded by fucking barbarians that wanted to fight and do weird things. *'…out of fear of contamination.'* Contamination. How many times in a day do I use that word!

Yeah, absolutely. And in the book as well.

Really?

Yeah!

'Can understandably lead to a reduction in social contact.' Sex!

Hmmm

Who needs it! Fuckinell. Disgusting! Not for an obsessive-compulsive! I would rather have, a cup of tea, in a new cup! Ha ha ha ha ...that's been sterilised.

I don't mean to go off on a tangent; there are no tangents in our ramblings! Thinking, like a thought process about my Mum. The number of times she's said, she expresses this really strong dislike of Welsh people, and I never thought twice about it - maybe it's because she's Scottish, or whatever - but suddenly I thought, my God! How bizarre! She's married to a half Welsh person, whose whole family, well basically whose Mother and in-laws were Welsh. How much hatred – I don't know, it's like a competition.

Yeah.

And then I thought, it's just a weird symmetry, I thought, I got the feeling that she wasn't very happy about having relatives or in-laws through me. Or through my Dad, it's like competition. But I also feel, it's strange because my parents have seen the first half of the book and they have, our relationship has changed. I don't perceive that they're getting on that well. I seem to feel, I feel like I'm better with them each by themselves. My Dad or my Mum. But my sister was saying the same. Again, we were talking about it, as we've said before, considering what our families went through, and every family must have these, I dunno. It astonishes me, how people function. With what's happened in their pasts. And not talking about it.

And how far in the past.

Yeah...

No one knows why. Why they're like this? Why were they like that? But for me it's huge. Learning about my great grand Mother being;

having her baby at the age of twelve. And then God knows how many more, and what kind of a life she had. It makes sense! Of course we're all fucked up. We're all indirect victims of probably rape. *Child abuse*, basically. I never thought of that – fucking hell! It is, apart from, it's legal. They were married.

Well exactly. It is, pretty much, well, how much more abusive can you get? The thought of having sex with a twelve year old.

Yeah!

Married or not.

With an old man. Not even a young guy. Apparently, he was an old – man.

'No good will come of it!'

Ha ha ha ha ha ha ha ha

Meanwhile, back at the OCD corner...

It's a funny one, about the Welsh, because so many people have got a problem with the Welsh.

Hmmm!

So so so many people.

Hmm!

And in a way, I've found the same, going to France.

Xenophobia, Jesus.

France and Australia - a few countries, but mainly France and Australia – where it's the same with the English. They hate the English and I'm treated differently when I'm with English people in France, and in Australia, than anyone. But the Welsh! So many people have said that there's something really weird, and paranoid, and 'chip on their shoulder', and almost backward in a way. I don't know what it is, but there is a difference. I'm not saying it's better or worse, because they've been – on the whole – very good to us. But then, thank God we had the English there. Because if we didn't have the English, maybe they would have hated us! Ha ha ha ha

I don't know, I don't know, I think there is a sort of – well, there's certainly a history of suppression by the English.

114. Enoch Powell. Conservative politician, notorious for his anti-immigration stance.

Control freak

Oh yeah! The kids thing. *'...Compulsive cleaning and compulsive checking is prominent among affected children....'*

But you only scored 13 out of 30 on the 'Am-I-OCD?' scale from the book.

Now, as an adult! But...

As a child?

And as a child it's 26. Yeah. Oh yeah! Children's stuff. *'Children display more repetitive behaviour.'* ...like counting? Also, it's like that recurring dream that I had through my childhood.

Hmmm

Sitting with various people on a rock near the sea, counting together.

That's, very strange.

Putting things in order, arranging things, tapping, touching. *'Affected children may go to some lengths to conceal their problems and keep their thoughts secret. Even from their family. They tend to deny the existence of the problem or to minimise its significance. In many instances obsessive-compulsive disorder is accompanied by other problems such as depressed moods, general anxiety and social isolation.'* All used to be me. *'Some children with obsessive-compulsive disorder are extremely demanding and controlling.'* Totally! *'They tend to become upset and angry when their compulsions are interrupted or blocked by others. They can even display open aggression. Some children with this disorder also control the entire family in almost a tyrannical fashion.'* I did. If I thought that any one in the family was gonna sneeze, like an animal I would shout aggressively "HAND!" and they'd stick their hands in front of their mouths. Otherwise, the whole room would be contaminated and I would have to go and wash. Or "DOOR!" I'd really, I'd be an absolute cunt the way I'd speak to them.

Maybe your parents have got together and they wrote a book about you.

HA HA HA HA HA HA

'Curse Of The Mummy's Child'!

I was vicious. I was ruled by this! But I fucked their lives up. I so controlled them with this – and, I was helpless… Much as I needed things clean, I couldn't clean them, because I'd be contaminated.

Hmmm

So I'd have to throw orders around.

'Catch 22.'[115]

Totally! And then, who was there to look after me? My Mother! To an extent, my Mother who stole my life! Saved my life, because she was there to do everything for me. Maybe she should have – you know – flushed my head down a toilet full of shit! It would help me get over it, but – you know – how many Mothers would do that?

Tough love…

I did it to myself. He he – with Mother Teresa. *'The psychoanalytical view'* – I'm not sure about this! *'Fixation, or getting stuck, at a particular stage of development caused by various factors during one's formative years, determines the nature of the neurotic symptoms that appear in this way in later life. Obsessive-compulsive disorder is linked in this way to the stage of development that is called, in this theory, the anal-sadistic stage.'* Anal-sadistic! *'Of which toilet training is a major feature.'* Locked in the toilet and I'm not leaving until I've shat!

Hmm.

Meanwhile, I come from a constipated family who aren't comfortable enough to let go, leave alone breathe properly! *'Anger and aggression are also associated with this stage of the child's development.'* I was talking to Billy today, and, from what I remember vaguely – I need to look this up somewhere – with babies; you might know this with Malaika. First the 'oral stage' everything goes in the mouth?

Hmm.

Then the 'anal stage'?

Yeah, as they become aware that they are doing 'poo' – I mean, she talks about poo a lot –

Yeah?

She doesn't do anything like sticking her fingers up her bum, or showing us her poo or anything. I think Malaika's quite – normal.

Yeah.

Thank God! Ha ha

Yeah. Because she hasn't been suppressed, I imagine.

Well no.

Or maybe different kids do it in different ways. Then, after that's supposed to be the – how do you pronounce it – 'pe-nile stage'?

'Genital stage'…

Genital stage! Then what? Because I think I'm over my 'anal' and getting into 'genital' and I wanna know what's… what's next!

Ha ha ha!

I want more fun!

I dunno. I suppose it's the integration of all the aspects. You're comfortable with…

Billy said, maybe it's "Other people's genitals stage!"

Ha ha ha ha ha ha

Sounds like fun! *'Therapy for primary obsessional slowness. The main feature of this disorder was excessive slowness.'* This is a quote about someone. *'...he took roughly three hours to prepare himself for work each morning. He bathed infrequently because he needed up to five hours to complete the process.*

Oh God...

'By the time he was referred for help, he was in danger of losing his job, because he was regularly quite late for work. Following this approach and dealing with all of his problems, a significant overall improvement, bathing, washing, teeth cleaning and dressing was achieved and he gradually learned to complete his daily self-care chores in an acceptable manner and period. The improvement ensured that he was able to retain his job.' I was; I couldn't; I was late for work! Because, I would need to do my rituals...

Really?

If I had my obsessive shower, wash and everything and a part of me, or my hair touched a wall that was considered contaminated, I'd do it all over again. I couldn't have a bath. If I had a bath, I'd have to have another bath to get the dirty water off me – and still I'd be a little bit edgy, because it's washing with dirty water. Uummm...

This is interesting, because, I remember last Christmas – it's funny the things I remember, you commenting on the fact that I burped, farted and then later on, John and I both said that we pissed when we shower.

YEAH!

With all those things, I thought, 'oh maybe I am just disgusting', but now, of course, thinking about...

Yeah

...what you are saying, all of those things would probably trigger

some, well, residual. I don't know, is it residual or is it still active?

I find people who piss in the bath and shower a bit iffy.

But, for me, I just like to do that. To me, that's nothing.

And they don't clean the bath after.

Farting; and... well I thought 'it's just cleaning itself', because you are pissing in the shower...

And I'm sure everyone would say that.

...yeah. It's just you! You are the freak! Ha ha ha...

No, I just don't bathe in other people's piss. He he he he he – no matter how 'with the Vedas'[116] it is! But yeah. I remember when I worked at, um, at that newspaper in London. Always late. And, for obsessive-compulsive reasons. Always. Self-employment, I would say, is, because of obsessive-compulsive. That's why...

You can go at your pace.

...exactly! And cancel things, and postpone things, and get staff to do things, and – same as the cleaning, or being cleaned. Get them to do everything. Work within whatever I could work with, but as long as I don't have to take; as long as I've got space for the obsessive-compulsive and I can manage life around obsessive; or I 'could' manage life around obsessive-compulsive. But...

Mmm

...excuses! I remember one excuse. Because I so ran out of excuses for being late! Once – you know, pretty much first job out of college – I just used every excuse and I just thought this has so got to be a good excuse! So I said something about '...there I was, sitting in the bus, and it stopped. Nothing was moving for ages! And it was only half an hour later, when we drove past, that I realised that the person in the car in front, whose car wasn't moving, had had a heart attack and had dropped dead at the steering wheel and that's why no one could go past!'

My God.

How desperate, a lie, is that?

That's fairly convoluted.

Then can you imagine all the lies I'd run through? I must have run out...

God... yeah, of relatives.

Servants used to do that! Their Mother's would die regularly, just so they could get – ha ha ha

And you have to remember who's dead.

Heh heh heh heh heh heh *'Other behavioural techniques'* This is the last bit! *'For example. A rather shy and timid young man who had severe obsessive-compulsive problems including obsessive avoidance of going out...'* Which I had. *'...was treated with standard behaviour therapy, but the results were short-lived. It quickly became clear that the disabilities caused by the problems - inability to go out, wash his own clothes, to do any outdoor work and so on - had the effect of his Mother doing everything for him and waiting upon him.'* After my Mother, I got best friends – more than girlfriends, even – best friends. Rob 'became' my Mother.

Hmmm.

To an extent; and I've never prepared food. Obsessive-compulsive. What if I don't cook it enough, what if there's a small, little animal in there that I should have seen and cleaned out and its gonna harm someone, or it's dirty, or what if, what if, what if. Whatever it is, what if – whatever. And, Lui! Made my meals. Billy is making my meals now. It's; I'm really quite helpless.

Hmmm

As you know, because you used to make my meals!!! Ha ha ha ha ha ha ha...

Thanks for reminding me; well, interesting that you said that's one of the things that you want to change at the community.

Big time!

Learning to cook.

And learning to fix things...

Yeah.

...and all the things that obsessive... so, you know. *My poor family. I terrorised them!* And they didn't even know what was going on! They took it.

And I can see the relevance of this to you – and I appreciate what you're saying, that other people will relate to it, but – surely this isn't true for most people!

No. It's an extreme case, but then... Bob's obsessive-compulsive, Billy's obsessive-compulsive, ummm, I don't know, I can't think from the top of my head, but... Rob is obsessive-compulsive, a good number of my friends – do you know Sheila, Bob's friend?

Is she?

Hugely obsessive-compulsive. I mailed her the book. A lot of people with sex problems. And I've had a good batch of sex, um, for the last little while. Clients, that is. Obsessive-compulsive issues partly, as well as issues of sexuality, not meaning that they are gay or straight or anything like that, but, they're not mature enough, or sexually mature enough to express any form of sexuality. So, asexual rather than bisexual. A lot of people that I've found that take ecstasy and go to, you know, raves and stuff. But just not sexually there yet! So they could be in a club, 'off their tits'[117], part of everything, dancing around, but um, 'no one could come near them'. They can't be touched. Do you know what I mean?

(Ed's face stretches into a yawn)

Don't worry, this is quick and easy.

No, I'm just - ha-ha - tiredness, that's all... it's not boredom. It's not that it's boring, I'm just thinking, is this relevant? And...

And... *I can't blame anyone!*

Oh, okay.

And... I can't blame my parents. The first half of...

Surely, this is just part of the - what's the word - part of the picture as well. I mean, like say, astrology. It's not the whole picture. Clues.

But this is; obsessive-compulsive. It was my secret. And if I was obsessive-compulsive, ummm, my parents should have done something about it. My parents fucked my life up. My; Idi Amin fucked my life up. The Welsh people...

So this is

...blaming everyone...

stopping being a victim?

...exactly! This is me. And my responsibility and the actual truth of what was going on. And, it's handy to have that, and to have the Oedipal book, and to know that all these things are 'quite normal'. Do you know the Lucis Trust mailing that they send to me every full moon?

Oh yeah. It's very interesting.

115. *'Catch 22' Joseph Heller (Vintage Press/Simon & Schuster) 1961. (Filmed 1970).*

116. *The Vedas. Hindu scriptures from 1500BC.*

117. *Off their tits. High on drink or other drugs.*

407

The Law is an Ass

Fucking good! This is a really juicy bit! I saw a film called 'Changing Lanes'[118], ummm, the guy – the black guy – from 'Pulp Fiction'[119]?

I can't remember his name. He's been in lots of Quentin Tarantino films.

Yup.

The name will come to me at some point, I'm sure.

Absolutely fucking excellent film! I didn't know what it was about or anything – saw it at John's – brilliant film. There, it's two years...

Samuel L Jackson[120]!

Samuel Jackson. It's two years since my ankle was broken because of this pot-hole on private land. Two years down the line, still being bullied by solicitors, the first solicitors just fucked up, fobbed me off, lied to me that I'd have my money by so-and-so time, so I borrowed money by someone - from someone else who knows the solicitor, and said "...well you'll be paid at so-and-so time because you'll have your money from the case." Meanwhile no. Meanwhile, this solicitor of mine's a dope-head. And, I can't do anything about it. So I heard the other day that the second solicitor would carry on running the case, and I need to pay this and I need to pay that in order to get something! Meanwhile, it bankrupt me! I needed to have enough money for Lui and I to survive, with no income, no money for food, no money for anything. It fucked-up our relationship, it closed the business down, blah blah blah, and what have I got? This has so fucked me up! So, this is what they wrote in the mail-out. Very briefly: Libra, the last full moon – not this one, but the one before was in Libra – *'Libra. The sign often associated with law and justice. In the law courts of the United Kingdom, the symbol of justice is portrayed as a woman, holding out a set of scales in one hand and a sword in the other. The sword is held in the right hand and represents the power of discrimination and judgement. Applied impartially, after weighing up the facts presented in the scales held out in the other hand. Furthermore, to show that judgement is made without prejudice, the woman wears a blindfold.'* Cool, eh. You know, you used to be a solicitor!

Hmmm. Well also, yeah. My Libra thing. Interesting.

Yeah. Exactly. What a FUCKED moon that was! I don't know how I got away with it, but everyone else around me 'died'! The next paragraph says: *'As one modern art sculpture reminds us*[121]*, in sympathy with the saying 'the law is an ass'* – who said that, was it Denning[122]? That the law is an ass?

Probably, I'm not sure.

'This parody of the original statue of justice wears the asses' ears, and the cap and belt of a jester, or court fool. The sword is replaced by the fool's mace, while in the other hand, justice holds the scales, but noticing that the pearls of truth in one hand are weighing heavier than the block of gold in the other, the little finger is extended to tip the scales in favour of the gold. The loose hanging sleeve of the finger is richly embroidered with the symbols of **those sections of society perceived as being immune to justice. Politicians, the famous and the wealthy.***'*

Hmmm

Ain't that the way it is! Have you seen 'Changing Lanes'?

No.

Fucking excellent! And it reminded me of when we went to go and see, that, David... Icke[123] with Matthew?

Oh yes.

That was ace, eh!

Yeah.

Conspiracy. I mean, you know, whether the Queen's a lizard or not...

Ha ha ha ha ha... was it Queen Lizard-beth?

...he he. But it was good. You don't need to take all of it!

Yeah!

What did you think in the end? Because it was your first exposure to him, eh.

Yeeeah... Um, well funny enough, he seemed like he'd assembled evidence the way a lawyer does. He seemed very... sober, and... rational, not at all... like a loon. Where, I'd heard... he was portrayed; I was, I was impressed. I mean, it's hard now to - sort of - look back and think. I mean, I remember thinking I hope he doesn't talk about the 'lizard thing' because that's really mad, but then, you know, he talked about the fact that there is the reptilian part of the brain.

Yup

So it does all make sense, maybe stretching the point. Sometimes. Yeah, like you say, like Goenka[124] says in Vipassana. That little story about the pudding that the Mother makes. Take out the things that you don't like and you keep...

I don't remember it.

...yeah, there was some little metaphorical story about a Mother who makes a luxury pudding for her little boy. He says he won't eat it because it's got cardamoms in it. And she says "Take it out and eat the rest because it's nice." And the metaphor of the story is, well, you can pick and choose. I can say that I think David Icke has got some good stuff, and I'm not sure that I agree with all of that.

Yeah, yeah.

Um, yeah! I haven't really formed a strong opinion, really. It seemed like another piece of the big puzzle.

Generally, I feel very bullied by society. By the legal system, by the capitalist system, by the de-humanisation of the whole thing…

Hmmm. But haven't you also said; I mean, to an extent – this is maybe being devil's advocate – I mean, you've done well in a sense through capitalism when you've charged say £500 – what is it £800 a day?

No £500 for a day and £300 for half a day.

I mean I feel, I feel an ambivalence about it. I mean, I can make £40 an hour doing massages. That wouldn't be possible in a world without money. On the other hand, I suppose, in some idealised world, we would all just give each other massages. We'd touch each other and…

Yup!

…but , whereas, again, it's like coming back to, for me it's like coming back to my twenties and being very political. What is the ideal world?

Hmmm

Like we were saying earlier, in the restaurant. People are just, seemingly, so distracted by day-to-day stuff that people aren't going to rebel and riot and burn the train carriage. They just shrug their shoulders and mutter, or moan, or go home and watch TV, or text on their mobile phone how pissed off they are…

And get more and more in debt.

…exactly, what are the options?

And get more and more disconnected from each other.

Yeah.

And more ill. And more… fed with… hopes, lies,

I feel I'd like to be part of some kind of revolution, but I don't see the kind of twentieth century revolutions as having achieved – well, they've obviously achieved what they've achieved – yeah, something new, but I don't know what, at this stage. If you sat me down and said 'what would it consist of', 'what would it look like', I don't know.

I don't see it as throwing stones at the Houses of Parliament or anything like that. I see it as the way that we, as individuals, conduct ourselves.

Hmmm

In our own lives, in our own communities, and let it pass on that way.

Yes, yes.

And, how that affects, err, litigation[125] – well it doesn't. Well, I'm not being bullied by that right now. And that will slowly, hopefully, change. How, I don't know.

I mean, everyone says everything's become more democratic, because your class and your origins don't matter as much. Anyone can be wealthy, anyone can be famous, but I think a lot of people are dis-empowered by the obsession with celebrity. I mean, coming in on the Tube the last couple of days I've noticed, every other person seemed to be reading either 'Metro'[126] or some other newspaper. And the articles are all about 'wouldn't you like to look like Victoria Beckham' or 'don't you wish you had David Beckham's four million pound property in Spain' or 'Dave spent four hundred thousand pounds on a hotel'

But isn't that, isn't that the same as Bollywood? Where the very poor people spend their last pennies going to see a movie to totally escape?

Yeah

And live their joy through someone else's filter? Meanwhile, stay small – and meet your minimum payment.

Yeah.

But check this! Isn't it Guy Fawkes today?

Yeah.

I read today in *'Metro'* – seeing as you talk about *'Metro'* – that Guy Fawkes was trying to blow up Parliament because of King James I, the way that King James I was persecuting the Catholics.

Exactly, yeah.

So the King James I Bible, was that what the religion is based on, isn't it?

What, Catholicism? No, isn't it the Anglican Church? I don't know to be honest. Not my forte...

And I don't know, but King James I Bible is 'the Bible' I think.

Hmmm. Well, that's the 'standard' Bible. Yeah. But, I mean, surely people have been having these conversations since time immemorial, that society is unjust. How can we change it? But, in a way, I suppose a lot of it is just; today it seems like a personal...

Well, it is changing.

Yeah!

And it's changing in leaps and bounds! In my lifetime probably more than the last three generations put together.

But then, I mean, don't people argue that we have a totally free press? For example, all this stuff that's going about...

Bollocks

...Princess Diana at the moment? You know, more conspiracies. How far that will go, I don't know.

Yeah, no. No answers, just bitchiness and bitterness.

What, from us?

From me.

Ha ha ha

You're being quite realistic and grown-up about it. I am - I suppose - 'throwing stones at the passing plane'.

Yeah, I mean, I don't I don't wanna give up – and I haven't – I don't feel like I've got to a point where I can see any – huuuh, I don't know. What is it? Engagement?

But in the way that you are living your life. You believe it and it's working for you.

Hmmm

And the way that I'm living my life. I believe it and it's working for me. We haven't bought into this... being bullied by society, as a lot of other people have. Umm, and I have litigation on my hands. And I feel fucked up by it...

Yeah, which I can understand.

...and I will be bitter about that. And feel helpless. Etcetera, etcetera. Anyway, on a lighter note, I thought you might like this one. Um *'Spiritual darkness teaches us the beauty of the immediate. The glory of the present opportunity, and the need to focus upon the task of service of the moment. These are the rewards of moving forward into the apparently impenetrable darkness.'* - Urrr... - *'for the initiate, this blindness is still more esoteric, as there remains absolutely no light what-so-ever. No earth light, nor any light between the worlds at all. Perhaps this helps us to understand why spiritually awakened people can sometimes feel so alone, and without tangible help from above or below, they've touched the vision, but the soul is now prompting them to turn their back on the light in order for it to flow through them and so lighten humanities path.'*

Hmmm.

Fucking gorgeous, innit!

I don't know if I completely get it. What's your interpretation?

Being... I suppose a very basic way is 'why hang out and preach to the converted?' Because that's just mutual masturbation.

Hmmm

Playing safe but no one's really moving on. Surely, you will take your light out into the world and into the testing ground, or – build a bridge...

Yeah

...into mainstream reality... to a more 'natural', which is not necessarily 'spiritual', because the 'physical', the 'emotional' and the 'mental' go to that 'higher frequency' too. It's gotta be all four, but it's all natural. Take your light into the mainstream and take nature back there. Over and above the shit. Or the ignorance.

What was I going to say? I mean, to some extent, like you say, it's just how, a lot of things we've touched on in these conversations, how we've interacted with a 'numbed' public on Tube trains and buses. And the way people are with adults and the way people are with kids – like Malaika can get away with things on trains that other adults would, we'd be locked up, or... people would just shun you? Strange. Yeah, as you say, just let your light shine and be friendly to people, in a... relatively hostile world.

It takes guts! To take the first step...

Definitely.

...but fuck is it worth it!

Yes.

Ninety nine per cent of the time, it gives everyone around permission – or at least one person permission – to join in.

Yeah

And this year, this winter has been the best winter!

Hmmm

It's not like a winter. It's like the summer, people still want to smile!

Hmm

And play and be nice! And hang out. On the Underground and in the streets, so many people – not only smile, but say "Hey, how you doin'?" THAT'S NOT BRITISH! No… it's fuckin' excellent! It's certainly not London. You know. You can't tar everyone with the same brush! People are a lot nicer in the small towns and villages and stuff. Shall I quickly run through the Oedipal so far, then go somewhere else?

Yeah?

You sure you haven't had enough?

Well, I'm not quite sure what we're getting at. I feel like I've slightly lost the plot right this minute.

I feel like, after all the bitchiness in the first part of the book, like I've been doing a lot of research and it's like… 'Oh that's what that is! And that's what that is! And that's what that is!' Getting over the guilt. Getting over the blame. Naming it! Getting over it. And thinking… rather than 'I'm a victim failed by my family, my world, society, it's – nah! This is what happened'

It's up to us to…

Exactly!

…accept it and live with it and move on.

Yup. *Name it – not blame it.*

And then I think, for me, it's the disappointment I feel when I still sometimes don't get on with my Dad, and my Mum annoys me, and I think, somehow, all this has been pointless and a failure, but, actually, that's being too perfectionist.

Yup!

You're gonna have rows, you're gonna have bad times, but it's how quickly you move on from it. That's...

And also, what you're getting from it, it think.

Yeah?

Rather than 'shouldn't have these things', it's 'thank God we have these things 'cos we're taking part.'

Yeah, that's true.

And we're all growing, shifting the boundaries as we grow. Interacting.

Well I suppose friction can be a sign of... change.

And closeness, as long as it's not the obsession. Hmmm.

Go on...

This will take no time!

... get your Oedipus out. Oedipusseee!

118. 'Changing Lanes' (2002) Roger Mitchell, USA.

119. 'Pulp Fiction' (1994) Quentin Tarantino, USA.

120. Samuel L Jackson. Leading character in the two above films.

121. Justice. www.iannorbury.com/carvings/touchstone.htm

122. Denning. Lord Denning, UK High Court judge.

123. David Icke. Controversial UK writer and speaker. www.davidicke.com

124. Goenka. SN Goenka, gave Vipassana back to the world. www.dhamma.org

125. Litigation. Any action in a court of law.

126. 'Metro' Free circulation daily newspaper.

Oedipus Complex

'Sigmund Freud drew on his clinical experience of self-analysis of the Greek cycle of plays by...'[27] – how do you pronounce this? 'So-fol...'

Sophocles.

Sophocles.

'Oh, I'm ever so over-educated!'

He he he he he – suits you! Fucking poof. 'In particular...

Ha ha ha

'... Oedipus Rex, in which Oedipus kills his Father and marries his Mother with disastrous consequences. Children from about three to six years have intense loving feelings towards one parent, and seek to possess that parent exclusively, while having strong negative feelings towards the other parent. At the unconscious level, these feelings are sexual towards the desired parent and murderous towards the same sex parent.' Do you remember I used to say that throughout my childhood *I*

wanted my Father dead?

Yeah, definitely. Me too!

And that wasn't just the bullying, it was... 'not us', it was 'Oedip-us'. Huh ha ha ha ha ha ha

Ha ha ha ha ha

'If all goes well in psychological development...' – which it didn't! Ha ha ha ha ha ha obviously – 'the child comes to see how he or she benefits from the parental union and learns to contain possessive and hostile feelings. The intense Oedipal feelings get reprised in

*adolescence when teenagers are typically rebellious, experiment with
their sexual identity and make trouble, sometimes serious trouble for their
parents.'* I didn't rebel!

Hmmm. No I didn't! Not really. I got drunk.

This is what we're doing now with the book. I'd say!

Yes. And some of our behaviour, as well.

Really?

Well, maybe, what I've described…

'No I'm not coming in from the tent!' Ha ha ha ha ha

**Yeah, well exactly! And the thing like that incident with Steven, you
know, kind of 'shocking your parents'. Bringing home…**

Yeah

…'somebody'…

Yeah

…so shocking that they'll…

Yeah

…throw up their dinner or whatever.

Hmmm

Which they didn't.

Yup. And… wait for them to tell you off.

Exactly!

And then having the tantrum.

Yes.

But it's so intellectual at our age. They almost wouldn't dare! Where do
we get a decent fight? Apart from the fucking bullies!

Exactly.

That 'we can't hit back because we might get their brains between our fingers'. Or should I speak for myself?

Ha ha ha

'The intense Oedipal feelings get reprised...' oh, did I do that bit?

Yes.

Yes! 'People who do not successfully work through their Oedipal complex are left immature, unable to get on, hung up about one or both parents, get involved in acting out rather than containing their psychological inadequacies and/or experience stasis in their careers and relationships, having impaired impulse control and difficulty with authority and are prey to all sorts of other troubles.' I know someone like that.

Me too.

Fuck you! Ha ha ha ha ha

Ha ha ha ha ha... isn't this what the book was hinting at earlier? But we didn't know the Oedipal Complex then. I'd heard of it and I knew a fair bit about it.

I vaguely knew about...

It's huge though! Because what it says is, there are no gay people. I mean, homosexuality is simply to do with – that!

Bollocks! There are gay people. And 'this' is why. Or this is a contributing factor.

Or, what I think – and I think we said this before –

Of course there are gay people! We've both had them.

Yeah, but – ha ha ha ha ha

Ha ha ha ha ha

But I think what's interesting is there seem to be gay people who are more – well, these terms are so loaded, but do you know, genetically more 'like that' and others who can't make up their minds or feel bad about it, who've had 'this' on top of it. Or 'this' separately, so it's like you could maybe be genetically pre-disposed – chemically, I don't know. Whatever. Plus, would 'Oedipus' make you definitely homosexual, whereas if maybe you've just had a domineering Mother...

I'm not even sure it's that strongly about sexuality. We are all victims – or products – of our childhood. I mean, if something doesn't work, or we want to sort something out, or get more pleasure from something, or more peace from something or whatever, then – do what we're doing. Check it out, get some awareness; throw some light on it and then make choices, rather than being a victim to Oedipiss or obsessive-compulsive disorder, or wicked aunts and step-Mothers...

And having to 'join the club'!

...exactly!

And go to meetings about being an Oedipus victim for the rest of your life.

Yup! Rather than just...shagging old women Ha ha ha ha ha!

Ha ha ha ha ha

Get on with it!

Hmmm...

Oh yeah, of course! Over to you... ha ha ha ha ha ha

My God, actually that's true. It's nearly the anniversary of that shag with Margaret.

Is it?

Eleventh of December, in Chippenham, after a strange day at Avebury. With a bunch of witches.

What a fast year! And fucking lot of - you know - fucking hell has this year thrown all the other years away, basically!

But I'm finding, I mean like yesterday, you know I was saying about this idea for interviewing people 'on the massage table', this guy yesterday that I have these conversations – not 'these' conversations – with. This guy has been married twice, has got an eighteen year old son and he lives with another bloke. He basically said he was more sexually attracted to men, but emotionally attracted to women…

Hmmm

…and, just fascinating! You know, this, this whole, what we've unearthed in the last year. Changes the way I interact with men and I was saying to you, I still… yeah I still sometimes look at men and think 'he's really attractive'. Some kind of sexual thing kicks in, but, there's such a strong urge. Oh, that's really interesting. On Friday, umm, on Halloween, with Five Rhythms, with Shane, we did this amazing dance, it was like – I can't describe it – it was rough! Wrestling. It was kind of; there was an edge to it that was soft. Just as we'd kinda get to the point where we threw the other person to the floor…

Hmmm

It was kind of like 'male ballet' but with female elements thrown in at the right moment. It was fucking brilliant! Amazing. So enjoyable. And that's kind of – almost seems to sum up a large amount of what I'd like from a male relationship.

You're lucky that you've got such freedom with your male relationships. I've got great male relationships. Generally, I don't want to touch them, I don't want them to touch me, it's cool to… you know, even hang around bare-chested with some of them – if it's a boiling hot day – but… I don't really want them to take their shirts off. I don't really want to see them. I don't want – you know – arm pits near each other. I'm cool for legs to touch and stuff like that, but, you know, and I've seen really beautiful bodies and huge cocks and stuff and I just think... 'I don't, wanna look at that', 'I don't like that', 'it's not attractive', 'keep it away from me', 'cover it up'.

Hmmm

I don't know. I'm not into it. And maybe I've got a block there again or something. I don't know.

Maybe for you the experiences you've described previously have dealt with that.

Yeah.

Whereas for me, it is what I enjoy.

Yeah.

It's not a question of 'going there and finishing it'. Yeah. It feels like a kind of 'aliveness'. I mean, I wouldn't want to 'do it', that just happened, spontaneously. We just danced.

Well now you've got choice, haven't you? Where, I think I've still got – I don't know if its obsessive-compulsive issues, or sexuality issues, or maybe it's just not my thing. It just doesn't seem like my thing. It seriously, honestly doesn't; and maybe when I was doing that, um, sauna thing, whatever, that was the same as when other kids do changing rooms or toilets.

I'm sure... claiming it.

I didn't go through that stage... Yeah. Exactly. So I claimed it this way! But now I've claimed it, I can make my choices, without claiming it how could I make any choices? And other people probably – you know – they have it easy, because it's normal. Everyone's claiming it at the same time. Going through the same thing. But, no. I skipped that. So, now I think it's different. I don't know what it is. But, you know, some of my mates are, very attractive. And naked, or half naked or whatever, at times. I don't wanna... I don't like it. It's not like 'Ugh – get away!' but it's... I look forward to them covering up.

Hmmm. Yes, funny, because when I'd visit you before I'd moved into Muswell Hill, and when I was there if I'd come out of the shower with a towel around me, I'd always feel a sense of, 'I'd better cover up around you'.

Yeah..

And I thought, 'am I just, am I being too free?' It was almost like the boundaries thing.

Yeah.

Is it you? Or is it me? Or is it somehow both of us?

Yeah. Yeah you probably picked up on the truth! Nah, the same with most people. I want them covered up. For some reason.

And yet, you embrace the nudity, like the nudist thing.

Yeah. Where everyone's naked.

Well maybe it's just an equality thing, I don't know.

But I didn't wanna necessarily want to get naked, with people. And it was a boiling hot summer! And also, that was an experience. But I think that was claiming it! It doesn't mean that every year I'll get naked with a load of other people and lie around reading my book. And be non-sexual. *Maybe I just needed to claim the normality of being publically naked.*

Hmmm

Probably. But, yeah, I'm surprised at how shut-down I am about other men not having their clothes on.

Hmmm

Maybe I'm still exploring my extremes. Fuck knows! And it isn't men, actually. Young bodies. No, that's not true because Lui has got a 'boy body' and I'm okay with him without his clothes on. Billy's got a 'boy body' and I'm not so okay with him for some reason. And Billy's naked quite a lot.

Maybe because he's older.

Yup. Maybe it is an age thing. Age, rather than stage of the body.

Hmmm

Dunno.

Hmmm

Anyway. Last bit of Oedipal?

Let's knock it on the head. Let's knock Oedipus on the head.

'A too strong attachment to a domineering Mother, coupled with a weak or absent Father, was a fundamentally important factor in the aetiology of male homosexuality in 'Suddenly Last Summer' 1958 (Tennesse Williams) Others hotly dispute the link.' and I think what we said is, 'contributing factors'.

Rather than, 'that's the explanation for it'. Domineering Mother, absent Father, equals...

Hm

...poof!

Hm. Which would kind of make sense. Maybe, schmaybe...

It's like I remember this bloke in Silchester saying to me – this gay guy – he didn't care why he was gay, he just accepted he was. I remember thinking 'God you're so fucking lucky!'

Yeah, good on ya!

Yeah!

Whatever it is, enjoy it! But, if there's something, like I said before, that needs to be enjoyed more...

Yeah

…or, be free from, or is an issue, or a problem, or is harming yourself or other people, or whatever, take a look at it and get over it! But if there's no problem – why dig?

Yeah! 'If it's not broken…'

Exactly!

Well, yeah! And I suppose that answers the question for me it was; it became this year, having relationships with men or women or both simultaneously. It's like, this is too much of a head fuck. So I'd almost rather, I'd almost rather, I'd almost rather leap one way or the other in a way, but then I don't…

But why not have the best of all worlds?

Yeah.

I mean, there are no men that I want to sleep with or anything and I'm really enjoying my relationship with Gina – not only sexual, but all of it! - even being mates - because she used to be a Tomboy anyway and I don't know whether that's a tell-tale. I mean, is this a pattern? Emma wasn't; she was very hot stuff in the 80's and she's not an unattractive woman at all, but she was quite masculine in a way I suppose. Or Tomboyish, or impish, like Enya[128].

Yeah

And, Grace, my ex. Hot as…! But, lesbian – now. Because that suits her and, you know, I want what's good for her.

Hmmm

My women are not… I suppose they're not feminine weaklings, because my Mother was.

Hmmm

And I don't want to look after them, I would rather have someone I can really play with, and hang out with, throw around sexually and not think

I'm going to break them. I remember when I first started shagging, I'd be really scared that I'm going to break some woman's rib by jumping on her too much or something. But now, I'd rather be chucked about and chuck about. You know, have fun. 'A Tonka[129] woman'. A 'Tank Girl'[130].

Ha ha ha

Feminine's cool, but not overly. But yeah. Maybe it's because I've got such a great relationship with Gina, I'm happy. I'm content. Maybe it's; I don't think I'd be able to have such a great relationship with Gina if it wasn't for this book. Or, with anyone else. Or have the life that I've got right now if it wasn't for the book. And the clarity and unfolding, or... it's like untangling a knot – that the book's done.

Hmmm

And I'm chuffed that it's documented. Not only for me, but hopefully other people can un-knot as well....

I think it's interesting that -

...and not think they're going mad.

- you've been far more putting the book out there. I guess maybe that explains why I feel more like, I'm not sure people are going to enjoy it, because... I never really got ; but I suppose I haven't really asked, from Shane or Angus, I don't even know if they've read it, which I think I got the sense both of them had stopped, and I thought, 'oh well, it must be boring then', or 'maybe it's just the people I know that aren't interested in it'.

Or maybe they've accepted – are, are they both gay?

Nooo. Shane is. Well, he doesn't totally accept he is, but his relationships have been primarily with women... I mean with MEN. For the same reason, maybe, because he doesn't want to box himself in and say 'I am this'. Angus. All relationships with women. But he's said he'd be interested in, he thought about having sex with men.

What does that mean? Huh. Maybe, maybe – I dunno – maybe I just haven't encouraged people enough.

Well maybe they're going through it, and this is cramping their style...

Could be.

...or they're enjoying where they are, this would force them to let go of something, or lose something...

Maybe.

...or maybe they're scared. Or maybe you're paranoid, so it's a panic. Ha ha ha ha ha ha... still.

You know, *you do have to fall apart, before you can consolidate again.*

Yeah. We'll, just like my family and I. We've had time apart. And it's been quite painful, scary, probably especially for my parents.

Hmmm

Probably, especially for my Mother. Because my Father's been used to being disconnected from. And maybe, to an extent, same as my brother. But my Mother must have felt it the most. But, with this time, and the understanding with me finding things out from the family, and, getting together and asking questions, looking at pictures and coming together the way we are... it's a million times better than it was. But it needed that painful, fucked up, without-any-promises disconnection. And all the rage that I must have expressed at the beginning of the book.

Hmmm... well I may have used this analogy before, but it's like going back to a bone that's been broken, that hasn't mended properly, you have to go back, re-break it, and allow it to set...

127. *'Ideas in Psychoanalysis-Oedipus Complex' Robert M Young (Icon Books) 2001*

128. *Enya. Female Irish singer / songwriter. www.enya.com*

129.   Tonka. Classic 70's indestructible toy trucks.

130.   Tank Girl. Cult cartoon chick who totes a machine gun and (apparently) fucks kangaroos. www.twisted.org.uk/tg

Pissing on the embers

Yeaah.

…in a more healthy way. At least that's the idea. Huh huh.

Last Christmas, with you, me and Bob was great! Funny, thinking about this Christmas. I've got no attachment. I could quite happily go and hang out with my parents, without a problem.

Yeah?

During the year or last year – no fucking way! Probably ever in my life. And I said in the book that I wouldn't want my parents near my kids. I've totally changed that! I wouldn't want my, God Mother, I wouldn't want my family – or my extended family – near my kids. I'm cool with my cousins from Liverpool, probably my aunt and uncle in Liverpool. And I'm cool with my parents, especially as they've matured, and changed, and grown, they're not the same panicked adolescents they were when they were my; not only adolescents, they were very fucked up. Not only with their fucked up lives, but with the situations in hand.

Hmmm

So, they've mellowed and matured and grown into wisdom, they'd be cool. *It's good to know who 'the enemy' is, rather than just throwing stones at anything that moves!* Ha ha ha ha ha ha ha

Yes, definitely. Well I think the enemy is anything left unresolved. Lurking.

And unboundaried. I can't blame other people if I haven't got boundaries, though.

No… No! All we can do is work out how to create them.

Yeah.

Hmmm

For me, looking at you, the big completion is moving from the woods, and having been through all that. I don't know what it is for me. Maybe, getting healthy, getting over addictions, whether it's to Lui, drama, feeling guilty, smoking dope, whatever whatever, it's feeling peaceful, accepting, safe and calm. Maybe that's my completion. Also, I suppose, in a way, maybe having a relationship with Gina. Nice girl, that I want to be with, that I like. Who I don't feel smothered by. She's living her life and I'm living mine and we're sharing. And also, coming back from Chester this morning. That feels like my last trip. I've seen the friends. I've seen the family. I've seen everyone.

That was your last lot of cousins?

Yeah. And really, I haven't properly seen my aunt and uncle in Liverpool and quizzed them, every one about every thing. I'm over the quizzes. I think I've found out enough to find out.

I think you're right. My experience of you is that something has really shifted. I think it's, um, more openness and more humility in your way of being in the world. Before it was sort of… I guess it was a certain amount of blag. 'You are this person… everyone worships because of the work you do.' And you've kind of thrown that out of the window, really.

Yeah. It's easy making a difference to other people's lives, but then…

What about your life?

…exactly. And, maybe I won't be doing the work I used to do, because, it's like they all say 'therapists need therapy'. Counsellors need counselling. Teachers need to be taught – blah blah blah blah blah – or need the school experience again, whatever.

Well, the other thing that's shifted – and I think it's true for both of us – is having… just the guys we've got in our lives. The ones who were around on Sunday. I couldn't have asked for a better group of men. There was no, no one I wished hadn't been there, or anyone I wished was there that wasn't. It was absolutely perfect. I think having that support of men who are not getting everything right, but are honest enough – like Bob was saying – he's still suffering pain, um, you know, we've all got, still got addiction to whatever, but…

Not so much, actually.

…no…

I think that's the difference with the people there. It's… most people are over most of the addictions most of the time.

Yeah

You're not an addict.

No.

Billy is getting over his, even if his addiction is to feeling guilty, or whatever, similar to me. Not a drinker or a druggie. You know, in other ways. Marius is not either. He's just sixteen, and quite clean. Bob has so got over who he used to be.

He has hasn't he! I was really amazed at the differences in him.

Hmm. So no, maybe, it was the addiction to having an audience and having people around who are still with their addictions, or whatever.

It just felt so real, having that fire in the woods. I just can't believe those two were Boy Scouts.

I'll tell you what… do you fancy schpeiling the story for the 'good people in TV land'? Your experience of it from beginning to end.

What, on Sunday? Well I felt quite nervous actually, when I was travelling up from Silchester. Umm, I don't know what the nervousness was. I think it was, sort of based in… yeah. Old experiences will I, will

I end up being someone I'm not? Am I going to be the centre of attention? Can I accept all of this – you know – praise and, being in the middle of it. Umm, but just the way it worked out. Meeting you lot in the pub...

Hmmm

...which felt like the first day of Winter, as you said...

It really so did!

...and then driving up, in convoy, to Box Hill. And just, yeah, to share it with you all, was just... I really felt, felt like Lord Of The Manor, but not in a...

Yeah!

...snooty way...

'This is my world.'

Yeah, 'Come and share it, have a look, I know you'll love it'.

We had no idea what to expect. And I had no idea whether Box Hill was a poxy little woodland, or something vast. And it was, it knocked shit off Hampstead Heath. It was the 'real' countryside. Old and magical with colours.

Yeah. And the atmosphere, that slight sort of misty...

Yeah! It was weird, wasn't it? Surreal! Vampires could have jumped out...

Huuh! Well I'm glad you weren't there when I was walking through the woods I had enough bloody people saying that!

Huh huh huh huh huh huh

It was great for us!

Hmmm. But again, no time to think or anything! We just got together, waited for a bit for Marius, picked up Marius, chatted in the car –

together or separately – about... all sorts of stuff. But it wasn't, it wasn't... um, blaggy laddie chat, about crap. Or putting each other down, or humiliation. It wasn't a pecking order thing. It wasn't cool stuff about chicks and drugs and... it was just honest. It was cool!

Hmmm

Well, whatever came up. It wasn't process – what a fucking relief! Yeah, process over. *'War Is Over'*[131]. And then, yeah, just sitting and waiting and waiting for you – not, like, 'where is he?' but it was almost like 'Santa's on his way...' or 'It's all gonna start soon!' or something. Do you know what I mean?

Yeah, yeah – totally. Well it's interesting that Marius is sixteen, because that's about the age I felt.

Really?

Umm... and yet. It's hard to describe it. That; but also a sense of having – yeah – having been through something really important in my life. Because I mentioned to you earlier, I met up with Rychard on the Monday, because I left a few things that we didn't pick up on Sunday.

Yah

And, um, I said to him, I mean, *"This is probably one of the most important things that I have ever done in my life"* and, coming at it from... not knowing that at all...

Yah

'...I've just got to live in the woods.' Totally following that intuition. I mean, I think if I'd, if I'd gone, thinking, 'Ooh, I must, you know I really must sort myself out.'

Yeah! 'It will take four months, and I might get cold, and I might get scared, and...'

434

Yeah.

Nah, it was just… it was honest, natural expression. Nothing more to think about really.

But just, as I say, having the fire was the crème de la crème – do you know what I mean? Or the piece de resist… - oh whatever, do you know what I mean? Or the best, the best bit. The jewel in the crown. And just, yeah, just hanging out and I mean, I can't remember what we talked about.

Whatever…

There wasn't any shit.

It wasn't 'doing' anything. It was 'being' together. And whatever happened to come up, it wasn't even about what's coming up and what's not – it could have been totally in silence.

Yeah. Well, I mean, there was that point when we were just fire-gazing and some of the stuff that Billy said about men, together, hunting… they don't speak that much. He's got such a great presence, that guy! I love the way he kind of, he just kind of acted out what you'd be doing if you were hunting.

Yeah.

It was so vivid.

'Gentle touch and a point.'

'cos he's got the same thing, that kind of… sixteen, but an elder. Like an elder, but he's on the way…

In a way, like an elder. I'm not sure

…well, in as much as any of us are.

Yeah. I think we can now access that part safely, where I couldn't before.

That'll be where we're going.

Yeah. And maybe he and Bob had done it. Had done it in the Cub way and the Scout way. And I think partly the 'bully' or 'bullied' way, or something, as well.

Maybe, yeah. Well there is that sort of, that 'have everything in order', 'I'll show you how to put up a tent' and all this kind of stuff.

Yeah, we avoided all that. And for us to come together with Marius to be the only one who's allowed to be that age, physically... ha ha ha ha ha ha

But also, it's felt like, um - things that I've written in my little books and diaries while I was in the woods - it felt like I was living through it again, but witnessed doing it, like with the owls. Because they really struck me. I wrote a lot about the noises they made. It was really comforting, hearing owls as you're falling asleep.

Wow...

And I think it was Bob and Billy both noticed the owls hooting. It's just, it was fantastic – and the best bit, the best bit was pissing on the fire to put it out. I thought that was...

That was the 'funny' bit for me! Because, I'd just emptied my bladder, and, I don't remember how it came about but we had to put the fire out. How did it come about, pissing on the fire?

Ummm, Billy and I jokingly said *"We should piss on it"* and then he started to get his dick out, and I thought, 'okay...'

He just can't wait to get his dick out! Really, he can not wait to get it out.

...but, that's how it happens. It's not, we all sit down and resolve...

Exactly!

...it takes one person who says it and another who dares, almost, first.

That was the only bit I didn't take part in. Firstly I'd just emptied my bladder and secondly, I've got a thing about getting my dick out... with other men.

Well, it is, a slightly unusual thing to do, it has to be said.

Yeah, but mainly – you know – like I keep wanking on about – so to speak – in the book. I didn't do changing rooms, I didn't do toilets through school and college...

Hmmm

...unless I had to, somehow, and then I didn't really take part anyway, I was invisible.

Hmmm. Well, it's funny 'cos I, I'd just emptied my bladder and I found my self actually starting to think things like 'Oh I probably won't be able to piss very much' and everyone had said – we were having a conversation in the pub earlier, weren't we? – Bob, and I can't remember, maybe everybody said they couldn't piss in 'urinals with an audience'.

Yeah, yes that's true!

And yet, then we all get our dicks out and pissed on the fire together. Because to me there was no pressure and I just thought, 'if I can't do this now... I'll never be able to do it'.

Aah, really?

It was like, kind of challenging myself. Just do it. You know, don't, I didn't think about it.

I think I've probably still got throw-back stuff from before. *Being checked out, being coloured*, urrr, I don't, I probably didn't even think about it that much, because I thought I've just emptied my bladder. I can get out of this!

That was...

Pure fear and panic.

437

But there was no body there taunting and saying 'Oh, why aren't you getting yours out?'

Yeah, yeah…

'What's wrong with you?'

…yeah.

It's just like, 'okay, he doesn't want to do it, can't do it, whatever'.

Yeah, absolutely. Same with anything, between all of us, is not everyone has to take part with everything all of the time. Or ever!

Well you and I didn't light the fire, and I probably could have rustled one up, but, it was great! By the time we had chatted and I'd packed all my stuff up from the tent, the fire was blazing outside.

That's it. Everyone contributes, and receives in different ways. Don't light the fire. Don't cook. Don't drive. I get very taken care of, and take care in different ways, it seems… but I don't think that – outside household chores, maybe – we look at who's giving what and who's receiving what. Because we're probably all quite ignorant as to what we're giving…

Yeah

…because we could do it, and it's not an effort, and it's not a problem. So what's there to think about? Where if it was something we couldn't do, or were scared of, apprehensive about, then it would be an issue.

Yeah. Well that's it – we just… get on with it! And that, to me, is the difference. Is that just 'being' with everyone on Sunday? There was no; I'd put no pressure on myself to do anything, other than anything that I felt like doing. I think I said to you, didn't I? I felt like – I can't explain why this came up, but it felt like – the Stag Night that I should have had…

Yeaaaahh…!

…when I got married. Just easy. You know, it's like I've always had this kind of love-hate relationship with being the centre of attention. It's like crave it, but when you get it – what do I do? How do I... show off, or...

'What's expected of me now?'

...yeah. And that was, there was no '...oh I just happened to be the person who lived in the woods'. I felt like I could talk about that, but it wasn't like I sat down and took centre stage. Everyone was there sharing their stuff. Sharing their presence. Their energy. I couldn't... I couldn't have asked for a better ending! And to have that – men – that group of mates. Men.

Another quality. Not only quantity – I mean, five of us, that's a lot of close friends – but the quality, more than anything.

Yeah.

It was just totally fucking cool!

And to have that sense of community is amazing to me. Because probably, if you hadn't suggested it, I probably would have gone there by myself, and schlepped the tent back, gone back and forwards to get my bags, it would have taken me twice as long, and it would have been really boring...

Not celebrated it.

Yeah. So that's it, that's one of your contributions. You are really good at bringing people together and making things into something different. And that's not my strength. And I don't beat myself up about it. And great you did it! Thank God you were there!

Ha ha ha ha ha ha ha! It was really really so touching. I could have cried! Listening to you and feeling your energy when you were saying about, um; I loved it when we were all passing the fire-stick with some of us talking, and talking about personal stuff, or giving something away, or up, or whatever. But at the end, when it was time to go, umm, me doing the 'okay Ed, blah blah blah... schpeil something if it feels right.' And what you said, I think everyone could have just cried.

439

Thinking, 'Yeah, this knocks shit out of any Stag Night', it was being together. Being on the same side. Feeling it. Living it. Honouring it. And stuff like that... but yeah, what you said. Perfect. And, who were you before you got married? Who were you with and what was going on? Do you know what I mean? And how pre-mature, in a way. Not to criticise it. But in another way, leaving the men to go to the women.

Yes.

But you can't leave the men until you're... one of the men. And you can't be one of the men until you're accepted by the men. *And the men can't accept you* until you're halfway accepting yourself as one of them. And it seems like the whole thing was completed from you drawing those naked, ummm, big dicked woodmen coming out of the trees...

...to, being...

one of those...

ha ha ha ha ha ha ha ha

ha ha ha ha ha ha ha ha ha

...well I'm not that big dicked, which was another issue when we were pissing on the fire! Do you find that? That was the old 'back in the loos' thing! I just, kind of, as I was looking down at the fire, I can't remember whose dick I noticed, but I was like 'Oh mine's really small...'

Huh huh huh huh huh

'...and it's cold...' so anyway!

I was behind everyone so I couldn't really see; because everyone else was around and I was just standing a little behind.

You couldn't make it up, could you!

What do you mean 'make it up?'

Well, as a story.

Huh huh huh huh huh huh

You would never think, pissing – I would never have thought 'and then we'll piss on the fire'

Exactly! A totally perfect completion. *Piss on the fire together*, rather than being… fucked up the arse! Couldn't ask for more.

Yup. I think I slightly got into my head a bit when, um, I realised that I'd have to go earlier than I thought to pick Mallie up, but it was actually, the timing was great!

Perfect timing. And actually so good that you did, because otherwise you couldn't 'go there and then come back', and demonstrate to yourself how to manage this.

Yeah. Because that's the thing. Going back with Rychard the next day to pick up the bits I forgot, in the dark, I just – Oh! – I really felt I could tap into the energy of us being there. It's like 'everyone was still there' the grey ashes on the forest floor. Oh, it was like a film, do you know when you hear these – it's almost a bit clichéd now – as a cinematic effect, the voices, or the snippets of conversation…

Like something from *'Stand By Me'*[132]

…yes! That's weird, that's the sort of vague image I had.

And what I loved – I don't know who it was – well, one or two people said, after pissing on the fire, "…smells a bit funny, too!"

Oh it did! Which is just…

…so *'Stand By Me'* and so honest! Finding out, rather than 'Oh, I'm cool, I know everything, I've been everywhere! I know how to eat fanny! I know how to mend this bike, and I know how to make so much money', and whatever! Nah! All on the same side exploring and sharing, rather than competing or putting down.

Yeah. And no one says "Well of course it smells funny!" You're right. We were like ten year olds.

And even words like 'sharing'. I'm getting over 'sharing'. I'm not sure that we 'share' any more. I think we more 'hang out', talk, joke and chat and stuff. Do you know what I mean?

Absolutely. It's baring, rather than sharing. Baring souls. Maybe. Or, no. Just being…

Hanging out!

…real. Yeah I think 'hanging out' is the best way to describe it.

And that's another end of an era. Like something you were saying earlier. Not doing the workshop stuff any more. Rather than that, getting on and living it! And, well we met doing workshop stuff. Ha ha ha ha ha ha ha

Full circle!

And now it's like, 'what workshop?' Playtime! Ha ha ha ha

Yeah.

But funny. The stress that I put myself under for about two weeks before?

Oh, about the press release!

About the press release? *The Guardian*? Probably, possibly - according to Emily - wanting the story? And whoever else. I could not write it. And usually… I love writing press releases. This is such a great story and…

We kind of wrote it as well, didn't we?

…we did, yeah, we got together! It wasn't, I imagine, meant to be that anyone else was there apart from us lot. Not a fiasco! But what a great opportunity for me to go through all this guilt, feel how I put other people before me, because it was all things to do for other people, and because it was us two, because we are so close and you're 'part of me' – therefore you're not 'part of other people' so much, maybe – which is an important thing to remember.

Hmm

I know with my Father, much as family came first in survival, but in day to day living, fun and who you wanna be with, we came last. Because we are part of him. And he'd need to 'avoidance addict' family and 'love addict' outsiders. So, similar pattern, in a way.

Sorry, what do you mean? I'm 'part of you', so...

So other people; if 'you're me', then other people come first.

...oh I see. Right. Because I was wondering about, are you thinking that doing the press release is putting me before your needs?

Putting 'us', and therefore me, and therefore the last to want or need or have anything. It's probably the first time that I put you in that bag. Because, I try not to do that any more. With anyone.

Hmmm

131. 'War is over' 'Happy Christmas (War Is Over)'. Yoko Ono and John Lennon anti-war anthem. (1971)

132. 'Stand By Me' (1986) Rob Reiner, USA.

Angry

You know, the closest people should be the ones cared for the most! Rather than the last ones, because 'they're in the bag'. So it's, yeah, the pressure that I put on myself. And then the shock that you were angry... or upset, or let down, or whatever the feelings were.

Umm, I'm not even sure what the word is, actually.

Well I think there were a few emotions.

Yeah.

But, for the two of us, not to be able to – between us, in the conventional way – be, you be angry at me, me be angry at the situation.

Yeah

Um, couldn't get into the anger thing. That morning I was rushing over to the Everyman Project[133] to be on their Management Committee, or help out in whatever way, because that's the bit that I haven't got, that I feel is missing, from *me being a man – is anger*. Errr, I feel like, the whole process of doing the book and the time around it has been me going through adolescence, finally. Getting over my complexes, fears, childish notions that have been built on. But, after that, thinking... well no. Being on the Management Committee is not the way to be angry. It's the way to intellectualise and stop other people from being angry. I don't know quite how I'm gonna do this, apart from... playfighting. Fighting. Going to the gym. Getting into; after seeing my cousin in Chester – really cool to hang out with my cousin, but he's an ex-fighter. He holds martial arts world titles. You know, that kind of stuff. He's always been into his martial arts and things and he's fucking excellent! I was talking to him about not being able to get angry or violent and he said, "Well, good." People don't want to fight with me and I thought, 'surely, your pecking order is 'the toughest is the coolest'!' but, it doesn't seem that way, for fighters, necessarily.

So what, he doesn't see it as a problem necessarily, that you can't get angry.

Not really, "…maybe you should just go to train, and figure it out, and take part." But he didn't seem to think; I said, well, my bones feel a little brittle, especially my ankle, because I've broken it, and the bottom line is, is that a drawback? And he said, "Well, yeah. But the bottom line is – get fighting! Go and do some classes, rather than think about it," or process it, or be on the Management Committee to stop violent people, blah blah blah blah. I need to learn to get angry! And then my other cousin, he said, "What do you need to be angry for? Good on you – you haven't got a short fuse." Nah, just a whole lifetime of understanding myself more, and other people, and why, rather than having tantrums.

Wasn't that what you, er, well what we both said, about rather than 'we don't get angry', it's more like, well how do we express these – kind of – unwieldy emotions?

Yeah, yeah.

Without getting into a fight, or getting pissed, or; I mean, I'll be honest, I'd love to train in something – but it's time!

Well for me, I was saying to my cousin, about his fighting. And, "How did you know that someone wasn't going to get killed? Or taken away by ambulance? Lose some teeth? Break a nose? Lose an eye?" And I'd be scared that if I'd lose it, that I'd hit someone and crack their skull, they'd probably slip, bang their heads, probably die! Or my hand would go through their bones and – you know, I've said this before – I am desperately fearful of that. Like I'm scared of driving and knocking someone over. Like I'm scared of saying or doing the wrong things and harming someone.

Well I had the same whatever, child or teenager, being very strong and physically able. Yeah, I was always holding back, because people would start howling if I pushed them to the floor.

Fear of getting in trouble with the parents!

Yah.

We were both addicted to parents loving us.

We talked about this. The whole thing about pushing people over.

And also the eldest brother! I didn't wanna hurt my brother. Once, I remember I lost my temper, I was in a rage with him, and *I found myself trying to pull his arm off!* And he was probably just looking at me like I'm stupid! And I didn't know how to stop. And then, when I suddenly came to my senses – I can't believe this – I started going 'tickly-tickly' under his arm-pit. As if to kind of pretend it never happened, because 'we were only kidding', you know; he probably just laughed at me and walked off.

Yeah

And I felt FUCKED about that! For a long long long long time. And then another time, he mysteriously went to hospital, something to do with his leg - for a while - and they found nothing wrong. And – maybe it was, maybe it wasn't – but I remember I kicked him, in his leg, on his leg, with my cowboy boot. And maybe that was it. There was no swelling, there was no mark, but maybe that was it. I don't know! But I'm desperately fearful of my own strength. Anyway, and my Mother going around like, anything would hurt her. And that's how she controlled us. So we wouldn't misbehave, we wouldn't do anything because, why would we want to hurt anyone? Dunno, but it, it's... that's another bit of adolescence that I missed, that I missed out on. Or the bit of me that I'd say is maybe still missing is, I'm too calm. I don't get angry. *(very long pause)* So you were going to *tell me why you have*

been angry with me all this time…

I haven't been exclusively angry with you.

You've been angry with lots of, lots of people, including me. But fuck 'em, I'm talking about me. Heh heh heh heh

You what?

Fuck 'em, I'm talking about me! Do you know what I mean?

Hmmm

Or do you think that's relevant? That sometimes angry people are angry at everyone. I'm not sure if that's true.

Hmmm…? I think I've only uncovered a lot of anger. I mean, take for example my sister. Last year and this holiday. So many people have said this to me. The older sibling, second child comes along, fucks them up!

Hmmm

Umm… Funny though, that process of trying to get the tape to work. I suddenly thought, one of the things with you, I often feel… very self-conscious. Almost like you're thinking that I'm a complete arsehole.

Ha ha ha ha ha

Do you know what I mean? Like you'd be thinking 'Why am I working with this twit'?

Ha ha ha

You know? Which comes back to what I was saying earlier, about, um, the the Father element that I – I don't know why, because, as much as we have had the Mother, 'Mummy's-boy' friendship-relationship, there's also been stuff I've laid on you about what my Father would have done, or, when I was a child, the way he would have got angry about something that I hadn't done right.

Do I come across in any way as authoritarian? Judgmental?

I think you can do sometimes, and I guess, recently, with what you were saying about not knowing your emotions, it's, that's thrown me; extra chaos then for me, because I don't feel that my Father was really knowing what his emotions were.

Hmmm

Or when he was likely to, just, lose it. You know it would be like everything would be fine, and then suddenly there'd be a, an explosion.

Hmmm

I guess I'm, I'm always expecting that of people. And for some reason that is an element between us.

Hmmm

I'm kind of waiting for you to go 'Right Ed... Fuck Off!' ...you know.

That was you, me and Bob last Christmas. Waiting for the argument.

Ummm!

The heaviness...

Ummm.

...or whatever...

Ummm

...but I had the same and my Father was probably the same. Waiting for an explosion, shouting, snap suddenly; like you were saying about your Father - over the phone, from when you were in Silchester - having a tantrum. Always nervous that your Father would have a tantrum – is that right?

Did I say that? That he'd have tantrums?

It's almost like, there'd be the slightest little thing – and he'd snap!

Ummm. Um-hum. I think I – this is getting very convoluted. I was talking, about probably, what Billy had said. Which totally rang a bell. Never knowing when, or how, or what - it might happen. Sort of like you said, the survival mechanism. Assume that that's gonna happen.

Yeah

And that's something else.

Waiting to respond to that.

Amazing conversation with Billy. Totally timely. I think it was the first day, or second day that I was down in Silchester for Christmas. I'd rung him and he was – great actually, he just said "I don't, I can't talk at the moment, I'm in bed, I don't feel like talking." Very nice and clear, rather than that sort of fluffy middle class... 'Oh how lovely to hear from you. Let's have a chat – about nothing.'

Hmmm

Well, between that and him ringing back, very small but very significant. My Dad was cooking and he'd knocked his glass of beer over - which was next to the hob, or whatever – and Malaika came up to look. And he just went "OH, JUST GET AWAY – STOP IT!" He didn't say anything else, but it was like, this, there's some hazard, you know, it was like he'd spilled - sort of - chemicals.

So he didn't make a noise? That was just his mood.

He did, yeah there was a kind of; flapping incoherence... Like, 'don't come near me'.

Right.

And then I didn't even really take in what was happening. I put something down as I was passing – because I was actually in another room when he spilled it – and he said "CAN'T YOU SEE THAT I'VE SPILLED SOMETHING?!" And I was like, 'Okay, alright, fine...' you know. Now I feel I understand what's going on. Anyway, then Billy rang. And I was talking to him about this. And he said "God this is so fucking weird because that's exactly what it was like in my house!" and he said something that amazed me. Which totally – um, how can I say it? – wasn't like 'Suddenly the scales had fallen off my eyes' and I don't know if there's any scales left, there always seem to be more! That was Billy's whole assumption for life. That's how people were going to react! He'd assume it and almost create the situation.

Hmmm

Um, and he said…

I think the Fathers are probably treated like that as kids.

Yup.

Criticised, so now he'd clear up the beer quick before he's criticised.

Yeah. And get almost hysterical before anyone else could.

Yup! Yeah.

"OKAYYY! I'M REAAALLY SORRYYY. I FUCKED UPPPP!!!"

Yup.

So your Dad was…

And in that case, um,

…God, how fucked up!…

fucked up people – fuck up and 'inside' have a tantrum. Have a caniption. Like, panic.

Umm.

Run on panic.

Our poor Fathers. You, me, Billy, and I'm sure ninety five per cent…

Oh yeah.

...of the male population! But what he said was, you know, he said for example that if you work in an office, you go to work and then something like that happens, people don't react like that. But, his assumption was they would.

Maybe they do 'inside'. Or maybe they dump it on whoever they can bully. For some people, the only people they can bully are the people at work, for some people it's their wives or husbands, for some people it's their children, for some people it's the shopkeeper, or the bus driver, or road rage.

But yeah, disowned emotions. I mean, that's why, or one of the reasons why I think I've had such a difficult relationship with my anger. Not knowing if I'm angry at you, are you angry at me, or should we talk about it, is it an issue, blah blah blah...

Yeah, and I suppose it's that kind of thought pattern that demands 'process'. Talk about it, talk about it, make it safe, make it okay, not actually 'do' anything, or live, or have any passion, or get out of the head.

Hmmm

But stress, worry. I know, that still, sub-consciously, semi-consciously, whatever, *I expect people to be angry with me.* Like now, for example, ummm, with Freya, John, etc we haven't texted or phoned for a few days, which is quite unusual, but it's Christmas, New Year and whatever, but there's a paranoia that they're angry with me...

Um-hum.

...like I've been found out about something – what it would be I don't know – and the same with Gina. Since last night we haven't phoned or texted. I noticed her phone charger is here. Maybe her phone is dead. Or still – maybe she's angry with me. Same with you. Same with everyone all the time.

Yeah

But then, I do, with you for example, I do feel it brewing, I feel it there; same with Billy. With Lui, maybe it's the other way around. Maybe the both of us are going for 'control through anger'. But yeah! With Lui, you can't get near. He keeps his boundaries through anger – and it could all be justified, or it could be because he's not well, or he hasn't got money, you know, whatever 'problem', but he keeps that *'ready to explode if you cross the boundary'* type-thing. But when I'm with him, I can't fault him. I can't argue. Maybe that's because I can't go that far! And he'd say "Why do we have to talk about it again…" which is the male way, isn't it? In a way.

Hmmm. Kind of, we get on with it.

In another way, it's absolute avoidance. Or talk so far, until something weird, something new, something scary or something out of control, and then the diversion or criticism or a laugh to throw us off the scent blah blah blah…

I feel like it's taken, for me anyway, between us, I think it's taken a long time, sort of, to be able to talk with you about this. Because I think, what you're saying with Lui is interesting. Makes me think. My experience of you, early on and quite a lot of the time, was – say living in Muswell Hill with our cleaning-living deal, those couple of times when I came and sat to 'have it out' with you. It was almost like, you know like, I felt like you were cross with me about housework, or, you know, you'd sent a text saying something like 'I felt abandoned by you in a filthy house, we need to talk to make it clear' and I was like, 'oh fuck, I kind of sensed it coming. It was like, there's anger. He's angry!' So I, I guess I came at it feeling like I had to – I don't know – how can I put it? It felt almost like you wouldn't get angry back, but you wouldn't totally receive it. It was almost like playing a ball game?

Hmmm

It's like I'd say how I feel, and you'd kind-of go 'Hmmm… that's because you're this, this, this and this.'

Hmmm

Rather than saying 'Yeah, I was angry with you.' Do you know what I mean? And now, what you said about not knowing whether you were angry or not, I'm kind of thinking 'Oh my God, what's going on here? Does Mickey know if he's angry, or is it just me?' Making an assumption…

Or maybe it's just being internalised.

…probably, because it's not really 'allowed', is it? From anyone. But I'm really struggling. Well, struggling's the wrong word. I'm really noticing that with Mallie. Because she's at that age now, where she really, she's pushing quite a lot… and, she wants to be emotional, you know? She gets upset, she'll start crying quite easily, I don't know…

Because you're scared of the emotions that she'll express?

…hmmm. And maybe we've talked about this before, but I just, sometimes think, 'Ahhh… what a job!' You know? What a job being a parent who has to negotiate this and try and work out – especially if you want to be quite aware and then allow her to be emotional, but not get sort-of hysterical and out of control. Do you know what I mean? It feels like maybe that's the key. Getting some balance, saying "OK, you go and express your emotions, there, feel them, go through them, sit, have your upset, and then we'll talk about it." Or then, we'll just get on. Because it's almost like, well, when they're expressed, they move out, they move through, and out. Rather than…

Name it and get over it.

Yeah.

If it's not named, then it's brewing somewhere.

I mean, so many parents – and I'm sure I've said this – say things like "Oh, don't cry…" or "Don't talk to me like that…" you know, "How dare you! Who do you think you are?" and…

"Don't answer back!"

"Be quiet!"

"Don't question me!" "Don't speak unless you're spoken to!"

And one thing I've; a gem from that book 'Emotional Intelligence'[134] which I have been ploughing through – though the Christmas break has interceded – was that 'formula' if you like. I'm a bit suspicious of it, but it's basically the way of addressing a child or an adult, which is meant to be non-aggressive. So, I might say to you "When you criticise me, I feel upset. I'd prefer it if you do der-der-der." So, do you see what I mean? There's three parts that are being named. "When you", "I feel", "I'd prefer".

Hmmm

Rather than "You're really annoying!" "You're making too much noise." "Be quiet!"

Basically, you need to describe it, otherwise they're guessing.

Yeah

Based on 'nothing'. They're basically learning that there are no rules for what's going on here, and our job is to speak 'the truth' and not necessarily 'break them with the rules' that aren't the truth. But is that asking for trouble and being irresponsible, or should they be 'broken and safe'?

Well that's it, exactly, um. Actually, it's funny, I, I so wanted to talk to you about this at some point. And I don't know if it fits in, but it feels like it does. When I dropped Mallie off yesterday, again, and um, Ayesha and I were talking about various things, like I was saying – and I could feel, I could feel the same energy as with my Dad. It was almost like 'I'm going to be very rational with her and, you know, reasonable, and say, '…if it's alright with you, I'm going to move to Stratford, to be near Mallie, once you've moved there, because I know that you don't want me in your community, and you don't want to bump into me.' All these things I've picked up, which she's never actually said. And we were just talking and she said, um, "Look, you're probably going to get really angry with me for this, but I'm going to say it anyway." She said "You know that song that you made up... can you not encourage Mallie to sing it?" I knew exactly which one she meant. Did I tell you? I'm sure I did tell you. Well we were sitting on this exercise ball bouncing together. We were having a really nice time, and I just started singing this song, to some kids' tune. The words were *'My little moggie goes miaow miaow miaow, my little doggie goes woof. My little Mummy is preg-a-nant, my little Daddy's a poof'*.

HA HA HA HA HA HA HA

HA HA HA HA HA HA HA! Mallie loved it!

CLASSIC! Wheeere are yooo coming from?!!

She was singing it and singing it...

Ha ha ha ha ha – where are you coming from...

I don't know.

A-mazing!

Outrageous.

That was channelled![135]

I blushed... when she reminded me of it.

HA HA HA HA HA HA HA... Say it again!

My little moggie goes – ha ha ha ha – miaow, miaow, miaow...

HA HA HA HA HA

...my little doggie goes – ha ha ha – woof...

ha ha ha

...my little Mummy is preg-a-nant...

ha ha ha

...and my little Daddy's a poof!

Ha Ha Ha Ha ha ha ha

Ha ha ha – as I say, I blushed, because she said, um, that Mallie started singing it in front of her and Ray...

HA HA HA HA HA

...and they were really shocked, and, like, 'Where did she get this from?' but of course, she must have told them that Daddy made it up.

Huh huh ha ha ha ha ha

Because, while I was talking to Ayesha, my sister Lizzie rang to say, um, "Oh Dad's left an answering machine message apologising for his behaviour on Saturday, blah blah blah, and what shall we, you know, what have you talked to him about? What was your conversation about?" and I was like, 'Oh my God, what is going on?' So, I rang her back, after I'd left Ayesha's and I was telling her about this, and she said that that's so weird, because, it's all true! You know, it's like the song. Why was Ayesha so upset? And I, I mean I said to Ayesha afterwards, "Okay, I don't want Mallie to make a fool of herself in the playground, or people kind-of-going 'Who is this four year old going on ten...'"

'...that we don't want near our children.'

Yeah... 'She's a freak! She knows too much. She's too... yeah, she's too grown up.'

Dirty.

Yeah! Yeah, 'How could she, does she know what she's saying? And who told her this? Who has corrupted her?' Kind of like wooh! You can see the witch-hunt brewing around this poor, innocent little child, singing…

And how did my Mummy get my Daddy pregnant? Or vice-versa – Ha ha ha ha ha

Ha ha ha ha ha – yeah, exactly! 'If her Mummy's pregnant, how come her Daddy's a poof? I don't get this! It doesn't make sense. Ve must investigate…' But my sister Lizzie said "It is so weird, because if it had been a song, if Ayesha had said "Oh, I'm really embarrassed, you know, I sang Mallie this little song (with the same words)" and she'd said "And I didn't want to upset you, you know, because – are you a poof? You know, where are you with your sexuality and all that kind of thing?"" It was like, it felt so honest to me.

Hmmm

But I also saw the whole situation typified what we were just talking about. You can't, you can't say that sort of thing.

Hmmm…

And especially, I can see…

…that's 'breaking' her.

…yeah exactly! I mean…

But is some 'breaking'… right? I imagine that's what your fear is saying. 'Should I be doing that, as a responsible parent? Should I 'break her'?
Should I 'dumb her down?'

Hmmm, yeah, and stop her being aware?

'Let me make her less, because I love her.'

Hmmm… and I want to protect her.

Hmmm

Or am I protecting myself?

Hmmm

And everybody else!

And there are only so many hours in the day.

It's almost like, yeah, it's like, 'shut the child up to protect everybody else's feelings.'

Hmmm

Which, as you say, can…

'don't run around saying…'

…maybe it's appropriate! Yeah…

What will people say?

Yeah, what will people think? Exactly! Phew. So that was very, um… interesting. But such a contrast, as well, because today I'd been with this…

Ha ha ha – does Mallie know what the words mean?

Well I don't know if she does! Because, then, the other thing is she; so I was singing that song about two weeks ago, then we went down to Silchester for Christmas – I think it was my Mum, or my Dad, or somebody. One of the other three family members who were there were pissing themselves, because Mallie had come into my Mum and Dad's bedroom and apparently she said – my Dad tried to engage with her, and she said "I'm not friendly with you today! Granny, Aunty Lizzie and Daddy are my friends. You're just a poof!"

NOOOO!

They said it was really funny and they really really laughed. I thought, 'Jesus, you know, if things were different…'

Hmmm

He'd be like, 'Where-did-you-hear-that-!'

Hmmm

'And how-dare-you-I'm-notapoof...' But thankfully – and I mean, that's the other funny thing. I'm rambling all over the place I know, but talking of poofs... in fact he seems to be totally okay. I mean I'll make, Mallie was talking about, oh that's right, Mallie also said, um – just over lunch, while Mum and Dad were sitting there – "I'm a flower fairy, and my Daddy's a boy fairy." And I just made a kind-of slightly jokey, slightly camp comment, like, well, 'many a true word...' or something. *My Dad roared with laughter* and I thought that that's really cool, that there's this real bond. It's not kind of like he's ashamed or embarrassed, which I always thought he would be. *(In Kenny Everett[136] expression)* "My son's had sex with a... MAAAN...!" *(Sharp intake of 'Kenny Everett breath' with bulging eyes and open 'blow-up dolly' mouth)*

What's been crossing my mind, loud and clear, is, um, from the first time I saw, I met you, I just thought 'Kenny Everett'.

Hmmmur

Every thing about you.

Hmmm

Shape, the way you move, the sense of humour, your irony, pain – in a way!

Hmmm

Urrr, the poofiness!

Yeah.

And you go more masculine and more feminine. You change. Not so much with the wind, but I'm sure something blows somewhere...

Ha ha ha ha

Heh heh heh

What are you suggesting? It's weird, actually, you're not – you're far from the first person to have said that. And weird that he was on that 'Simon Dee Show'[137].

That's what reminded me!

Yeah, because he was married, wasn't he, and yet…

Yup, yup, I don't know the story – did he have kids?

I don't know about kids, I'm sure he was married, but I'm sure he had sex with men as well. Hmmm…

Or the other day, I was looking at Elton John, for some reason, walking around a bookshop. He was married to a woman called Renata? Or Renee? Or something or other.

Yeah? That rings a bell. But so many of these pop stars… Funny, I'd also mentioned that I'd seen Cliff Richard performing, really 'hamming-up' this song. Um, and he was supposed to be, wasn't it the tennis player that was supposed to be his girlfriend? Sue…

Sue Barker.

Yeah. All those years, and it was almost 'counter intelligence' wasn't it? The gossip was he was gay, but look, he's got this girlfriend.

Really?

Yeah-yeah-yeah. When I was growing up, that was the gossip!

I thought it was a secret and he is only now living with a 'friend' somewhere, in the sun.

I've no idea. But, in a way; well it is relevant, 'cos it's like this double, double standard or…

And it's against the Born-again Christian rules.

Well I suppose so… what, to be happy with somebody, even though they've got the same genitalia as you? 'Awful!'

Hmm – having to live with his genitalia…

Funny, this came up after this conversation I had with my Dad, um, which I felt was soooo – well, it was a bit dry, emotionally. I mean, there wasn't a lot of emotion. But at the end of the conversation I was saying to him, "And, I don't know how you feel. I have the feeling that you're comfortable with the fact that; you know, I've told you about my life and what's happened, and why the marriage broke up, and this and that and the other…"

They didn't even know why the marriage broke up?

Oh yeah yeah yeah they knew all that! No no, but it's more like, because we'd talked a bit about how we don't share each other's private lives. We don't seem interested, we don't have anything really in common. And he even finished my sentence. He said "So, you find my life really boring." And I said "Yes."

Wooooow…

It was such an honest conversation. But it wasn't like – I don't know, I could be wrong, he could be at home sobbing his eyes out, but I don't think so, because it was like, 'Well this is how I feel.' 'Alright! Well this is how I feel.' How refreshing.

Yeah

We don't have to go *(in an American accent)* 'Well I love you really…'

Ha ha ha ha ha

Despite everything – although I did send him a text telling him that. No, what I was going to say was…

Ha ha ha ha ha ha ha – AND THAT'S WHAT MAKES YOU A GREAT POOF…

Exactly. Well in that moment, I was just like, yeah, after he had seen me and Mallie off at the station – and there wasn't the usual panic, it was all just… calm. From him, actually. And I just said to him, "Look, you know, don't want to tell you about who I'm shagging, or who I'm seeing, or whether it was a man or a woman or that or that." And if it comes up in conversation naturally, fine! But I'm not going to come home and *(clears throat)*. Right, 'Well, okay, in answer to your question 'How are you?' this is what I have been doing. I've been having sex with 'this' person and 'this' person... um...'

Is this your stuff, or his? Is he interested, anyway?

I don't know. It's almost like I've felt I needed to say it. Just to kind of clear it out the way.

In case that part of anger was brewing...

Well that's true, yes. Coming back to what we were saying... *(deep breath)* Oy-yoy-yoy...

I had a funny one, I've been chatting with my folks on the phone over Christmas. It's been nice. It's been fun! And then, I was chatting to them and Tony said *"I've got crabs!"* As if to say 'Woow, I'm gonna be cooking crabs...

Ha ha ha ha ha

...I'm going to be preparing crabs' and stuff like that. And I said "Aw yeahhh maaan, I had crabs when I was in Australia and I was so embarrassed that I went to New Zealand, not knowing what they were going to do, and they just gave me some 'special' shampoo..." and after they'd been gone for a while "...and I quite missed them when they were gone...

Ha ha ha ha ha – your pets!

"...my little friends that would say 'hi' by itching and tugging at me, and I'd have a scratch and see who's under my fingernails, waving their little arms and legs at me...

Can you see them? I have never...

"...I quite enjoyed it!...

I don't know anything about…

…I know it's strange, it must be a very strange thing to say, but it was fun for a while."

Uh-huh-huh

And they never knew that I ever had crabs, or that's what I did when I went to New Zealand, or that I was doing anything in Australia in order to get crabs. I would never talk like that! It wouldn't be discussed…

For the same reason? Because he might be angry? Or…

No no no, sex. Sex didn't exist.

'No genitals', so how could you possibly have crabs? 'In the plastic zone'

Well, on one extreme 'no genitals', in the other extreme my Father was always making dirty jokes and making comments, so he was wrong and bad and dirty saying it. But all the same, there were two extremes. Neither of which was helpful in any way.

Yeah, exactly. Are you going to spend the rest of your life as Kenneth Williams[138] or Barbara Windsor[139]?

HA HA HA HA HA HA HA HA HA – own it!

Well I haven't made up my mind yet!

Ha ha ha ha ha ha ha ha

I'll lose the tits first!

You got so upset…

Ha ha ha. But that's, that's the other thing, I think… so many men of that generation simply have not had enough sex. And I don't, I'm not saying – you know – it's time for them to go off and be adulterous and leave their wives…

How did the War affect all this? There was a baby boom when the men came back, a Depression, it was – you know – does it all fit into a picture somehow?

Well, it was all, almost like; I guess the majority of people in Britain must have been poor...

Was it our Fathers that didn't have Fathers to show them how?

Yeah, pretty much. I mean, well my Dad's Father was away, and my Dad was born in '34, the war started in '39, so his Father must have been gone pretty much after that for six years.

So it's either Fathers that weren't there, or Fathers that came back fucked up,

Or didn't come back at all.

...hence, our Fathers - or our parents - were the first ADHD[140].

Hmmm... I don't know. I think more of that...

All our Fathers sound ADHD.

That's true, actually. That's interesting, because that's one of the things I was talking to my Dad about. I said, no he said "Well you never ask me anything about my life." And I said "Well, you don't do anything!"

'You haven't got one!' HA HA HA HA HA HA HA HA HA

And that's where the 'you think my life's boring' quote comes from. But it was like, well, what do you expect me to ask about? There isn't anything.

You know what's funny? Um, I enjoyed being with your parents. Everyone loves being with my parents.

Hmmm, everyone likes every one else's parents.

Exactly! And my parents are fucking... great! And your parents are great.

Yeah. Except when they're with their own children. Ha ha ha

Exactly.

We should just swap regularly, I think. Family-swappers. But I think, what it is – you're probably right about the inability to pay attention, because it's almost like with my Dad, he might say "So how's the massage course going?" and I'd start to answer and he'd be kind of distractedly looking off at, I don't know, at the boiler.

'I asked a short question' – now come on, I'm busy...

'I'm interested', but I'm not...

Hmmm, it's not that 'I'm interested', I've said the words...

Yes

But maybe it's just 'appreciating' to them, because they've got so much inside that they want to find out, or know, or whatever...

Hmmm

...but they're not even allowed to think about it, leave alone join in any way and I think that was a big issue with my Father. *He didn't know how to join in.*

Hmmmmmmmmmmmmm! That is a huge one. You've just pulled the lid off something. Absolutely. I said this to my Dad in that same conversation! I said to my Dad that "I feel that the only way we can connect is for you to be critical..."

Hmmm

"...pessimistic, worried," and it's all, it is! It's obviously care, or love, or concern and as you said, desperation to be part of it all, but not knowing how, so... with my Mum monopolising the 'loving caring' part of the relationship, what's left for him? And that's not to say that she's bad, or he's bad.

Both 'panic reactions' but opposite extremes. Neither of which is very helpful.

But isn't this the amazing thing? I mean this; I came away from Silchester yesterday feeling quite relieved, and there'd been quite a lot of heaviness. Because, just the dynamic. You know, everybody. Grown up sister, Mother, Father, me, whatever. But I also thought, actually, it's been amazing, because I've been really really honest with both my parents. 'Cos you know, like I said to my Mum, "You're too much…

Hmmm

"…you're over enthusiastic, you're over interested and Dad's not at all interested." Somewhere in the middle everyone's like – really confused. I'm really confused…

Over-compensating for each other.

'…tell me every little detail about, you know, what colour shoes were you wearing when you were walking to your massage course. You know, who you spoke to, and what the flowers were like on the table' – and he's like, 'Yeah, right, whatever, I'm gonna make a cup of tea.'

And in a nutshell, my issues with women are that they're gonna smother me and my issues with men are that they are gonna abandon me. Ummm, and with Gina, it's just been ab-sol-utely fucking perfect in every way over this little break and Christmas and whatever. Ummm, and, if we think hard or try hard to find an issue, or 'what's up?' then all I can come up with is, she knows my 'fear of being smothered'. Meanwhile, in bed, I'm always chasing and chasing and chasing her and she has to wake me up and push me over so she's got some space and doesn't fall out of the bed. And, um, during wake time, um, she kisses me a lot, which is cool, but I know I've got issues about kissing, and I don't know whether it's smothering or obsessive-compulsive, or a healthy combination of the two - at least.

Hmmm

But, like I've said to Gina once or twice – you know, we'd talk about something, whatever it is – "If that's the extent of our problems, FUCK we've got it good!"

Yeah, definitely!

And we have! Yeahhh…!

What a relief, though, I mean that… yeah. I was saying this to Lizzie yesterday on the phone, "Aren't we lucky! It's really hard – and it sounds really corny or Pollyanna[141]-ish to say that *we are so*

lucky to have had the parents that we've had,

because otherwise, I'd be; I don't know what I'd be doing now!"

Hmmm

But yeah, you're right! Thank God. The possibilities. The absolute possibilities that are available. I'm losing my thread now.

So, in a nutshell, why are you angry at me? Ha ha ha ha ha ha

Ha ha ha ha ha ha – Oh, God. In a nutshell… but I'm not at the moment.

Or why do you get angry at me? Or what do you get angry about? – Because it's not me, it's my behaviour.

Yeah.

Like a button being pressed.

I'm trying to think… Well one, one instance is, a recurring one where we're doing, we're transcribing, that I'd just get very impatient and, ummm – now why is that? – I think it's because you appear to be really enjoying it and flowing with it and I'm struggling and thinking 'Oh fucking hell… I wish I was – whatever – drawing, or doing nothing.'

I didn't know that.

Yeah sometimes, that's come up. Um, and it's, maybe it's that.

Other people are having a good time, why can't I? and I said, do you remember I said to you about listening to the tapes, how you have a lot more laughter...

What while we're talking?

...yeah! It seems like you get, you get the laughs HA HA

I enjoy the conversations more?

Yeah, whereas I'm kind of like, um, 'Yeah!' or going off into thinking about 'Ummm? Yes, what does that mean?'

Hmmm

Rather than just enjoying the silliness of it, or, or yeah, self-apprec...; it's like I don't appreciate myself, so I get angry.

Hmmm. So, like a jealousy?

Possibly, yeah.

That would make sense, because what I was saying before is that for me it's something around the way people treat me, you not liking it, or... I have it too easy, or... I don't join the drama or join in an argument, or a, it's like always being right, or always being 'smug'!

Hmm.

Self-righteous is what Lui calls me.

Yeah, it's almost like you've... you've said you don't like people treating you like some kind of – you know – guru[142] on a pedestal, but at the same time I imagine there's a part of you that does quite like it. It's like, if it happens to you, if it comes to you, then there's a part of anybody that would love it.

I just want to join in.

Hmmm

Same as my Father did.

But, do you know, I guess the bottom line is, it's probably... I hate to use the word abandonment but it's, it's, I guess what it is is that it's the sense that I'm – God this is going to sound so honestly raw! – but almost like, for this work we're doing, for the conversations that I'm... serving – I don't mean serving a purpose, but it's almost like I question, well, 'What's our friendship?' You know? 'Is it just, we get together to talk about the book and to tape...'

And *you will be abandoned after that?*

Yeah, and, 'Is this a friendship?' And almost, yeah, like I said to you last night.

You're being used.

Yeah. But equally, I suppose it's, it's confused because 'am I being used or am I using?' I'm just as much responsible. I think, yeah, it's the kind of 'helpless child'. When I get angry it's the helpless child thinking 'Well I'm, I didn't ask to do this, yeah, I'm being used!' and the whole sense of my own responsibility and choice in the matter just flies out the window. Evaporates. So it's like yeah, okay, I'm being exploited by somebody. By you.

Which is like we were saying last night. Something about, you know, fears, and something-or-other am I fucking you up? Fucking your life up. Or will this process fuck your life up?

Hmmm

What was it you said to me? Umm...

Something about making the 'right' choices. You know, about following this, and having faith in the project, that it actually is something. Amazing.

But on the other hand...

Could it be just a complete...

…it'll fuck you up!

…illusion.

…rather than make you great.

Yeeaahhh… And yeah, it's funny, the other thing I said to you last night, about, um, the friendship that we talked about in the first part of the book, Jude. You know, the friend who I basically cut off from.

Yeah

And abandoned him in school, to be with the cool people. It's almost like, I'm kind of assuming that will happen from you to me, when there are times when I think, I suppose I'd better do it first. You know, it's like in a relationship…

Ahhh…!

…I'd better chuck you first!

So you believe that's gonna happen, because that's what happened with you and Jude and that's where 'we' are.

Almost like my karma[143], because 'I've done it', right, so 'people will do it to me'.

Yeah. That's an interesting one.

And yeah, it's funny how it manifests in anger. Also, I wonder why, there are some people I have found it very difficult to be angry with, like clearly and honestly angry with.

Hmmm

There's very few people I can do that with. It's like we were talking last week, or whenever, about sort of passive-aggression.

Hmmm

Rather than active and out. Billy and I were talking about this. Both saying that we really have experienced it. That's how we'd mainly expressed anger. Sort of snippily, sarcastically, little kind of hand-grenades thrown into the conversation. And we both said that what we really admired about Lui was that ability to just be angry. And again, it's like it goes too far. I don't say I want to be like that, all the time, but I'd love to get the art of treading that line and saying right, 'This is how I feel!' Explode and then go... 'right, now, what shall we talk about? Where shall we go for dinner?'

But then I think we can only have one person like Lui, or my Father, or whatever, in the house.

Hmmm

And the others passive-aggressive because that won't blow 'his top'. It's all we can get away with in the form of communication.

Hmmm

Or it could be the other way around. Which came first? But they seem to be co-dependent, or whatever.

Hmmm. Definitely.

But yeah. Lui is an absolutely amazing person. Ummm, and I love him!

Yeah, it's just, even if he had no other qualities, the ability to be really honest, openly, emotionally, even if it's just that one emotion 'anger'. Fucking powerful one! And what most people are lacking. Our culture doesn't like anger and it's, I don't know, unless it's on television or you're allowed to witness a brawl in the street but, you know, you can't express it in your family apart from; yeah, well it's just everywhere. I was really struck by that glasses ad. You know, the one we saw last night? The man looking for his glasses and his really sarcastic bitchy daughter. 'Me and granny got them!' and the Mum in the background making – like everyone's angry with Dad and Dad's angry with everyone. And it's like 'Wow, who started it?'

I was upset by the way he lifted up the dustbin and emptied all the rubbish on the ground, for someone else to clear up, or whatever.

Yeah

Because it says, well that form of - umm - violence, in the house, is acceptable!

Yeah

And funny.

Well and also, his wife – presumably it's the wife standing behind the cooker – said something really like 'Tut, ohhh, what did you do that for? Clear that up!' It's like she's turned into his Mother and he was the stroppy little boy, who never got his way…

It's like spilling a glass of milk. And the acceptability of that is the same as violence in the house like that?

Yeah

Disgusting. What are they making okay? Even the stuff that's like, you know, 'Eastenders' for crying out loud. So it makes those kind of lies – normal. It normalises fucked up lives.

I was just, you know, funny you were talking about spilling, like the glass of beer that I mentioned earlier. All of those things have a huge impact. I mean, Lizzie said to me that when she's got Malaika, or when she's with her, if Malaika spills something she had gone completely the other way. She's like, 'It's fine, it doesn't matter, at all…'

Hmmm

And they'd clean it up together; so in a way it's great, because they've learned – my sister's learned – well it's only a spilled… storm in a fucking tea cup or whatever.

Isn't that the, um – oh, how do you put this? – either running off cortisol[144] or adrenaline, the aggressive stuff rather than endorphins, and – what's it called?

Serotonin?[145] I think so, yeah, the 'feel good'

Coming from the mellow place. It's a choice, it's just raw energy – you know, if you give it your negative, you're gonna get negative; and if you give your positive, you're gonna get positive. Where the 'negative' automatically kicks in, when it's self-preservation.

Yeah

And the one thing I haven't, one way, like Lui's, is, aggressive. 'Keeping everyone at arms' length.' Mine is 'I go cold'. I go prickly, I withdraw, when I do get angry it's unnameable. Unfindable.

Ungraspable. Like, yeah, exactly. Like trying to get hold of smoke rings.

Hmm. Hmm.

It's interesting because you really have 'named' that completely. Good point!

But how it comes on, and how to stop it and how to deal with it. Dunno... it's a really funny one. It's a tough one.

But maybe, like, in Vipassana. 'Notice how your body is feeling'. I've noticed that, with, with fear. I really feel like somebody is pushing into my abdomen. Um, do I mean my abdomen? Yeah. Solar plexus. With anger I usually feel hot. Cold. Prickles running up and down my back. They're really strong feelings and I can't imagine I'm unusual.

I get like that when other people are angry at me, or when I'm being smothered. When I need space.

Claustrophobia.

When I don't set my boundaries.

But get; ah, I've just remembered something amazing. My Dad has always said that he's not interested in navel-gazing – as he calls it – so psychotherapy, all this – as far as he's concerned – is too much too far. But when we were driving back, on Sunday, after that big conversation that I've been going on about, I'd gone out with him just for a drive,

so he could recycle the papers. It was great because we don't actually get that much time alone. He said to me at the beginning, "So what did you want from Tesco[146]?" I said "I didn't. I just wanted to spend some time with you. Just the two of us." And we were talking about his behaviour, my sister, his relationship with my Mum, all in what twenty minutes? And nothing very very big or dramatic, in a way, but at one point I found myself getting quite emotional because I was talking to him about things we've talked about in the book and recently transcribed, like, um, he made some comment about my Mum, which I don't feel like I can say, really, because, he said "Oh I've never told your Mum this…" but it was about insecurity and competitiveness in the family. There, I've just said it, oh fuck it!

HA HA HA HA HA

Neh-neh-neh-neh-neah…

That's terrible.

It felt incomplete. I wanted to say to him later on, 'Well, why haven't you told her? This is crucial. Absolutely crucial, because if you feel that she's competing with you, and you're being pushed aside, this is affecting every time I come home, my sister comes home, every time you've got Malaika.' Do you know what I mean? It's massively important, but what I was saying to him, what made me emotional, was I suddenly really felt that I was in both their corners, fighting for them against, not against their parents; I said to my Dad, you know, "If you don't mind me getting all psychobabbly, or whatever, um, you both share massive abandonment issues. From your families. They, basically, you know, your brother comes along, the golden-boy, you're the older child who's displaced. With Mum it was all to do with, you know, 'Your Mother's run away, she's dead, she abandoned you, and here's this wonderful step-Mother who cares about you and you're always upsetting her, so she's packing her suitcase and blah blah" …and I could feel the anger rising. I, I just said – as I said with Felicity – you can't… how can people treat children like that? You know? How could you… how you… blackmail a child like that?

And I suppose, like I said earlier, maybe there was no other release.

Ummm.

And maybe they didn't, didn't think about the reactions of the child, because the child will forget, maybe.

Yeah

Or it's like the cat. Take it out on the cat and who's the cat gonna tell? Huh huh huh huh he he huh

Oh my God. Fucking hell!

So, why are you angry at me?

What, don't you believe what I said?

Well I do, but in a nutshell. Because it's just… a lot. And it can kind of go over my head, or I can almost not get it…

Because you're human and I'm human. That sounded like it was going to be really good, but it wasn't… I think it's just, every relationship has…

Abandonment. Is it the abandonment? Because I remember a while ago, a long long time ago, when we were first transcribing the first part of the book, this came up. And I said, "Well if that's the case, then consider yourself abandoned!" Ummm, because that's the only truthful way to go on, because it will happen. Ammm, even if it's only a matter of perception.

I think, maybe I'm angry with you because I feel I can be.

Aaarrrrr…

And with other people I don't feel I can be. Because there's some history, some block from the past, like you don't get angry with this type of person, or this type of person.

Or, it crossed my mind that when Lui and I had that fight. And I wouldn't back down. And he wouldn't back down. You don't get angry with someone that's not gonna back down. And it'll get out of hand, if you get angry with someone who will keep the peace – it won't get out of hand.

Yes, yeah.

With Lui and I, it went the length - because I wouldn't back down.

Hmmm

And ordinarily I would. Because I know he'd go further. And vice-versa with other things.

I guess fundamentally, yeah, it's a fear that you won't like me. If I, and I, you know, I really enjoy our friendship. I like our friendship a lot.

But wouldn't that mean that you'd need to prove that I don't like you, sooner rather than later?

Yeah. Probably.

So you're reacting to a belief that I don't like you. And you'll be angry at me…

Not so much that, but a sense of, well, all friendships seem to come to an end. And I haven't got many long term friendships.

So you're reacting to the end of the friendship, rather than what's happening in the friendship here and now.

Yeah! Yeah. Something's – and I don't think it's you – something's; you just bring up my anger. And, um, and coming back to the transcribing is a good one. I sometimes feel that I would like to take more breaks. I feel like I'm letting us down, so I kind of internalise that. Kind of like, instead of saying to you 'I'd like to do this and you actually saying yes or no, I have the conversation in my head and then you become a tyrant, a slave driver who is making me do this…'

And you're again *reacting to what's going on in your head, rather than what's actually going on* in life.

Yes. I'm glad you persisted. That's good actually, that's – oooff. That's opened quite a bit.

And for me, for me, I naturally, normally, most of the time assume that everyone's angry with me, until we're together and, um, I'm over thinking that they're still angry but they're just not showing it – and not only that, I shouldn't ask what they're angry about, because 'I should know!' Because 'I've done it!' and…

Yeah.

That's an old line now.

But what about you? I mean, do you, since we're talking about, between us, I mean, do you feel angry with me?

No.

Never? Ever?

No.

I mean that's probably part of it. I mean, I think – well it's probably legitimate for me because you're probably angry with me… you know? So I'll get angry with you!

I'd say, sometimes maybe frustrated. Sometimes maybe disappointed. Sometimes maybe smothered. Sometimes maybe manipulated. You know, all those things. But all of those I can observe, and not, not negative, I don't have negative feelings towards you. Do you know what I mean? And I'm okay with all those things, because…

What, it's just part of human relationships?

Yeah! And it's more like 'the truth' than tantrum-my angry nonsense.

Yeah

I'm just not ADHD enough.

It's funny. My Dad said something when we got back, after the end of this conversation that I've mentioned, and, he said "Well you"; well I was kind of like, so what do we do? Where do we go from here? Which is very much my way of thinking, you know, well we've talked about this, and so things will be really nice in the future, won't they, because we've had this conversation. Things will change. We'll all be like, well at least just able to communicate. Like, for me what happens is, you can pull the scab off all this crap, and then next time you go back it's started to grow back again, and then it's like, am I gonna pull this scab off, again?

Hmmm

Is it, is it the right thing to do? Do I feel like it. And he said, "Well, life isn't about formulas. You can't apply a formula." So, with what you've just said, you know, I can't expect you to say 'Ed, sit down, I feel like I'm being manipulated by you…'

Ha ha ha ha ha ha ha ha

'…and it's making me feel upset.' But, I don't know. It feels like that, I was thinking about that this morning. It feels like that's the massive rift in history. There's been a kind of 'let things evolve' approach. And then there's been the far more 'we have to plan things' you know, 'humans are flawed'. Do you know what I mean? Say, take historic Capitalism or Communism. One way was, okay, 'humans are mechanical things and we can change them'. That's the sort of Communist approach. If we do 'this', 'this', 'this' and 'this' and we take away property and we take away money. We take away; we make everyone cooperate. 'Everyone live together in a utopia[147]'. And the other's like, fucking hell, you know… 'If you took away everyone's money and re-distributed it, within a year the rich would be rich again and the poor would be poor again'. It's just the natural law of the jungle. And that sometimes feels like it's been the rift with me, between me and my Dad. I do have this, kind of, idealistic – a utopian thing.

Also, I'd say, the more you get in your head, the greater the concepts and preoccupations…

Hmmm

...rather than 'bringing it down here', into the here and now. And live your life.

133. Everyman Project. Counselling programme and helpline for male abusers and their victims. 020 7263 8884 (helpline).

134. 'Emotional Intelligence' Daniel Goleman (Bantam Books) 1995.

135. Channelled. Communicated through a channel (human) from a higher source.

136. Kenny Everett. UK comedian and broadcaster. www.kennyeverett.co.uk

137. Simon Dee. 1960's-1970's radio and television presenter.

138. Kenneth Williams. UK comic actor, co-starred in many 'Carry On' films.

139. Barbara Windsor. UK actress from the 1960's 'Carry On' films to present day 'Eastenders'.

140. ADHD. Attention Deficit & Hyperactivity Disorder.

141. 'Pollyanna' Eleanor H Porter (Harper Festival) originally published 1913.

142. Guru. Teacher – usually referred to in a spiritual flavour.

143. Karma. Cause and effect. 'What comes around – goes around'.

144. Cortisol. A hormone from the adrenal glands released in response to stress. www.stress.about.com

145. Serotonin. A natural chemical that helps maintain a happy feeling.

146. Tesco. Chain of supermarkets.

147. 'Utopia' Thomas Moore (Penguin Books) originally published 1516. A programme of total social and political reform with the object of bringing about a perfect society.

Perfect party pressure

So, a recent discomfort was around the New Year's Eve thing with the Eva thing.

For me?

No, for me. Aaahmm. I feel like I want to tell the story of how the whole New Year's Eve thing came around, you cancelling Lizzie in Scotland, are you allowed? Wanting to be with Gina and Billy and me, having another offer... do you know what I mean?

Hmmm

It would be interesting to hear the story in your words. In light of what we are talking about, *relationship is equal to unexpressed anger...*

Hmmm

...abandonment...

But you said 'recent discomfort', you mean your discomfort?

Yeah

Well, let's hear your bit first. Go on...

Well no, I'd rather hear, then I'll tell you during your story where mine is. I think it'll be a lot clearer that way.

OK. Um, well what? Was it this month or, it must be over a month ago. I said I was going to go up, by myself, to Edinburgh to be with Lizzie for New Year. Umm, and even as I was doing it, I felt a bit like it didn't feel right, but I still booked the ticket and whatever. And I don't

know how much of it is because of what happened last year. You know, the big bust-up with Lizzie at New Year, but I thought 'No, this will be different, because it's just me and her. We haven't got Malaika with me and it's just kind of easier in the winter'. Whatever, blah. Um, and then I actually realised that house-sitting here at Lisa and Yannis – it felt like a really nice space to be in and I didn't have to rush off anywhere to do anything, or be anywhere. And, so, what, it was just gonna be you, me, Billy and Gina. And I thought 'That's perfect! That's just the right number of people...'

Umm

...and I feel like I have got a relationship that I feel very comfortable with – not that I desperately wanted to be comfortable with people, but – those are the people that I felt very much, that I was on the same wavelength with. And then I think you mentioned... Eva.

Before that you had to cancel you sister, or find out.

Errr, oh that's right, so you... yeah, yeah, I did. Oh that's right. I left a message for her and she was very very upset. She'd been going through a really shitty week. But...

Is it a case of her being angry?

Yes. And angry, but not really expressing it.

This is the big one, always pressure on 'how you're spending New Year's Eve?'

Hmmm

Or even Friday nights, for some people.

And that's it! I've only, I've only woken up since the bust-up last year, to how much I've been worried about her anger. Probably in the same way as with my Dad. 'I failed', or 'I'm fickle and I can't make up my mind, and it upsets people', ur, and...

Hmmm

No, you're absolutely right. It was… well she's going to be emotional in some way. Probably angry. But at the least disappointed.

I think that's, that's the same for me. And probably for Lui. Is *the only emotion I will show you is anger, because that way I'm not vulnerable.*

Hmmm

Or that way I reclaim my boundaries. Or that way I can hold it together. Or whatever it means.

Yeah, because it takes a lot to be vulnerable.

Hmmm

And to be fair to her, she really just said "Well I am disappointed. But I'm not angry." And that was amazing. Very honest. So then, then I think that must be when you mentioned something about, would it be okay if Eva and Marius…

You were really chuffed about who was gonna be here, and… Eva

And I realised it wasn't – it was nothing to do with her at all. It's just, I had this little sort of picture-perfect image 'that's what New Years is going to be! And these are the people who are around.' And yeah, I'm kind of thinking, 'was I being in control? And is that wrong?' because yes, I think I did want that control. It didn't feel, wrong, it just felt like 'no, that's nice – because that's what 'I' want New Year to be like'.

So I phoned Billy and Gina, and straight away they were cool. And I phoned you, and you needed time, and I can understand why and how, but that left me in a familiar situation because I was in between.

Hmmm

Do you know what I mean?

Hmmm. But I wasn't, I wasn't really clear whether you'd asked her, or she'd asked you. Or it had just been… and that's right! And then I said, "'cos this is what my brother's always done!"

Yeah.

You know, it's like "It's gonna be you, me, Lizzie and a small group of friends" – and then it's like "Do you mind if my friend Robert brings his friend Dave, who brings whoever whoever. And it's like suddenly you've got…"

And you're out of control. And maybe not as safe to be as open?

Yeah, I think, yeah that's true, actually. Yeah I think that's the time when it does feel okay to be in control. So much of the time we're in a world with people that we don't really know that well, or acquaintances, or colleagues, or whoever and you can't, or I can't just relax and be really myself with; plus the other thing with Eva – well there were two other things. One was – and again, you know, nothing against the boys, but I didn't want kids around. I love kids, I really like them, but it was just like, I almost had this vision of a – not a cocktail party, but something, you know, quite – sort of – cool, mellow and relaxed. And I knew kids would change the dynamic; plus I don't really know Eva. And plus, there was guilt, because she did let us use her house for transcribing.

Hmmm

'I owe her'.

And we said we'd take them out to dinner.

Well I mean, that may well happen. Maybe that, maybe that was partly another thing. Maybe another factor in the anger with you. It's like, well, for me, we'll do it at some point, or whatever. It doesn't feel like we have to take them out for dinner. But I almost feel like you wouldn't say 'I want to do it now. I'd feel comfortable if we do this sooner rather than later. Take them out for a meal.' Whereas I would just say 'okay, we'll just take them out in January or February'. That's when the balance, if you like, would be, kind of, readjusted.

Hmmm

So what was next? Well, talking to Billy, then you mentioned something about Billy's thinking of not coming. And I realised, actually then what it was, and again – this sounds like I'm going to be anti-woman – but then I thought, okay. Gina is a woman I feel comfortable around because, not because she's boyish, or anything, but just – it felt fine. But then when Billy; I then rang him and he said, he explained, perfectly reasonably, and cool and he said "I would normally feel guilty about changing my mind, but, you know, some very old friendships have reopened, some people I haven't had a chance to see for ages." We talked about it, really, at length and I said "Well yeah I do feel disappointed that you're not coming, but at the same time, it made me realise that I really really wanted to hang out with you and Mickey!" And so, with him gone, I suddenly saw it as with you and… women and children. And that wasn't what I wanted. So then, this other thing coming up, with dancing, drumming, singing whatever.

That came after the thing with Billy.

Well I kind of knew that was floating around and I was wondering if there was a way that we could - ha ha ha - do all that. It's kind of like all these offers suddenly coming in, and at one point I imagined saying to you "Why don't we all get in a van and drive down to Hastings and we can all drum and dance?" Blah blah blah… So it had gone from really wanting that cozy little foursome, to…

Wanting the people that would allow you to be open, and safe.

Yeah. I mean, I think, well I think it's okay to want to feel safe sometimes. I really do. But sometimes I know I might feel guilty about that. You know, I'm being too controlling, 'control freak' or whatever. Yeah I think there is something. Like you said, it's New Year, but it's also Friday nights. So, I think more it was New Year – because it just feels a bit different – and after last New Year I thought, I really would like this to be… nice.

What happened last year?

I had a massive bust-up with Lizzie. You know, where she said, she thought I was cold and indifferent to her. But really what was happening is that we were starting to see how much our relationship was just unhealthy. And, and corrupted. Because of all the things we'd talked about. We'd talked 'about' my parents so much, um, I was starting to notice that she was angry with me over things that I didn't think I'd done wrong, or – you know – feeling like the scapegoat. And also feeling like the scapegoat and also, feeling like, um, the person she'd turn to when she was in trouble. So it felt like, 'okay, slap the one side of my face – stroke the other cheek'. Do you know what I mean? It's kind of like, 'Well, what am I gonna get?' And so again, that's not just her, I think that's from the family. Like one side's Mother and one side's Father. So anyway; yeah, the upshot was, then, phoning you up and feeling, suddenly feeling like I didn't know how to say what I wanted. Which comes, probably comes back to, you know, with Dad and whatever. Not being clear. I wasn't sure whether I wanted to say to you 'How do you feel about me doing this?' or 'Can I do this?' Do you know what I mean? It was almost like…

Asking for permission.

Yeah

Or explaining why, before I get angry.

Yes. Yes. Yeah, which was an old pattern. Funny, because I don't do that with my Dad anymore. I used to.

Hmmm

And with my sister. 'I know you're going to be angry and upset…' – like Ayesha said to me about the song that Mallie and I sang

You're older, and as we've left home, they're not bullying us anymore…

No

…and we are, maybe, part of the outside. And therefore treated 'nicely'. Rather than just part of home, and therefore not in the same way, or, you know...

Except when we go home. Because people, generally, revert to that, whatever relationship it was last time, or whatever it usually is. Father said this to son; Mother, Mother treats her daughter this way.

Hmmm. Yeah, it was a funny conversation.

But, yeah, in a way, it comes full circle with what we were describing with, with children and with Malaika. Owfff... it's not exactly about boundaries, it's more like, um, how can you... what's going to; getting the balance between doing what you want to do, behaving in a way that feels right, and sticking to agreements, and... doing things for other people, do you know what I mean? It's almost like, the things with the song. Should Mallie be told that song is not appropriate. She can sing it with me, but only with me – and we'll have a laugh – but if she dares to sing it at school, or somewhere, other people will be upset. You know, it's like, how confusing! Was I asking, was I disappointing, afraid of disappointing you? Yeah. That you'd say 'Ed, you were the one who didn't want Eva to come, then you said she could not, and now she's coming and now you're not coming', and it's kind of like 'pwhor'... and then last night, Gina said "Oh it was really cool. You're doing what you need to do." Which is what you said as well! And as I was hearing your words, you know, you were saying "I don't need to get angry with you. You know. If you're doing what feels right, that's absolutely fine!" but, there was a tiny part of my mind just thinking 'Can I trust this? Is this the truth, or is this just... politeness?'

Will this be taken down as evidence and held against me at a later date?

Yup. But I saw, I so saw that. You know, this conversation I keep talking about with my Dad. It basically came about because, um, - Oh, I don't know what! - The family dynamic at Christmas, with Lizzie, she very much, you know. I mean I don't enjoy being in my parents' house all the time at Christmas, so, you know, going out, for walks, going out, whatever. And this whole thing brewed up and erupted. Lizzie's being much stronger with my Dad, saying she wanted a yes or no, whether they wanted to come out to lunch. His side of it, well both their side of it is, she said, "Um, let's go out for, I'd love to go out for lunch." And he went "Hmmm." And she said "That's not positive enough. Forget it!" Then she was talking later to me about "What shall we do? Blah blah blah…" And I said "Well frankly, I don't care. You know, I don't… let's go out for lunch. If they want to come, they can come. If they don't…" And she said, suddenly it was like, she went from being quite angry to saying "Well, I feel we should ask them." And I said "Well, okay, well that; if it's 'should' then that's, that's very clear. You know, you're doing it because you're being polite."

Hmmm

So then this caused more shenanigans. Da da da, lots of tension, really really difficult afternoon, and we all had lunch together, and then she was dropped off at the airport, and then my Dad and I 'had words', so the next day I thought, 'God I've just got to clear this with him.' And one of the things he said was, he felt that he ought to say "Yes." And I said to him "This is ridiculous! Everyone's being so fucking polite! You know?" He's thinking 'Oh well, well they'd really like me to come, but I'm not sure if I want to go, so I'll say yes, even though I don't really want to.' And she's thinking 'I don't really want them to come, but they'll be upset if I don't ask them.' It's kind of like, all this 'second guessing' – it's exhausting! I mean I felt…

Meanwhile, it's all a lie. No one gets what they want. And no one even knows what's going on. And I think they call it 'normality'.

And funnily enough, both my Mum – when she came back from work, she'd asked at work if people had had good Christmases. And she said "You think we've got a dysfunctional family. You should hear these other stories. Nobody had a good Christmas. They all had a dreadful time." Then talking to Lizzie yesterday, apparently lots of people at her office said "Oh, so how was Christmas?" and she said she was about to lie, and say 'Oh it was fine.' And she said "I really didn't enjoy it!" and then, apparently, everyone else said the same. And I said to her,

"My God, if you're that honest, it really is so true. It gives other people absolute permission to say 'Oh, oh you didn't? Oh. Because you know, I didn't really, either'." Why do we do this? Why? What the fuck's it all about?

And then change things, for the better, for everyone.

Yeah. I mean, for me, that's, that, the bottom line for me is okay, we've identified 'that'...

It's named, get over the blame, and we can move through it.

What do you do? So, I mean, for me, the question is, 'Do I go back with Malaika?' Or do I just say to my parents 'Okay, you come and pick her up.'

That's not the issue right now. The only issue now, is, changing your reactions to things...

Hmmm. Which I did!

...Change your perspective...

Massively.

...Own yours and change it. Which gives other people permission to own theirs, and change it. And we can all live happily ever after...

Hmmm, hmm, yeah. Yeah, 'cos it was funny just talking to Lizzie. She was saying – when I was talking to my Dad when we were dropping her off at the airport, and he started going on about, "Oh you do know where you're going?" Because I was driving, which was quite unusual. I drove them all, we had a pub lunch on the Saturday so everyone was drinking except me. And, it was really, it was just a typical behaviour. All my life of him, saying, it's like the assumption is that I don't know what I'm doing. So, '...you need to take a left here...' and eventually I said to him "Look, I appreciate the fact that you are trying to be helpful, but if I want your help, I'm perfectly capable of asking for it!"

Ha ha ha ha ha

You know, in the past it would have been hysterical, and I'd have snapped at him, screamed or said, you know, "Why are you always doing this? Well, you always do this." Bring all the past up.

Give him…

Exactly! Give him the opportunity to be as aggressive back as I was being to him.

Hmmm

Lizzie commented on this. She said, "You sounded like a parent, and he, his reaction was like an angry little child."

I remember my Father saying to me "If you're going to behave like a child, we'll treat you like a child." Meanwhile, he was probably behaving like a child when he was saying it.

Yeah. And so many parents are still in, in that kind of 'childhood default mode'.

It's as if they're competing with their siblings…

Yeah!

…rather than realising they've got children.

Yeah, and, you kind of, we have said, time and again that we do recognise that they did do the best that they could. Yeah, but, fuckin-hell! Once I've seen all the 'stuff' they were carrying around with them…

Ummm!

…and do you know, I was thinking that I was from a relatively normal family – well I am, in a way because everyone 'normal' is 'fucked up'.

Hum hum hum hum hum hum hum… yeah, so after that position I felt put in between you and Eva…

Hmmmm

…that I didn't want to be in.

But that's interesting, you felt put in it, because I saw you more as putting yourself in it.

I couldn't, I didn't want to say 'hurry up…' or put pressure.

Oh that position. Okay. Right. I thought you meant whether she could come. Go on… go on…

Then, you changing things. And that being fine! Working out perfectly for everyone.

Yeah

Maybe the only thing that didn't work was the control aspect. And the reaction to abandonment.

Perhaps, yeah, but I think I wasn't – I wasn't sure whether I was being controlling in a 'good' way, as in 'I feel really happy with all of these friends. These people who I really do feel comfortable with'.

You needed time to think about it, I'd say.

Yeah. But that's, you know, coming back to that thing with my Dad and my sister. That's what we often don't give each other, or allow ourselves to take. I mean, my Dad gave the classic reaction, 'cos I said, eventually, "Well Lizzie and I talked about going to the Inn At Thrashwater last night and that's where we're going to go." But he said "Well it will take about an hour and a quarter." Which I knew wasn't true, because I've driven it in forty five minutes. But, afterwards I was saying to him, "Well, what's your point? It will take an hour and a quarter. Is that 'yes, you want to come', or 'no you don't'? Are you coming, or aren't you?" That's, like completely off the question. 'So what if it takes an hour and a quarter? Are you going to be in the car, when it takes that length of time? Can we just have a bit of clarity?' But I suppose what he was saying, was that he wasn't sure. And so, when you're not sure, do you plump for yes? Or do you plump for no? Do

you disappoint yourself? Do you disappoint the other people?

Do you say your thoughts out loud?

Yes, which I think, actually – you know, you were saying about the anger. Again, me coming back to that 'doesn't it annoy you?' because I always got the feeling it annoyed my Dad. You know? I'd be referred to as 'gibbering', 'chuntering', or whatever. But what I was doing was just trying to work out how I was feeling. Out loud. I think kids do. Kids talk their thoughts a lot more. I know Mallie does; but, coming back to the anger thing, I don't do it so much. Occasionally it slips out. But, I realised at one point that Mallie was my scapegoat. You know? This gorgeous, lovely little child, is, is… you can be angry with your children. Because really they have no defence. They shrink. They shut up. They do all the things that we want our parents to do. Our wives, our husbands, our friends. And they do it – (snaps fingers) 'like that!' And it has an immediate effect… and it's awful. But it's easy, because there's no defence from them.

In a way, bringing it back to us, this is new. This is interesting. Because at least now I know what it is. Because it seemed to be an anger at how well I get on with other people. Do you know what I mean?

Hmmm. No I don't think that's really the bottom of it!

That's what it's, maybe that's what you 'piggy back' in on.

Possibly, yeah… I think, in a way, what I'm suddenly getting now, take away all the justifications and explanations. It's easy, it's possible to get angry with you because you have that defencelessness that Malaika has.

Hm. First time I've heard this one!

Hmmm. I mean, okay what I mean by 'take away all the justification' is, I know, you can be like, you know, like we've said, 'trying to get hold of a smoke ring'. So that, in a way, is a form of defence. Possibly a childhood defence. I mean, you know, kind of side-stepping and ducking, rather than facing it full on or pushing it back. Not owning it.

But yeah, there is that sort of... almost naivety that a child has. Kind of like 'Oof, what's this all about?' you know, 'Aah! Someone's angry with me.' It's complicated though, isn't it?

The clear light

Anger – schmanger. *'Bad Boy Bubby'*[148] – how was it for you?

Well I trusted your taste in films after *'Wings Of Desire'*, *'Good Will Hunting'*[149] and *'Brother Sun Sister Moon'*[150] last Christmas, and you pointed out things that I never ever got when I first watched them. Because you said that *'Wings Of Desire'* was like your story, as was *'Sixth Sense'*[151], where *'Good Will Hunting'* was the early you and Lui.

Yeah... yeah! Films that 'are me'. That make me feel like, yeah, I'm not the only one coming from that perspective. So, what did you think to *'Bubby'*? What effect did it have?

It's what effect didn't it have?! It was, it was just everything. Every emotion I think I could name – I felt. There were moments when I just wanted to leave the room, or turn it off, or say it's crap, or hear someone else's voice. Well I think I said, didn't I? I could imagine my Dad just looking at me and... sort of in confused horror. 'Why are we watching this?' 'What are these perverts?' 'These people are sick!' 'What are we gaining from this?' And, yeah. There were some really really emotional moments. Really, amazing. And the music! Really, whoever made that film understood the power of music. Fucking hell!

Huh hum hum...

'cos all of it was great! Whether it was, sort of, Baroque music, or that punk, 'New Wave-y' sort of band.

Hmmm

I thought it was amazing. And then afterwards, going into the garden with you, just made me realise, you know, thinking that I had been an emotionally accessible person all my life. But then, I think as you put it, a lot of it has just been processing how I was feeling, rather than actually feeling the emotion.

Umm, humm, same as me. Otherwise I wouldn't say a word, obviously.

But then, it just – I don't know. I don't know what it was – some, a couple of things triggered it. As we were starting to talk after the film I could hear the birds twittering. Something about that makes me feel very uncomfortable. It's like I've stayed up too long?

Ahhh

It feels wrong. Then we went in the garden for a smoke, and the birds were really singing and you said "Look at you. Have you seen that film 'Birdy'[152]?

Oh yeah.

When I was crouching like in the film, which felt very comfortable. And then I found myself shaking and shaking and shaking. And I felt, it wasn't just the cold, it was… fear and releasing… anger and emotions. Unexpressed emotions really, because that's one thing that; who was I talking to? Somebody I was talking to about the other downside of the whole Christmas / New Year thing is, most people don't move much, or they don't make much noise. It's like, all people tend to do is be in a house full of people they don't necessarily get on that well with…

He he

…eating lots of food that they don't really want…

He he he

…watching television that they don't really want to watch - and then wondering why they all feel so crap at the end of it and then vowing to do something different next year and usually doing exactly the same, and then thinking '…but I felt this last year! Why am I doing it again?' So I really felt that. I haven't moved enough and I haven't stretched. I hadn't danced around – even though I had, with Mallie.

Hmmm

But afterwards, when we were sitting together, I really; I almost felt like coming over and touching you in some way... not sexually, or dramatically, but just, sort of being connected.

Hmmm – I felt you feel that, and I felt that that would have been, that would have pressed a 'smothering button'...

Yeah

...but then I felt, as soon as I had that feeling – is it self-protection? – beyond that feeling, er, what I'd probably say, which is, um, *"Sit in it, rather than connect with someone else – sit with it."*

Well, which is what we both did. It was almost like we were, we were on the same psychic track. I felt I was 'reading what you were feeling' and I felt like you were feeling what I was feeling.

Hmmm

That expansiveness was amazing! Huge.

As a kid, I would be petrified of that feeling. It would be 'stuff'... feelings that I would have when I was semi-conscious, you know...

Falling asleep!

...yeah. Or waking up. And feeling that huge expansiveness and my place in it, and out of control, or threatened, or; it would be, you know, I've got two or three 'funny dreams'. And I don't think I've talked about this. One of them is as if I was sitting in an old classroom, on my own, and I'm just sitting there, um, in this state of expansiveness, and, um, God has given me the task of counting all the molecules in the room, including the end of the pencil, the paper, the chair... and I have to start counting, but it's just too huge a task. It fucks me up. And then the molecules move and I lose control and it just fucks me up. That's one. And it would make me petrified! And another one would be being at the edge of this huge huge huge blade.

What… 'glade'?

Blade!

Oh…! Knife blade.

Yup. More like a chisel. And under the blade – and I'm just like a tiny molecule, so I can see all the imperfections of the blade – and under the blade is running huge planks of wood. And from the outside it feels like the most perfect, perfect cut. But from that perspective, it's just so imperfect and so… messy and wrong and fucked and out of control, that, again, it's me screaming and going mad because I can see the imperfections. Umm, but I can't do anything about it. Meanwhile, it doesn't seem that with the imperfections, people are aware of it.

So what's all that about then?

Fuck knows! Ha ha ha ha ha

That's why it used to scare me. Kind of lying, almost asleep but still awake, um, looking at the curtains at the end of the bed. One minute they'd be tiny, like I'm looking at a piece of furniture in a doll's house a hundred feet away, then they would be huge and then I would be tiny and they'd be huge. And last night I was feeling that again.

Yes!

It was almost like 'Alice In Wonderland'[153] but I haven't; do you know I was really aware of the fact – this is amazing, okay, I'm… more or less – I don't smoke cigarettes and I don't smoke dope anymore. And I was having this feeling, I was thinking…

You never did, really – smoke dope.

…well I suppose not. It doesn't seem to make any difference. You know, this is like one cigarette, okay, we've been through an intense film, talked, and I felt very very… I can't even say I felt close to you, I felt like part of you – and like you were part of me – and there was

this whole kind of one-ness, expansive-ness took over. And it reminded me of Vipassana. The first time, feeling like something massive was bubbling up, wanting to come out and I didn't have the courage to go with it. But on my second retreat, feeling the same and thinking 'Okay, this is like being on a wild horse!'

Yeah

'My main fear is that I'm going to fall over, land on somebody and embarrass them and myself, or throw up over them – that's the other thing. It's like, I'm spinning. Totally aware of being just molecules. And the same, as a child, I don't think I ever even mentioned it to my parents, because I thought, 'is it madness, or…'

It doesn't make sense.

'…what's it all about?'

I remember, not only the same nightmares, I remember also that paralysis thing. Not being able to shout, or scream, or ask for help, or move, or fall out of my bed, or somehow indicate to the outside world that 'I FUCKING NEED HELP - Because *I think I've died!*'

Exactly, 'what is happening?'

Really fucked up.

They probably are, I think I've probably said this to you already. In the massage course, there's a term which I think in Reiki[154] they call 'Reiki land' but it's that state of not being awake and not being asleep. The Tibetans call it 'the clear light', which is exactly what it felt like. Yeah, 'Is this what it feels like to die?'

Hmmm – ha ha ha

And maybe that's it. That's what I felt like when I woke up this morning, after a kind-of broken sleep, that, I felt like, I felt like I'd been skinned.

Yeah. Ha ha ha ha ha ha ha

Every noise was just so loud. I could feel my blood rushing through my veins. I could feel my heart pounding. And that's what I actually realised – or I hadn't realised. I'm only realising now I'm saying it – maybe when I wake up in the mornings, it's not that my heart is pounding any more than it ever has, but I'm just more aware of it.

Yeah

It's not wrong or bad, it's just how it feels.

Or maybe automatic panic.

Yeah…

Automatic something-or-other that's not even from here and now, that you don't even realise it's going on.

Hmmm

But going back to the sleep thing, I remember being upstairs, petrified to go to sleep, being left, being moved to a room on my own, away from my brother, being in the dark, the absolute dark, hanging to be checked on.

You what? What did you say?

'Hanging to be checked on' by my Mother, or…

Oh, yeah yeah yeah

I can't remember who even checked. But I'd make them promise AND I WAS DESPERATE. So scared that I would hold hands with my brother in the bottom bunk and pray out loud. Fucking petrified!

Cor the mind of children, eh? Fucking hell.

But *kids shouldn't have to go through that.*

But then how, how on earth would you… what would you say to your child? What would I say to Malaika? 'Are you, thinking you're dying?' Ha ha ha…?

Just being, surely, somehow just being able to relate. And then 'name' that they can talk about anything and everything. And ask what's normal and what's real. Because they're working out what they're allowed to talk about and what is their – what are the 'secrets'.

Yeah

What shouldn't be talked about in front of people. Or, what's not normal, like...

'...my little Daddy's a poof!' Ha ha ha ha ha ha

Yeah, exactly! Or that you can see something, you know, maybe children see things that adults don't see. Like dogs hear things that humans don't hear...

Yeah, yes.

...but no one ever talks about it, so it 'shouldn't be talked about'. Or feels things, within the family – meanwhile, it's the most important thing to talk about.

I was talking to Malaika about angels. 'Thanking in advance'. And she just started talking about, she started naming all these names of her angels.

Yeah??

It was just so amazing. And, like you said, my gut instinct was just to listen and make it normal, rather than going "You what?!"

Heh heh heh hu huh huh huh hu

148. 'Bad Boy Bubby' (1993) Rolf de Heer, Australia / Italy.
www.angelfire.com/movies/badboybubby/interview.htm

149. 'Good Will Hunting' (1997) Gus Van Sant, USA.

150. 'Brother Sun Sister Moon' (1972) Franco Zefferelli, Italy / UK.

151. 'The Sixth Sense' (1999) M Night Shyamalan, USA.

152. 'Birdy' (1984) Alan Parker, USA.

153. 'Alice In Wonderland' Lewis Carroll (aka Charles Dodgson), UK (originally published 1865).

154. Reiki. A form of energy healing.

Don't 'have to' shag

There's so much, so much beyond – *(points)* look at that girl! Pink and purple…

So what is going on in your fucking sexuality? Or don't you know? Or isn't it an issue? Or is it an issue for other people and you feel like it should be an issue for you?

I think it's an issue for other people. I've said this to you before. I thought at one point that you felt quite pleased, because you'd 'cured me' of homosexuality…

Ha ha ha ha ha ha

…when I couldn't stop shagging Maria after a one-off with Margaret. I think it's just…

No.

…no that was what I picked up. I mean, I think you said something in a conversation once about 'That's another reason for your Mum to hate me, was because I stopped you being a poof'.

Ah ha ha ha ha ha – did I say that?

Yeah.

Terrible.

You do say some very brazen things, don't you?

He he he he he he he he… very rude.

I just feel very comfortable with who I am. I feel, I do feel very – I'll tell you what it is, I've realised I can talk to you, or Billy, or Bob about fancying other men. And there's no assumption that you will think 'Uh-oh… backs to the wall' as they used to say in the changing rooms at school when this allegedly gay teacher came in. Do you know what I mean? Maybe I'm wrong. Maybe you are all secretly thinking 'Hang on, why am I hanging out with this poof, then?'

Maybe we are all secretly all talking about it.

What do you mean?! Oh yeah exactly – well that's the other thing, you know, it's kinda getting that line between bitchiness and honesty about your friends. Accepting that people probably do talk about each other.

Umm

It's not necessarily bad. Or malicious. It's just…

Out of control!

'…Ed can be a cunt, sometimes, can't he?' 'Yeah, he can.' 'Mickey's a right bastard sometimes…' do you know what I mean? So, anyway, maybe I'm being evasive, but I don't think I am, um… I'm not totally sure. I know I just; there's a rampant part of me that just wants to shag… endlessly, and another part of me that…

Anyone and everyone?

No, I'm really, I think I'm in a 'man phase' at the moment. I really see attractive men. But, it's not the, it isn't anyone and everyone. Because with friends it's different - if that makes any sense - I wouldn't shag my friends. Why are you being so quiet?

Ha ha ha ha ha

You don't believe me, do you? Yeah, Shane was saying, "Oh it's nice to have friends you can sleep with…" when I talked to him on Sunday night, and I said "I don't quite know why I'm saying this, but I don't feel, I wouldn't want to shag you." and I said, "In a way, I get on really well with you, you know, you're physically…"

Do you mean me, or Shane?

…no, talking to Shane. Um, and I think he, I think he understood it wasn't like I was rejecting him before he could make the offer…

Yup

…um, but, he said "It's alright, I'm not going to pounce on you!" and I said "No, that's not what I'm talking about. It's more I don't feel like I need to… have that experience with you, because, maybe with some of your – sort of – gay friends, you do sleep with them occasionally and it's not like you're having a relationship and you go shopping in IKEA for furniture together, because you slept together once." That's maybe it, that is maybe a big difference between men and women. With women, you shag 'em and next thing it's, you know, arrangements for the wedding.

Yeah

Whereas with a man, it's like, 'Yeah that was nice. So, when are you coming around again? Oh yes. See you in a fortnight.' No but I want to be, I want to be intimate. And with you, last night, as I said, there was that sense of wanting to somehow connect and realising that it doesn't always have to be physical. I even – when I was in Silchester – totally, without any addictive, compulsive behaviour, thought 'Oh, yeah maybe it would be good to just get my rocks off with a stranger, just to see what it feels like from this place-of-awareness.' That I'm not needy, and desperate, and that I'm not running away from home because I'm so upset and angry that I need to have sex with the first person I come across. But it didn't happen!

And that's another one to add to the list. That's how people get rid of their unexpressed anger.

Yeah. Well I would regularly go from my parents' house in Silchester…

Rather than dumping it on anyone!

…go and shag it away. Wank it away. And, yeah, there is that easy

'no questions asked' 'no words exchanged' possibility, where it's just;
but then I thought, 'I don't, I don't want to just have my dick taken in a
man's hand, he wanks me off, I wank him off and nothing else
happens. I feel beyond that, I don't feel like I can, I don't feel I can do
that'. And not that it's wrong to do it, but

You want more connection than that?

Yes.

Same. I don't want sex with my friends. I don't even really want to get
naked with my friends. It's far more comfortable with the naturist thing,
doing it with strangers and hanging out.

**Or doing what we did last night. Feelings that the other person is
feeling. A desire to connect somehow and just thinking, hmm, just sit
with it rather than coming over and gushing.**

Yeah, that's just being. It's not even about the other person. In fact it
never is. In truth. And then the second-guessing and the over-thinking
comes in.

**Yeah, 'should I say that?' 'should I do that?' In fact I was saying this to
Billy, that quite often I know when I've got something wrong, in my
own mind. I've had a thought about something, in advance, like how a
situation will be. And I turn up in that situation, and it's different. And I
still say the kind of clever, or funny thing that I thought would be
perfect to say in that situation. 'Won't everyone laugh!' But everyone's
different in the situation that I go to, but then I say it anyway, and I
think... 'Naah, that was crap! It didn't work.'**

Yeah? —?

**But the other thing is this assumption - a very kind of casual
assumption - about people who sleep with men or women – or
whoever they sleep with, I don't mean children. Men or women,
consenting adults. I read a review of Nicholas Ray[155] in 'The
Guardian'. He did all of these film noir[156] 40's-50's like Humphrey
Bogart[157] films. He did 'Rebel Without A Cause' as well – this article**

just said, it was really judgmental, it said, it had titillating mentions of bisexuality, and then when it actually came to the bisexuality – it was all talking about his marriages, and very blithely said something like 'Oh he seduced Natalie Wood[158], and the scriptwriter Gavin somebody-or-other, and possibly James Dean[159].' And then later on went on to say something about '...the untidiness of his life.' I thought, how dare these people judge this man? And what do they mean by 'untidiness'? He didn't live in a nice suburban semi with two point four children? So what do you want your fucking film directors to be doing?

Ha ha ha ha ha ha ha ha

Shopping at B&Q[160]? With his girlfriend or their wife? I think that's it. It's almost like, I suppose I can relate to; in a way it can be chaotic. But, I wouldn't want to be shagging loads of people simultaneously and having relationships with men and women at the same time, I think. It's too complicated. But, as you've said, just to feel – this is what you're feeling. And act on it. If that feels right.

It's interesting. Gina and I didn't have Christmas, our Christmas meal, lunch or dinner or whatever you call it, until 10.30pm. Ha ha ha ha ha ha ha ha We were just so busy hanging out and doing whatever we were doing, and um, I think it was Boxing Day, or the day after that – I just needed male company. And I thought of seeing Anna and Simon – because they're really cool – and, um, I fancied hanging out with Simon. And if anyone was there, whatever. And for Gina, I thought – perfect. Hang out with Anna. Perhaps they can speak in Italian and they wouldn't even have to think that much. You know, to translate or whatever. And it was great! And I said to Gina, I think, that evening, "It's really cool, because probably, if I wasn't with a girlfriend, I'd wanna hang out with girls, as well as boys. Attract the situations where not only may I meet a – I might meet a girl, but I could get female company. But now I'm getting so much female company, that I need a balance. Male company."

U-hum?

And, fucking excellent. All of it! As long as we can keep the balance, and not… play games with each other, we're great! We're just telling the truth! We have a perfect time.

I felt the same though, with um, my family that being at home with my Dad, and he was the only other bloke. It was 'female heavy'. You know, my Mum, my sister, Malaika, whatever the dynamics. Yeah, as you said before, there's that potential tension that a lot of men have between going off and hanging out with their mates, usually down the pub, and having "er indoors' …complaining!

It's not, it's not fair to say that men only hang out down the pub.

Yes, yes.

Some men go fishing. Some men do volunteer stuff, or fight, so many bloody things. Men don't only hang out together at the pub. Actually…

I was using it as an example.

Ha ha ha ha ha

With awareness!

Yes, but I love being with women, and I love being with men, I love being with both. Um, probably to do different things with, or, depending on my moods, or if I want to be – I don't know – I love being loved by women. I love their smell. I love how clean and soft they are, and how they give me attention, and how I can be a man.

Hmmm

Play with them, or… flirt! I suppose. Different things for different people.

I suppose that's sometimes what, if I do get into my head about my sexuality I think, 'am I… Am I attracted to men sexually?' Which I think I am. That, that's been a recent revelation to me. I am sexually attracted – in ways that other men aren't – but it probably was overlaid with confusion from my parents. You know, I was saying to my Dad the other day, it wasn't particularly reassuring, when I was

growing up, that he talked about 'queers' and 'poofs' and all this kind
of thing, and it's like, yeah, I'm really going to tell him, that that's "Oh,
I feel like that too." Do you know what I mean?

Or maybe that's his way of making sure that you don't.

Yeah.

Maybe he's yet to deal with it.

Yeah. But I think, there's been a shift for me, that in the past I thought
that all this is very Freudian and I'm just basically – like you said – I
don't want to be smothered by women, so I'll shag men instead,
because it's safer, and less emotionally engaging. But then I read
something, Boy George[161] said in an interview and someone else was
saying the same, that *so many gay men are afraid of
intimacy*. It's not as simple as, you know, not being smothered by
women because men don't give a shit. You know, men want emotional
engagement as well. Well, that's what I've found.

There are so many different reasons. So for men who are scared of
fanny, who haven't seen one, who are scared of women, or
humiliation, who have very small cocks, or have very big cocks, or
whatever the issue is, maybe it's their way of avoiding it. Or making the
most of it. Or the stage that they're at. Or the place that they're at. It's
about the journey, rather than – winning.

Yeah. I would not categorically now say that I'm going to have
relationships with men exclusively for the rest of my life. Because, you
know, if a woman comes along, there's a strong attraction, you know,
and I don't rule out – God forbid – having more kids. Because I love
kids, I think they're great! You know?

Hmmm!

But there is a part of me that is just very very unconventional. I mean,
these two absolutely lovely women I know, who've had relationships
with men and are in a relationship together, at the moment. One of

507

them just happened to mention - we were at this gig and there were all these gorgeous kids around dancing to this drumming and they were just being totally pure, and everyone loved them, and it was like 'sharing the children'. So, so beautiful. And I looked at my friend and I said, you know, "Do you want to have kids together?" She said that "A lot of people have said that they can see us with kids." It's almost like she was saying "We're two women and we're not sure..." and so on. But then suddenly my mind just drifted into this little fantasy about, well you know, I've got a really nice looking kid, and I'm a good bloke, maybe I should offer – hah ha – but then I immediately thought, 'Hmmm, that could be complicated!' maybe just give them *a little glass jar full of fresh sperm*, and, do you know what I mean? And then it was, then my mind immediately was thinking that 'I would want to have a relationship with this child, and surely it would need to have a strong male influence in its life, and what would that be? And would I have to pay maintenance?' It's so funny...

Going 'round to their house shouting

"...YOU WON'T LET ME SEE MY SON – YOU BITCHES!"

Ha ha ha ha ha ha ha ha ha

All from me thinking about giving them some sperm... Quite funny, because it's like in that little Vipassana book, the author said they call it a 'Vipassana romance', where you see somebody walk into the meditation room and you think 'Oh, they're a bit of alright...' then while you're sitting on your little cushion, supposedly meditating, you've gone through courtship, marriage and kids, divorce, settlement, peaceful old age and death, just from one glace at somebody.

You just don't know where to look, but you end up looking.

Yeah, totally.

All part of the journey.

155. Nicholas Ray. US film director, 'Rebel Without A Cause' amongst others.

156. Film noir. Atmospheric (usually black & white) film, 1920's-1950's-present day, depending on the mood!

157. Humphrey Bogart. US actor and star of many Nicholas Ray's films.

158. Natalie Wood. US actress and co-star in 'Rebel Without A Cause' amongst others.

159. James Dean. 1931-1955, US film / gay / straight icon, the 'Rebel Without A Cause'.

160. B&Q. UK DIY superstores.

161. Boy George. UK singer, dance music dj. www.veryboygeorge.com

Joan, Bette & Kiki

Hmmm… what?

What were you going to say? Obsessive-compulsive – your Father being, and your sister already knowing…

Oh well, one of the things I said to her over the Christmas break was "I want to tell him! I want to tell him that he's obsessive-compulsive."

Yup!

"But I don't know how… and I don't know what; well he'd probably deny it. And here I am, already assuming his reactions."

Heh he he he he he

So that's that over and done with! Heh heh… but yes, it did make a difference in absolutely seeing that he doesn't want his routines interrupted. Um…

Knowing 'the nature of the beast' and working around it.

Exactly. So in a w…

Rather than guessing what the rules are, and sometimes getting it wrong and being hurt.

Yeah

Playing too small to take part.

Yup – so maybe it…

Don't take part, just like him.

So maybe in a way it doesn't have to be that I say "Look, here's this little book I've got – whether you agree with it or not, this is what I think your problem is."

Is this what we're doing with the book? Justifying why they are victims? Saying to people, look... maybe not.

I hope not. I mean, whether or not – and I have no doubt that massive things will potentially come of it, as you say, if we're right about it. But apart from anything else, it's changed my relationship with everything. Which is... plenty, to be going on with. And it's opened up; thinking about, in our letter to the different people we sent it off to initially, about who we were.

Yup

And I was thinking, 'Sexually, spiritually, creatively frustrated' – I'm not any of those now!

Huh huh huh huh huh

I mean, through this, like I was saying to you last night, I was brimming with ideas for children's books, because to me that's the next step for me, logically. Okay, we've talked about what kids aren't allowed to speak about, or see, or do... and I just want to have books with characters who are... whatever.

Permission.

Yeah, exactly.

'Normalised'

Hmmm. But not a big song and dance...

Take responsibility as well.

Yeah, definitely. Because there will be plenty of people going "You can't expose children to that sort of..." I mean, think of all the Clause 28[162] furore. Remember about Thatcher banning, um, that book with the little girl's name. Something like *'Somebody lives with Tony and Guy'*[163] or whatever – not the hairdressers...

511

Ha ha ha

It was like you can't even tell children that it's alright for a child to be brought up by two men. And I thought, 'Well okay, that was of its time. I don't want to write books that are bashing you over the head with a hammer saying that it's alright for men to cross-dress. Or it's alright to have half brothers and sisters. Or lesbian couples, or whatever. But just make it normal.'

I think we have, like I, we have talked about doing other people's books – 'Talanoa'[164].

Definitely!

But also, if I do the trilogy, one with you – which brings out a certain side of me – and I was saying to Gina recently, it's a side that doesn't often come out, because I only know one of you, while so many of my other friends are more similar to each other.

Right

In a lot of ways. So, doing (working title #3 for this book) 'What Will People Think?' with you, which is very much, if I think of you, it would be standing in that posture with your arms folded thinking 'what will people think'? Meanwhile, after that, doing 'Fuck 'em' with Lui, and that is very much Lui.

Yeah

Then doing 'Dark Side Of The Spoon' with John.

So seeing all your sides, basically.

Yeah!

Hmmm.

I do feel more like a man, though. Because the impression I give in this book, would be quite different from the other books.

God, when you looked at me just now, I felt really embarrassed. I could see real liking there. It was like, 'oh, I don't know if I can handle

that!'

Ha ha ha ha ha ha ha ha

You know, even whether it's '...he likes me globally, or in this moment – we're good mates!' It's like a real shock! And I noticed that with my Dad actually. That I was looking at him and noticed that he doesn't make much eye contact. And I was really, almost - kind of - following him around the room with my eyes thinking, 'I don't, I'm not playing a game here.'

'Where are we?'

And then, when we had this, I guess it was a man-to-man talk, it felt like – we looked in each other's eyes a lot more, because we were both being honest and we weren't trying to gauge... but that's why it was so important to be with just him. And that could, so easily, have been a big drama, with me saying 'Look Dad, I've realised that you are obsessive-compulsive – and I can help you...' you know, like they'd probably do in a crass American film. But it was just like, well...

Kenny Everett!

...exactly, yeah! A drama, and I've got a big blonde wig on probably – ha ha – and the most ENORMOUS TITS... '...they're beautiful.'

Ha ha ha ha ha '...angel tits!' 'Bad Boy Bubby' – fuckinexcellent!

Ummm!

I can't wait to watch *'Betty Blue'*[165]. Maybe first the cut version, then the un-cut version.

I've never seen the un-cut version.

Whoooah! It kind of changes the film.

Is that the scene where she's... done something to her eyes?

There are a few things...

I would love, I'd love to see all these films again. We were talking about all those Peter Greenaway[166] films...

Well that's why I can't wait. It's like I say, I think *(Californian accent)* 'my inner child' - or wherever I'm stuck in my unconscious - is in Wales. That's what we'll get when we do the final tape there.

Yeah

I think yours is these films, which I can't wait to see. What's her name Betty Grable?[167]

Um, Bette Davis[168]. Well that's the classic thing. Bette Davis and Joan Crawford[169] – they're the gay arche... sort of, not archetypes, um you know, I mean...

Are they? And do they dramatise around 'what will people think?'

Yeah, I mean that one I mentioned, *'Mildred Pierce'*[170] which I remember locking myself in the room – well, not locking myself in, but a dark room, all alone, while everyone else is off being healthy - must have been around thirteen? - and it's the story of this woman who is a waitress, who's got ambitions, she's a real social climber. One daughter hates her – she's the oldest daughter – there's no Father, interestingly enough. Lots of men just flit through her life. The Mother's life played by Joan Crawford. She has this really difficult relationship with the oldest daughter and the younger daughter, who's brilliant, she's just so real and alive, and not pretentious at all – she dies, basically. It's really melodramatic, but, yeah, I'd love to see it again, because – it's like I was thinking last night. I don't feel I got half of what these films are about.

Yeah. Yeah, like I said last night, you just bought into the moods and the flavour, rather than the emotions.

Yup. Drawn to it, without knowing why. Kind of intrigued. And then people say "What did you think about it?" "Oh, it's good."

Did it bring up those emotions? Allow you to express those emotions? Did it express those emotions for you? Or is that a way of dealing with things? Well like Kiki Dee[171] and I! And other music from the 70's. It was my escape. It made me feel happy.

Hmmm. Yeah, I suppose that's it. A sort of fantasy world where you can see; well that's what I thought watching 'Bubby'. The first scenes were… half of my reaction was 'this is gross and over the top!' and another part of me was 'well this is what drama is all about!'

Yeah!

You know, it, it kind of writes in ten foot high letters, 'this is what happens in lots of families, but it's not as obvious.' That's what I got from the first few scenes.

Hmmm

You know, you were saying about that book on the Oedipus complex. That whole, the first scenes in the film were all about that, weren't they?

Hmmm, yeah, totally.

And brilliantly acted out.

Yeah

In quite an obvious, but somehow subtle way, as well.

That's where they were coming from. They weren't doing anything wrong or dirty – that's where they were coming from! That was their survival.

And it was never, what was good about it was, there was no kind-of justification, or – you know – she's in the situation because of, this, and this is why she's treating him this way.

It just 'was'.

Yeah. So yeah, and it's like we've said, feeling sixteen again. I feel like all these books and films and things that teenagers are given to read. Like 'great' literature, like Dickens or whatever. I'd love to read them now, read them as an adult, with some perspective, rather than trying to analyse it and take it apart and say, well these are the themes, this character is this and that – but actually feeling it.

Changing your role in 'Lord Of The Flies'[172].

Ummmmm… But that was what was so good about last Christmas. Watching 'Wings Of Desire' with you and hearing Bob asking all these questions, and all I wanted to do was sit there and feel. I knew I was, I was getting it – without having to ask, and make a big show of the fact 'Oh, I get it, now!' it was like, it was falling into place.

Yeah

I mean, I would never have watched, say 'Fight Club' if you hadn't told me about it.

162. Clause 28. In British law, section 28 of the Local Government Act 1988 prohibits local authorities promoting material, or by promoting the teaching in state schools, of the acceptability of homosexuality as a 'pretended family relationship'.

163. 'Jenny lives with Eric and Martin' (limited edition, currently £90 from www.amazon.co.uk)

164. Talanoa. Fijian for 'tell your story'.

165. 'Betty Blue' (1986) Jean-Jacques Beneix, France.

166. Peter Greenaway. UK arty film director. petergreenaway.co.uk

167. Betty Grable. US film actress and World War II pin-up.

168. Bette Davis. US film actress described as 'the queen of the American screen'. www.bettedavis.com

169. Joan Crawford. US film actress / legend.

170. 'Mildred Pierce' (1945) Michael Curtiz, USA.

171. Kiki Dee. Mickey's fave! UK singer. www.kikidee.info also www.kikiandcarmelo.com

172. 'Lord Of The Flies' William Golding (Faber & Faber) 1954. Filmed 1963 & 1990.

Process, process, process...

It doesn't surprise me that what we'd taped had not come out at all. It just felt... it felt like it was kind of a volcano blowing its top. Being pissed off and – I wonder that now I'm sitting here, I was thinking... 'I just wanted to have a fight with you when you were talking'.

What...

Physically. I just wanted to... start something.

Big big difference between the two of us, is like, I don't want to fight, I don't want you to touch me.

That's not because I, that's not because I want to touch you.

Yeah I know, but you know I don't want either. Both ideas totally turn me off. But, um...

It struck me the other day, um, and I was thinking about our relationship - our friendship - as much as I think you're an amazing person - and I love you - I know where Lui has been coming from all this time. There's a part of me that just... almost wants to kill you.

Hmmm

Physically. *Just take you by the neck and* – like you see in films? You know, when someone just bashes their head against the floor – and I don't know what it's about.

You don't have a clue what it's about?

Well no, no, I mean I don't know why I have such a strong reaction. I think I know what it's about... it's the things that we talked about before. Ummm, I think it's to do with... yeah! This book has brought out a different side of me. Before, I was, I couldn't, I couldn't get in touch with that sort of feeling around other blokes – maybe I'd feel angry sometimes, but I wouldn't know what it was all about. It's a whole range of things. It's, it's feeling like... well the other day when we were in the City, afterwards I thought, 'why did I not; why didn't I feel what I'm feeling now, which was... ahhh... manipulated, pushed into something, hurried along', I felt like my decisions and my input were just kind of pushed out of the way because you decided that – you know – making copies of the book was the most important thing. And it, yeah! It unleashed a whole lot of anger. Um... and also I guess, you know what you were just saying, downstairs - which didn't record - about you don't want to process any more. I just thought, 'Well, what's it all about?' You know, what. Are we just, this is now just to do with the book. Just getting it finished and, you know, kind of, I mean I don't question why I'm coming to Wales with you, but I think... it's all getting very odd in a way. It's kind of, I feel like our lives are being distorted by the process.

What do you mean?

I feel like we're, you're saying you don't want to talk, you don't want to process, but that's what this book has been all about. And so it continues to be about...

Hmmm

...but just for the tape, it's almost like, I feel a bit... that... you wanna talk about the book, but I'm not bothered any more. Since, I really feel that something big changed the other day, when we were in the City. Umm, for the first time, when I was talking to the guy behind the counter about getting the copies done, and whatever, again, I just picked up utter utter rage from you. And I found it quite funny. For the first time I thought 'I don't feel guilty about this – I don't care'. It was like, 'feel fucked off!'

This is about what?

About the fact that, you know, you might be cross and you might; I got the feeling that, you know, I was standing there, negotiating with this bloke about the copies and the price, whatever. And from you, I was getting just massive impatience. Irritation. Then when we walked back I got the feeling, you know, that you were trying to sort of chat and talk about various this and that. And I just didn't feel like talking. You know, I felt like... hmm. I felt like I was living what you'd described before, that you didn't realise that you were angry. Remember that day when you walked out of the house in Finsbury Park, wherever it is and I said to you "You're really angry" with Lui or whoever it was, and afterwards you phoned me and said "Oh, I didn't realise I was angry."

No, you didn't say that until I phoned you, and then when you 'named it', then I thought back to the day and the morning and I thought 'Yeah, I have been angry, but I didn't know that that's what it – that that was called'.

Hmm

You didn't say it that morning, because otherwise I probably would have thought about it, which was probably better, because when you did say it, then I had a whole day to review.

Hmmm

And realise that I was.

Hmmm – well I mean I didn't not say it, because... it was nothing...

You probably thought I knew!

Well yeah, exactly. Yeah!

I don't even remember what I was angry about that day.

It was because Lui had rung you in the middle of an evening with Gina and I...

Oh, yeah, I remember.

...you had gone into, you kind of suddenly looked like a whipped

dog.

And he'd said, something like, it was about this 'best friend label' wearing...; not an appropriate label any more because I wasn't calling him back when he phoned me and I saw his name on my phone as a missed call, even though he didn't leave a message. I wasn't answering the phone to him all the time and saying "I'll call you straight back mate, I'm with someone!" I was just leaving it, so he must have felt...; especially in the vulnerable time that he's been through since he's been back. He must have felt abandoned. Errr, so responded in that way. And, that was the first conflict that we had since he came back. And it wasn't even a proper conflict. And from there, I did recover from it straight away thinking, 'Well, yes it is an old label. And labels don't really come into it. *It's the quality of the relationship and how the relationship's being expressed* that comes into it.' And, I've got over it, but, it took me time to get over the old reactions...

Which are what?

...and the panic.

The next day you seemed furious and I seem to remember later on you were saying that you were angry because you felt you'd been bullied, but you hadn't expressed it to Lui, or fended him off, or told him to fuck off, or something.

Probably similar thing with; well this would make sense, actually. A similar thing with us two, with Lui and I, where I would chase Lui – because I'd need to talk, or 'name something', or sort something out and get clear and feel safe again, whatever. Ummm, where Lui is probably the only one that I do that with. Because other people do that with me.

Hmmm

Aammm, but they want to, ummm, justify themselves, blame themselves, sort out anything that I may be thinking that they might not want me to think, ummm, and process, and blah blah blah, and I don't really – I'm not into it. I'm just not into it anymore.

Except perhaps when you want to do it.

Ummm…

Which is maybe where that sense of manipulation; or I don't know, or maybe it's, it's to do with ego or something. Because I said something to you when we were walking there the other day.

Walking to?

Walking to the photocopiers'.

Right.

Ummm, and it was to do, I don't know, it was to do with the exchange of energy, money, time, etcetera of whatever we're putting into this project.

Hmmm

And, from when I said that, I sensed a change in you. You seemed to go very quiet, then there was that feeling of suppressed rage in the shop. And then when we came out, I thought probably in the past I would have wanted to process it, but I felt myself kind of laughing inwardly about it. 'just like, so what. You know? If you're angry – I almost, like, don't give a shit'. Do you know what I mean? It's kind of gone to the other extreme.

No, it's quite different for me. Because for me, I felt that um, once we'd done it, that what we'd agreed was to print it out and make copies. So I went to John's – because he said he'd print it out for me for free, and, you know, help out in whatever way – so I went to John's, printed it out, once it was printed out I thought, well the next thing's copies. And then the first and the second parts of the book can be read while the last bit was being done. Because by the time the first and second parts have been read, this last bit will be completed. So, as far as I knew, I was doing what we wanted. And I had no problem that I was doing it.

Umm, because I know John and if I've got the resources I'll put them in and I imagine if you've got the resources you'll put them in...

Hmmm

...whether it's money, or time, or friends, or favours, or contacts, or whatever. So I didn't realise that there was an unmade decision, that I was kind of enforcing. And then, at the copier shop, it wasn't anything apart from, I felt that you were just 'getting into one' with this guy and you had a lot to say, where he didn't have a lot to say, I didn't have a lot to say.

Well I disagree with that. That's totally your projection. That's what - I guess that's what's starting to change - is I now feel much more able to, almost to tell you how fucked off I feel, rather than see how you're feeling. I think that's the big shift as far as I'm concerned. Like, instead of saying "So what was it about for you?"

Hmmm

Saying "Well I felt fucked off!" You know, it doesn't have to go into any great depth or drama. And in a way we're doing what you're saying you don't want to do.

Well no, I love 'naming things' and carrying on, but it's just the going 'round in circles that; and I think that's something that I'm learning to do now. Rather than – and I think 'naming and carrying on' is not having the fear of the consequences. Where the 'going around in circles' and processing and second-guessing and whatever, is to make sure that the other person isn't going to abandon, or inflict violence, or blah blah blah. It's just... because that, for me, I had no problem, apart from the money thing, which we hadn't talked about, ummm, and... I felt the change when the money thing came up. But then, I would have been cool to talk about it, I would have been cooler to have made time aside to sit down, look at a business plan, a list of whatever you've spent, and I've spent, and to do it from there. But, no, there and then, it wasn't, I'd had quite a time printing the thing out and checking out over a thousand Emails that had landed.

Hmmm

So I wasn't too chatty. And I felt very raw after the intensity of…

The lack of chattiness didn't bother me. It was only afterwards I thought we'd somehow steamrollered into this sort of; okay it's not a lot of money, but neither of us are particularly 'flush'.

I didn't know that until you said that it was an issue for you. Because I thought that we'd agreed, as soon as it's done, we'd print it out, make copies, my parents, you, William[173]…

Well that was all in your head then.

Well it must be.

Hmm.

Yeah. Either in my head, or you forgot. I imagine that it was more likely that it was in my head than you forgot. Otherwise, if it wasn't in my head, then I would have brought it up and said "Okay, well we've done this, what are we gonna do next?"

Hmmm

So for me, it was kind of 'keeping the momentum going'. Because I really want this done as soon as poss – and we're so near. Almost done. And I'm, I'm low on it, because I haven't read it for a while. I feel like it's taken a lot of intense work with the, um, not only the transcribing - but I think you had quite a hard time transcribing, in that you found it…

No, I had a hard time with the punctuation. That's the bit I found tedious as hell.

Yup. But I didn't so much.

But like you said, we enjoy different parts. I really enjoy reading it through. I enjoy that kind of, it's like, almost like play-acting. Getting to play yourself and hearing the lines that you said, that I've said – and I enjoyed that at school. You know, so for me that's great!

I've also got an old pattern, with ummm, Lui to an extent, but I think, no not so much. With ex-business partners, Rob, maybe Timmy – certainly Timmy in Australia – and other people, but rather than doing the work, they'd wanna talk, and talk, and talk, and do therapy type thing. And with us, I just wanted to… do the work. Not to stop and talk and talk and make sure everyone's okay and everything's fine. Just finish it.

But that comes back to what I said earlier. I think that's why I find you quite difficult to work with sometimes. Because there's this kind of simmering rage, which is actually hard to be with. It's not that I want to know what it's about, or I want to, you to say "I'm fine it's not your fault" but it's just it's, it's hard. It's hard going. You know? It's like being with somebody who's tense and angry.

This is what I'm beginning to understand. That I don't know. This is new. Umm, so this is when we were doing the corrections?

Yeah.

Yeah! For me, I'm not sure whether, it may be a simmering rage. What my perspective of it was, was you're finding it difficult, not very happy about doing it, whatever whatever. And I just wanted to focus, whatever you're going to do, or whenever you needed a break, or whatever, go and do it, but not talk about it, not deal with it, focus and work. And once it's done, maybe then we can…

Yeah but that's part of making it; this is like a circular talk we're having here. Being with you when there seems to be a mood underneath it. It's not that it – as I say it's not that I want to understand it, why you're in a bad mood, or even why I'm in a bad mood, because I knew I was. Because it was boring. Um, it's yeah! It's just… it's hard going. It's like – I don't know – it's like any relationship with somebody. If somebody appears to be brewing about something, it's not much fun to be around. And to actually work in that environment – yeah.

Well that's the difference then. Because I didn't feel anything but focussed.

Hmmm

I didn't feel angry, or brewing, or anything apart from *'shut the fuck up let's get on with this.'* Or, 'if you need a break, or you need to whinge, or you need whatever, do it. But I don't wanna give it energy. I wanna hold this focus. Get this done.

But it seems to me that you can't own the fact that you were enraged. Because that's what was coming across.

Well rather than that, I don't feel like I was.

Well isn't that the same old thing of, you know, you saying that you don't know when you're angry, or when you're this, it's like a kind of game, it's like *'Catch 22'* or something. I don't know, it's – that's what I mean, it's hard to be around, because I'm used to being with people who at least know if they're pissed off, or, yeah, I guess I know when I'm angry. I remember you saying once, at that time when we were at the 'Publish Your Book' seminar and that absolute twat got up and did a summary of the day in poetry form. I wanted to get up and kick him in the fucking balls! Just walk out kicking people. You know, it's like violence.

Hmmm

And, you said afterwards that you envied me because you felt that, you know, you were saying, you were sitting there feeling odd but you didn't know what it was about.

It's like, 'Does everyone else think this is great?'

Hmmm

'And if I get up and do that, will every one else think I'm a tosser because – whatever?' But, I'd say, with this one, either, you put on me that I'm angry – because you're uncomfortable, where I just wanted you to shut up so we can get on working – or, I was…

Or you put on me that I was really uncomfortable

You said you were really uncomfortable!

Yeah, but I'm saying that I'm able to know how I'm feeling

So rather than putting on you that you're uncomfortable, maybe I just thought, 'Well, I'm not angry, he's uncomfortable, I'll hold the focus and we can carry on.'

But maybe what you do, is you surround yourself with people that are able to say what they're feeling, and explore that and become the sort of therapist figure, rather than having to look at your own self. I mean, you said earlier that it's easy to fix other people's lives. Much easier than fixing your own life…

Hmmm

…and finding your own emotions, finding out what you're pissed off about rather than being with people who can say, quite easily, "Yes, I'm frustrated." "Yes, I'm feeling anxious." "Yes, I'm feeling this." Or whatever. Because then you can talk about that, you and the other person can analyse and delve as much as seems right, rather than, you know, you saying, "Well actually I am really fucked off." But maybe you were angry because you wanted focus and you weren't getting it. I'm only speculating. What came across loud and clear to me was a kind of, like I say, simmering. Absolute simmering. Same with the other day, but the other day, as I said the difference is I just thought 'Okay that's yours.' You know, you deal with it, you simmer, or whatever. I'm not going to try and work out, or say 'Ooo I'm sorry!' 'It's to do with money, it's to do with this, it's to do with blah blah blah blah blah…' I mean, in a way I think I was, I was as bored of the processing process, as you say you are.

Hmmm. Well it seems to be totally different perspectives. Because the other day I had no problem with you, until I suppose I saw you and I got into your energy and you seemed really worked up about something. Or uneasy. Or, there was something – I don't know what it was.

Well we're both pretty much saying that we both felt the other person.

Or something that that person doesn't seem to think they were.

Because I was quite chuffed that the night before I'd got a lap top from John, that day I'd managed to print it out, and it was just done by the time that you were there, and I thought we were both going to do the wonderful thing! Like 'hooray!! We've got it in our hands, this is complete and now we can print out copies for us…'

Well that was the difference. I didn't think that there was any point in doing that.

And that's what I was saying. I didn't know that there was a discrepancy. I had nothing to be sad or upset about. I was chuffed that…

Well I wasn't sad or upset about it. It was just like, I didn't have, I wasn't in the mood to be particularly challenging and say 'No no, I don't want to do this, absolutely.' It was only that evening that that strength came through…

So why didn't we… because we were initially gonna sit down in a café and talk it through.

Yeah.

Why did you decide not to? I was quite happy to and you said, well let's walk while we're talking.

Ahhhhh, now now, this is why I get annoyed with you. Because suddenly, you are the calm, cool headed person who wanted to do all the right things. I've seen this pattern a lot. And it really pisses me off a lot, because you were just 'Right. This is what we're gonna do. We're gonna go and get five copies done, we're gonna go, right, where's the nearest photocopier, let's go into Snappy Snaps[174], no that doesn't do copies…' So I ended up saying that there's a cheapie place which does bulk copies, so…

Before that, we met at The Spitz[175], we were gonna sit down,

Nahhh… Well, we talked about that, but again it was all vague. I just

feel like, yeah, I was probably feeling, yeah, well I have been feeling quite strange this week, you know, first we finish, literally the day Lisa and Yannis were coming back, then we tidied the house, after we'd finished transcribing, then Billy came over, then I moved house into this new place that's – you know, I'm moving; again, I mean I'm not going to go into all the details, moving to be nearer to Malaika. 'Is it right? I don't know!' But it, it's weird. It feels like, like you said, wanting to have; I'd love to have a space, just a studio or something completely my own.

Hmmm

But at the moment, I don't seem to have the resources to do that. So all that's going on, so I'm not able, I wasn't able when I met you, you know, like suddenly the goalposts shift massively from you saying you've printed out – well I assumed you've printed out two copies, or printed out a copy...

Aah, I see!

...we were going to sit, talk about the business plan, talk about whatever. When the next thing I know, okay, I've been steamrollered into making five copies and not really being sure why, but not thinking... it's kind of like, I think sometimes you come across with your absolute confidence, or, I think as I said to you the other day, it sometimes, it's like the flip-side of self-confidence is excessive ego. Like this is what were gonna do, this is the right thing to do, this is what's happening! Yeah? You know?

I had no idea...

Then coming from a place of uncertainty. As we were walking, I was thinking 'well why?' and arguing with you a bit in the beginning and saying "Well, does William need one? Surely, do you want your parents to have one?" And it suddenly brought up, well my parents have seen the first part, I'd rather they see it all together – maybe the same with your parents. You know? And your memory is now that you wanted to sit quietly. I feel, I feel a bit like – what is it? Like false memory syndrome or something? I've noticed a couple of times in the past since I've known you that you'll say "Oh yeah, well I, you know I was quite calm and happy…" and I'm like, 'What? You were in a fucking awful mood!' or 'No you didn't say that.' Or, do you know what I mean?

Hmmm

It's like we're both looking back at a series of events and we're looking at totally different scenarios.

With this, I had no idea that you thought I had a copy each and that we were going to sit down and discuss. Ummm, if you weren't coming over so we could make copies and do what we're doing with the copies – I didn't know why you were coming over.

First of all it was talking about the business plan.

Yeah. So we had absolutely, totally different things in our heads about what was going on. Because I didn't know we were talking about the business plan.

Well no that's what you said. All you said to me was "Come over, I'm printing out copies, - plural! - at John's. And I thought I'm just picking up those, you know, great! And that's it. And if we need to go and read them… but then it was, you know, it was kind of, suddenly…

Hmmm

And yeah, okay, I'm not pretending that, I know it's not about the money, the money was part of it, because I thought, well, seventy quid, for copies that; because I remember this happened before, when, back in, when we finished the first part of the book, I remember you saying "Right, we need a copy for you, a copy for me, a copy for Lui, a copy for someone else…" and I paid for x-amount to be printed. Which were just binned, you know?

That was the stage we were at, though.

Yeah. But I don't think it's necessary, every single time, to do it the same way. I don't think, for me, that the people you talked about seeing the copies of the book at this stage, necessarily need them.

Yeah.

Which we talked about yesterday.

Hmm. But then obviously one each for us two, I'd discussed that I was going to give - or told you that I was going to give - my parents two, one for William and I imagined your parents would want one...

Well I don't know.

...Or whether you want to give one to your parents or not – that's up to you. But, um, yeah. We had totally different things that we thought were going to happen, umm, so in that case, *we were 'going to different parties', when we thought we were going to the same party together.*

Hmmm. But it's hard being around you, because apart from anger, I'm trying to think what emotions I've really experienced with you. Do you know what I mean? Like, you know, the things we've just talked about, I'm not trying to create a drama out of it, but to me there was a lot going on. Probably for both of us, but I was picking up what I felt were quite strong emotions from you and I don't see any reaction from you. It's kind of like somebody's just described that you've just bought, I don't know, egg and chips or something, or... do you know what I mean? It's like...

Well, what reaction would you like?

I don't know what I want. I just feel..

What do you feel would be 'normal'? If it's not 'what you want'?

Well, now I'm just thinking, you know, you were saying recently that you felt like you were passionless. In a way, it's what it feels like. It's like, I don't know. As I said to you before, you know, you talk about how you don't criticise people – you give them feedback.

When did I say that?

On a number of occasions. In the flat, a lot, a lot's come up in the last, you know the last six weeks has really… ahhh, it's been very very intense. And I think it, yeah, it's changed my relationship with you.

I think the, um, the things that make me shut down and move away from you — mainly intensity. The feeling that, it's like you look *startled?* There's something up and you're *brewing?*

Hmmm.

It's very very *intense…*

Yeah. Well we

…and there's a lot to step in to.

But this is what we were saying the other day. Exactly this, and I remember you saying exactly that to me and I said, "Well, what I get from you is quite the opposite. *Detached…*

Hmmm

"…*flat, unemotional,*" so the two extremes. You know, no wonder you attracted, say Lui, because he just seems to be 'on anger', all the time. Or maybe me - it's just a range of high-level emotions - or Billy, or Bob, or John - who's, I don't know, he's stoned most of the time, in my experience, or doesn't get very excitable. I'm just trying to see whether there's any pattern. You know, it's almost as if… maybe you, maybe you need to have people around you to express the emotions, but then you can reject them. But it's wearing, I find it quite wearing, in the way that you say you find intensity wearing. You know?

Hmmm

And it doesn't make for the easiest of partnerships. I mean, maybe it fuels it, maybe that's right, but the personal – cost is the wrong word –

but the personal – I can't think of a word...

And like I say, in the past, I think I'd say if it was a while ago, we would have been the perfect partnership, but I would have been more 'that way'.

Hmmm

Where I would be, I would need to always know how I feel, how you feel, what's going on and, um, I'd need to process. I'd need to know, feel safe. And, um, all that kind of stuff. Which, like I say, was my relationships with Timmy, Rob, blah blah blah. And now I've made that change where I'm less like, brashly speaking, you, Billy and Bob – and more like Lui, maybe John to an extent. Ammm, in a way, less with the feminine and more with the masculine. And in the past, for most of my life, I've just thought 'Well, *if that's the masculine – it's fucking stupid!* It doesn't help any one or any thing. It's absolute avoidance, blah blah blah...' Um, I don't know where I am with any of them right now. If you want to call them the masculine, or the feminine, or the... 'live and the dead', whatever it is.

Those are such... blunt labels, I don't know.

They are.

I'm not sure they're particularly helpful, I think they, for me they kind of turn me off rather than anything else. I just think 'Oh yeah, here we go. The old put-everything-in-a-box and push it away, or bring it towards, or something.'

I'm sure that we both discussed this in the book in those terms quite a lot.

Maybe, I don't know, but maybe, yeah. Maybe when we re-read it we'll find out how much of it is just irrelevant dross. I remember saying to you, you know, not long before we all moved out of Muswell Hill, that, you know, you talked about confronting your bullies, and I felt that, for me, you were one of my bullies. Umm, and it's been a process

of realising that and, yeah, standing up for myself more.

Hmmm

And I sometimes feel, like - rightly or wrongly - there's a sub-text of '...if you don't want all of that feminine stuff around' – yeuch! – push it away – don't want it near you. And I think, well, you know, maybe, goodbye to your friendships with Bob, Billy and me. Unless somehow... we change. But that doesn't bother me now. I think, 'Well fuck it then, okay...'

Hmmm

'If you wanna hang out with angry people, or stoned people, whatever...'

But then it doesn't need to be that extreme.

I don't know, but it's very hard, it's hard to be around somebody who's constantly saying 'Oh I don't like this, I don't like that, I don't like this characteristic...' it's quite corrosive. Like I remember that time on the bus after David Icke when you were saying something to Matthew which was what you were describing to him as feedback. He just turned around and said "My self-esteem is low enough without you kind of kicking me any more..."

Hmmm

And I don't know if you know that you do that.

Hmmm

If you don't; again it's almost like I don't care. I'm not, I'm not going to - sort of - do what you don't want to have done to you, in order to help you understand yourself. Do you know what I mean? It's like 'You don't want to process, well fuck off then!' You know? That's not my sole mode of operation. I kind of resent the implication that that's all I ever do. Or that I'm 'startled' – do you know what I mean? It's like, it's getting to the point now where it feels like it's criticism, criticism, criticism and I think, well, if you don't like it, why are we doing this?

You know?

Hmmm

Okay maybe it's to change the world and write a best selling book, or whatever – and I'm sure, I trust the process – but at the same time, that's what is behind the anger. And it's only been, sort of peeling off all these layers that I've noticed it. And I think that's probably how you've changed as well. So in a way, it's almost like you're saying you don't, you know, you've got to the point where you feel you're more masculine, or whatever, so you kind of push away whatever it was that helped the process. And I don't think that's about abandonment, it's not that I'm feeling abandoned – quite the opposite. I've, in the process for me...

Have got over the fears.

Yeah!

Yup, same.

And got to the ability to express anger far more. Like Billy was saying the other night, he couldn't express anger, apart from with his Dad. And I used to be like that and now it's healthy, you know? I'm able to do it and not care about the consequences.

Hmmm

You know, I mean, for me, now, if we have a bust-up, we have a row, whatever, at any point, I don't give-a-fuck, really.

Hmm

You know? If it means the book doesn't get finished. My life is more important than anything else. Any product or any creative process. You know, these people who say they want to suffer for their art –

well fuck them, let them suffer for their art.

Hmmm. Yeah, that's what the book's done for me as well. I feel like it's got me over all the fears, all the restrictions, all the unsaid things that controlled me, or the said things that controlled me. It's got me over it, thinking, 'well, fuck all of it – now it's time for me'.

Hmm

Pretty much, in a nutshell, that's what it's done for me, maybe.

I mean I would, I... feel that sort of five years ago, yeah! I did massively need a dose of more masculine energy. Which is what started with Steven, and then discovering about my Father and all this stuff. And I feel like I'm, I'm far better balanced than I was before. And I think, I don't think it's a point of reaching a satisfactory level of masculine versus a satisfactory level of masculine (he meant 'feminine') – I think we all express it differently.

Different for me. Very different. Because, um, I wasn't, I wouldn't, over and above what anyone says, um, I wasn't masculine and I wanted to claim the masculine.

But what were you then? Because you've said recently, sometimes, in contradiction to what you're saying now, you've been claiming your feminine and becoming more feminine. But...

Um, yeah.

Well, what does that mean? I don't understand it anymore.

Well I would expect to be bullied, by someone like Lui, and I'd want someone else there to be, to play that role, to get their hands dirty, to make the noise, to fix things, but maybe in the feminine to cook things, because I was impractical...

That's a bit of a fucking generalisation. What, women do all your cooking and

No men, while I..

What, feminised men?

I wouldn't call Lui feminised.

Well, you've said Rob was far more feminised! You can't remember what you've just said ten minutes ago, which is that Rob and you were 'processing Mummy's- boys'.

Yeah, totally.

Now he's not feminine. Well, which is it?!

Well I wouldn't call him feminine, but he did those, he did the fixing and the cooking and the practical and those kind of things, where I did... other stuff. Business stuff. Got clients. Got the business thing happening, got clients, brought money in.

Well, women do that, doesn't mean they're masculine.

No, not at all.

I mean, is that...

I'm not saying masculine or feminine.

Well this is all getting to be a head-fuck with all that stuff, because you have been saying that. A lot.

I'm lost in this masculine and feminine thing now.

Yeah.

And, um, I'd say I'm lost with that within myself as well. Because, as I'm saying, um, as I've said, I feel like I'm changing with this and it's all quite new, and it may quite simply be me being quite intolerant, because I'm tired, umm, I want my own space, I want my own home, and I want this done. I can't wait to read the book and to start the business plan and courses and stuff like that.

Hmmm

But I can't have that now. I can have that in two weeks or so, once I've got a space and I've got my things around me, where now I'm carrying bags around. Ammm, and it's gone straight from the intensity of us being together and the book, and a very heavy full moon, and darkness, and not great weather. For me the worst part of the winter so far. To… not knowing where to put myself. Basically. Meanwhile, who have I got to tell this to to make it better or anything – well, no one, really. Ummm, so that's going on. Maybe it's not all, about the book. The book, I'm inclined to keep up with and do my best, but, I'm going through a load of shit myself.

So maybe your habit is wanting to process, but there's no one to process to. I mean, I've felt, a couple of times, since I've moved, very very alone. But the people that I could have phoned, or would have phoned in the past, I just haven't felt like talking to. Yeah! Maybe internalise it more. Just… be with it, rather than thinking somebody's got to – like you said – somebody's got to make it alright by talking about it.

Well it's not process I want. It's like I had…

Yeah, exactly! That's what I'm saying.

Sitting in a space together. Same with tonight. I just want to… be with Gina. And last weekend we didn't see each other. Before that, it was a long time of spending a lot of time together. And it's one extreme to the other. It's all very extreme, emotionally extreme, and emotionally insecure, financially insecure. It's extreme and insecure. So… so I'm not running perfectly. I'm not making perfect sense. I'm not hugely – I may have conversations in my head, I may make assumptions, I may have a shorter fuse than usual. That's the truth of what's going on right now. It's just a very tough time of change in my life. And a huge huge shock to the system, after three years of shit with the legal battle thing, or court case, to find that no solicitor's gonna touch me because the people that I'm suing have got no insurance.

Hmmm. Well like you said in a previous talk, the legal system is pretty crap.

Yup!

To say the least.

It's for the rich. Not for the workers.

537

Well it's more, now, the two extremes. You can get Legal Aid if you're very very poor, and you can pay for it if you're wealthy. Most people are in the middle. In fact, it's funny, Billy – when he gave me that Christmas present – his card said *'Bollocks to the meek, it's the middle classes who should inherit the earth.'* I think the so-called middle classes in this country are getting the worst deal of everything. They're being squeezed, pushed and attacked for everything. You know, all the things – well I don't know about your parents, but my parents thought the things to aim for are turning out to be…

Empty.

Yeah, exactly. Illusions, or a mirage.

I think, I hope that I feel with this conversation, more than anything, the truth of the matter is, I'm confused.

I think this country's confused. Billy, when he dropped me off, Billy was saying that someone had said to him 'This country's past it's sell-by date.' Everywhere I look; there was a review of a play about the railways and how fucked up they are, called *'The Permanent Way'*[176] and it was basically saying, a play about a system, and a country, in crisis. I think this country is in massive crisis. But what we're going through is a part of that.

Yeah

And I was massaging some people today, and on the radio – funny, it reminded me of Lui, what's he called, Gary Jules[177]? That version of 'Mad World' that's at number one. That really mellow, well, melancholy version.

Yeah

I wish I'd written that song. Because it sums so much up…

Hmm

...that we've said in the book. But in how many lines, twenty lines? Also made me think, there's an advert on the Tube for the *'Spanish Property Show'* that says that fifty six percent of British adults want to live abroad.

Yeah.

Fuck! It's mad. It really is... mad.

173. William Bloom. Writer, teacher, healer and Mickey's friend / mentor. www.williambloom.com

174. Snappy Snaps. High Street chain of film developers.

175. The Spitz. Live music, gallery, bar & bistro. www.spitz.co.uk

176. 'The Permanent Way' Current play by David Hare.

177. Gary Jules. With Michael Andrews, covered Tears For Fears' 1982 hit 'Mad World'.

a nice cosy night. And he was... But their focus was more on... time
some work, more work. Always gotta... More work. It's so important. It's
important to me. But it's not about that. Work is a big... but it isn't
everything.

Bully

Hmm. It's a trap. It's a very difficult trap to get out of. Leaving this
country. And when I left it, life was much much easier. I had a lot
more... time, money, energy, health, life, ways to express myself, peace
- I had more of everything.

Hmmm

Where, this place, it's like having, it's like being leeched on.

But not realising it. I don't think people really realise what's going on.

No. And it is really; I do feel so cheated. And abused by the whole
thing. As soon as I set a foot wrong, um, I pay a fortune for whatever.
As soon as any of the corporations, or the government, or – you know
– the banks, and the legal system sets a foot wrong, or isn't there for
me, 'Well tough! You'll have to pay for it. Or keep schtum about it.' But
yeah, I feel very very bullied. And unable to express my rage at the
court case. Or, a lot of other things that I just don't 'buy'.

Hmmm

So I don't know how to express any of that. That's fact. I do hope that
something comes of going to Wales. Something that just 'flips it'.
Changes it. Shifts it. What it could be...

Well it better then.

...well I don't know.

**Well maybe it's not about changing our families, it's about changing
our relationship to them.**

No, I'm talking about me. Not even my family or my relationship to
them, it's me. It's like, why can I not – whatever it is. Express whatever it

is that doesn't work for people. Do you know what I mean? It's not like I don't want to be expressive. Or I think it's clever not to be, or I'm holding control or whatever it is – I don't even know what's going on. And if I don't know what's going on, then how can I – you know – get a better deal out of it, or give a better deal out of it? So if there is a 'pause button' there or something, you know, fuck everyone and everything else! I'd like to un-depress the 'pause button' so I can work better, and then surely everyone and everything in my life will also work better. It's as simple as that! It's like having a dirty great rock on the path that's invisible. So once it's located, the invisible rock can be blown, or something.

That's what I mean. I'm not necessarily sure that it can be 'blown'. Maybe that's an option, but how you do it...

Awareness.

But that doesn't necessarily mean the rock can be blown up. It might just mean that you become aware that there's a fucking huge rock, that you walk around every time, rather than walking into it. Cracking your head open on it.

Hmmm

But yeah, I'm, I'm intrigued. I also suddenly thought the other day - assuming you do have copies of the book to give your parents - if they start reading it while they're there, 'will your parents react against me the way that my Father seems to have reacted against you?' And it doesn't bother me. It's more like a detached intrigue. You know, I think maybe over the last six weeks we've, well I thought we had exchanged qualities, to some extent. You know, you living in a fairly filthy house and me becoming more sensitive to that. I felt that somehow by being in such close proximity we'd somehow picked up each other's characteristics. You know, I had a feeling of what it must be like to be obsessive-compulsive, through living so close to you. Yeah, you know, it's like I was saying to you, the fear and anger that I could feel with my Dad, when I'd asked to borrow their car, but I hadn't asked if you could stay over on the way to Wales. That was his fear!

Hmmm

And then, talking about that with Shane, and both of you saying that you'd had the same pattern.

What Shane and I?

Hmm. Well we all had the same pattern in our childhood. That our parents – on some subconscious level, or whatever fucking level – disapproved of our best friends, or they weren't particularly comfortable with them...

'Were they bad boys?'

Yeah, or if something went wrong, if we got into trouble it was always the other person's fault rather than we've got a bad side, we've got a naughty boy side. Anyway, I don't know.

Yeah, I don't feel the need to, the obsessive-compulsive in some ways is still a big thing, in other ways, like at Lisa's and Yannis' house, umm, I was very comfortable. I wasn't even looking around. I needed to transcribe. Work. That was it. Didn't really mind so much about anything else. It's not such an issue. And I think – I've got over it. In so many ways. I've really got over it. And I think the Community will be great for me and I'll be great for it. I'm looking forward to it. I hope so, obviously. But no, the idea - I thought you knew this - was always to hang out with my folks and then give them the book as we leave. I never talked about giving it to them while we're there.

Yeah.

But such focus at Lisa and Yannis' house has been incredibly intense. And I wasn't prepared for that, or what I faced afterwards, which has been – in a very dramatic way – out in the cold with, um, no real plans. Suddenly my fallback with money and whatever it was with the case whipped away from me, and it was suddenly like, 'Well who the fuck am I? Where do I belong and what's going on?' It's been quite a thing to suddenly - *out in the streets.*

And yet, what are the options? Your 'alternative life' could have been a nice conventional safe career...

What, if I didn't choose Fiji?

...well, whatever. An alternative you, a parallel life, you'd have probably been brewing for something else.

I don't understand what you're saying.

Well what I'm saying is, the life you've got is the creation of all those choices. Not having a safe, secure career pattern. The path that the majority of people opt for. But I don't think that makes them really happy either.

Yeah

I'm not sure what I'm saying. I don't know.

Well what occurred to me, maybe, umm, I didn't have that same secure lifestyle, because I didn't have a safe secure beginning in my life - or in this country - and I couldn't just join in and do that. I had too many paranoias and things going on. Ummm, and given the option, maybe I would have taken that option. I don't know. I don't think I would have, but I'm not sure that I even had that option to take, because of how damaged I was inside, but I don't feel like I had that option, anyway. And maybe this book is one big whinge about why I didn't have that option. *To become a boring empty suit.* Ha ha ha ha ha ha. *With loads of money and no life.*

Hmm

With *children and a wife that I don't know what to do with.*

Well I've been realising how under the surface of what I've described as quite a civil relationship with Ayesha is simmering. A massive amount of simmering. You know, I was thinking the other day, the last two years – okay I've learned a lot and I've grown a lot and blah blah blah – but underneath it I have felt at the mercy of Ayesha. She hasn't ever said 'you must do this, you must do that!' but something she said in front of me the other day with Mallie - I think I was talking to Malaika about why I left and what happened at Wilmington - and Ayesha said to Malaika "...and I left with you." And I could see that she suddenly thought that Malaika might feel that I wasn't upset. That I didn't want them to go? So she said, "Oh, and I didn't give your Dad any choice." And I suddenly thought, that moment, a few weeks ago, really underlies what's gone on in the last two years. I haven't had; you know, I'm not trying to play the victim and I don't like hearing you talk, and you sound like a victim, and I don't like hearing me talk, and I sound like a victim, because I don't think it's particularly great to live the life of a victim. But, at the same time, there's a fuck of a lot going on at the moment about men's powerlessness and identity crisis, we don't know what's going on, and then, in a way I think that's partly what we're all talking about.

And we are sometimes victims. That's fact. There's nothing wrong with it. If that's the truth and that's what's going on, then it's simple fact.

And I wouldn't be moving to the part of London that I'm moving to if Ayesha and Malaika weren't going to be there. And, you know, with the pregnancy, with the new partner, with the new flat and everything. But I've spent so much of my time in a bad mood, with Malaika, on a train, taking me an hour and a half to get somewhere because the trains don't fucking work properly. Or, you know, we said there's a lot of pent-up rage. Nothing works. Even if you've got money. You know? The times I've had money, it doesn't necessarily feel any better.

Hmmm. I feel, in a way, I think that I probably have - since I don't know when, but quite a while, with the book, that in a similar way - I have a fear with you and the book, that you'll say "Right. We've finished it. It's changed my life. Now I'm gonna bin it! It's not gonna go out, it's not gonna happen, end of story, we're both walking away from it, you've got no choice, that's it. Done!"

So, perhaps that's your - you know, we've talked about, you've said - did I feel abandoned? Maybe that's the same for you.

I don't understand.

Maybe that's your abandonment. Your fear of abandonment.

Yup! Right.

But I think, actually, what underlines... I've been wondering this for the past few days. Now-a-days so many people are lonely, or alone, or spend most of their time by themselves, living alone – I don't know all the statistics, but more people live alone...

Isolation.

Yeah! So maybe the theme of modern life is abandonment.

Yup.

From your childhood onwards.

And control through abandonment.

Hmm. You know, everything from school, to employers, is the surrogate family.

Hmmm

And I've noticed a really insidious trend in businesses is to describe the company as '...become part of the so-and-so family' you know 'the GRAB Bank family'.

Yeah, yeah.

The 'Big Royale Burgers family'. 'Fuck off... you're not my family!'

Absolutely.

And if; that's the ultimate abandonment. Not having a job, being homeless...

And who will stick with who? No one. Very few people stick with each other. Whether it's a marriage, or with your own kids, with your own family, with your own best friends, with anyone. It depends on, you know, what's the price?

Hmm

A Father will leave his family to go and be with his friends and get a fix of popularity. The Mother will leave her family to; you know, without pointing the finger, every one has a price, and does it, and it's normalised in society as okay. But who stays with who?

I think, as you say, it's actually okay to allow that you are a victim, you feel like a victim in order to clear it out of your system. Because a lot of things are beyond our real control.

Yeah.

It's like I said to you the other day. You know. My choices with Malaika. I sometimes think 'Am I staying around for guilt? Am I staying around so that she doesn't feel abandoned? Because I love her more than anything else? Is it a mixture of all of that?' But what I got, what I really got the other day was a very strong sense that, umm – I've forgotten what I got, it's all getting very fucking confusing – is it better to have a Father around who's struggling financially, emotionally, is feeling isolated, is feeling alone, and then has the child two or three days, whatever, a weekend, a day, and then… doesn't feel like he's giving his best to his child? Or *is it better if the Father completely disappears.* You know? Out of the life at an early age?

Hmmm

Like I was saying to you. If I was going to abandon Malaika, it would have been when she was fifteen months old, when Ayesha left Wilmington. Now, I know I've got a relationship with her, and a bond. I would feel shit, she would feel shit.

Yeah. Too late!

You know, I might as well have a mortgage and a family.

I love...

One thing that really came up – today, and while we were in Wales – even listening to this music. Well this music just reminded me now... how much I absolutely love Rob. We went through a long time of being in pain, thinking about it, whatever. The pain and the hassles that we had. – The Isley Brothers[178] were clients of ours, amongst other... pop stars. Rob and I did it! Rob and I ran; started our business on Priory Road, just behind this restaurant, from my bedroom, basically. And we used to do the Isley Brothers, James Brown[179] and fuck knows who else – from my bedroom. But so many things, going to Wales reminded me of Rob.

Ummm. Your Mum obviously loved him.

My Mother absolutely loved him. My Father was really cool with him as well.

Hmmm. So he wasn't just a Mummy's-boy? He was a Mummy's-boy plus.

Yeah. Amongst my friends he was a bit of a Mummy's-boy, in a way, but he wasn't really a wuss. Um, he was nice. He had a pure heart. He's a lovely lovely bloke. But... I treated him badly. But I so see the way that I shouted at him. I bullied him, basically. But, I didn't know it. I treated him exactly the way my Father treated me. Which I hated! But it's normal. And I think I did pretty much to him, the same as I did with my brother.

I would argue – sounding like a lawyer for a moment – that you've probably been doing that quite a lot in your life. Until quite recently.

Yeah. It's true! Who is my brother now?

That reminds me, have you heard anything from your parents since you left the book with them?

Spoke to them a couple of times, didn't even mention the book.

Do you think they've started reading it? Would you know if they had?

I'll ask them next time.

Oh, I'm just curious.

Yeah, me too, in a way... but whenever we've talked, we've had other stuff to say. Things have been absolutely fucking amazing with them.

Ummm

It was just the best when we went to Wales, eh... Great fun, chatting, driving, laughing, hanging out. Same, actually, as we were just saying about music. So many things that we couldn't talk about, they wouldn't allow us to talk about, we knew not to 'go there', or whatever — it's okay now.

I think maybe we have to go back to our parents' homes to appreciate that they have changed, maybe in ways that we don't always notice.

Ummm.

Where as we change. We live what we've talked about.

Ummm.

It enables them — as well, it's funny, I think like I was saying to you, I don't know if you remember, you were talking to Ann? Lisa's Mum.

Yup!

And we've been saying that maybe this is also a book for that generation of parents, to try and understand what their children went through.

Hmm

Not understand, rather than be understood.

548

Yeah. One line that that rings in my ears that Ann said, *"No matter what you do, or how you do it, you'll never get it right."*

Hmmm – tell me about it…

WHAT MY PARENTS WENT THROUGH WAS TRULY HORRIFIC.

Hmmm. I was very impressed by your Mother's – openness, actually! Her willingness to talk about things. And it seemed like, very honest.

Yeah

It didn't seem like she was trying to hide anything.

Yup!

Or try to edit anything, or try to make it better. And even though your Dad's a bit more reticent, or whatever, he's just not obviously as chatty about it as her. But I just got a really nice vibe off both of them.

You and my Father had a really good chat while I was on the phone to… was it Matthew?

Yeah, yeah. It was really great! In the past I probably would have thought, 'Well I'd better not speak my mind. I'm in his house and I don't want to cause a disagreement or an argument!' but I just thought it was important to explain to him how much impact the book has had on me and my family.

That's what the conversation was about?

Pretty much, yeah. Yeah, what it boils down to was he was saying, okay, he was saying, basically, that *"you have to turn the page on the past and move on."* And I was saying "Yes, to an extent, but *first of all you have to see what's written on the page."*

Yeah, yeah!

I just felt very adamant about it.

That's very very well put.

Yeah. Otherwise, it's just, it's buried.

Suppressed… and ruling the life.

And my next counter-argument — why am I sounding like a lawyer today? Must be a legal sort of day, m'lud.

Hm hm hm

That's right, he was then saying "OK, fine to dig and delve, but do you have to share it with the whole world?" and I think, just as you were coming off the phone, I was saying to him "Before I would have agreed with you. I had doubts about the book. I wasn't just doubting - I questioned the whole process. But now I definitely agree with Mickey. Because, it kind of shows people… what's possible."

Yeah

I mean it is 'speaking the unspeakable'.

Yeah

Even if it's not necessarily that shocking. Which it fucking is…

And I really hope that the main outcome from this book is that people read it and think *'Fuck-it! I want my life back…'*

Yeah

'And I'm gonna stop whatever my addiction is, whatever my abuse is, whatever my playing small or victim is — I wanna get my life back!'

Yup. One thing that struck me while I was up in Kilburn High Road buying more tapes and looking around, I remembered about twelve years ago, when I was doing my legal training, how most of the time — this is in retrospect and I'm not sure I realised it so much at the time —

but most of the time I felt this oppression. Not even depression, just a sort of heaviness. Everywhere seemed heavy with the past. Everything seemed ugly. Shitty and dirty and horrible and everyone seemed down. I'm not saying that's massively changed, in terms of society. But what's really shifted is, just, I don't feel that anymore. I obviously get those moods from time to time. But it's not the overall mood.

Are you saying that's since the book?

Yeah! Plus all the other things that I've done. So much has dissipated – it's been so odd. I'm gonna have a big talk with Ayesha on Sunday.

Are you?

Yeah. I suddenly realised that I've just surrendered so much of the decision making and; well no I haven't even surrendered, it's just assumptions that she's the one in charge of Malaika, and the catalyst for it was them moving. And Malaika's not going to nursery, um, until she starts school. And, um, Ayesha's Mum was; as usual I had to wheedle information out of Ayesha, who told me that her Mum would have Malaika one day and Ray will look after her another day. And again there's that split reaction, it's like 'Yeah, that's good! But...' and I said "Well I'm, that's fine. But I'd like to have been consulted, at least."

So legally, you've never got an arrangement together with money, or when you see her, or anything?

No, and things are now changing with her moving out of her parents'. It's kind of like...

In what way?

...I mean, we're probably gonna look at money... and also, I want to challenge her basic underlying assumption that she makes the decisions and checks with me if this is alright; rather than including me.

One thing that this might change is you might spend a lot more time together.

Who, me and…

You and Ayesha. Researching things…

Possibly, yeah.

Um, just discussing things. Sussing things out.

Yeah. But like you were saying, about bullying. I imagine you have been bullied; well it's like the pecking order. You were probably bullied by your Father. So you then learned to bully other men, and anyone else that would allow you to bully them.

Yeah, you're right! *It's either bully, or be bullied.*

Yeah. I think, I think I've done both. But I've only really recently realised how, how much I've allowed myself to be bullied. There's being a bully in many different ways.

Manipulative, rather than humiliating. I think. Do you think that's right?

Ummm, I'd say more subtle. Kind of points to manipulation, rather than direct.

Yup! Absolutely.

"Shut up you stupid little bastard." It's more likely to be… well I don't know. That woman you were talking about on the Tube. Maybe it's a bit of a class thing, too. The quote, unquote, working classes. They are more vocal and

They're more 'yang'.

Hmm.

Where as the middle classes are more…

178. *The Isley Brothers. Legendary soul group, USA.*

179. *James Brown. The Godfather of soul, USA.*

You twat

I had another amazing incident on the Tube. I was so pleased with myself afterwards, although I was shaking. To cut the story to its bare bones – if that's possible! – I got on the Tube – the Victoria line – and these two guys got on. One of them – they were both kind of, really dirty looking. I couldn't work out much about them, apart from, one of them was absolutely pissed, and the other one had a really strange squeaky Mancunian accent. But they were both big big men. Big, fat, unshaven bastards!

Ha ha ha ha ha ha ha ha

Anyway, to cut a long story short, the big fat one – well, the particularly fat one – said something about cigarettes, and I thought 'Nah, he's not gonna light a cigarette!' but he did, he lit up a fag. And they were sitting in the doorway, the two of them, and there was something about them, and I just turned to them and said "Look, it's non-smoking." And he like waved, in this kind of gesture of absolute derision, like just a wave of the arm, he didn't even look at me. So I sat there, fuming...

Was anyone else there?

Yeah. It was a packed train. All the seats were packed.

But everyone else was 'invisible'.

Everyone else was invisible, exactly. You've got to the nub of the story already. I sat there thinking 'What's stopping me from really speaking my mind? Yeah, there's fear, probably, there's two of them, they're big fuckers...' So anyway, some more people got on, and the fat bastard on the floor was saying to them "Step ova ma baag." Because his bag was in the doorway. And there was this one guy, standing there in the door, I think he was in his fifties or sixties, and the fat bastard said to him "GO ON THEN, step ova ma baagg!" Really aggressively. The bloke looked at him and said "I don't want to. I'm not coming into the carriage. I'm getting off at the next stop." And the fat bastard started giving him all kinds of lip and the other guy started arguing, and I thought 'I'm gonna join in.' So I said to him; or no, that's right, I heard him say "Ahve pay'd fo ma teekeet…" He was behaving like a schoolyard bully or a spoilt child.

Obviously scared shitless.

But really really annoying. And angry angry angry little brat. So I heard him say this thing about ticket, and I got up and said "Actually, you're not; you don't respect anybody else, never mind your fucking ticket." And he went "Ooo wrattled yoor faakin caige?"

A ha ha ha ha ha

"You fucking did!"

A-HA HA HA HA HA

"By not listening to me when I said 'No smoking'!" and he said "Wot's yoor problerm?" and I said *"You're my fucking problem! Who do you fucking think you are – you twat?"*

That is so excellent!

I was absolutely livid.

You called him a twat? That is so cool!

And he just sat there. Deflated in the corner. And this woman was looking at me as if to say 'well done!' but I just couldn't look at anyone.

Yeah. It's all very well for you to say 'well done' now…

That's; I really thought about all the things that we've talked about on the tape, things that we haven't taped, um, it's magical to be able to do that. I did think afterwards of Lui, I thought, wow, to have seen the ways that people are. To reclaim the missing parts. And I thought, I'm making up for a lifetime of suppressed anger. And it is coming out, sometimes, maybe inappropriately. But it's, like, if I can do that, with someone like that, then I probably won't scream and shout at my daughter.

Yeah, you won't take it out on her.

Or you, or any of my friends, or family, or – do you know what I mean? So I felt really thrilled, afterwards. WOW! And I kind of did that in my early twenties. Really intervening in, like a couple rowing in the street. I'd go up to them and say, you know, "Do you need any help?" But this felt different.

That wasn't about you... this was about you. It was confrontational.

I love it. I absolutely love it!

That is just one of the best stories you have ever told.

Hm. Finding clean expressions of anger almost is addictive. It's like, I cannot let anything past now. I can't stew.

Well I'm, I'm lost. I'm really quite lost. Somewhere between where I'm leaving – and it's been, like we were saying, 'like a woman'. Nice, manipulative, passive-aggressive, appropriate, non-confrontational, and it's all 'between the lines'.

Yeah

And now I'm 'playing' and that's a lot more 'yang'. Basically. And I don't know how to do it. And people get hurt by the tiniest little things, because they're basically nice and reasonable and whatever, and they can get away with being cunts all the time. But if I do it for one minute, then the whole world knows about it.

Ha ha ha ha ha

And I'm still totally ruled by my guilt, but it's difficult. Because I don't know where I am anymore. I'm lost. I'm really really quite lost. It feels much better and I tell the truth. I so tell the truth. I live the truth and I don't get confrontation, but – like I think I've said before – I'm astounded at the people that look at me on the Underground and say "Hi" and stuff like that. And it's the people I'd have been scared of, or lesser than, or whatever. But, I suppose, more than anything, I feel quite equal. I don't feel that anyone's any better or worse than me. Umm, and I'd realised how I'd make it one thing or the other. Either they are better than me, or they are worse than me.

Hmmm

Equal I couldn't deal with. Then what do you do?

Exactly. Then you might have to have a conversation with them.

Yeah, yeah. Rather than an argument, or ignore in fear. It's so easy to be a victim of something or other. Hide behind a personality. It's so easy to have a mission, or whatever. Anything but... myself. Whatever that is. And I think that's what's emerging now.

Out of the, uh – slumber.

Be it ever so humble...

And out of the absolute fear, I mean, we were talking about that 'slavery wallpaper'. Um, a whole lifetime of being told that basically, that the Welshpool community accepts us, but we have to behave, and basically don't pick fights, don't challenge, basically don't do anything to turn them against us.

Hmmm

And then it was that deep deep deep deep secret – almost knowing – that at some stage, something's going to change somewhere. It will probably be in 'a city', and because of that, *all the black people will be made slaves again*, and they obviously – from thinking that we are anything from cannibals to Red Indians to God knows what else – we would be enslaved. That's another good reason to be nice to people.

Hmmm. I really got the sense in Welshpool, that your experience, and the things your Mother was talking about and her experience were quite different. Which makes sense, although probably living in absolute panic and terror and fear, having been through all that shit in Uganda, umm, she was still an adult – at least, hah ha, I'm kind of saying that with a wry laugh because of what you said about you being the 'parent', but yeah, as a kind of...

Yeah, *she was a protected innocent.*

What, you protected her?

Maybe that's what she was, over and above being a child, maybe she was so protected, and so innocent, and so pure, so from... I was thinking, coming here, that we went from Staffordshire – which gave us; the only problem with Staffordshire was our own family, those people now in Swindon that totally fucked us up, otherwise, people were just amazing. They were lovely lovely people. And the only incident I can remember is, like I was saying, walking to school and walking back, on ice, with chilblains, and some kids, a couple of kids harassing us. My Mother, my brother and I. We'd never had anything like it in our lives before! He was walking funny, putting on Indian accents, wobbling his head, whatever and in the end my Mother said something or other to one of the kids and it stopped. And other than that, I don't remember; I think the first few days in school, people staring at me to see whether I know how to use cutlery - and obviously if they stare at you that much *the fucking mashed potato's gonna fall off your fucking fork!*

Um-humm.

But, then we moved to Wales… and they were like – in the majority – fucking animals, compared to the 'cotton-wool' that we were brought up in! Not just to us, but to each other. To their own kids. To everyone. It was vicious! Just the way they were was so so so different. Really different.

I got the sense from your Mother that she was just astonished about how friendly people were to her.

In Wales. They were. They were amazing! But – I don't think my brother said anything – but I didn't tell them any of my problems. Because, we were glad to be alive, I didn't want to make any problems, because we would be the representations of all coloured people, or all people who were non-Welsh, Irish or English; just get your head down and get on with it! And don't tell them what's going on. They never told us any of their problems. Fine. That's what we all needed to hear. We never asked questions about the past, because that would cause problems. So, many of my problems and my own fears – and hugely, my obsessive-compulsive – that they didn't know, or understand, I didn't know, because a lot of it was 'secret' anyway, and… like my parents. Much as they were perfect in every way, and I've just loved being with them in the last few days, *I wanted to shout at them when they talked with their mouths full.* It really, it really made my blood boil! *(in a Mr Bean*[180] *voice)* "It really made my blood boil!" Heh heh heh heh… Big time!

'Writing the script.'

Yeah, yeah. Not as huge, because it wasn't a problem now. I could recognise it and let it go. But then, that kind of stuff, or any kind of behaviour that 'attacked me', as in obsessive-compulsive, that's what I reacted to! That, plus my own notions, my own fears, the things that were unspoken, what was going on… it was a very very fucked up time.

But you said something when we were out driving around with your folks in that secluded valley, I saw the way that, the way that you were with your Dad, and Mum, it reminded me so much of my Dad.

Yeah?

Yeah, like seeing you, although you were there as an adult, the dynamic of you and your Mum hanging out, and looking at things in that craft shop and bric-a-brac shops, and whatever, and really loving it – she was lapping it up – your Dad sitting in the car - not fuming at all - but that would have been my interpretation as a child. Because he's not joining in, he's bored and frustrated. And maybe that was the vibe he was giving off. Maybe your Dad was, a little bit. And you said something like – when we got back in the car – something about "Oh, can you turn the volume down?" it was the way you said it, something about a Hammond organ.

Oh, "Hammond-a-go-go?"

And just to my ear – again, it was probably the childhood thing – was 'Oh, that sounded critical! There's something happening…' you know?

You're annoyed with him. He's annoyed with you. None of it was manifested, or was really obvious. I could see that. The pattern was the same...

The 'Hammond-a-go-go' thing is almost like a private, family joke, as a reference to one of the first records we had, that we all actually quite enjoyed. That we'd laugh at, take the piss off, or whatever. But we all quite enjoyed it.

But coming back to what you were saying about being a woman or the 'girlie stuff'. I always felt safe with my Mum. She'd be supportive and talk – *I was totally out of my depth with my Dad, because his silence could have been anything.*

Yup!

Same with your Dad.

Silence amongst the adults... would be absolute fear of the unknown. Every child and every adult, I think, basically.

Hmmm

It was my Mother and I, up against all odds, trying to make the most of everything, trying to create a home, a house, a place of support, love, trying to make the most of it, making the most of our situation. Meanwhile, we both felt very very abandoned by both Father and brother.

Hmmm

But both in very different ways. My Father was out, um, I don't know what he was doing. On one hand, perpetual meetings and committees, paying the community back for accepting us and being a good person; on the other hand, being the 'love addict', going out to play and coming home whenever he wanted to, and not being the Father, and taking my teens and my childhood.

Yeah

Forcing me into Fatherhood.

There was a sense I got from your parents. You know, they really didn't have a lot. They really didn't have money to buy...

They had nothing. More than that, they didn't know how to buy things. Or how to prepare food. Or, um, decorate, or even that certain things are free, like education, medicine; they were starting from scratch. How to catch a bus!

I think that's why I enjoyed - I hadn't thought of it, but I think you'll love that book 'The Curious Incident Of The Dog In The Night-time'[181] that I've just lent you. It made me realise how complex the world is. And where do we learn all these things? You pick them up, or you don't.

Yup.

Like you said, if you come from a totally different culture, and in effect, you are reduced from being comfortably-off 'whatever class',
living in a bungalow, with servants, to living in a council house with nothing **in Wales.**

And also, my Father, being used to being 'the black sheep in the family', 'in the dog-house', blah blah blah, because he was used to that, he was re-creating that. He'd never fight back, never stand up for himself, he'd act guilty and inside - I now realise - there wasn't even a point. Meanwhile, to a child, that's saying that all those things that are being said about him, and how he is and who he is – are true. So, we had to live from that truth. He's not around, we're in refugee camp, and God knows, while the absolute shit's hitting the fan, meanwhile he's meant to be a bad person. Because that's the way everyone talked. That's the way everyone acted around him. So, you know, he came back a very different person. Very fucked-up – he was a huge mess. You know, he didn't know who he was, but, his behaviour, everything about him had changed.

A lot, you'll probably never really know, necessarily. But interesting that you and he were talking about how he'd; why the Uganda Secret Service wanted to kill him.

Hmm

Because he was basically very brave. And he was helping Indians and various other Asians get away or take stuff out of the country.

Absolutely. And going into the place where everyone is; where everyone is – where everyone goes and don't come out!

Hmmm

Going in and getting people out. That's outrageous! Plus he smuggled – what's that book that they made the film out of? He smuggled out a manuscript of someone's story, it was published and then made into a film.

Hmmm

But then same old… taking care of the community, but generally, crap at home. Because you can't be in two places?

That's very true.

He told you about us being sent to this country without him, being smuggled to Italy while they were waiting to pick him up at the Kenya terminal and all that, eh?

Yeah, he ran a refugee camp in Italy before being allowed to join you here a few months later.

Yeah, so he was a genuine do-gooder – apparently *to keep himself sane he took care of other people who were also ready to top themselves*. So he kept taking care of others and we never really talked or caught up properly. It's as if a totally different person turned up in this country to take the place of my Father - who I'd lost in Africa.

It's very very – what's the word? – with parenting, what your parents went through, and what most parents go through, I don't think, um, I don't think that everyday parenting is given enough praise. It takes a lot, when you haven't got enough money, or community, or support, not to leave your child, I mean, it's tempting – I've been incredibly tempted on a couple of visits with Malaika recently, just to literally abandon – either take her with me, you know, rush to the airport, fly off, just leave it all behind; or just leave her behind. And I don't know, I still haven't found, it must be this inexplicable... love, that you have.

Inexplicable love?

Yeah. And it goes so deep.

Yup.

That even through adversity, you know, what your parents went through – I'm not comparing my experience with theirs. But sometimes it's boring, it's grinding – not the child, but, you know, if you haven't got money, or whatever, the child wants things, to do things, it exhausting. And I think nowadays, it's even more exhausting. There are so many pressures on people - I'm not quite sure how that relates to what you just said - the days when I feel worst are when I'm tired. I can't seem to muster the energy to play or to run around and that kind of stuff. So that's when I find myself thinking 'Oh, I'll buy a video, or I'll buy this, or I'll buy that...' something to, kind of distract her. It's okay, I suppose it's like anti-depressants, in a way, maybe. I don't know, I'm not medically qualified.

Resting on a plateau to reconsolidate before moving on?

I so envy you sometimes. Your life path, in a way, and I was saying this to my Mum and Dad the night before we went to Wales. I was really honest – and if this doesn't sound like a total paradox... I almost wish... that I'd never had children, but I'm very glad that I've got Malaika.

So many people say that! They wish they hadn't, because of what it's done, because of how it's affected their lives. How they've lost their lives, in a way.

Well, partly that, but for me...

But on the other hand, how they've gained, by having this most loveable being in their lives that makes their lives worthwhile.

But then, the wheel turns full circle. I end up feeling – not exclusively, because I have a hell of a lot of fun with her, and good times, but as she gets older and gets to school age, my God, there's this event coming which is really; everyone says, you know, their child had changed so much when they went to school, they became this, or that, they wouldn't talk as much, they weren't as open, they're gradually...

Being squashed down.

...yeah, and I think, why? Why did we have this child? And I may have said this already, err, it's painful. It's really painful. I feel powerless. I want to take out all my rage. And I'm probably thinking about Ayesha and how, well, *sometimes I feel I'd like to kill her*, quite frankly.

Hmmm

I mean, I was thinking of a novel, all of this being a novel, and describing all the thoughts I've had. Not because I hate her, but just because I feel powerless.

Yup, yup! And that's life. That's so much of life. Feeling powerless, and then where does that rage go?

Hmmm

Internalised, you get ill, or it's dumped on someone, or perpetuated, maybe.

Hmmm

You fuck me up, I'll fuck him up, he'll fuck her up, and so it goes on.

Hmmm. But, how good to be honest. I felt so pleased I could say that to my parents. They didn't really say very much, because I think they understood. But saying that, the best times I've had with Malaika have been just playing, or makings things up. It hasn't been when we've been playing with expensive toys, or dolls, or...

Isn't it a fuck-up when you spend a lot of money, and a lot of time, buying the right present for a child, and then they find a comb...

Yes, exactly.

Heh he he he he

And yet we all keep doing it.

It's the fix of having it, for a few minutes. Same as adults, same with a lot of my friends. They've got flash cars, big houses, tropical fish tanks that cost £10,000, whatever. It's that having it. Then you get bored of it after a little while. They're as lost and empty as the next poor person.

It's so true! It' like when I asked your Mum and Dad - when we all went for a drink at the posh hotel in Welshpool – I think you'd gone off, talking to one of your old school friends. I just asked them where they thought the obsessive-compulsive had come from. Your Dad said he'd thought that you were quite like that in Kampala. That you didn't like dirt and whatever, even then, but your Mum was very adamant that she thought it came during the refugee time. You know, when the Indians didn't know how to use the toilet and it was all disgusting and filthy and dirty.

It's just a different culture. I kind of agree with my Mother. I personally feel, more than the refugee camps, it was Staffordshire, and it was more emotional than physical. I think the African OCD behaviour was partly learned, because that was how my God Mother was. Being fucked up big time by my God Mother and uncle and the situation that we were in. But I'm almost over finding out.

Yes. Well I think that's why this is definitely the last bit of the book. It's *not about finding the answers, it's about*

living the questions.

180. Mr Bean. Comic alter-ego of Rowan Atkinson.

181. 'The Curious Incident Of The Dog In The Night Time' Mark Haddon
(Jonathan Cape) 2003.

Doing the questions

180 My Book of Good... ...espasa of Ra...

181. The Curious Incident Of The Dog... ...or: Time, Mira Hadden
Chambers 20...

Follow your heart – live your truth

What was my New Year's text this year? I remember last year I woke up singing – what's the Nat King Cole song?

'Nature Boy'[182]

'Nature Boy'! *'The greatest gift, that you will learn, is just to love and be loved in return.'* And this year, I was a few days late, with *'Mellow 2004...'* – I had to, because it was, I was late – *'...may all your problems turn into questions, and may all your questions bring fulfilling passionate answers, because then you know you've got it right!'*

Hmmm. But even that, it's not even looking for the answers. But maybe that's it.

Follow your heart. Follow the signs? Rather than the appropriate, or the right answer - the one that feels right. Which could be, leave your family. Because that could save your life. And your kids' lives. And everyone might have a chance of having a bloody good life. Or it could be, don't leave your job, because you feel you should, or, you know, something really exciting or something really boring. The judgement of what it is doesn't come into it.

Funny you should mention that, because after I was reading *'The Curious Incident Of The Dog In The Night Time'* the wife leaves, because she feels she's not needed and that she's actually causing trouble. Same in that film *'The Hours'*[183]. Brilliant!

Well, look at the Findhorn Foundation. Eileen Caddy, well both the Caddys had families, Eileen apparently had her head in the oven, err, trying to kill herself – and then she pulled it out through 'Divine intervention' as they were both told to leave their families, give everything up, and they followed guidance, where they were gonna

go, what they were gonna do, where they were gonna plant –
because they'd never planted before – and then up spring the 1960's
'Goodies'[184] type huge vegetables that initially made them famous.

Yeah

All through following inspiration.

And they never saw their families again.

They have seen them again, as far as I know. Who, what and how
much I don't know. I really don't know. But they both upset their
families, 'following the word of God'. Same as my other 'spiritual
home'. Ummm, um, Halcyon. They are more theosophical, but I had no
idea of the similarities. Not only do they have the same problems on
the dark side - as well as the goody-goody nice spiritual stuff - but they
started in a similar way. They followed guidance. They were told where
to plant the seeds and what to plant. They were also, I mean, the locals
stopped them from entering competitions because their marrows were
the size of Bill Oddie's[185] marrows. So to speak...

Ha ha ha ha

And Tim Brooke-Taylor's[186] courgette, I imagine.

Ha ha ha ha ha

But that's it. Huge huge vegetables. So weird! But, um, you know, I
don't know how many people's lives it affects, but it's been a huge
influence in my life, um, The Temple of the People in Halcyon,
California – a few hours from where Rob and Carrie live. And now
people go from all over the world. They've apparently been in some
Russian book and that's how people are beginning to find out about it
more, but it's all, it's all the people who went to 'the essence' of all
these things that we're now still wanking on about, like Blavatski[187], and
Alice Bailey[188], and Judge[189] and God-knows what. It goes to the
essence of humanity. Not only ours, but back into the other cultures and
civilisations, and where and why and how and whatever.

Yeah

But I suppose the bottom line conclusion that they've come to, come to think of it, is the same as us. It's the way you live your own life. That's the beginning, and end of it.

I'm glad you said that, in a way, because I have to say that I've recently thought that maybe Malaika would be better off without me. The last few times I've got really tired, I thought, I thought '...she's got the family, in a way. You know, she's got her nice little nuclear family.' But just thinking it was actually enough to admit that I was even feeling that. It's the worst thing you can do, isn't it? Abandon your children? God.

I had a, I went to see a client the other day - a guy I'd previously met - and said "Man you look so skinny, what's gone on?" because before, he was comfortably podgy. This was the first time he really spoke of his private life, so basically, he told me that his wife is dumping him. He's got kids, but he's being so bullied and manipulated by his wife that he's beginning to actually believe her lies. Months ago, before there was any talk of a split, she started getting her finances in order, bought this, hid that, anything to fuck the poor little man up. He's a lovely guy, and he's a real mess. And his hugest concern is that the kids are being turned against him. It sounds like she's being an absolute manipulative bitch. Planning all this and kicking him while he's down. He's so scared of what's going on, and I said, "Well the bottom line is that the kids will probably hate you at some stage. But then they probably would if you stayed with them, or not. And, no matter what goes on, the most important thing is – *be yourself.*

Yes

"Don't try and jump into dramas and jump through hoops of fire. Just be yourself and carry on that way. And it will take time. Who knows when they'll come back. Or when things will be uncovered or what will go on. But, maybe the easiest way to deal with it is to accept that you will be hated, there'll be lies flying around, you'll feel like shit – but even while still living in the same house, start building your own life with the community, with your own friends, so when you do need their help it's kinda gonna be like a natural progression, rather than life being, um, about being victimised by her". So he's fucked! And he's got two kids that he cares about more than anything else. And what about his money? But how does he deal with this? Because he's gonna need money. If only to look after himself – so he's staying for the kids. And he needs the love of his kids because he didn't wanna split – he didn't want any of this to happen. Again, back to Lisa's Mother.

"Do what you can."

"…and what ever it is, it's not going to be enough or it's not going to be right." Down to the same old again. *Live the truth*, no matter what anyone says, live it! And *you know what it is because of the way it feels*, rather than what other people have to say.

182. 'Nature Boy' 1948 hit for legend Nat 'King' Cole.

183. 'The Hours' (2002) Stephen Daldry, USA.

184. The Goodies. Classic 1970's BBC comedy.

185. Bill Oddie. One of the three 'Goodies'.

186. Tim Brooke-Taylor. Another of the three 'Goodies'.
(Graeme Garden was #3!)

187. Blavatski, Helena Petrovna. Founder of theosophy. www.theosophical-society.org.uk

188. Alice Bailey. Esoteric philosopher. www.lucistrust.org

189. Judge,William Q. Theosophist writer and philosopher

Waking up

Yeah. Hmmm. So have you seen Billy... whizzing about the place?

I haven't really gone back for about a week or more. This morning, he said that he couldn't remember the last time he woke up scared. And that's something! Even in chat rooms on the internet, watching what people are saying. Loads of them talk about what I've had, which was waking up scared. At the end of the day, it was pointless. *The only way out was suicide*, because I couldn't see how anything else was going to change. So why not just remove myself from the equation? And for Billy to say that, it's fucking excellent! And that gives everyone hope, surely!

Hmm

But, waking up scared, surely that's the worst. During the day, you can phone someone, you can do something, whatever. But waking up in the morning, I'd roll myself a little spliff that would get me out of bed, and have a nice shit – and the loo's always been my safe place – hardly a solution. But how many people are on their uppers and downers? Drugs and whatever. 'Trisha'[190] during daytime, TV to keep them sane.

Yeah, I think that's the scariest thing. Like you say, that's something new, for me in the last year, I've actually been waking up feeling really scared. It's horrible, because I feel like it's an invasion. Because if sleep isn't safe, what is?

Yeah, that's so spot on. Especially with dope smokers. Stoners can't sleep unless they've had a smoke. Something to knock them out to order, taking away feeling. The pain. There's all that space for being, and the being is not good, because reality might creep in. Helplessness. What's really going on? And where it's going? And there are so many old stoners around and all they've done is smoke. They come up with great ideas and concepts and stuff – but they've generally not done anything. No one wants to meet an old stoner. Ha ha ha ha ha ha ha ha

But I've noticed, recently, the times when I tend to wake up in a good mood – I mean, Malaika still shares my bed, because that's how we started off. And I haven't got another bed. Huh huh huh huh – but, it's lovely, because I wake up and she's usually kind of cuddled up, and we always smile at each other. Like big smiles.

That is lovely.

It's so sweet, but then I think, 'God,' – I hadn't thought of it before now, but as I'm speaking, maybe that's why we cling to each other. Why people stay in couples. They don't, at least they've got someone to snuggle up to when they wake up in a panic.

Yup. Yup. That's something Billy and I talked about, about one of his ex's. That he'd wake up in the morning and he would be holding on for dear life. He was just fucking scared. Scared as if it was his worst nightmare. Love, touch, intimacy – none of that came into it. It was terror!

What I don't want is to make Malaika into my substitute relationship.

Yeah, don't do to her what our Mothers did to us, at whatever level.

Yeah, like Lisa's Mum Ann said, don't mix up your priorities. The way she said *she always put her husband first, kids second*. And I remember my Mum saying that given the choice, the kids would come first.

Same with my Mother, though I'd think I'd like to demonstrate an ace relationship with my partner, so my kids can get the same for themselves. Meanwhile, practise makes perfect, eh!

Talking of which, what I need is a 'fuck buddy'. I think, because I've been in quite a, well, a very intense relationship for so many years, maybe I'm never gonna...

Yeah! That is very very true. And you've really – you've had a fair innings. How many years?

In relationship, for about fifteen.

That's a long time. For someone of your age, that's almost half your life.

It is! Exactly.

That's a lot.

But it was that; I was just thinking, looking out of the window. Little triggers, like you were saying about how old music triggers things for you. Watching someone smoking, remembering myself when I was with Ayesha. It wasn't unrelentingly bad at all, but just sometimes this darkness, this heaviness, and I couldn't put my finger on it. And it wasn't just the relationship. To an extent it was a lot to do with that. It's like being handcuffed to somebody. You go out together, you go to bed together...

You say "This is what 'we' think about this, this is what 'we' don't agree with..."

190. *'Trisha' UK television talk show.*

I love you

And what you were saying is true. I can say "I love you" to a male friend far more easily, because it's casual, it's simple, and maybe this is exactly what women say about no commitment. But I do feel committed. I feel committed to friendship. Like I never have before. For me, the relationship was everything. There wasn't much room for friendship.

Because the relationship wouldn't abandon you – and the friends might. Or humiliate you, or whatever. Or at least that's how it was for me.

Yeah.

But, like I was saying earlier. I am astounded at how Lui and I can not only tell each other that we love each other, but joke about it, like we joke-texted the other night when I was at a party. And it was all about loving me, him loving me and getting over it and stuff. And then Matthew, who is a good bloke. He's a bloke's bloke. Umm, phoning up and saying really nice things and then saying that he loves me. Marius even. Billy, and stuff like that. I find it very comfortable to say it to bloke blokes. Because it's the truth. And it's just like "Love you mate..." type thing. (They say it to me, actually)

Yeah

Meanwhile, I've known Gina for, it'll be a year on the fourteenth of February. We've been a so-called 'item' – what a horrible word – 'going steady' – horrible word! – 'courting' horrible word! – etcetera etcetera since the beginning or mid July, and I haven't told her that I love her. We show it, we express it, it's wonderful, but... I don't feel like I need to. Or want to. Or that it's an issue for anyone – but maybe for her. And I think generally it is for girls. They like to hear it, to know it, for it to be said, and then it's so cool, chatting on the phone like she's a close friend, rather than someone that I have to be mushy-mushy around…

Yeah

… and "I love you" at the end of the conversation. It's much more fun this way! Brilliant! But chatting about the 'I love you' thing with John and him saying it took him a year to properly say it to Freya, and then how he slipped it in, you know, typing it, writing it, putting it in a text before he could properly spit it out.

And that's it. It's like, eventually, you're going to have to say it sometime.

But I've had such pressure on myself, that that's what Gina wants to hear, it's looming, I'm withholding, not checking in, whatever.

You're not in love with her…

Um. And yeah, we've never even said whether we're in love with each other or not. But we both know, we've both said how brilliant our relationship is. It has been by far the – not only the best relationship, but better than we've ever imagined, or we don't know what to do or how to do it, and then saying "How great was that!" because we don't need to know, and how could we? The other day I bought this book. Umm, *'Jaybirding'*[191]? and it's about nudity. From the 20's to date. And how so-and-so guy had to campaign so that in his magazine he gets to show – he didn't show fannies or anything. But at least 'bush'. Just *lots of pubic hair*. You weren't allowed to show pubes, leave alone anything else. It's just really funny, for us to see, like my favourite picture in the whole thing is this girl, totally naked, just sitting there and looking a little confused, like Betty Boop[192]. And on either side of her parting – what do you call those, where the parting is on top of the head?

Oh, bunches, or whatever.

No, no. She's got two different men's dicks just sitting on her head like they're two horns, and she's just sitting there all innocent and not knowing what to do. And it's hilarious! But we were just sitting there and laughing at some things, comparing my dick, comparing her fanny, and so much of it was an appreciation society because *she has a* **beautiful, lovely fanny — and I do have rather a remarkable dick**. Well, balls anyway... well, dick as well. Well, just the whole package. Ha ha ha ha ha — but it was such good fun! But the sex thing has been fine with us, but it's been 'claiming it'. Same as the relationship. And we just enjoyed looking at bodies. And it was quite a thing. Like I said to Gina, where do you see naked people? Well, porn. What's that got to do with anything? They're models, they're chosen because they've got implants, or ridiculous donkey dicks, or they've got ridiculous abs, all the bastard things that I haven't got that I want...

Hmm.

They're not real. Disconnected.

That book that you had. *The Book Of Tantric Love*[193] or whatever? There's a picture in there of a man and a woman. They're just embracing — it's not clear whether they're meant to be fucking as well — and they're kissing, and it's such... aah! That image! It turned me on. Big time! Because it's reality. Lovely.

But with the 'I love you' thing, I always felt a bit 'funny' about kids that would say it to their parents, parents that would say it to their kids, especially young adults where no one really means it, and they've just left a fucked-up family to go to college. But it was the way of holding it together. But the way they said it was kind of needy and desperate. And generally, I don't know, my parents never said it to me, but then, I don't think they've actually said it to each other either. Maybe some people find it really embarrassing, but there are times when it's said when it shouldn't be said. Because it's just a lie. Yeah, or a cover-up.

But also, I've noticed with my Dad, he never used to say it when we were younger. Occasionally on the phone he'd say "Lots of love" but

after, particularly after this Christmas and all that shenanigans we've talked about. When I spoke to him – and it hasn't lasted – he would say it every time. And there was real sincerity in his voice. Maybe that's it. Maybe it's not about noticing when it starts and when it stops. Or 'ooh, he doesn't say it any more'. Maybe there are just times when it's intense and you feel it. And other times you don't. You feel like saying *"I hate you."* Or "I don't like you." Like children do.

Kids do that all the time. "You're not my favourite today." Or "I don't love you any more." But then we all learn that we have to say it because it pleases the other person. And they'll stop loving us if we don't love them.

And it's the same, with love, for me. Me and Lui, for example, I can love him - I can love him all the time – I'm not sure how often I actually like him. His behaviour or attitude rather than Lui. I think if it wasn't for that love thing, there wouldn't be a Lui in my life. I don't know. But, there have been times where I've had the need to say it, but I would avoid saying it because it is too emotional. Because I'd want to cry. And other times I'd just be plain embarrassed. And emotional expression – including dancing and singing, or expressing a feeling – was embarrassing.

Well, I think when it's intense, it can be quite overwhelming. But there is nothing for me so simple and meaningful as somebody saying it. And they somehow convey to that other person that they know the other person doesn't have to say "And I love you too".

Yeah!

Sometimes, it's just that simple. So when are you telling Gina that you love her?

Fourteenth February.

191. 'Naked As A Jaybird' Dian Hanson (Taschen) 2003.

192. Betty Boop. 1930's glamorous 'cartoonette'.

193. 'Tantric Love; A Journey Into Sexual & Spiritual Ecstasy'
Ma Ananda Sarita & Swami Anand Geho (Gaia Books Ltd) 2001.
www.schoolofawakening.com

Epilogue #2

A zig-zag course; a roller-coaster. My Dad's words (from the intro) are in my head this morning as I wake after five hours sleep. Mickey and I have steamrollered ahead to get the final 'beast' of a book ready for artworking/formatting by him today. Despite the howling wind and driving rain of this prematurely cold Autumn (after a non-Summer; thank Christ I wasn't in a tent this Summer). Zig-zag course; I recall - from one of the dozens of self-help workshops I have been to in the last five years or so - that aeroplanes, between take off and landing, are constantly changing their course; by small degrees their voyage is totally altered...

Re-reading the book in its entirety has been truly amazing. How often - if ever? - in life, do we get to re-read, let alone re-interpret or understand our own words? It's like a by-the-moment diary. But because it's a conversation, very, very different to a diary for both Mickey and I, the people we were when we began, and here we are now are so far apart as to be unrecognisable. For myself, reading about my problems ('challenges' in alternative language) with Ayesha and Malaika has shown me that I've totally used this book – and Mickey – as part of the road map of radical change.

Ayesha and I have been through the mill together these last three years, and now she's a new Mother, with Ray as the Dad and Malaika has a baby sister. We've rowed and exploded and snarled and accommodated and now, remembered that, deep, deep in the mists of time, before Malaika, we had a relationship, for better or for worse. Somewhere, deep, deep, down, we have that core of friendship and the book has helped point me back to that. My – sometimes ambivalent – relationship with Mickey has also been a huge help (despite me never 'wearing the best friend label'). One of his favourite phrases 'get on the same side' has reminded me that Ayesha and I have not just a daughter in common, but a shared history and a lot of shared love. Her new kid is cute too! Ray is a good bloke. And so am I, I remind myself.

Going back this last weekend, for the final read (partly for legal reasons) remembering those confused years of casual sex with blokes, I notice how I've 'erased' so much of my past with Ayesha in my current life. (Mickey also pointed this out). And also noticed that nowhere in the book, do I 'justify' or explain that I was 'out' to her sexually with all my confused good intentions. It strikes me again, how many married men are living in marriages where their liaisons – gay or straight – are a double life that they've somehow learned to manage. Difficult and painful though it was, to be honest, Ayesha always knew what was going on outside our relationship. The unspoken rule ('don't fall in love with another bloke') snapped into pieces when my passionate love for Steven burst out and spilled over to create the beginning of this new landscape I now inhabit, one in which I still often feel confused and scared. But alive and vulnerable, with many, many deep connections.

The book (and Mickey) remind me that it's only when I get in my head and 'anal'yse up my own arse, that panic steps in; when I lose the present moment. So many memories of the life and pre-birth of this book. So much fun and insight and what a trip – like our varied, extraordinary footnotes – from the extremes of wisdom and insight (everything from 'The Power Of Now'[194] to the poignant, clever, melancholy, clarity of 'The Royle Family'[195]). I see, and interpret, so much through my post- 'MenSpeak' eyes.

Bringing us, and the book, here and now, ready to publish (and I take my hat off to Mickey for his energy and dedication, not to mention his genius for design and marketing ideas). But also for the continuing depth of friendship. His obvious interest and love for Malaika – and all kids; his gifting me his T-shirt that says 'Daddy' on it boosted my self-esteem at a time when Malaika, who through her new life circumstances, often 'slips' and calls Ray 'Daddy'.

'Zig-zag' is also the name of the main road in Box Hill from the bottom to the top (or the top to the bottom). I climbed that hill daily for several months. A bit like this journey, climbing the hill from the 'near dead zone' back to life again. The elusive and 'out of control' book has edged out and out and now, several re-reads, lots of punctuation, a large amount of legal advice, endless layers of skin and cups of coffee and chocolate digestives later, it's waiting.

Things need to change. We seem to be on a threshold, a lynchpin time in history. People are ripe and ready for change. I just pray that this strange, lovingly nurtured, raw, beautiful, unique beast-of-a-book will make some difference to the lives of those who read it. As both Mickey and I have remembered only recently, it's very likely neither of us would be here to tell the tale without it. I hope it inspired people to step out of conditioned fear. I'm sure it will ruffle a few feathers. But then there are a lot of turkeys who need a lot of ruffling.

On a more personal note – Ed's big dating opportunity – if there are any bold, pioneering women (preferably bisexual – no, definitely bisexual as I'm not putting any woman through, or going through that again myself) who are also gorgeous and courageous out there, willing to share the journey with me, please drop a line to personal@menspeak.co.uk once you've read the book.

We live in truly exciting times. For all the darkness in the world, there are so many people groaning for change, myself included. Frightening and exciting, like the storm blowing outside the window, it's time to launch the good ship 'MensPeak' on to the foaming seas and see where it travels.

Bon voyage!

Ed Seeker, Mickey's spare bedroom, Oakwood Community. October 5th 2004.

194. 'The Power Of Now', Eckhart Tolle (Namaste Publishing Inc) 1997.

195. 'The Royle Family', (1998-2000) UK 'favourite' sitcom.

The beginning... now it's your turn!

& now you've read the book, you may wish to join the

Private Members Area of our website (for free) at

w w w . m e n s p e a k . c o . u k

Just quote your hand-written 'copy number' from the front
section of the book in your Email and we're away!